The educator's guide to Texas school law
KFT1590.K314 96   29266

Kemerer, Frank R.
Wright Library

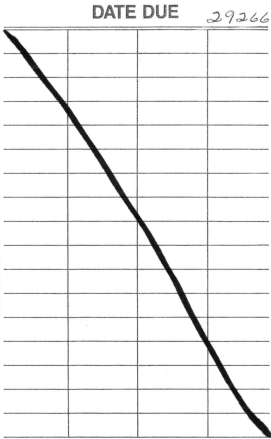

DATE DUE   29266

THE EDUCATOR'S GUIDE TO TEXAS SCHOOL LAW

FOURTH EDITION

The Educator's Guide to Texas School Law

FOURTH EDITION

by Frank Kemerer
and Jim Walsh

 University of Texas Press, Austin

Requests for permission to reproduce material from this work should be sent to
Permissions, University of Texas Press, Box 7819, Austin, TX 78713-7819.

♾ The paper used in this publication meets the minimum requirements of
American National Standard for Information Sciences—Permanence of Paper for
Printed Library Materials, ANSI Z39.48-1984.

Library of Congress Cataloging-in-Publication Data

Kemerer, Frank R.
    The educator's guide to Texas school law / by Frank Kemerer and
Jim Walsh. — 4th ed.
        p.   cm.
    Includes bibliographical references (p.   ) and indexes.
    ISBN 0-292-74324-6 (alk. paper). — ISBN 0-292-74325-4 (pbk. :
alk. paper)
    1. Educational law and legislation—Texas.   2. Educators—Legal
status, laws, etc.—Texas.   I. Walsh, Jim, 1950- .   II. Title.
KFT1590.K45   1996
344.764'07—dc20
[347.64047]   96-4490

To Anne, Jenny, Sarah, and Devin

Contents

Figures

Preface

IN PREVIOUS editions the authors have admonished readers to understand that the law never stands still and that the longer the period between the date of publication and the time the book is read, the more cautious one must be in accepting its contents. The events occurring in 1995 certainly demonstrate the point. That year, the Texas Legislature enacted Senate Bill 1, the most ambitious overhaul of the Texas Education Code since 1949. In the process, many sections of state law were eliminated and new provisions added. In addition, the Code was entirely renumbered.

The revamping of state law, coupled with the steady pace of change instituted by judicial rulings and the decisions of the Texas Commissioner of Education, has necessitated a new edition to *The Educator's Guide to Texas School Law*. This Fourth Edition reflects all the changes that occurred up to the date of publication. Changes in state law have resulted in complete rewrites of the chapters on governance, employment, and student discipline. Many portions of other chapters have also been rewritten to reflect the current state of the law.

This book is intended for all Texas school personnel—superintendents, principals, teachers, supervisors, counselors, and coaches—as well as school board members and school law attorneys. The authors endeavor to explain in lay language what the law is and what the implications are for effective school operation. The goal is to help professional educators avoid expensive and time-consuming lawsuits by taking effective preventive action. College and university professors will find the book an especially valuable resource in teaching school law courses.

The book begins with a review of the legal structure of the Texas school system. Given the changes in school governance instituted by Senate Bill 1, readers are urged to read this first chapter before going on to other sections. Education law is a complex interweaving of state and federal constitutional, statutory, administrative, and judicial law. It is important to understand the nature of this interrelationship before reading other sections. Following this chapter, major topics of education law are presented in some detail. Statute and case references are kept as simple as possible; a complete index of case citations is included, should readers want to consult the cases themselves. The appendixes describe how case law is reported and where to find it, provide a listing of other sources on Texas school law, and present an expanded glossary of legal terms.

Other format-related matters include the simplification of legal terminology and the periodic use of summaries and reviews to clarify complex material. It is important to note that this book is designed to provide accurate information regarding the subject matter covered. It is published with the understanding that neither the authors nor the publisher is rendering legal service. If specific legal advice or assistance is required, the services of a competent professional person should be sought.

The authors and publisher are gratified by the wide acceptance accorded the *Educator's Guide* through the years as an authoritative source on Texas school law and hope that the educational community will find the latest edition a valuable professional resource.

THE EDUCATOR'S GUIDE TO TEXAS SCHOOL LAW
FOURTH EDITION

ONE
An Overview of Education Law, Texas Schools, and Parent Rights

IN THIS CHAPTER, we begin by examining the sources of school law and describing the basic roles of the state and federal governments in the establishment and operation of the Texas school system. We also look at how the legislature restructured the Texas schooling system in 1995 and review the culmination of the long-running lawsuit over the financing of Texas schools. The chapter ends by examining parent rights, including the right to have their children educated in another district, in private schools, or at home.

SOURCES OF LAW

Constitutional Law

Since education is not a power specifically delegated to the federal government by the U.S. Constitution, it is a state function. The Tenth Amendment to the Constitution declares that all powers not delegated to the federal government are reserved to the states. This amendment gives state governments their traditional power over schools. Viewing the school as an important socialization device, states gradually expanded public education in the nineteenth century. By 1918 all states had compulsory school laws.

It is important to note that states do not have to set up public school systems. The U.S. Supreme Court decided in a 1973 case, *San Antonio I.S.D. v. Rodriguez*, that education is not a fundamental right available to all persons. When a state decides to provide public education, as all the states have done, it has established an important benefit, which, as we will see later, it cannot take away from students without following due process procedures.

Consistent with the Tenth Amendment, the Texas Constitution of 1876 establishes the legal basis for a public school system in the state. Section I of Article VII reads: "A general diffusion of knowledge being essential to the preservation of the liberties and rights of the people, it shall be the duty of the legislature of the

State to establish and make suitable provision for the support and maintenance of an efficient system of free public schools." The long-running Texas school finance case, *Edgewood I.S.D. v. Kirby*, centered on whether a finance system resulting in substantial inter-district disparities is "efficient" within the meaning of this constitutional provision.

Since the mid-1960s, the Bill of Rights and the Fourteenth Amendment to the U.S. Constitution also have furnished a basis for litigation against public schools. Claims to freedom of speech, press, religion, and association, due process, and other rights have a constitutional basis, just as the state's power to establish and operate schools stems from the Constitution. The Bill of Rights of the Texas Constitution, which protects many of these same civil liberties, also is being asserted more frequently in litigation against schools. Constitutional law at both the federal and state levels thus is an important source of education law.

Statutory Law

A *statute* is a law enacted by a legislative body. Most of the statutes passed by the Texas Legislature that directly affect education are grouped together in the Texas Education Code (TEC). The code is an important source of law because it applies to the daily operation of schools, detailing the responsibilities and duties of the State Board of Education (SBOE), the Texas Education Agency (TEA), school boards, and school personnel.

Since the early 1980s, the Texas Legislature has taken an increasing interest in improving an educational system that it regards as deficient. The result has been a plethora of reform laws. At first, the reforms were top-down in nature. For example, the legislature in 1981 mandated that all schools offer a well-balanced curriculum consisting of specifically designated subjects and in 1984 passed House Bill 72, a massive reform package that changed much of the operation of Texas public schools. By the late 1980s, the legislature began shifting authority and responsibility back to school districts and district personnel in the face of evidence that top-down mandates were having only marginal effects on increasing educational quality. Indeed, some commentators argued that the mandates were having a negative effect. In 1995 the legislature embarked on a complete reworking of the Texas Education Code—the first major overhaul since 1949. Not only did the legislature produce a more systematic, readable code, it took the opportunity to change, and in some cases streamline, many features of the Texas schooling system. Thus, the legislature significantly downsized TEA, gave local districts and school personnel more independence, and provided parents with more authority over the education of their children.

Many other state statutes besides the Texas Education Code affect the activities of the local schools, and we will discuss them in the succeeding chapters. One point worth emphasizing now is that, despite their essentially local character, public school districts are legally part of state government. The present system of some 1,045 Texas school districts and nearly 6,200 individual school campuses could be changed should the legislature desire, given the latter's authority over public education under the Texas Constitution.

Federal statutes also have significant influence over the operation of public schools in the state. Some of the more important are described later in this chapter. Since establishing and operating schools is not a power that the U.S. Constitution delegates to the federal government, most federal laws affecting education are passed pursuant to the Congress's power to collect taxes and spend for the general welfare. As the late Supreme Court Justice William O. Douglas noted in a famous case, *Lau v. Nichols* (1974), "the Federal Government has power to fix the terms on which its money allotments . . . shall be disbursed" (p. 569). Thus, these laws contain the "strings" the federal government attaches to the use of its money. Schools receiving direct or indirect federal assistance must comply with the conditions the government attaches.

Administrative Law

A third, often overlooked, source of law is administrative law, which consists of the rules, regulations, and decisions that are issued by administrative bodies to implement state and federal statutory laws. Special education personnel, for example, are familiar with the extensive "regs" accompanying the Individuals with Disabilities Education Act, as developed by the administering agency, the Office of Special Education Programs. These regulations are designed by the implementing agency to apply the law to the realities of day-to-day schooling and of necessity must be quite detailed in order to eliminate as much ambiguity as possible. The length of a statute's regulations often exceeds that of the statute itself.

Administrative law also includes the rules and regulations that state agencies establish to carry out their responsibilities. When promulgating rules, administrative agencies are said to be acting in a quasi-legislative capacity. In the education context, this responsibility lies with the State Board of Education. The rules that it enacts are grouped together in volume 19 of the Texas Administrative Code (TAC). As a result of the downsizing of the Texas Education Agency in 1995 and the recodification of the Texas Education Code, the state board rules previously adopted had to be readopted or deleted in areas where state board authority was curtailed.

The policy manuals and handbooks developed by local school districts are excellent close-to-home examples of administrative law. TEC §11.151(d) provides that school trustees "may adopt rules and by-laws necessary to carry out [their] powers and duties. . . ." Board policies and administrative directives represent the law of the district, and it is a condition of employment that all personnel observe them.

Administrative law also has a quasi-judicial character. State law provides that anyone aggrieved by the school laws of the state or the actions or decisions of any school district board of trustees that violate the school laws of the state or that violate a provision of a written employment contract, causing possible monetary harm to the employee, may appeal in writing to the commissioner of education (TEC §7.057). This section does not apply to student disciplinary actions, however, nor to the termination or nonrenewal of professional employee contracts. These matters have their own appeal procedures, as we will note in Chapters 4 and 8, respectively. In the past, the majority of the cases appealed to the commissioner annually have involved certification and employment.

Before appealing to the commissioner, the person first must exhaust administrative remedies within the school district. As the commissioner noted in 1992, this includes seeking redress before the school board (*Havel v. Gonzales I.S.D.*). When the commissioner hears an appeal against an action or decision by a school district, the commissioner most often reviews the written record of the school district hearing to determine if there was substantial evidence to support the board's decision. In some instances, the commissioner conducts an evidentiary hearing and has much the same authority as a state district judge to issue subpoenas, take depositions, and order production of documents in an effort to determine the facts. However, unlike those of a judge, the powers of the commissioner are limited to directing districts to comply with state law. The commissioner cannot issue restraining orders, assess fines, or order contested items removed from a personnel file. Also unlike a judge, the commissioner does not hear the cases personally. Rather, licensed attorneys acting as TEA hearing officers conduct the hearings and draft decisions for the commissioner to review and sign.

The commissioner has developed a set of rules governing these hearings and appeals in the interest of efficiency and fairness. Both the rules and the hearing decisions from the local board on up are classified as administrative law. Figure 1 illustrates the overall structure of Texas administrative law.

Judicial Law

A fourth source of law is composed of state and federal court decisions. When disputes arise under constitutions, statutes, and administrative law, some authority must have final say. The courts serve this function. As we have noted, when a person wants to contest a decision of a local school board, that person has a statutory right of appeal to the commissioner. If, after appeal to the commissioner, the matter still is not resolved to the appellant's satisfaction, that person may appeal to a district court in Travis County, Texas (TEC §7.057(d)). As noted earlier, employment and student discipline appeals are handled differently (see Chapters 4 and 8, respectively).

Before filing an appeal in state district court, the aggrieved party must pursue administrative remedies. Courts generally refuse to become involved until all administrative remedies are exhausted. The reason for the exhaustion requirement is obvious. Administrative agencies are staffed by persons familiar with the educational setting and, theoretically, more qualified than judges to arrive at satisfactory and workable solutions to disputes that arise within that setting. In fact, judges are not educators and, generally, will be the first to admit that the resolution of educational disputes is best left to educational professionals. Further, the exhaustion requirement has the effect of channeling and resolving most conflicts before they reach the judiciary. Only approximately 10 percent of the cases filed with the Texas Commissioner of Education are appealed to state district court.

There are, however, exceptions to the general exhaustion requirement. For example, student expulsion decisions are not appealed to the commissioner but instead must be taken directly to the state district court of the county in which the school district's administration building is located (TEC §37.009(f)). Further, in 1984 a Texas appeals court ruled that exhaustion of administrative remedies is required only when there is a factual question to resolve. When there are no facts in dispute or when a school board acts outside its statutory authority, a party may proceed directly to state

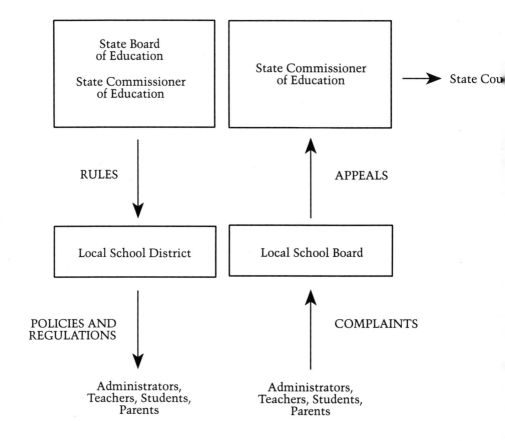

Figure 1. The Overall Structure of Texas Administrative Law

district court without first pursuing administrative remedies before the commissioner of education (*Benavides I.S.D. v. Guerra*). Indeed, TEC §7.057(b) recognizes that the commissioner appeal process is not intended to deprive a person of a legal remedy. As a practical matter, however, most disputes involve some factual questions, and the commissioner provides the initial forum for most litigation involving school laws and school district actions.

Regardless of whether litigation is filed initially in a state district court or as an appeal from a decision of the commissioner, the state court system plays an important role in the resolution of educational disputes. Therefore, it is important to review the composition of the Texas judiciary. District courts are the major trial courts in the state judicial system, having jurisdiction over major criminal and civil matters. From a district court, an appeal goes to one of the fourteen courts of appeal located throughout the state and, finally, to the Texas Supreme Court. An appeal from a Travis County district court goes to the Third Court of Appeals in Austin. The Third Court, by virtue of its jurisdiction over appeals from the district courts of Travis County, has great influence over the development of educational and other public law matters. Only the Texas Supreme Court, however, can speak for the entire state in civil matters. For criminal matters, the highest court is the Texas Court of Criminal Appeals. Thus, in Texas we have two supreme courts, one concerned with civil matters and one with criminal matters.

Although the Texas judicial system provides a theoretically efficient structure for adjudicating disputes, frivolous lawsuits present a generally recognized problem. In an effort to deal with this problem, the legislature enacted two provisions providing that a person who files a frivolous lawsuit under state law against a school district or an officer or employee of the district who is pursuing official duties may be liable for court costs and the defendants' attorney fees (TEC §§11.161, 22.055). It is important to note, however, that state law provides specific protection for persons who report suspected violations of law. The Texas Whistle Blower statute is discussed at some length in Chapter 6.

If the matter in dispute involves a *federal question*, individuals often can avoid administrative law procedures and state courts altogether and go directly to a federal district court in the state. Federal questions are those involving some provision of the U.S. Constitution (e.g., freedom of speech), a federal statute, or a federal treaty. Since many disputes involve constitutional or federal statutory rights, the number of disputes going directly to the district courts in Texas's four federal judicial districts continues to increase. Figure 2

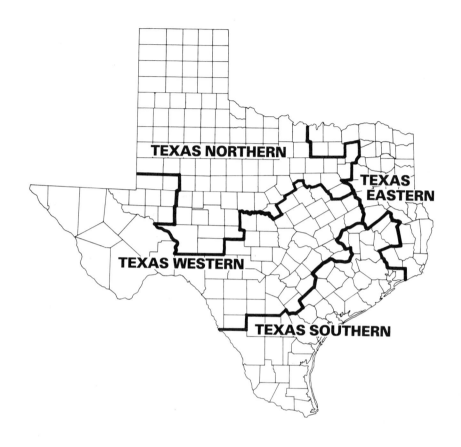

Figure 2. Geographic Jurisdiction of U.S. District Courts in Texas

illustrates the geographic jurisdictions of the four Texas federal judicial districts.

The most important function of federal courts is to adjudicate
disputes arising under the Constitution and statutes of the United
States. As a general rule, disputes arising under state law must be
tried in state courts. Decisions of the Texas federal district courts
are appealable to the U.S. Court of Appeals for the Fifth Circuit in
New Orleans, one of thirteen circuit courts in the nation. Prior to
1981, the Fifth Circuit encompassed six southern states and the
Canal Zone. But the population growth in this region of the country
convinced Congress to create another federal court of appeals—the
Eleventh, with headquarters in Atlanta—to hear the increasing volume of cases coming from Georgia, Alabama, and Florida. The present jurisdiction of the Fifth Circuit includes Louisiana, Mississippi,
and Texas. Decisions of the old Fifth Circuit constitute binding precedent in both the current Eleventh and Fifth circuits unless these
courts decide to the contrary. On occasion, a decision of the Fifth
Circuit will be reviewed by the U.S. Supreme Court in Washington,
D.C., which, of course, has the last word for the entire country. Unlike most other courts, the U.S. Supreme Court has the authority to
decide which cases it wishes to hear. From as many as eight thousand cases filed annually for review, the justices will select fewer
than two hundred for a full hearing. Thus, most federal questions
are resolved by the U.S. Courts of Appeals. For this reason, the pre-
cedents established by the U.S. Court of Appeals for the Fifth Circuit are particularly important in the context of Texas schooling.

One might assume that state and federal case law has relatively
little impact on Texas public education, compared with state statutes and administrative rules and regulations. Up until the last
twenty years or so, this was generally true. Since the late 1960s,
however, courts have been increasingly involved in a maze of litigation involving the day-to-day management of schools. The rulings
they hand down have become an important part of school law and
are ignored at one's peril.

Other sources of law besides the four primary types discussed
above also have an impact on education law. For example, contract
law plays an important role in the context of employment. For our
purposes, however, separating school law into the four previously
discussed types—constitutional, statutory, administrative, and
judicial—will help us understand how the system works. Table 1
provides an outline of the four types, and Table 2 shows how they
interrelate.

Table 1: Basic Components of Texas Education Law

Types of Law	Source	Impact on Texas Schooling
Constitutional	Tenth Amendment to U.S. Constitution	States that "the powers not delegated to the United States by the Constitution, nor prohibited by it to the States, are reserved to the States respectively . . ." Since education is not delegated to the federal government, it is a power reserved to the states.
	The Bill of Rights and the Fourteenth Amendment to the U.S. Constitution	Protects certain civil liberties of employees and students in the public schools.
	Texas Constitution of 1876, Art. 7, §1 and Bill of Rights	Authorizes the state legislature to support and maintain an efficient system of public free schools and provides for individual civil liberties.
Statutory	Acts of the U.S. Congress	Acts of Congress guarantee various civil rights and establish the conditions upon which states and political subdivisions may receive federal funds.
	Acts of Texas Legislature; most pertaining to education are found in the Texas Education Code	Sets up the State Board of Education and the Texas Education Agency to carry out limited educational functions. Actual operation of schools is left to school districts. School districts and school personnel are a part of the state.

Administrative	
Federal administrative regulations	Both TEA and local school districts must comply with the regulations promulgated by federal educational agencies implementing federal statutes.
Policies and rulings by school boards, Texas Commissioner of Education, and State Board of Education	Boards of trustees develop policies to be utilized in operating their schools. State board and commissioner have the authority to establish rules that govern school district activity in areas designated by the legislature. Any person aggrieved by the school laws of Texas or actions of school districts involving school laws or impairing employment contracts can appeal to the commissioner. Policies, rules, and appeal decisions are classified as administrative law.
Judicial	
Decisions of state courts	Any aggrieved person can appeal an adverse administrative ruling from the commissioner into state courts. Highest state court (civil) is the Texas Supreme Court, which has the last word on matters of state law, subject, of course, to the ultimate authority of the U.S. Supreme Court to review questions of state law in light of federal statutes and the U.S. Constitution.
Decisions of federal courts	Any person alleging state interference with a right granted by the U.S. Constitution or federal law can bring an action in a federal court. The lowest federal court is the district court. There are thirteen intermediate appellate federal courts (ours is the U.S. Court of Appeals for the Fifth Circuit). At the top is the U.S. Supreme Court, which has the last word on matters of federal law. The U.S. Constitution provides that any state action, law, or constitutional provision that conflicts with the Constitution or a federal law is null and void.

Table 2: Relationship of Law to Establishment and Operation of Texas Public Schools

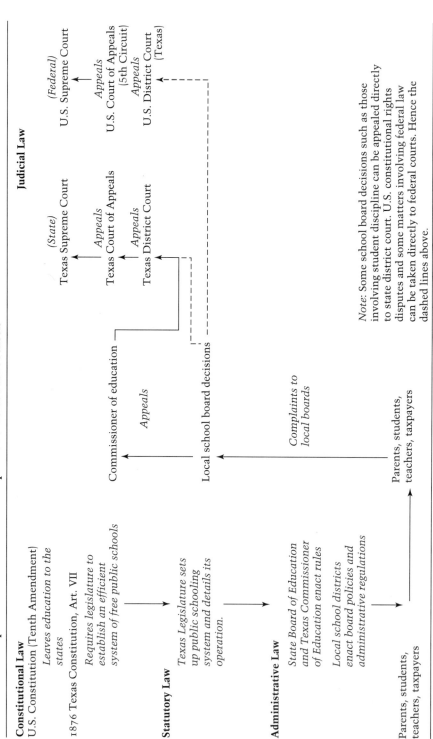

Constitutional Law
U.S. Constitution (Tenth Amendment)
Leaves education to the states
1876 Texas Constitution, Art. VII
Requires legislature to establish an efficient system of free public schools

Statutory Law
Texas Legislature sets up public schooling system and details its operation.

Administrative Law
State Board of Education and Texas Commissioner of Education enact rules

Local school districts enact board policies and administrative regulations

Parents, students, teachers, taxpayers

Complaints to local boards

Local school board decisions

Commissioner of education

Appeals

Judicial Law

(State)
Texas Supreme Court
Appeals
Texas Court of Appeals
Appeals
Texas District Court

(Federal)
U.S. Supreme Court
Appeals
U.S. Court of Appeals (5th Circuit)
Appeals
U.S. District Court (Texas)

Note: Some school board decisions such as those involving student discipline can be appealed directly to state district court. U.S. constitutional rights disputes and some matters involving federal law can be taken directly to federal courts. Hence the dashed lines above.

Parents, students, teachers, taxpayers

THE STRUCTURE AND GOVERNANCE OF THE TEXAS PUBLIC SCHOOL SYSTEM

Texas Legislature

The Texas Legislature, acting pursuant to the Tenth Amendment to the U.S. Constitution and Article VII of the Texas Constitution, is responsible for the structure and operation of the Texas public school system. The nearly continuous flow of reform legislation since 1980 makes it readily apparent that the legislature is the biggest player in Texas education. Thus, those wanting to influence the way Texas education is structured and conducted are well advised to focus their efforts on the Texas Legislature. Both school districts and educators are becoming increasingly sophisticated in this regard. However, TEC §7.103(c) prevents a person who registers as a professional lobbyist from serving as a school board member or acting as the general counsel to the board.

State Board of Education and the Texas Education Agency

Formerly the policy-making body of the Texas Education Agency, the State Board of Education was separated from TEA by the Texas Legislature in 1995 and given a reduced role in the public school system. An elected body of fifteen members, the state board is limited to performing only those duties assigned to it by the state constitution or by the legislature. While many of its functions have shifted in recent years to the Texas Commissioner of Education, the state board is still a powerful entity. Among its designated duties as set forth in TEC §7.102 are establishing a state curriculum and graduation requirements, determining the standard for satisfactory student performance on assessment instruments, adopting and purchasing state textbooks, adopting rules governing extracurricular activities, and investing the permanent school funds. The board is also charged with granting up to twenty charters for open-enrollment schools, a subject to be discussed later in the chapter, and adopting rules for the accreditation of school districts.

The Texas Education Agency is now composed of the Texas Commissioner of Education and the agency staff. Like the state board, TEA can perform only those duties specifically assigned to it by the legislature. The legislature's disenchantment with top-down control is clearly evident in the wording of TEC §7.003: "An educational function not specifically delegated to the agency or the board [of education] under this code is reserved to and shall be performed

by school districts or open-enrollment charter schools." TEC §7.021
lists fourteen educational functions that TEA is to perform. Included among them are monitoring district compliance with federal
and state programs, conducting research to improve teaching and
learning, developing a teacher recruitment program, and maintaining an electronic information system. TEA is also authorized to enter into agreements with federal agencies for such activities as
school lunches and school construction. In addition, TEA administers the capital investment fund established by the legislature to
provide grants to school districts for improving student achievement. With the downsizing of TEA has come a reduction in staff.
By the start of the 1996–1997 school year, TEA will employ
889 people, down nearly 200 from the year before.

Other than the legislature, the most powerful state-level player
is the Texas Commissioner of Education, whom the governor
appoints and removes with the advice and consent of the Texas
Senate. Like the governor, the commissioner serves a four-year
term. The only qualification for serving as commissioner is U.S.
citizenship. The legislature designates the commissioner to be the
educational leader of the state. The commissioner also serves as the
executive officer and executive secretary of the State Board of Education. Included among the forty responsibilities the legislature has
assigned the commissioner are adopting an annual budget for the
Foundation School Program, reviewing school district waiver requests, adopting rules for optional extended year programs, performing duties in connection with the public school accountability system, and reviewing school district audit reports (TEC §7.055). Other
sections of the Code give the commissioner added responsibilities,
e.g., taking sanctions against low-performing campuses and school
districts including closure (campuses) and annexation (districts)
(TEC §39.131). Several of the commissioner's current responsibilities previously belonged to the state board, such as adopting a recommended state appraisal process for teachers and administrators
and performing duties associated with the guaranteed bond program.

A necessary adjunct to the activities of the Texas Education
Agency are the twenty Regional Education Service Centers located
throughout the state. Operating under the auspices of the agency,
the service centers assist school districts in improving student
achievement and increasing the effectiveness of school operations
(TEC §8.001(b)). Their core services include teacher training, assistance in providing specialized programs like compensatory and special education, assistance to low-performing districts and campuses,
training in site-based management, and assistance in complying

with state law. Funding for these services is provided by the state through the Foundation School Program. The centers provide additional services under contract to school districts and, in partnership with school districts, seek grant support for various purposes. Each service center is governed by a seven-member board as established under rules developed by the commissioner of education. The commissioner also approves the selection of service center executive directors. Districts increasingly are relying on the service centers for computer and media services, staff training, and technical assistance.

Local School Districts

The governance of schools is clearly left to local boards of trustees. Section 11.151 of the Texas Education Code states that "the trustees as a body corporate have the exclusive power and duty to govern and oversee the management of the public schools of the district. All powers and duties not specifically designated by statute to the agency or to the State Board of Education are reserved for the trustees, and the agency may not substitute its judgment for the lawful exercise of those powers and duties by the trustees." Accordingly, the local school board may acquire and hold real and personal property, sue and be sued, receive bequests and donations, levy and collect taxes, sell minerals and property belonging to the district, and condemn property for securing school sites. While the school board also has the authority to make employment decisions, the board by policy must accord the superintendent the sole authority to make recommendations to the board regarding the selection of all personnel other than the superintendent (TEC §11.163). The board may delegate final authority for hiring to the superintendent. Taken together, these provisions give the local school board a status very similar to that of a municipality.

TEC §11.157 allows districts to contract with a public or private entity to provide educational services for the district. Sherman I.S.D. became the first Texas school district to take advantage of this provision to contract with the Edison Project to operate one of its elementary schools starting in the fall of 1995. The Edison Project is a for-profit corporation started by entrepreneur-businessman Chris Whittle to revolutionize the schooling process through a rigorous curriculum, increased time in school, and the innovative use of technology. When a district contracts with a private vendor to provide educational services, the district must ensure that the vendor complies with state statutory requirements applicable to public school districts (*Att'y. Gen. Op. DM-355*, 1995). The Texas Attorney General noted that nothing in the contracting statute exempts the private vendor from complying with these statutory requirements, nor denies to participating students the benefits the statutes provide.

TEC §11.158 allows school boards to charge fees for a number of activities such as membership dues in voluntary student organizations, security deposits for return of materials, and parking. The board may not charge fees for school lockers, required field trips, and library books, to name a few. TEC §11.162 allows school boards to require school uniforms, provided that the uniforms are furnished free of cost to the "educationally disadvantaged" and that children of parents who have a religious or philosophical objection to the requirement are exempted.

One of the more interesting provisions of the Code is TEC §11.160, which allows the board of trustees to change the name of the district. All kinds of interesting name changes have been proposed in jest, such as "Way Above Average I.S.D.," "Schools-R-Us I.S.D.," and "The Fiercely Independent School District."

The majority of Texas school districts elect their board members in at-large elections. Increasingly, however, minority voters are asserting that single-member districts should replace the at-large system. In a single-member system, the school district is divided into five or more separate election districts, each with its own trustee position. Thus, each election district will be assured at least one trustee who is from that area and represents the special concerns or needs of that election district. TEC §§11.052–11.053 governs the changing of an at-large system to a single-member system. A single-member system must be submitted to the U.S. Justice Department for approval under the 1965 Voting Rights Act.

School board trustees serve a term of three or four years (TEC §11.059). Elections for trustees with three-year terms are held annually, with one-third expiring each year. Elections for trustees with four-year terms are held biennially, with one-half expiring each biennium. The staggered terms assure continuity to school board functioning. A person must be an eligible voter to be qualified for office as a trustee. Trustees serve without compensation. The state board is required to provide a training program for school board members through the regional service centers. Other training programs are offered through professional associations such as the Texas Association of School Boards (TASB). TASB is a comprehensive organization that provides a host of services to school boards, including model school board policies that most districts have adopted. TASB also is influential in the legislative arena on behalf of its members and provides financial support to districts embroiled in expensive litigation.

Charter Schools

Freeing up public schools from state regulation and giving parents more influence over the education of their children have become major legislative agenda items in the 1990s. Texas is no exception. In his 1994 election campaign, Governor George Bush promoted the concept of "home-rule school districts," which would allow local communities to shape the functioning of their schools. Key figures within the Texas Legislature also wanted to increase school district and campus autonomy through locally developed "charters" that are granted by school boards or by the State Board of Education. Three forms of charter schools emerged from the 1995 legislative session: home-rule school district charters, campus charters, and open-enrollment charters.

Home-rule school district charters allow school districts to free themselves from most state requirements. A school district is required to appoint a fifteen-member charter commission if at least 5 percent of the registered voters of the district sign a petition or two-thirds of the school board members adopt a resolution. The charter developed by the commission must address such matters as the educational program to be offered, the governance structure of the district and campuses, acceptable levels of student performance, and the budgeting process (TEC §12.016). If the secretary of state determines that the proposed charter changes the governance structure of the district, the charter must be submitted to the U.S. Justice Department or the U.S. District Court for the District of Columbia for preclearance under the 1965 Voting Rights Act. The charter also has to be submitted to the commissioner of education for a legal review. The proposed charter becomes effective if adopted by majority vote in an election where at least 25 percent of the registered voters in the district participate. The 25 percent requirement will be a significant hurdle for many districts to overcome. The State Board of Education is given authority for revoking or placing a home-rule district charter on probation. Other provisions in the Texas Education Code describe the process for voter amendment or rescission of the charter.

TEC §12.012 provides that home-rule districts are subject only to those state laws and administrative rules that specifically apply to them. Thus, for example, since neither Texas educator employment law nor student discipline law specifically mention home-rule districts, home-rule districts arguably are exempt from these provisions. In addition, home-rule school districts may determine their own curriculum. However, home-rule districts are not autonomous. In addition to federal law requirements for such matters as special education and nondiscrimination, TEC §12.013 sets forth a list of state requirements that must be followed. Included are those pertaining to educator certification, student admissions and attendance, high school graduation requirements, class size restriction for low-performing schools, public school accountability, state purchasing, and accreditation sanctions.

Under the second charter option, a school district board of trustees or governing body of a home-rule school district may grant a charter to parents and teachers to operate a campus or campus program free from most regulation including district instructional and academic requirements if presented with a petition signed by the majority of parents and teachers at the school (TEC §12.052). Cooperative charters involving two or more campuses may also be approved. A school board may not arbitrarily deny approval of a charter. This means that, while boards have discretion in approving proposed campus charters, they can only reject a charter for cause. It will be interesting to see how school boards handle innovative proposals that might be competitive with the district's existing schools and programs. Considerable tension and infighting have occurred in Minnesota and other states where local school boards have the authority to grant charters.

The proposed campus charter must describe the educational program, acknowledge that continuation of the charter is dependent upon satisfactory student performance, specify the conditions under which the charter may be placed on probation or revoked, prohibit various forms of discrimination, describe the governing structure, specify health and safety measures, and provide for an annual audit (TEC §12.058). The governing body of the campus or program is subject to the provisions of the Texas Open Meetings and Public Information acts. These statutes are discussed in Chapter 9. While the campus charter school has a good deal of autonomy within the district, the school board retains legal responsibility for its activities.

Campus charter schools and programs remain public schools and are subject to federal law and to those state statutes that specifically apply to them. Among matters specified by the latter are the Public Education Information Management System (PEIMS), high school graduation requirements, special education and bilingual education requirements, prekindergarten programs, extracurricular activity provisions, and health and safety measures (TEC §12.056).

But charter schools are exempt from most other provisions of the Code. TEC §12.064 provides that geography and residence are to be given first priority in student admissions, thus preserving the concept of the nonelite neighborhood school. Age, grade level, and academic qualifications are secondary considerations.

How responsive campus parent bodies and teachers will be to the opportunity campus charters afford for innovative approaches to schooling remains to be seen. For some time, the annual Gallup Poll of Education has shown that most parents give high marks to the public schools their children attend, even if they also express dissatisfaction with public schooling in general.

Open-enrollment charter schools constitute the third charter option. The State Board of Education is given authority to grant up to twenty charters for the operation of these schools in a facility of a commercial or nonprofit entity, a school district, a public or private college or university, or governmental entity (TEC §12.101). Open-enrollment charter schools are public schools that may attract students from either within or across school district lines in competition with existing public and private schools. Open-enrollment charter schools can provide instruction at one or more elementary or secondary grade levels as long as students perform satisfactorily. They operate much like new school districts, except that they do not have authority to impose taxes. Revenue in the form of state and local funding follows the student. Open-enrollment charter schools may not charge tuition and must provide transportation on the same basis as existing school districts.

Like the other two forms of charter schools, open-enrollment charters are exempt from most state laws and rules other than those specified in the TEC. A list of the latter is provided in TEC §12.104 and is similar to those for the other forms of charters, except that open-enrollment charter schools must offer the state-required curriculum. The components of the charter are also similar, with the addition of such items as specification of grade levels, qualifications of professional employees, facilities, and enrollment criteria. Open-enrollment charter schools may not discriminate in admissions on the basis of sex, national origin, ethnicity, religion, disability, academic or athletic ability, or school district the student would otherwise attend. Charter schools may reject students who have committed criminal offenses or have a history of disciplinary problems.

Senate Bill 1 required the State Board of Education to develop approval criteria and procedures for the open-enrollment chartering process. The board took little time doing so, with a set of criteria and procedures in place by the fall of 1995. The criteria address stu-

dent performance, innovative programs, and potential impact on existing districts. In addition, the legislature also requires the state board to select an impartial organization with experience in evaluating school choice programs to conduct an annual evaluation of open-enrollment charter schools. The evaluation is to encompass costs, student performance, and impact on existing school districts (TEC §12.118). Previous research on school choice consistently shows that choosing parents are different from nonchoosing parents. They are more likely to have higher incomes, more education, fewer children, and greater ambition for their children's education.[1] At the same time, there is little reliable research on how school choice affects student performance, controlling both for the socioeconomic characteristics of families and the bias inherent in the act of choosing. Open-enrollment charter schools may provide an opportunity to learn more about the impact of school choice on students, parents, and schools. The fact that they must follow the state-mandated curriculum, however, diminishes their ability to be innovative.

School Administrators

The superintendent is the chief operating officer of the district, responsible for implementing the policies of the board. TEC §11.201 lists eleven superintendent duties. Included among them are responsibility for the operation of the educational programs, services, and facilities of the district and appraisal of the staff; assigning and evaluating personnel; and making personnel recommendations to the school board. The superintendent also is responsible for developing a budget, organizing the district's central administration, overseeing the development of administrative regulations to implement board policies, and performing other duties assigned by the board of trustees.

The school principal is the front-line administrator, with statutory responsibility under the direction of the superintendent for administering the day-to-day activities of the school. Principals have seven major functions, as listed in TEC §11.202. Based on criteria

---

[1] See, for example, Valerie J. Martinez, R. Kenneth Godwin, Frank R. Kemerer, and Laura Perna, "The Consequences of School Choice: Who Leaves and Who Stays in the Inner City," *Social Science Quarterly*, September 1995. See also Valerie J. Martinez, Kay Thomas, and Frank R. Kemerer, "Who Chooses and Why: A Study of Five School Choice Programs," *Phi Delta Kappan*, May 1994.

developed in consultation with the faculty, they have approval
power for teacher and staff appointments to the campus from a pool
of applicants selected by the district or of applicants who meet the
district's hiring requirements. However, the superintendent or the
superintendent's designee can override the principal regarding
teacher placement resulting from enrollment shifts or program
changes. Principals set campus education objectives through the
planning process, develop budgets, and have responsibility for student discipline. They also assign, evaluate, and promote campus
personnel, as well as make recommendations to the superintendent
regarding suspension, nonrenewal, and termination of personnel. Finally, they perform other duties assigned by the superintendent.

The certification requirements for principals developed by
the State Board for Educator Certification—a topic addressed in
more detail in Chapter 4—must be sufficiently flexible so that
an outstanding teacher may substitute approved experience and
professional training for part of the educational requirements
(TEC §21.046). Further, qualifications for certification as a superintendent or principal must allow the substitution of management
training and experience for part of the educational requirements.
The legislature has increasingly emphasized the importance of recruiting and retaining the highest caliber of personnel for the principalship. School boards are required to institute multilevel screening
processes, validated comprehensive assessments, and flexible in-
ternships with successful mentors to determine whether a candidate for certification as a principal is qualified.

Believing principals to be the persons with the most responsibility for school improvement, the legislature has given them more
authority to operate their schools. At the same time, principals are
held more accountable for their work. The appraisal of a school
principal must include consideration of the performance of the
campus on the academic indicators set forth in TEC §39.051 and on
the campus objectives established under TEC §11.253. The legislature appears particularly serious about administrator appraisal.
School district funds cannot be used to pay an administrator who
has not been appraised in the preceding fifteen months. In addition,
TEC §39.054 provides that the campus performance report as-
sembled each year by school districts shall be a primary consideration of superintendents in evaluating principals. Likewise, the district performance report is to be a primary consideration of school
boards in evaluating school superintendents. These reports will be
discussed in more detail in the next chapter. With increased respon-

sibility also comes increased liability. For example, principals must be familiar with employment law in order to carry out their personnel responsibilities effectively and without legal liability.

While local school boards and administrators have substantial power, they must manage and govern the public schools in accordance with both federal and state law—law that is constantly changing. And they must do so economically. TEC §42.201 directs the Texas Commissioner of Education to determine annually a cost ratio of administrative to instructional expenses and to require school district compliance. Failure of a district to reduce administrative costs to the desired ratio can result in a reduction of state aid or a requirement to remit the amount in excess of the ratio to the state comptroller.

District and Campus-Level Decision Making

Despite the authority given to local school boards, the Texas Legislature since 1990 has increasingly sought to "flatten the decision-making pyramid" by involving others in district and campus governance. Over the years, these requirements have become more complex. TEC §11.251 requires the establishment of committees at the district and campus level to participate in establishing and reviewing educational plans, goals, performance objectives, and major classroom instructional programs. The committees are to be broadly representative of professional staff, parents, community members, and business representatives. The latter need not reside in the district. In partnership with the district-level committee, the board is also required to delineate the roles of those involved in planning, budgeting, curriculum, staffing, staff development, and school organization at both the district and campus level.

TEC §11.251 requires each board to have a procedure for the nomination and election of professional staff representatives to the district-level committee (two-thirds must be classroom teachers; one-third must be professional staff) and to establish procedures for selecting the other members and for holding meetings periodically with the board or board designee. The statute stipulates that the committee process is not intended to limit the power of the board to manage and govern the schools and is not to be construed as a collective bargaining statute. Nor is it to restrict the board from conducting meetings with teacher groups or receiving input from students, paraprofessional staff, and others.

A companion statute, TEC §11.253, requires that the school principal regularly involve the campus committee in planning, bud-

geting, curriculum, staffing, staff development, and school organization. Otherwise advisory, the committee does have approval power
over the portion of the improvement plan addressing staff development. The membership of the campus committee and its selection
are similar to that of the district-level committee. Like the district-
level process, campus-level decision making is not to be construed
as any form of collective bargaining. Whether or not mandated site-
based decision making will be any more effective than centralized
decision making in improving student achievement remains to be
seen. At present, there are no reliable research findings on the issue.

Utilizing the deliberative processes set forth in these statutes,
school boards and campus administrators are required to engage in
an annual planning and improvement process linked to student
achievement. Each district's improvement plan is to encompass
such matters as a comprehensive needs assessment addressing student performance on the academic excellence indicators set forth in
TEC §39.051, performance objectives, and strategies for improving
student achievement. Among the strategies to be discussed are the
need for special programs, dropout reduction, integration of technology in instructional and administrative programs, discipline
management, and staff development (TEC §11.253). Each campus's
improvement plan must assess each student's performance using
the academic excellence indicator system, identify how campus
goals will be met, determine the resources and staffing needed,
set timelines, and establish a periodic assessment process (TEC
§11.253). At least every two years, school districts are required to
evaluate the impact of their planning and decision-making processes on improving student achievement.

That the site-based decision process remains essentially advisory appears clear both from the wording of the current statutes and
from early commissioner decisions predating Senate Bill 1. In three
1995 decisions, the commissioner rejected teacher contentions that
they had been illegally excluded from decision making. The first
case involved the hiring of a new principal without involvement
by the campus-level committee. The commissioner noted that
TEC §21.931 (now TEC §11.253) gives school districts considerable
discretion in deciding the role of the campus committee. Here, the
committee had not been given a direct role in the selection of a
principal. This being the case, the district did not violate its own
policy by electing not to consult the committee (*Clear Creek Educators Association TSTA/NEA v. Clear Creek I.S.D.*). Similarly, the
commissioner determined that the statutes did not require a school
district to involve either district- or campus-level committees in the

restructuring of the district's junior high schools, since the matter was more a matter of location and less a matter of instruction (*La Porte Education Association v. La Porte I.S.D.*). In the third decision, the commissioner concluded that the school board retained authority under its plan to reject the school committee's block scheduling proposal, which would have varied the schedules and instructional time at the district's two high schools. The commissioner noted that site-based decision making is not designed to limit the board's governance authority in such matters (*Shoffner v. Goose Creek C.I.S.D.*). In a fourth decision, the commissioner determined that a district's existing policies and procedures met the statutory requirements for implementing site-based management (*Classroom Teachers of Dallas/TSTA/NEA v. Dallas I.S.D.*). All four decisions involved pre–Senate Bill 1 provisions, and thus are not necessarily indicative of future decisions involving the slightly altered wording of the current statutes.

HOW THE U.S. CONSTITUTION AND FEDERAL GOVERNMENT AFFECT TEXAS SCHOOLS

Key Provisions of the U.S. Constitution

Until recently, the role of Congress and the federal courts in education matters was quite limited. However, the quest for individual rights and greater procedural safeguards triggered by the civil rights movement of the 1960s spilled over into the schools. In the past twenty years, a new generation of constitutional rights law has evolved. The changes have been significant and are discussed in detail in subsequent chapters. Nonetheless, the advent of a more conservative majority on the Supreme Court, led by Chief Justice William Rehnquist, has tempered the Court's recent extension of constitutional protections to students and school district employees. As a result, plaintiffs are beginning to bring suits on these issues in state rather than federal court.

We begin with the Bill of Rights of the U.S. Constitution. Most of our basic civil liberties are included among its provisions. The First Amendment is particularly important, for it lists several liberties inherent in a democratic society: the right to be free from governmental control in the exercise of speech, publication, religious preference, and assembly. However, the First Amendment, like the other nine in the Bill of Rights, applies only to the federal government (the first word in the First Amendment is *Congress*).

To determine what U.S. Constitutional rights we enjoy in the state setting, we must look to the Fourteenth Amendment. For our purpose, two clauses from the first section of that amendment are important: "nor shall any State deprive any person of life, liberty, or property without due process of law, nor deny to any person within its jurisdiction the equal protection of the laws." These two clauses—the due process clause and the equal protection clause—together with the federal laws that implement them, provide the basis for constitutional rights suits against public educational institutions and personnel. Congress passed a statute after the Civil War to enforce the Fourteenth Amendment by enabling aggrieved persons to pursue their claims in federal court. That statute, known as 42 U.S.C. §1983, is one of the major sources of litigation against both school districts and school personnel. The statute provides that "Every person who, under color of any statute, ordinance, regulation, custom, or usage, of any State or Territory, subjects, or causes to be subjected, any citizen of the United States or other person within the jurisdiction thereof to the deprivation of any rights, privileges, or immunities secured by the Constitution and laws, shall be liable to the party injured in an action at law, suit in equity, or other proper proceedings for redress [in federal court]." As will be noted often in this book and particularly in the last chapter on legal liability, the consequences can be severe.

One may wonder how schools can be affected by the Fourteenth Amendment, phrased as it is in terms of states. As we already have noted, local school districts are legally viewed as state political subdivisions. Therefore, the Fourteenth Amendment applies to public school districts and personnel, but not to private schools, since they are not state related. Neither the Bill of Rights, the Fourteenth Amendment, nor most provisions of the Texas Education Code apply to private schools. This is an important point, for many educators assume they are entitled to the same rights in the private school setting as in the public. In reality, the "rights" that a person has in private schools depend to a large extent on the wishes of the private school. For the private school, contract law is of great importance, since it defines not only the teacher-institution relationship but also the relationship of the student to the school. Thus, it is important that contractual provisions be carefully developed and reviewed.

Over the years the U.S. Supreme Court has held that almost all provisions of the Bill of Rights are binding on the states through the Fourteenth Amendment. In other words, the Supreme Court has gradually incorporated these rights into the Fourteenth Amendment, specifically through the "liberty" provision of the due process clause, thereby ensuring that neither the federal government nor the states can abridge them. Courts have differed, however, on the extent to which teachers and, particularly, students in the public schools enjoy the same protections as do other persons.

Neither liberty rights nor property rights are without limits. They can be regulated, even denied, provided that the state or school follows due process: "nor shall any State deprive any person of life, liberty, or property without due process of law," meaning that, if due process *is* followed, the curtailment of rights *can* occur. Due process rights for employees will be discussed in some detail in Chapter 4 and those for students in Chapter 8.

Behavior that is not constitutionally protected as a liberty or property right can be regulated relatively easily. Smoking and the possession and/or use of hallucinogenic drugs fall into this category. The legislature has banned smoking by all persons at school-related or school-sanctioned activities on or off campus (TEC §38.006) and has made student possession or use of hallucinogenic drugs an expellable offense if punishable as a felony (TEC §37.007).

Of course, the fact that the U.S. Constitution does not protect certain types of behavior does not mean that a state legislature or school district cannot decide to do so. For example, some school districts grant students personal grooming rights, though they are not legally required to do so.

In sum, the Fourteenth Amendment protects persons from state government repression of basic civil liberties guarantees, such as those in the Bill of Rights to the U.S. Constitution. Since public schools are part of state government, the Fourteenth Amendment applies to them and to their employees, but not to private schools. Exactly what constitutional rights students and teachers have in the public school setting will be discussed in subsequent chapters.

A second major source of constitutional litigation in the public school setting relates to the Fourteenth Amendment equal protection clause: "nor [shall any state] deny to any person within its jurisdiction the equal protection of the laws." This amendment, coupled with civil rights laws designed to enforce it, has furnished the grounds for antidiscrimination suits against schools. While desegregation suits have abated in recent years, so-called second-generation equal protection issues have arisen over such matters as in-school tracking and competency-based testing.

Important Federal Laws

There are a number of federal statutes that directly affect the day-to-day operation of Texas public schools. Several also apply to private schools. The most important are briefly set forth here and will be referred to periodically in later chapters.

42 U.S.C. §1981 accords all persons the right to make and enforce contracts free of racial discrimination in both the public and private sectors. This law recently has been amended to apply to discrimination occurring during the contract term as well. Thus, a minority child subject to discrimination after being admitted to a private school would have a cause of action. Penalties include both injunctive relief and compensatory damages.

42 U.S.C. §1983 allows suits for injunctive relief and compensatory damages against public school districts that through policy or practice deprive persons of U.S. Constitutional and federal statutory rights. Public employees are also subject to suit under this statute. This law is very important in the enforcement of federal rights under the Fourteenth Amendment.

Title VI of the 1964 Civil Rights Act prohibits intentional discrimination in the context of race, color, or national origin in federally assisted programs. Injunctive relief and monetary damages are available. This law was instrumental in the desegregation of schools during the 1960s and '70s.

Title VII of the 1964 Civil Rights Act prohibits discrimination on the basis of race, color, religion, sex, or national origin in all aspects of public and private employment. In addition to equitable relief such as back pay and reinstatement, this law has been amended to allow money damages for intentional discrimination.

Americans with Disabilities Act of 1990 accords persons with disabilities meaningful access to the programs and facilities of public and private schools as well as most businesses in the country. The statute also prohibits discrimination against persons with disabilities in public and private employment, and requires employers to make reasonable accommodation for disabled persons to enable them to perform the job. Money damages are available for intentional discrimination.

Title IX of the 1972 Education Amendments prohibits discrimination against persons on the basis of sex in any federally assisted education program. Penalties against school districts under this statute can encompass compensatory damages as well as termination of federal funding. Title IX has gained major significance in the context of student and employee sexual harassment. For example, the school district can be liable when an administrator sexually harasses a teacher or when a principal fails to act when a student complains about unwelcome sexual advances from a teacher.

Individuals with Disabilities Education Act requires public schools to identify and provide children with disabilities a free appropriate public education in the least restrictive environment. Together with §504 of the 1973 Rehabilitation Act, IDEA provides a comprehensive legal framework for serving children with disabilities. Both statutes will be discussed in detail in Chapter 3.

In addition to these, there are a number of other important federal laws that will be discussed in subsequent chapters. Included among them are the Equal Access Act, the Family Educational Rights and Privacy Act (Buckley Amendment), and the Equal Pay Act.

SCHOOL FINANCE

School finance is a complex subject, generally beyond the scope of this book. However, it is important to have an overview of the subject since it is central to the operation of the school system and remains contentious. In recent years the issue of equalization in school finance has been the focus of a dramatic struggle between the Texas judicial and legislative branches of government.

As previously noted, the 1876 Texas Constitution left to the legislature the duty to establish an efficient system of public education. That same year the Texas Legislature established the Available School Fund, with monies for education apportioned on a per capita basis. The Available School Fund consisted of revenue from an endowment and from designated state taxes. Funding was to be provided on a per capita basis, though for many years the amounts distributed were meager. Most of the funding for public education originated at the local level.

With the growth of population centers, the imbalance between urban and rural districts created by reliance on local property taxation became increasingly apparent. But it wasn't until the enactment of the Gilmer-Aikin Bill in 1949 that substantial reform occurred. The Gilmer-Aikin Bill later became the focus of the *San Antonio I.S.D. v. Rodriguez* equalization lawsuit filed in federal court in the late 1960s. The bill established a Minimum Foundation Program (MFP), whereby state funds for personnel and operations were distributed via a complicated economic index that established a basic minimum below which no district could go. The MFP involved both local and state contributions to a special fund. Eighty percent of the funding came from the state, with the rest coming from local districts on an ability-to-pay basis. Thus, each local district had to levy a property tax to support its contribution. But inequities continued because local districts remained free to enrich their contributions for their schools beyond the MFP local fund assignment. At the time of the *San Antonio I.S.D.* suit, all districts did so, though the amounts raised varied considerably. For example, in 1967–1968, Edgewood I.S.D., one of the parties to the suit, contributed $26 per student above its MFP local fund assignment at a property tax rate of $1.05 per $100 of valuation. Alamo Heights I.S.D., serving an affluent portion of San Antonio, was able to raise $333 per student above its local fund assignment at a tax rate of $0.85 per $100 of valuation. Similar interdistrict differences occurred elsewhere in Texas and, indeed, throughout the nation.

The plaintiffs in the *San Antonio I.S.D. v. Rodriguez* lawsuit tried to convince the courts that this system of educational finance violated the equal protection clause of the Fourteenth Amendment. While the lower court agreed, the U.S. Supreme Court did not. In a five-to-four decision, the Court ruled that the plan had a rational purpose, did not deprive anyone of a fundamental constitutional right, and did not discriminate against any particular group in violation of the Fourteenth Amendment equal protection clause. The high court noted that, while not perfect, the Texas MFP program did alleviate some of the vast differences in school finance among districts. For example, Alamo Heights I.S.D. derived almost thirteen times as much money from local property taxes as Edgewood did in 1967–1968, but the MFP reduced the ratio to approximately two-to-one.

While ruling against the plaintiffs, the majority on the Court urged the Texas Legislature to end the glaring discrepancies between rich and poor districts. Despite some legislative attempts to improve the existing system of educational finance after 1973, significant inequities remained and, in fact, increased. These inequalities persisted despite the passage of House Bill 72 during the special session in the summer of 1984. House Bill 72 fundamentally changed the school finance system by establishing a basic allotment for each student in the state and by introducing other mechanisms intended to foster equalization.

After *Rodriguez*, the next episode in the Texas equalization fight was *Edgewood v. Kirby*, filed in state district court in Travis County. The property-poor districts, having failed to find an enforceable right under the U.S. Constitution in *Rodriguez*, sought to find such a right under the Texas Constitution in *Edgewood*. The case was tried before Judge Harley Clark, and in 1987 Judge Clark declared the existing system of school finance in Texas unconstitutional. Judge Clark ruled that, because education is a fundamental right and because wealth is a suspect classification under provisions of the Texas Constitution, disparities between property-rich and property-poor districts violate the equal rights provision of the Texas Constitution, Article I, §3. That provision provides in part that "All free men, when they form a social compact, have equal rights. . . ." Judge Clark enjoined state officials from enforcing the challenged school finance statutes but "stayed" the injunction until September 1, 1989. His intention was to give the 1989 legislature an opportunity to enact a constitutional school finance system.

The defendants appealed the district court decision to the Texas Court of Appeals in Austin. In December 1988, the court of appeals, closely following the reasoning of the U.S. Supreme Court majority in *Rodriguez*, reversed Judge Clark's district court decision. With this development, the legislature was off the hook and, predictably, failed to address equalization in any significant manner.

The plaintiffs, having won in the district court and lost in the court of appeals, filed a further appeal in the Texas Supreme Court. The Supreme Court handed down a decision reversing the Third Court of Appeals on October 2, 1989. The court noted in *Edgewood I.S.D. v. Kirby* (*Edgewood I*) that "if the system is not 'efficient' or not 'suitable,' the legislature has not discharged its constitutional duty . . ." Thus, the Texas Supreme Court mandated that the Texas Legislature remedy the inefficiencies in the Texas school financing system by May 1, 1990, although the court purposely provided no guidelines as to how this should be achieved. Finding the present system in violation of the Texas Constitution, the court did offer this guideline:

> Efficiency does not require a per capita distribution, but it also does not allow concentrations of resources in property-rich school districts that are taxing low when property-poor districts that are taxing high cannot generate sufficient revenues to meet even minimum standards. There must be a direct and close correlation between a district's tax effort and the education resources available to it; in other words, districts must have substantially equal access to similar revenues per pupil at similar

levels of tax effort. . . . Certainly, this much is required if the state is to educate its populace efficiently and provide for a general diffusion of knowledge statewide.

The Texas Legislature struggled mightily to address the court's objections in enacting yet another finance plan during the sixth called special session in the summer of 1990. In January 1991, the Texas Supreme Court once again unanimously declared the plan unconstitutional because it did not correct the deficiencies noted in *Edgewood I*. The court suggested in *Edgewood II* that the legislature could effect systemic change by consolidating school districts, thus removing duplicative administrative costs, and by consolidating tax bases. Nothing in the state constitution, the court noted, prohibits tax base consolidation. The justices reinstated the injunction against continued state funding of education but delayed the order until April 1, 1991.

Shortly thereafter, the high court was faced with a motion for rehearing filed by property-poor districts. The motion asked the court to overrule its 1931 *Love v. City of Dallas* decision holding that local property taxes could not be used to educate students outside the district. The property-poor districts argued that since local districts are creatures of the state, local property revenue could be considered a state tax and thus could be used to fund other school districts. In an order of February 25, 1991 (known as *Edgewood II½* and appended to the court's published *Edgewood I.S.D. II* decision), the court refused to overrule *Love*, noting that tax base consolidation could be achieved through the creation of new districts with the authority to generate local property tax revenue for all of the other districts within their boundaries.

But then, interestingly, five members of the court went further. Noting that property-rich districts as defendants had filed a brief in which they urged the court to clarify whether unequalized local enrichment was still possible under the state constitution, Chief Justice Thomas R. Phillips responded, for the five, in the affirmative. "Once the Legislature provides an efficient system in compliance with Article VII, §1, it may, so long as efficiency is maintained, authorize local school districts to supplement their educational resources if local property owners approve an additional local property tax." This comment set off a scathing attack by Justice Lloyd Doggett, with whom two other members concurred. Doggett accused the five of responding to newspaper editorials decrying the effect of equalization on wealthy districts, which would see their locally generated revenues siphoned off for use elsewhere. "Today a judge expounds on social policy preferences rather than resolving a motion," he wrote. "The underlying need for writing arises from the fear that the Legislature may otherwise fail to satisfy certain judicial desires, not that it may inadvertently pursue some further unconstitutional course. The restraint observed by a unified court has become the activism promoted by a majority of a divided one."

The Texas Legislature once again tried to reform the system by enacting Senate Bill 351 in the 1991 regular session. That measure sought to consolidate school district tax bases by creating 188 county education districts (CEDs) to levy, collect, and disburse property taxes in a way to minimize interdistrict disparities. But the Texas Supreme Court was not impressed. In January of 1992, Senate Bill 351 was declared unconstitutional in *Carrollton–Farmers Branch I.S.D. v. Edgewood I.S.D. (Edgewood III)*. The central problem was that the county education districts violated constitutional provisions requiring local voter approval of local property taxes and prohibiting a state property tax. The court, however, did allow the county education district plan to operate for the 1992–1993 school year and gave the legislature until June 1, 1993, to reform the finance system. After that date, all state funding for education would cease. Three justices favored no extension of time. A fourth, Justice John Cornyn, took the opportunity to shift the discussion to a different level. He noted the absence of evidence showing a direct correlation between expenditures and student achievement and suggested the time had come to focus more on ways to achieve equalization of educational results.

Now expressing considerable frustration and uncertainty, the Texas Legislature opted to let the voters have a chance to pass a constitutional amendment upholding the CED plan, which effectively would moot the Supreme Court decision. The voters rejected that measure in the spring of 1993, along with two others designed to help financially strapped districts. With time running out before the June 1 deadline, the legislature passed Senate Bill 7. The law required school districts above a certain wealth level to engage in tax base reduction by transferring wealth to poorer school districts. Five options for school districts were listed: (1) consolidate with one or more districts, (2) detach territory with another district, (3) purchase attendance credits from the state, (4) contract to educate nonresident students, or (5) consolidate tax bases with other districts. The last three options required voter approval. No sooner was the ink dry than lawsuits were filed by both property-poor and property-wealthy school districts. Finally, late in 1994, the Texas Supreme Court upheld Senate Bill 7 as constitutional "in all respects." The

Court found that the plan provided an efficient system of education. However, the Court cautioned that "Our judgment in this case should not be interpreted as a signal that the school finance crisis in Texas has ended." The basic provisions of Senate Bill 7 remain in effect.

PARENT RIGHTS

In 1923 the U.S. Supreme Court noted that parents have a constitutionally protected right to control their children's upbringing (*Meyer v. Nebraska*). While the parameters of the right in the education context have remained unclear, growing pressure has been evident in recent years to increase parental influence and control. In this section, we examine how Texas law protects parent rights in public schools, the right of parents to choose private schools, and the right of parents to educate their children at home.

Rights within Public Schools

In the recodification of Texas school law in 1995, the legislature added a section identifying parent rights and responsibilities. TEC §26.001 recognizes parents as partners in the educational process and encourages their participation in "creating and implementing educational programs for their children." To that end, the statute requires boards of trustees to support the establishment of at least one parent-teacher organization in each school of the district and to establish a parent complaint procedure. The term "parent" means anyone standing in a parental relationship to a child. Excluded are individuals whose parental rights have been terminated or who do not have access to or possession of a child under court order.

　　While TEC §25.031 gives school officials the authority to assign students to particular schools and classrooms within a district, parents have the right to petition the board to have their child placed at a particular school or to contest the assignment to a particular school under TEC §26.003. That section of the Code also gives parents the right to ask the school principal to have the child reassigned from a particular class or teacher within a school if the change would not affect the assignment of another student. Parents have a right to request, with the expectation that the request will not be unreasonably denied, the addition of an academic class to the curriculum if it would be economical to do so, the right to request placement of their child in a class above the child's grade level, and the right to have their child graduate early if all course requirements have been completed. If the child graduates early, the child has a right to participate in graduation ceremonies. The board's decision in these matters is final and nonappealable. This curtails the ability of parents to enforce the statutory provisions against a recalcitrant school board unless they can convince the commissioner or a judge that the board has acted illegally—for example, by engaging in illegal discrimination. As we noted earlier, in this sense nothing is ever truly "final and nonappealable."

Parents of children attending low-performing schools are entitled to a public education grant so that their children may attend a school in another district (TEC §29.201). This provision is a watered-down version of a voucher plan that did not pass in the 1995 legislative session. The voucher would have enabled parents to choose private, as well as public, schools. Under the public education grant program, a low-performing school is defined as one having 50 percent or more of the students performing less than satisfactorily on state assessment tests or as one identified as low performing by the commissioner of education. The education grant consists of the state and local funding the student is entitled to in the residential district. The chosen district may not charge additional tuition. If the chosen district's expenditure per student is less than the public education grant, the difference remains with the residential district. Districts have the right not to accept students from other districts under this program, but they may not refuse to accept them for reasons of race, ethnicity, academic achievement, athletic abilities, language proficiency, sex, or socioeconomic status. This essentially leaves available space as the selection criterion. If there are more applicants than places, the district must select by lottery, giving preference, first, to choosing students from the same family or household and then to at-risk students. The residential district is required to provide transportation to the school the child would have attended. The parent is responsible for transportation beyond this point. It will be interesting to see how many parents take advantage of this school choice provision once it becomes better known and whether school districts will be willing to accept children from other districts. It is likely that the legislature will expand parental choice options in the future, particularly if parents are frustrated in their attempts to have their children escape low-performing schools.

Texas law reinforces federal law in giving parents access to all written records concerning their child, including attendance records, test scores, disciplinary records, psychological records, and teacher and counselor evaluations (TEC §26.004). It is important to point out that the federal provisions require that parent rights in this context transfer to the student when the student turns eighteen or is attending a postsecondary institution, though parents do not lose their right of access if they claim their child as a dependent. The federal Family Educational Rights and Privacy Act is discussed in Chapter 9. In addition, parents have a right to see state assessment instruments administered to their children. However, TEA is not required to release questions that are being field-tested and are not used to compute a student's score on a particular test.

Parents also have a right to review all classroom teaching materials and tests previously administered to their child. School districts are required to make these materials readily available to parents and may charge a reasonable copying fee. While parents have always had the right to attend school board meetings, TEC §26.007 reinforces the right and requires school boards to hold public meetings within the boundaries of the district, with two exceptions: joint meetings with another district and meetings outside the district required by law. This provision restricts the ability of school boards to hold retreats where public business is conducted.

With the exception of child abuse reporting (discussed in the next chapter), parents have a right to all information concerning the activities of their child at school. School employees who encourage or coerce a child to withhold information from the child's parents are subject to contract termination or suspension without pay.

TEC §26.009 requires school employees to obtain written parental consent before conducting a psychological examination, test, or treatment unless related to child abuse reporting. This right extends a right accorded parents under federal law regarding evaluations and assessments (see Chapter 9). Students cannot be referred to an outside counselor without written parental consent. The district must tell the parent about any relationship between the counselor and the district, and must provide the parent with information about other sources of treatment in the area. Referral also requires approval of appropriate school personnel (TEC §38.010). The purpose of this statute is to prevent collusion between districts and outside counselors. Written consent is also required under TEC §26.009 before making a videotape of a child or recording the child's voice unless for safety purposes in common areas of the school or on school buses, for purposes related to cocurricular or extracurricular activity, or for classroom instruction. However, it is important to note that videotape and audiotape recordings may constitute protected records under federal law and cannot be released without parental consent. TEC §33.004 requires districts to retain signed consent forms in the student's permanent record.

One of the more notable provisions emerging from the 1995 legislative session is TEC §26.010, which accords parents the right to request temporary exemptions for their child from a class or activity "that conflicts with the parent's religious or moral beliefs if the parent presents or delivers to the teacher of the parent's child a written statement authorizing the removal of the child from the class or other school activity." Note that both religious *and* moral beliefs are recognized. The right is limited to the extent that a parent cannot remove the child from a class or activity to avoid a test or to prevent the child from taking a subject for the entire semester. Nor does the provision exempt a child from satisfying grade level or graduation requirements.

Choosing Private Schools

The right to control a child's upbringing identified by the U.S. Supreme Court in the 1923 *Meyer* decision does not restrict the state from requiring all children to attend school. However, the state cannot require all children to attend *public* school. In 1925, a unanimous Court ruled that an Oregon statute to this effect was unconstitutional because it deprived private school operators of their property right to operate a business under the Fourteenth Amendment (*Pierce v. Society of Sisters*). Citing the earlier *Meyer* decision, the Court also noted that the Oregon statute "unreasonably interferes with the liberty of parents and guardians to direct the upbringing and education of children under their control." The justices observed that the concept of liberty "excludes any general power of the State to standardize its children by forcing them to accept instruction from public teachers only. The child is not the mere creature of the State; those who nurture him and direct his destiny have the right, coupled with the high duty, to recognize and prepare him for additional obligations" (p. 535). For this reason, the Texas compulsory public school attendance law provides an exemption if the child "attends a private or parochial school that includes in its course a study of good citizenship" (TEC §25.086).

In the past several years, private schooling has received considerable attention from educational reformers who view the public school system as too resistant to change to be successfully improved. Rather than provide money directly to public schools, these commentators urge the adoption of some type of voucher system whereby public money goes to parents, who then choose a public or private school for their children. Not only would such a system stimulate healthy competition within the educational system, proponents assert, it would give parents a greater stake in their children's education. Critics assert that a voucher system would destroy the common learning experience fostered by the public schools and would be both economically and racially discriminatory. They also point out that private schools likely would experience an increase in state regulation. While the debate rages, some states are moving toward such a system. Voucher measures have been introduced into recent Texas legislative sessions but have yet to garner sufficient support for passage.

Educating Children at Home

A critical problem with the Texas compulsory education statute is that the word *school* is not defined. This uncertainty led to the dispute surrounding what generally is called "home schooling." A state district judge ruled in 1987 that in Texas a home in which students are instructed qualifies as a private school, subject to certain conditions. Chief among them are that the students actually are taught by parents or those standing in parental authority, that there is a specific curriculum consisting of books and other written materials, and that the curriculum is designed to meet basic educational goals of reading, spelling, grammar, mathematics, and a study of good citizenship. The court further held that TEA lacked the authority to enforce a more restrictive interpretation of the compulsory education law previously adopted by the State Board of Education. The decision was affirmed by the Texas Supreme Court in 1994 (*Texas Education Agency v. Leeper*). The high court recognized that TEA has the authority to set guidelines for enforcement of the compulsory attendance law, including requesting achievement test results to determine if students are being taught "in a bona fide manner." The Court then added this confusing statement: "While administration of such tests cannot be a prerequisite to exemption from the compulsory attendance law, we do not preclude the TEA from giving this factor heavy weight." To date, the State Board of Education has not promulgated rules relating to home schooling.

Since the case was brought as a class action lawsuit, the holding applies in all Texas public school districts. Attendance officers are prohibited from initiating charges against parents simply because they are instructing their children at home. The trial court did recognize, however, the legitimate need of attendance officers to make reasonable inquiry of parents to determine whether a child is in attendance in a home school that meets the requirements approved by the court. Thus, information can be requested about the students, the curriculum being offered, and student test scores, if they exist.

In 1992 the Texas Commissioner of Education was confronted with a case in which a parent who home-schooled his daughter requested the local high school to enroll the girl in a one-period choir class. When the request was denied, the parent appealed to the commissioner. Noting that the school required all students except seniors to be enrolled in a seven-period school day, the commissioner denied the appeal. "This policy is rationally grounded to foster several goals of Respondent's board of trustees, including, among other things, maintaining discipline and obtaining state funding," the commissioner observed. The school district had argued that the girl's enrollment would cause complications with choir competition under University Interscholastic League (UIL) rules and would cause logistical problems in student supervision. The commissioner upheld the board's decision, concluding that it was not arbitrary or capricious (*Michelle S. v. Beeville I.S.D.*).

While permitting part-time enrollment of home-schooled students is left to the discretion of the district, such is not the case if the student has a disability. The Individuals with Disabilities Education Act (IDEA) requires school districts to provide special education and related services designed to meet the needs of private school handicapped students who are living in the district. Since home schooling qualifies as private schooling in Texas, school districts have an obligation to serve these students if parents request special education services and agree to allow the student to be dually enrolled in the public school for the amount of time identified in the student's Individual Education Plan.

When home-schooled students seek to return to the public school, placement decisions are left to the school. There is no requirement that school districts recognize the previous grade-level placements of home-schooled children.

SUMMARY

In this chapter we have reviewed the several sources of education law and their relationship to the structure and operation of the Texas public school system. It is apparent that local school districts have considerable authority to operate schools. Included in this authority is the right to develop local policy manuals and handbooks. School employees are required to follow these rules and regulations as they go about their assignments. At the same time, both federal and state law impose restraints on school boards and personnel by requiring compliance with certain constitutional and statutory provisions.

Education reform has been a central concern of the Texas Legislature since the early 1980s. At first, the legislative focus was on establishing state-level mandates that all districts and personnel had to follow. More recently, the legislature has sought to return greater decision-making authority to local districts and educators. At the same time, the legislature has recognized the need for innovation in schooling. A system of charter schools was enacted in 1995 to give local communities, campuses, and entrepreneurs the opportunity to develop new educational approaches and thereby stimulate reform across the education landscape.

While the U.S. Supreme Court has ruled that interdistrict disparities in per-pupil expenditures do not violate the federal constitution, the Texas Supreme Court and the Texas Legislature have spent years addressing the matter. Though the current financial system has been upheld by the Texas high court, the issue of equity in school finance remains a central concern.

Parent rights have increasingly come to the forefront of the policy-making agenda. The Texas Legislature has given parents more influence over the schooling of their children, including the right to request exemptions from programs and activities they find objectionable on religious or moral grounds. Further, parents with children in low-performing schools can take advantage of a public education scholarship to enroll their children in the schools of another district. Constitutional law accords parents the right to choose a private school for their children, though the state has no obligation to finance the choice. Texas law affords parents the right to educate their children at home.

In short, the trend in Texas is decentralization of the educational enterprise, together with parental empowerment.

TWO

Student Attendance and the
Instructional Program

THE MISSION of the Texas public education system is "to ensure
that all Texas children have access to a quality education that en-
ables them to achieve their potential and fully participate now and
in the future in the social, economic, and educational opportunities
of our state and nation" (TEC §4.001). To that end, the Texas Legislature has specified nine objectives for public education. Included
among them are parent participation as a full partner in the educational enterprise, development of full student potential, reduction
of the dropout rate to zero, a well-balanced curriculum, recruitment
and retention of highly qualified personnel, exemplary student performance, a safe and disciplined learning environment, utilization
of creative and innovative techniques to improve student learning,
and implementation of technology.

This is an ambitious agenda, and the legislature has enacted a
host of measures to address it. In this chapter, we discuss the law
governing student attendance and the instructional program. Included will be a discussion of topics that are tangentially related
to enrollment and instruction, such as a safe school environment,
library censorship, the federal copyright law, and extracurricular
activities. The chapter ends with a discussion of how the school
program must accommodate the needs of special groups of students.

ATTENDANCE

Texas provides that children who are at least five years old and
under twenty-one on September 1 of the school year are eligible to
attend school on a tuition-free basis (TEC §25.001). The law also
requires that children of certain ages must attend school. Simple
as this may seem, there has been considerable litigation over the
years regarding school attendance. This section begins with a discussion of various forms of discrimination in attendance, then looks
at the specific requirements of school attendance in Texas.

Impermissible Discrimination

In 1954 the U.S. Supreme Court began the effort to eliminate de jure racial segregation (segregation by law) in our society. The means to accomplish this was the last sentence in the first section of the Fourteenth Amendment: "nor [shall any state] deny to any person within its jurisdiction the equal protection of the laws." Beginning with the *Brown v. Board of Education of Topeka* ruling, the Court repeatedly struck down laws that treated people differently solely on the basis of their color or racial heritage. In 1964 Congress added its legislative backing by passing the monumental Civil Rights Act, which prohibits discrimination on the basis of race, color, or national origin in public education, in any federally assisted program or activity, in public and private employment, and in privately owned places of public accommodation (hotels, restaurants, and so on). In 1968 the Court ruled this law to be constitutional. About this time, the Court began to require not only that de jure segregation be ended but also that adequate remedies be provided to the victims of prior purposeful segregation.

The remedial mandates of both the federal courts and Congress have been the focus of controversy for some time. Since desegregation alone would not place the victims of segregation where they would have been had there been no segregation in the first place, the Supreme Court, Congress, and federal enforcement agencies have required good-faith integration and affirmative action efforts. It is beyond the scope of this book to describe the history of school desegregation. However, Table 3 provides a kaleidoscopic view of important U.S. Supreme Court rulings in the years since 1954, some of which have provided the basis for lower federal court rulings on racial attendance patterns in Texas public schools.

Districts still involved in the original desegregation suits conduct their affairs in accordance with the court orders issued in their respective cases. Those under court orders must file with the responsible courts periodic status reports describing their progress toward desegregation. The ultimate goal of this process is to be declared "unitary," a status denoting the eradication of all aspects of a segregated, dual school system.

In 1991 the U.S. Supreme Court handed down a decision in the most important school desegregation case since the mid-1970s. By a five-to-four vote, the Court concluded in a cautiously worded opinion that once all the vestiges of de jure segregation have been eliminated, federal court supervision may end, even if one-race schools reemerge (*Board of Education of Oklahoma City v.*

Table 3: Major School Desegregation Decisions, 1954–1995

Supreme Court Cases	Decision	Significance
Brown v. Board of Education of Topeka, 1954	Public education facilities that are racially segregated are inherently discriminatory even if equal.	Overruled the "separate but equal" doctrine of *Plessy v. Ferguson*, 1896, and began the movement to end de jure segregation in the public sector.
Griffin v. Prince Edward County, 1964	Ordered public schools that had been closed to avoid desegregation to be reopened.	Beginning of increased Supreme Court involvement in implementing its *Brown* mandate.
Green v. County School Board, 1968	Outlawed freedom of choice plans that do not result in integrated schools.	Demands more than a color-blind approach in areas of previous de jure segregation in the interest of establishing unitary school systems in which discrimination is eliminated "root and branch."
Swann v. Charlotte-Mecklenburg Board of Education, 1971	Approved a variety of court-ordered remedies, including cross town busing, to achieve school integration.	High tide of Supreme Court support for remedies designed to achieve integration in former de jure segregated school systems.
Keyes v. School District No. 1, 1973	Burden of proof placed on school officials to show that intentional discrimination in one section of a school district has not been repeated elsewhere in the district.	First northern desegregation case; majority now speaks in terms of "segregative intent."
Milliken v. Bradley, 1974	Five-to-four decision limiting remedies to the school district(s) where de jure segregation previously occurred.	Makes it clear that the federal courts will not use Fourteenth Amendment to eradicate de facto segregation in North and West; for remedial efforts to be required, there must be evidence of illegal segregative acts by school officials.
Runyon v. McCrary, 1976	Used 1866 civil rights laws to prohibit racial discrimination by most nonpublic schools.	Dampened efforts to start "white academies" but raised questions about bona fide exemptions and meaningful enforcement.

Case	Holding	Interpretation
Pasadena City Board of Education v. Spangler, 1976	Struck down court directives to enforce periodic adjustments to original desegregation plan.	Demographic changes occurring after desegregation order is in place are beyond judicial remedial powers.
Columbus Board of Education v. Penick, 1979 / *Dayton Board of Education v. Brinkman*, 1979	Upheld systemwide desegregation orders for two northern school systems.	Appeared to be reaffirmation of Court's willingness to uphold extensive remedies for past segregative acts.
Crawford v. Board of Education, 1982	Upheld a California constitutional amendment forbidding state courts to order busing unless necessary to remedy a violation of the U.S. Constitution.	States are under no legal obligation to go beyond the equal protection clause to require busing as a remedy for de facto segregation. This California constitutional amendment caused state courts to lift a busing order in the Los Angeles school system, which had never been found to have engaged in intentional segregation.
Washington v. Seattle, 1982	Struck down a state law prohibiting local school boards from using busing to desegregate schools.	Majority found the law unduly restricted local schools trying to integrate by lodging decision power regarding busing at the state level.
Board of Education of Oklahoma City v. Dowell, 1991	Held that once all vestiges of de jure segregation have been eliminated, federal court supervision may end, even if one-race schools emerge.	Described the process by which federal district courts must decide whether a district has become unitary.
Freeman v. Pitts, 1992	Held that federal courts can relinquish supervision of those areas of school operation that have become unitary.	Unitary status can be achieved incrementally.
Missouri v. Jenkins, 1995	Held federal judge exceeded his powers in ordering adoption of a magnet school plan to attract white students from the suburbs.	Curtails federal judicial power to foster integration, even if schools remain substantially one-race and student test scores remain low.

Dowell). Justice Thurgood Marshall vigorously dissented. The five-to-four split among the justices was an indication of disagreement on the Court over the appropriate time to end judicial efforts to eradicate the effects of prior state-maintained segregation. The question the trial court should ask, wrote Chief Justice William Rehnquist for the majority, is "whether the board had complied in good faith with the desegregation decree since it was entered, and whether the vestiges of past discrimination had been eliminated to the extent practicable." In making this determination, the court must consider "every facet of school operations," ranging from student assignment to faculty hiring, facilities, and extracurricular activities. A year later, the high court ruled unanimously that a trial court can relinquish supervision over those areas where a school district has achieved unitary status, yet still retain authority to oversee continued desegregation in other areas. In effect, unitary status can be achieved in incremental stages (*Freeman v. Pitts*, 1992).

In 1995 the Supreme Court continued its curtailment of federal judicial power to foster integration by ruling five-to-four that a federal judge exceeded his powers when he ordered the adoption of the magnet school concept in the Kansas City school district in the hopes of attracting suburban white students to a district that had become predominantly black (*Missouri v. Jenkins*). The majority also criticized the judge for basing his integration remedies on continued substandard performance of minorities on national achievement tests. In a concurring opinion, Justice Clarence Thomas, the Court's only black member, argued against continued judicial oversight of school districts to bring about integration long after state-enforced segregation has ended. "It never ceases to amaze me," he wrote, "that the courts are so willing to assume that anything that is predominantly black must be inferior."

These decisions will likely affect the continued viability of *United States v. Texas*, the statewide school desegregation order handed down by Federal District Court Judge William Wayne Justice in 1971 (the order known as Civil Order 5281 is outlined in the preface to the *Texas School Law Bulletin* that TEA has published biennially). As affirmed by the U.S. Court of Appeals for the Fifth Circuit, Civil Order 5281 applies to all districts except those under separate federal court order. The order requires integrated bus routes; an end to discrimination in extracurricular activities and use of school facilities; nondiscrimination in personnel decision making; a prohibition on student enrollment and assignment on the basis of race, color, or national origin; TEA approval of student transfers; nondiscrimination against students on the basis of

their first language; and the establishment of a complaint procedure. TEA has responsibility for enforcing the order. Violations can
also be reported to the U.S. Office of Civil Rights. State officials
can be expected to seek an opportunity to show that the conditions
outlined in *Dowell* for declaring Texas school districts unitary have
been met and thus court oversight is no longer necessary. In the
meantime, the order remains in effect.

The new charter school provisions and the public education
grant program for students in low-performing schools are also subject to the terms of Civil Order 5281. For example, the order requires compensatory education in racially and ethnically isolated
schools and restricts interdistrict student transfers that change the
racial composition in either the sending or receiving district by
more than 1 percent.

In a related matter, the Fifth Circuit in 1990 affirmed a lower
court ruling that Fort Worth I.S.D., which was under separate court
order, had achieved unitary status despite the existence of some
deficiencies, e.g., some schools had not met the required black-
white faculty ratio (*Flax v. Potts*). "If, as in this case, a 'deficiency'
is not so serious as to render nonunitary a particular aspect of a
district's policies, such as student assignments, then the sum of
such non-serious deficiencies, no one or more of which renders a
particular aspect nonunitary, will usually not render the overall
desegregation plan nonunitary," the court noted. The appeals court
observed that the district had employed a panoply of measures to
eliminate the vestiges of the prior dual school system, including
busing, school pairing, magnet schools, redrawing of attendance
zones, etc. The continued existence of fourteen one-race schools
was attributable to a drop in white enrollment (thirty-three thousand fewer students in 1984 as compared with 1968) and residential
housing patterns, not to any action by the school board. Declaring
that "further measures would be both impractical and detrimental
to education," the appellate court concluded that the trial judge
had not erred in declaring the district unitary. In 1994, a unitary
order was entered by the trial judge for Dallas I.S.D. even though,
as with Fort Worth I.S.D., deficiencies existed, such as underenroll-
ment of minorities in the district's magnet schools (*Tasby v. Wool-
ery*). Though a gap continued to exist in Dallas in the test score
performance of Anglo and minority students, the judge concluded
that most of the gap could be explained by socioeconomic factors
rather than a legacy of racial discrimination.

In 1991 the Fifth Circuit ruled that once unitary status has
been declared, plaintiffs bear the burden of proving in a new lawsuit

that a school board's actions were based on intent to discriminate. The case involved a new Austin I.S.D. student assignment plan which increased the number of racially identifiable elementary schools from six to twenty. The appeals court agreed with the lower court that the school district had redrawn elementary school attendance zones in the interest of curtailing crosstown busing time and promoting neighborhood schools, not with intent to discriminate. The fact that the minority schools were in a state of disrepair was attributed to budgetary problems, not racial animus (*Price v. Austin I.S.D.*). That school districts now can become legally resegregated after court-ordered integration plans are terminated raises significant pedagogic and public policy questions.

In 1982 the U.S. Supreme Court ruled that the state could no longer exclude the children of illegally admitted aliens from a tuition-free education (*Plyler v. Doe*). A narrow five-person majority differentiated undocumented children from their parents, noting that the children cannot be responsible for being in Texas illegally. The Court was not persuaded that the law retards the influx of illegal aliens into the country or that providing a tuition-free education to these children would constitute a serious drain on the state's funding for public education. Writing for the majority, Justice William J. Brennan, Jr., concluded, "It is difficult to understand precisely what the State hopes to achieve by promoting the creation and perpetuation of a subclass of illiterates within our boundaries, surely adding to the problems and costs of unemployment, welfare, and crime."

A federal district court issued an injunction in 1992 curtailing abusive actions by Immigration and Naturalization Service (INS) agents used to apprehend illegal aliens at or near Bowie High School in El Paso (*Murillo v. Musegades*). The court agreed with plaintiffs that INS agents were violating students' and school employees' Fourth Amendment rights to be free from unreasonable searches and seizures by detaining and questioning persons of Hispanic descent without reasonable cause and by conducting searches without probable cause. Such actions based solely on an individual's racial and ethnic appearance also constituted illegal discrimination under the Fifth Amendment.

In 1988 the commissioner of education considered the situation of children of foreign graduate students attending the University of Texas at Arlington on F-1 visas. An F-1 visa holder is an alien who is in the United States to pursue a course of study. The commissioner concluded that the school district could not charge tuition to these alien children while they lived within the boundaries of the school

district. Such a policy would violate both state and federal law
(*Islam v. Arlington I.S.D.*).

In 1988 the U.S. Supreme Court confronted a case alleging discrimination against the poor in school transportation. The dispute
arose when North Dakota school districts began charging an annual
fee for bus transportation pursuant to a state law authorizing such
charges. The parents of one student were unable to pay the fee and,
as a result, bus service to their child was discontinued. The parents
challenged the termination of service in federal court under the
equal protection clause of the Fourteenth Amendment. The U.S.
Supreme Court ruled in a five-to-four decision that the state of
North Dakota need only advance a rational reason in defense of the
statutory provision authorizing the fee. The Court concluded that
the statute rationally encouraged school districts to conserve general revenue funds and, therefore, was constitutional even though it
had a disproportionate impact on the poor (*Kadrmas v. Dickenson
Public Schools*). While TEC §11.158 allows districts to charge fees
for various services other than transportation, subsection (f) requires school districts to accommodate students and parents who
are unable to pay. The *Kadrmas* decision, however, could be relevant to the public education grant program, which requires the residential district to provide transportation to the school the child
would have attended but makes no provision for transportation
beyond that point to the chosen school (TEC §29.201(e)).

Section 504 of Title V of the Rehabilitation Act of 1973 prohibits discrimination against individuals with disabilities in federally assisted public school programs. The Individuals with Disabilities Education Act requires that any school district receiving
financial assistance under the act must assure a free, appropriate
public education to children with disabilities within the district and
must assure that the rights of these children and their parents are
protected. Both statutes and the obligations they place on school
districts to serve children with disabilities are discussed in the next
chapter.

Title IX of the 1972 Education Amendments prohibits intentional discrimination on the basis of sex in programs that receive
federal assistance, while §106.001 of Title 5 of the Texas Civil
Practices and Remedies Code prohibits discrimination by public
officials and employees against persons on the basis of race, religion,
color, sex, or national origin. In addition, Article I, §3a of the Texas
Constitution provides that "equality under the law shall not be
denied or abridged because of sex, race, color, creed, or national
origin." Together with court decisions, these laws restrict dis-

crimination in a number of areas, including denying school attendance or participation in school activities on grounds of marriage or pregnancy.

Title IX has been given new significance by the U.S. Supreme Court's 1992 decision upholding the right of victims to sue for compensatory damages (*Franklin v. Gwinnett County Public Schools*). Previously, the only remedy available under Title IX was the termination of federal funding. The *Franklin* case involved a female student who alleged that she was harassed and pressured into sexual intercourse by one of her teachers. She sued the school district for damages because of its failure to take corrective action. The addition of damage remedies, coupled with increased sensitivity to sexual harassment, has made Title IX claims a major concern of school districts. In one 1995 ruling, a federal district court in Texas ruled that school districts can be liable for such claims whether school officials knew about them or not (*Leija v. Canutillo I.S.D.*). Other courts have imposed a less rigorous standard of liability under Title IX (see, for example, *Rosa H. v. San Elizario I.S.D.*). While Title IX cases can be filed only against organizations, public employees themselves can be sued for sexual discrimination and harassment under 42 U.S.C. §1983. Together, these statutes have raised the stakes for not taking employee-to-student sexual discrimination and harassment claims seriously. While several recent federal district court decisions in Texas have held school districts not liable for student-to-student sexual harassment (see, for example, *Young v. Austin I.S.D.*), the law remains unsettled. From a preventive law standpoint, school administrators are advised to undertake a careful investigation when allegations first surface of any kind of sexual discrimination or harassment and to take whatever corrective action is warranted. Liability for failure to act can be extensive. Further discussion can be found in Chapter 10.

Residency and Guardianship

The cases discussed so far address the right of children present in Texas to a free public education. The more troublesome question has been whether a student who does not reside with a parent or legal guardian has a right to attend school in the district where the student happens to be. Under TEC §25.001 students are entitled to attend the schools in the district in which either of their parents reside, their guardian or other person having lawful control of them under a court order resides, or they reside if they are younger than eighteen and have established a separate residence. A district may allow a person showing evidence of legal responsibility for a child, e.g., power of attorney, to substitute for one possessing legal guardianship or lawful control under an order of a court. Section 25.001 also requires the admission of homeless children within the district on a tuition-free basis and, unless a hardship waiver has been granted to the district by the commissioner of education, of students who are participating in a nationally recognized foreign exchange program and living with the host family in the district. As defined by federal law, homeless children are those who lack a fixed nighttime residence or live in a shelter. Students living in the district who are eighteen years of age or more, but not older than twenty-one, are also entitled to attend school on a tuition-free basis. So too are students who are younger than eighteen and are or have been married or have had their minority status removed by a court because they are living apart from their parents and are self-supporting and managing their own affairs. Children placed in foster care by a state or local agency are entitled to attend school on a tuition-free basis in the district in which the foster parents reside. These children may not be required to serve a period of residency before they can participate in extracurricular activities. High school–age students who are placed in temporary foster care outside the attendance zone of their school or outside the school district by the Texas Department of Human Services are entitled to attend the school they were enrolled in at the time of placement.

The commissioner ruled in 1984 that it is the student's burden to prove to the school district that his or her presence is the result of a bona fide intention to reside there (*Moreno v. Harlingen C.I.S.D.*). TEC §25.001(c) gives districts the right to request evidence of residency and requires districts to establish what constitutes the minimum level of proof of residency.

Students who are less than eighteen years of age, unmarried, and have established residency in the district separate and apart from their parents, guardians, or other persons having lawful control of them under a court order have a right to attend school in the district on a tuition-free basis if they are not there for the primary purpose of participating in extracurricular activities (TEC §25.001(d)). The district need not admit students in this category who have been placed in an alternative education program or expelled within the past year. The district also need not admit students in this category who are on probation for having engaged in delinquent conduct or conduct in need of supervision or for having been convicted of a criminal offense. Conditions of this sort have been upheld by the U.S. Supreme Court (*Martinez v. Bynum*). A person who falsifies information on an enrollment form to admit an ineligible student is liable for the student's tuition (§25.001(h)).

Can school officials require persons with whom students live to secure legal guardianship? The answer is no. The leading case on the subject is *Byrd v. Livingston I.S.D.*, a 1987 federal court ruling. That case concerned whether three children living with their grandmother in Livingston I.S.D. were entitled to attend school in that district without the grandmother's becoming the legal guardian of the children. The court concluded that they were, noting that the statute allows students the right to attend schools in a district where they live, separate and apart from their parents, guardians, or other persons having lawful control of them. While school officials cannot require legal guardianship, they can encourage persons with whom students are living to secure power of attorney for use in emergencies. Furthermore, having such persons establish power of attorney can be a precondition for students' participation in extracurricular activities and similar events.

The court in *Byrd* specifically disagreed with two Texas courts of appeals that previously had addressed this issue. A court of appeals ruling in 1982 upheld a school district's policy limiting a tuition-free education only to school-age children residing with their parents, guardians, or managing conservators (*Jackson v. Waco I.S.D.*). Similarly, in 1983, the Texas Court of Appeals for El Paso upheld an Ysleta I.S.D. board policy which required other adult caretakers to secure legal guardianship for children living with them and attending Ysleta schools (*Rodriguez v. Ysleta I.S.D.*). Although the court in *Byrd* disagreed with the Ysleta and Waco cases, it did acknowledge that illegal immigration (the problem in Ysleta) and white flight (the problem in Waco) are two prime examples of important state concerns in questions of residence requirements.

Although such unusual situations might justify restrictive residence requirements, a school district would have difficulty successfully defending the sort of residence requirements at issue in these cases in light of *Byrd*. Thus, not surprisingly, the Nederland I.S.D. lost in 1991 when it refused to admit a student who was living with her boyfriend's parents in the district so that her homelife could be stabilized. The student's mother had executed power of attorney giving the boyfriend's parents authority to make decisions regarding the student's education and health care. The federal district court concluded that the district could address problems of white flight and overcrowding of its schools without enacting an overly broad policy that violated state and federal law (*Major v. Nederland I.S.D.*, 1991). The district was ordered to change its policy and to pay court costs, the student's attorneys' fees, and nominal damages for the days the student was excluded from school.

What if a student lives with his or her parents, and the entire family moves from the district in which it had resided? This was the situation in the 1984 case *Daniels v. Morris*. Officials in the Arlington I.S.D. learned that the Daniels family had moved during the school year to a new residence located in the Grand Prairie I.S.D. The Arlington principal, upon learning of the move, ordered the children to withdraw from the Arlington schools. In this federal lawsuit, the children contended that they possessed a property right to continue attending the Arlington schools, which could not be taken away without due process. The children based their claim upon the statutory reference to residence "at the time he applies for admission" (this provision is now codified as TEC §25.001(b)). The *Daniels* court concluded that this statutory provision does not imply either a right or a duty on the part of the student to continue attending the school in which he or she enrolled at the beginning of the school year, tuition free, even after the child and the parents have left that district and established a residence elsewhere. A school district is not required to provide a free public education to a student after both the student and the family have moved to another district.

TEC §25.002 provides that within thirty days of enrollment the parent, other person having custody of the child, or the former school district must provide the enrolling district with the child's birth certificate or other document proving the child's identity, a copy of the child's records from the previous school, and an immunization record. If the child is enrolled under a different name than the name on the submitted documents, the enrolling district is to notify the missing children and missing persons information clearinghouse. The notice is confidential and may be released only to law enforcement personnel. If the information is not provided, the enrolling district is to notify law enforcement authorities and request information whether the child has been reported as missing. Failure of those enrolling the child to furnish the information at the request of the police is a Class B misdemeanor. A Class B misdemeanor is punishable by a fine not to exceed $1,000 or a jail term not to exceed 120 days or both. School districts are required to inform those enrolling children that presenting a false record is an offense under Texas Penal Code §37.10 and may require the payment of tuition or costs under TEC §25.001(h). However, failure to produce the required documents does not justify a district's refusal to enroll the child.

Thus far, we have discussed the right of a student to receive a free public education from the state of Texas and issues involving the right to attend one particular district as opposed to another. Another issue is that of attendance at a particular school within a district. This was the question in *Citizens for Better Education v. Goose Creek C.I.S.D.* (1986). That case involved a decision of the board voluntarily to revise school attendance zones in the interest of improving ethnic balance between the two high schools of the district. The court held that students have no constitutional right to attend a particular school. As a result, where there is no allegation of an illegal discriminatory motive in revising attendance zones, students have no right to a due process hearing when they are required to attend a different school as a result of rezoning. However, TEC §25.033 gives parents the right to petition to protest a particular school assignment or to have their child assigned or transferred to a particular school. While the board of trustees has the final say in these matters, the board does have to accord the parent a hearing if requested. The board must grant the parent's petition unless there is a reasonable basis not to. The board's decision is final unless the parent alleges a violation of the U.S. Constitution. In that event, the statute gives the parent a right to file a lawsuit in state district court.

The Compulsory School Law

While the free public school is open to students who are as much as twenty-one years of age, the compulsory school law requires that "a child who is at least six years of age, or who is younger than six years of age and has previously been enrolled in first grade, and who has not completed the academic year in which the child's 17th birthday occurred shall attend school" (TEC §25.085). The provision also applies to children who are enrolled in prekindergarten or kindergarten. By "attend school," the provision means that the child shall attend for each day of instruction. Currently, the school year consists of at least 180 days of instruction, and the school day shall be for at least seven hours, including intermissions and recesses, except for prekindergarten and kindergarten. TEC §25.084 allows schools to operate on a year-round or multitrack schedule (staggered instructional blocks and vacation periods) for the same length of time. Nonemergency interruptions for nonacademic announcements are to be limited to no more than once a day (TEC §25.083).

A student who is seventeen years of age or older and has a high school equivalency certificate or high school diploma is exempted from the compulsory school law. TEC §25.086 includes a long list of others who are also exempt. Among them are students attending a private school (including home schooling) that "shall include in its course a study of good citizenship," students who are at least seventeen and taking instruction for the high school equivalency certificate, students who are at least sixteen and preparing for the equivalency certificate upon recommendation by the public agency responsible for the child under a court order, students who have been expelled, and students temporarily absent for physical or mental reasons.

In accordance with TEC §29.151, districts must provide either half-day or full-day kindergarten classes to children who are at least five years of age at the beginning of the school year. Districts with fifteen or more children who are at least four years old must also offer half-day prekindergarten classes unless the commissioner of education grants a waiver because of the need to construct facilities. Districts may offer prekindergarten for three-year-olds if there are fifteen or more eligible children in the district. A child is eligible for enrollment in the latter if the child is unable to speak and comprehend English, is educationally disadvantaged, or is homeless. A district need not provide transportation for prekindergarten, but if provided, it is part of the funded transportation program. If schools contract with a private agency to provide for prekindergarten, the agency must comply with the licensing stardards adopted by the Texas Department of Human Services. The content of prekindergarten programs must be designed to develop skills necessary for success in the regular public school curriculum, including language, math, and social skills. The impetus behind these provisions is the need to provide special help to the students in question as early as possible.

Absences

Parents commit an offense under §25.093 of the Texas Education Code if, after being warned in writing by the school attendance officer, with criminal negligence they fail to require their child to attend school and the child has unexcused voluntary absences for ten or more days or parts of days within a six-month period or three or more days or parts of days within a four-week period as specified in Texas Family Code §51.03(b)(2). The attendance officer is required to file a complaint against the parent in the appropriate court. If the child has not been referred to a particular court, the attendance officer must refer the child to the county juvenile probation department.

Failure to have the child attend school is a Class C misdemeanor. A Class C misdemeanor carries a $500 fine. Each day the child remains out of school may be considered a separate offense. Interestingly, if the court probates the sentence, it may require the parent to render personal services to the school as a condition of probation. One-half of any fines collected are remanded to the school district, thus increasing the incentives for districts to pursue truant students. A court may also order parents of truant students to attend a class offered by the school district that provides instruction in effective parenting skills relating to school attendance. In addition to parent liability, students who are truant under the terms of the Family Code §51.03(b)(2) commit a Class C misdemeanor under TEC §25.094. If a juvenile justice court determines that a student has been habitually truant, it may order the student to attend school. The Texas Attorney General has issued an opinion that a child brought into court on truancy charges is entitled to an attorney at all stages of the proceedings. Further, tardiness to class generally does not constitute an "unexcused voluntary absence," as defined in the Family Code, for which truancy charges may be brought (*Att'y. Gen. Op. DM-200*, 1993).

TEC §25.095 requires school districts to notify a student's parents if the student has been absent without excuse five times for any part of the day during a six-month period. The notice must stipulate that if the student is absent without an excuse for ten or more days or parts of days within a six-month period, both the parents and the student are subject to prosecution under the sections described above for thwarting the compulsory school law.

Texas Education Code §25.087 allows temporary student absences from school for any reason acceptable to the teacher, principal, or superintendent. In addition, this section requires school districts upon written parental request to excuse students who are observing religious holy days, including the time traveling to and from the observance. School districts also must excuse a student who has a medical appointment if the student returns to school on the same day of the appointment. Students who are attending religious observances or are seeing health care professionals are not to be penalized and are to be counted as present for purposes of calculating the average daily attendance. They are also to be allowed to make up missed work. If they do so satisfactorily, the days of absence are to be counted as days of compulsory attendance.

TEC §25.092 requires that a student may not be given credit for a class unless the student is in attendance for at least 90 percent of the days the class is offered. The section requires that school districts appoint attendance committees made up of a majority of teachers to hear petitions for class credit by students who do not meet the 90 percent requirement. These committees may give class credit to a student who is in attendance fewer than the required days because of "extenuating circumstances." School boards are required to establish guidelines to define what are extenuating circumstances and specify alternative ways for students to make up work or regain credit lost because of absences. The section further specifies that professional employees are not to be assigned additional instructional duties because of this section unless they are compensated. If credit is not given, a student may appeal the decision to the school board and from there to the state district court of the county in which the district's central office is located. The overall approach is to enact strict requirements calculated to put pressure on excessively absent students but to establish an appeal process to grant some flexibility for the student whose absences have been because of legitimate extenuating circumstances.

MAINTAINING A SAFE SCHOOL ENVIRONMENT

Concern among the general public and parents about discipline in schools has prompted the Texas Legislature to strengthen provisions for assuring a safe school environment. In particular, the mandated student discipline procedures described in Chapter 8 reflect this intent. There are other provisions in the code that also relate to keeping schools safe. Some of the more prominent are briefly reviewed here, since maintaining order is a prerequisite to an effective instructional program.

Students, like other citizens, are subject to the laws of the community, state, and nation. Under certain circumstances, they can be held accountable for their illegal acts on school premises in the criminal or juvenile justice systems whether or not they are also subject to the authority of the school. To be subject to the juvenile justice system, a student must meet the statutory definition of a child. The term *child* is defined in §51.02 of the Texas Family Code as a person (A) who is ten years of age or older and under seventeen years of age, or (B) between seventeen and eighteen who is charged with, or found to have engaged in, delinquent conduct or conduct indicating a need for supervision as a result of acts committed before becoming seventeen. Persons under the age of ten cannot be legally held responsible for their acts. But as noted below, parents may be held responsible for the actions of their children. Over the age of seventeen, a person is considered an adult and is within the jurisdiction of the criminal justice system.

TEC §37.101 provides that the criminal laws of the state apply to areas under the jurisdiction of the school board. School boards have the authority to adopt their own safety rules, including rules governing the parking of vehicles on school property (TEC §§37.102 and 37.106). A violation of these rules is a Class C misdemeanor. Public school officials can request identification of any person on school property, can refuse to allow those with no legitimate business to enter onto school property, and may eject a person from the property if the person refuses to leave (TEC §37.105). A person who trespasses on school grounds commits a Class C misdemeanor (TEC §37.107).

It is a Class B misdemeanor for a person alone or with others to engage in disruptive activity on the campus or property of any public or private school (TEC §37.123). "Disruptive activity" is defined to include such acts as obstructing entrances or hallways, preventing school administrators from conducting assemblies, and preventing persons from entering or leaving the campus. TEC §37.124 makes it a Class C misdemeanor to disrupt classes or other school activities within 500 feet of a public school. Contrary to common assumption, this statute does not extend school administrative authority to areas within 500 feet of the school; rather, it gives police the right to arrest someone who engages in disruptive activities within this area. It is a Class C misdemeanor for a person to disrupt transportation of children to and from public school or to a school-sponsored activity (TEC §37.126).

TEC §37.125 provides that a person commits a third-degree felony by exhibiting, using, or threatening to exhibit or use a firearm to interfere with the normal use of a public or private school or school bus. Penal Code §46.11 provides for a weapon-free school zone and enhances penalties for violations of this provision which are committed within 300 feet of a public school, school function, or UIL event. The federal Gun-Free Schools Act of 1994 requires a one-year expulsion for students who come to school with guns. This act is part of the Improving America's Schools Act and is unrelated to the Gun-Free School Zones Act that was declared unconstitutional by the U.S. Supreme Court in 1995 (*United States v. Lopez*). The Gun-Free School Zones Act was enacted in 1990 and made it unlawful for anyone—not just students—to bring a firearm within 1,000 feet of a school.

State law permits a person who obtains a license from the Department of Public Safety to carry a concealed weapon. However, §46.03 of the Penal Code gives school boards and the operators of private schools the authority to restrict the carrying of weapons including concealed handguns on school premises, on grounds or in buildings where school-sponsored activities are being conducted, and on school transportation vehicles. Security officers are exempted. Section 46.035 of the Penal Code makes it an offense to carry a concealed handgun on the premises of a school sporting or interscholastic event unless the license holder is a participant and the handgun is used in the event. The statute applies to on- and off-campus events (*Atty. Gen. Op. LO-96-009,* 1996). The term "premises" in §46.035 means a building or portion of a building, not a driveway, street, sidewalk or walkway, parking lot, or parking garage where a sporting event is held. The attorney general has defined "premises" in §46.03 to mean the portions of land and buildings under school control. TEC §46.035 also makes it a Class A misdemeanor for a license holder to intentionally, knowingly, or recklessly carry a handgun into a meeting of a governmental body. It is a criminal offense for anyone to take a concealed handgun to a school board meeting.

Section 28.04 of the Texas Penal Code makes it a Class C misdemeanor to recklessly damage or destroy property without the consent of the owner. Section 54.041 of the Texas Family Code provides that, when a minor engages in conduct resulting in damage to district property or personal injury, the district may proceed against the minor in juvenile court, or through his or her parents, to obtain full or partial restitution to the district. Section 41.001 of the Family Code provides that a parent or other person responsible for a child is liable for property damage caused by the child if such conduct reasonably relates to the failure of the parent or the other person to exercise the duty of a parent or if the act is caused by the willful and malicious conduct of the child, who is at least twelve years of age but under eighteen. The limit of liability is fixed at $15,000 per act plus court costs and reasonable attorneys' fees.

School districts must ban all smoking or use of tobacco at a school-related or school-sanctioned event on or off school property (TEC §38.006). Students also must be prohibited from possessing tobacco products at school or at school-related or -sanctioned events. Similarly, school districts are required to prohibit use of alcohol at a school-related or school-sanctioned activity on or off school property and must attempt to provide an alcohol-free environment for students coming and going from school (TEC §38.007). It is a Class C misdemeanor for a person to possess an intoxicating beverage at a public school or on the grounds of an athletic event (TEC §37.122). Each public school with a grade level of seven or higher is required to post an antisteroid law notice in the gymnasium and other locations where physical education classes are conducted. Finally, a school board may prohibit students from possessing paging devices while on school property or at a school-sponsored or school-related activity (TEC §37.082). The district can dispose of the confiscated paging device in any reasonable manner after giving the student's parent and the pager company thirty days prior notice or can charge the parent or owner of the device a $15 fee before releasing it.

Thus, in addition to internal discipline measures described in the school's student code of conduct, there are numerous measures available to school administrators for maintaining an orderly environment conducive to teaching and learning.

THE INSTRUCTIONAL PROGRAM

The Required Curriculum

To assure consistency across the state in the instructional program, the Texas Legislature passed legislation in 1981 requiring a well-balanced curriculum in Texas public school districts. The law is presently codified at §28.001 of the Texas Education Code and requires school districts to offer both a foundation curriculum and an enrichment curriculum. The foundation curriculum consists of English language arts, mathematics, science, and social studies. The enrichment curriculum adds health, physical education, fine arts, economics with emphasis on the benefits of a free enterprise system, career and technology education, and technology applications. The law directs the state board, in association with educators, parents, and corporate representatives, to designate the essential knowledge and skills of the foundation curriculum and to require that they be taught in the state's public schools as a condition of accreditation. Prior to Senate Bill 1, the state board had designated the so-called "essential elements" of the required curriculum. A good portion of Chapter 75 of volume 19 of the Texas Administrative Code, a collection of rules enacted by the State Board of Education, is devoted to setting forth these components. While the state board can specify the content of the foundation curriculum, it cannot designate either the methodology or the amount of time to be used in teaching it. That is left to the discretion of local districts. The state board is also to designate the essential knowledge and skills of the enrichment curriculum, but only to serve as guidelines to local districts. A district is encouraged to exceed the minimum curriculum, and many districts do.

In recent years, sex education programs have been the focus of considerable conflict and debate at both the local and state levels. Some assert that sex education should be left to parents, while others point out that most parents either don't teach their children about sexual matters or provide them with wrong information. After several years of controversy involving the Texas Education Agency's ill-fated attempts to introduce a sex education curriculum into the public schools, the Texas Legislature in 1995 enacted a provision establishing how school districts are to teach these courses and to select teaching materials. In essence, TEC §28.004 requires districts to establish a local health education advisory council to assist in ensuring that local community values and health concerns are reflected in the district's human sexuality instruction. Contrary to the thrust of other provisions of the Education Code that return more discretion to local districts, this provision requires that courses on human sexuality must present sexual abstinence as the preferred choice of behavior for unmarried persons of school age. Curricular materials related to these courses must be available for public inspection, and parents are entitled to an opt-out option for their children. In addition, school districts are prohibited from distributing condoms.

TEC §29.085 authorizes public school districts to offer an integrated program of educational and support services for students who are pregnant or who are parents. The program must include counseling and self-help programs, day-care services at or near campus, transportation services, and instruction in child development, parenting, and home and family living (TEC §21.114).

TEC §28.023 requires school districts to develop advanced placement tests for each primary grade level and secondary academic subject for advancing talented students from one grade to another under State Board of Education guidelines. The legislature has encouraged school districts to take part in the college-level advanced placement program operated by the College Board and Educational Testing Service and in the international baccalaureate program. Assuming funding is available, the Texas Advanced Placement Incentive Program offers schools based on need a one-time $3,000 equipment grant for offering a college advanced placement or international baccalaureate course and $100 for each high-achieving student (TEC §28.052). Participating teachers may also be awarded incentive grants. In addition, subsidies for test fees are available to students who demonstrate need.

Student Assessment

The legislature has endeavored to end social promotion in Texas public schools by requiring that students may be promoted only on the basis of academic achievement (TEC §28.021). While the Code in the past has specified a passing grade of 70 to receive course credit, the matter is now left to the discretion of local districts. However, the "no pass–no play" provision specifies that a student who does not maintain a grade of 70 in all courses except honors or advanced classes must be suspended from extracurricular activities for at least three weeks or until the grade is raised to 70 or higher (TEC §33.081). The student can still practice or rehearse with other students. The absence of reliable evidence on the effects of the "no pass–no play" rule coupled with concern about the dropout rate convinced the legislature in 1995 to reduce the suspension period from six to three weeks. Application of the "no pass–no play" rule against a student with a disability that interferes with meeting regular academic requirements must be based on the student's failure to meet the terms of the individualized education program (IEP).

A flurry of litigation greeted implementation of the "no pass–no play" rule in 1984. The Texas Supreme Court ruled in 1985 that the rule does not deprive students of any recognized right to participate in extracurricular activities and is not discriminatory (*Spring Branch I.S.D. v. Stamos*). The plaintiffs continued to argue their case in state court on the grounds that the "no pass–no play" rule discriminated against minority children and children with disabilities. This argument was rejected by a state appeals court in 1991 (*Texas Education Agency v. Stamos*).

Since the enactment of House Bill 72 in 1984, the Texas Legislature and the State Board of Education have wrestled with the best way to assess student achievement. As a result, the statewide testing program has undergone considerable modification over the years. The legislature has directed the state board to establish a statewide student performance-based assessment program (TEC §39.021). The testing provisions require TEA to adopt appropriate criterion-referenced tests in reading, writing, mathematics, social studies, and science. TEA must also administer a secondary exit test in mathematics and English language arts. TEA must adopt end-of-course assessments for selected subjects. A student cannot receive a diploma until the student has performed successfully on designated end-of-course assessments or on the exit-level assessment. Exemptions from the state assessment system are allowed for children with disabilities whose IEP allows the exemption and children with limited English proficiency. However, the legislature has directed the commissioner to develop a separate assessment system for these students. Districts must offer special instruction to students who do not perform satisfactorily on any state assessment instrument.

In addition to the state-required tests, school districts can use other criterion-referenced or norm-referenced tests at any grade level; however, a norm-referenced test must be economical, nationally recognized, and state approved. The law now allows private schools to administer any state-mandated assessment instrument under an agreement with TEA.

A student may receive a diploma when the student completes the required curriculum and the exit-level assessment or the designated end-of-course assessments (TEC §28.025). Students with disabilities can receive a diploma when they meet these requirements or complete the components of their individualized education programs. School districts may award a "certificate of coursework completion" to students who complete the curriculum requirements but fail the exit-level or end-of-course assessment requirement. In 1995, the legislature clarified a litigious issue of the past by specifying that a school district may permit a student who receives such a certificate to participate in graduation ceremonies. The legislature further directed the state board to propose an alternative assessment system whereby these students can demonstrate sufficient mastery to receive a diploma. The transcript form must specify whether the student received a diploma or certificate of coursework completion.

A related issue involving graduation relates to the withholding of diplomas until students return books. According to TEC §31.104, a district may not withhold a diploma or deny a student the opportunity of graduating or participating in graduation exercises for failure to return books or pay the price of the books, but the district can withhold a student's records. However, under an attorney general interpretation of the Texas Open Records Act, the student has the right to secure a photocopy of the records, including a transcript (*Att'y. Gen. Op. ORD-152,* 1977; *Att'y. Gen. Op. ORD-431,* 1985).

Another area of concern relates to teacher evaluation and accountability. Senate Bill 1 changed the teacher evaluation system to require that one of the appraisal criteria must encompass the performance of the teacher's students (TEC §21.351). The appraisal of a school principal must also reflect how well students on the campus perform (TEC §21.354(e)). Almost certainly, disputes will arise in the future over the extent to which an educator's success depends upon student performance. Suppose a teacher gives all the students in the class grades of 70 or above but only a small proportion are actually at or above grade level as demonstrated by test score results. Most commentators agree that a teacher probably can be held accountable for student test performance and that discrepancies between grading practices and student test performance can be negative factors in teacher evaluations. A case in point is a 1984 decision of the Texas Commissioner of Education involving a teacher who contested her nonrenewal. In *McLean v. Quanah I.S.D.* the commissioner of education observed that significant lack of student progress can be a reason for nonrenewal. However, low grades alone do not establish a teacher's level of competence. In fact, low grades may signify a teacher with high standards. The commissioner further noted that, while parents may be dissatisfied with teacher grades or disapprove of a teacher's methodology in the classroom, such dissatisfaction and disapproval cannot be cited by the district as grounds for nonrenewal. Actual competence, not community perception, is what counts. Because the district did not have sufficient evidence of teacher incompetence to support the nonrenewal, the commissioner reversed the district's nonrenewal decision. The best advice for teachers is to be honest in grading. The best advice for administrators is to have sufficient documentation linking teacher behavior to poor student performance. For a helpful manual that describes how to document effectively in the classroom and how to link teacher behavior to student behavior in growth and assessment plans, see F. Kemerer and J. A. Crain, *The Documentation Handbook*, Second Edition, published by the *Texas School Administrators' Legal Digest.*

In recent years, the commissioner of education has been confronted with several appeals involving disputes over student grades. The commissioner has used a substantial evidence standard of review in considering these cases, meaning that the action of the school district will be sustained unless there is no rational basis for it. A case in point is a 1995 decision involving a student who received a zero on a long-term English assignment because illness prevented his being in school on the day the assignment was to be submitted for credit. The English teacher's class rules specified that no credit would be given for submission of the paper after the due date, regardless of whether the student's absence on the due date was excused or not. Students were given the option of turning in the assignment early or having a friend submit it on the due date. The student argued that failure to let him turn in the paper after the absence violated his right under TEC §21.305(f) to make up missed work following an excused absence (this section was recodified by Senate Bill 1 as TEC §25.097). The commissioner disagreed. The student had been given ample notice of a nonnegotiable due date. The appeal was dismissed (*John A. v. La Vernia I.S.D.*). Similarly, the commissioner was unsympathetic to a student who complained that her low geometry grade was attributable to the "whim" of her teacher. His review of the matter supported the teacher's conclusion that the student had received too much assistance on her homework from friends and had not mastered the mathematical concepts taught in the class. The commissioner noted that the professional judgment of the teacher had been respected by the school board when it backed the teacher "and is entitled to deference here" (*Kimberly C. v. Ingleside I.S.D.*). See Chapter 6 for a discussion of teacher grading as related to the concept of academic freedom.

Texas law provides that a person under eighteen years of age will not be issued a driver's license unless the person "has obtained a high school diploma or its equivalent or is a student enrolled in a public, home, or private school who attended school for at least 80 days in the fall or spring semester preceding the date of application, or has been enrolled for at least 45 days, and is currently enrolled, in a program to prepare persons to pass the high school equivalency exam" (Texas Civil Statute 6687b, §7(a)(3)).

School District Accountability

With public school effectiveness questioned and with school finance continuing to generate controversy, the Texas Legislature has placed considerable emphasis on school district accountability. TEC §39.051 directs the State Board of Education to establish a set of academic excellence indicators for school campuses to include such items as results on state-mandated assessment instruments, dropout rates, student attendance, high school exit-level assessment, Scholastic Aptitude Test (SAT) results, percentage of students taking end-of-course assessments, and percentage of students exempted from the statewide assessment program. TEC §11.253(c) requires that school principals must consult annually with their site-based planning and decision-making committee in reviewing and revising the campus improvement plan relative to performance of the campus on the academic excellence indicators.

Each year, TEA prepares a "campus report card" that compares the performance of the campus on the academic excellence indicators, student-teacher ratios, and administrative and instructional costs per student with the performance of the district and other schools in the state (TEC §39.052). These report cards are to be distributed annually to the parents. In addition, school boards are required to publish an annual report describing the educational performance of the district and each of its campuses on student achievement and other measures, including the progress of each campus in meeting campus performance objectives (TEC §39.053). These reports are to be subject to public discussion at a hearing and thereafter widely disseminated. To help make the reports meaningful, they include TEA-generated comparisons with past performance of the district and its schools, as well as with the performance of other similar districts and campuses.

The thrust of these statutes is to make districts and individual campuses accountable to the community for the quality of education they impart. And they also make teachers and administrators more accountable for their performance. As a result of accountability measures, pressure is likely to increase on district personnel from parents who do not want their children to attend mediocre schools.

School districts and individual schools are also more accountable to TEA through the accreditation process. Based primarily on performance on the academic excellence indicator system, districts are classified as exemplary, recognized, academically acceptable, and academically unacceptable. Sanctions for low-performing districts can range from a public notice of deficiencies to annexation with an adjoining district (TEC §39.131(a)). Sanctions for low-performing campuses can include appointment of a campus intervention team to render assistance, selection of a board of managers from district residents, and closure if the school has been deficient for two years or more (TEC §39.131(b)).

School districts and campuses exhibiting exemplary performance may be entitled to certificates and even financial rewards under the Texas Successful Schools Awards System (TEC §39.091). Exemplary schools may also be entitled to exemptions from selected statutory and administrative requirements (TEC §39.111).

Removal of Objectionable Library Materials

Legal controversy over school library censorship has diminished somewhat following a 1982 decision of the U.S. Supreme Court. In a five-to-four decision, the Court affirmed a lower court decision ordering a trial to determine why a school board removed controversial books from the junior and senior high school libraries (*Board of Education of Island Trees v. Pico*). The fact that five justices ordered the case returned to the lower court supports the view that the First Amendment is involved when books are removed from public school libraries. Some of the books involved in the *Pico* case were *Slaughterhouse Five* by Kurt Vonnegut, Jr., *The Naked Ape* by Desmond Morris, *Down These Mean Streets* by Piri Thomas, *Soul on Ice* by Eldridge Cleaver, and *A Hero Ain't Nothin' but a Sandwich* by Alice Childress.

The majority, however, were not consistent in their reasoning, so no definite set of guidelines can be derived from the decision. Prior to trial, the school board voted to replace all the books, so a trial was never held. Most school districts have developed a set of criteria for both book selection and book removal as well as for describing the steps a person can follow when bringing a complaint. Some criteria are easy to defend as legitimate reasons for a book removal: obsolescence, mutilation, absence of shelving space, redundancy, lack of funds. Others are harder to defend: bad taste, inappropriateness to grade level, threatening to the emotional or intellectual growth of students. In some districts, a school psychologist serves on screening committees to lend credence to recommended removal decisions based on such criteria.

The U.S. Court of Appeals for the Fifth Circuit had an opportunity in 1995 to apply the *Pico* rationale to a Louisiana school district's removal of a controversial book on African tribal religion from the school library (*Campbell v. St. Tammany Parish School Board*). After the parent of a middle school student sought to remove *Voodoo & Hoodoo* by Jim Haskins, study committees were instituted at both the school and district levels to review the complaint. Both committees recommended that the book be retained but with restricted access. *Voodoo & Hoodoo* traces the evolution and practice of religious subcultures in African-American communities in the United States. The latter half of the book offers a prescription for over 220 spells to bring about certain events. For example, one spell requires taking a piece of the intended victim's hair and a piece of his clothing, together with a piece of parchment with the person's name and age written on it, and placing all three in a bag with graveyard dust. If the bag is then buried under the person's doorstep and left undisturbed, the person loses all his energy. Most of the parent's objections centered on the spell portion of the book. With the support of the Louisiana Christian Coalition, the parent continued her quest to have the book removed by appealing to the school board. In a twelve-to-two vote, the board voted to remove the book from all school libraries in the district.

Following this action, a lawsuit was filed by other parents who objected to the removal. The federal district court granted summary judgment for the parents, whereupon the school district appealed. Noting that the plurality of justices in the *Pico* ruling viewed the library as a marketplace of ideas not subject to school board plenary control, the Fifth Circuit sent the case back for a determination of what motivated the school board's action. The appeals court added, "we are moved to observe that, in light of the special role of the school library as a place where students may freely and voluntarily explore diverse topics, the School Board's non-curricular decision to remove a book well after it had been placed in the public school libraries evokes the question whether that action might not be an unconstitutional attempt to 'strangle the free mind at its source.' That possibility is reinforced by the summary judgment evidence indicating that many of the School Board members had not even read the book, or had read less than its entirety, before voting as they did. . . ." (p. 190). The court also was troubled that by not considering the recommendations of the two review committees, the board disregarded its own procedures for channeling and resolving complaints of this kind.

Behind the censorship controversy are two conflicting ideas about the purpose of schooling: Should schools inculcate community values as reflected in school board decisions or should schools foster a marketplace of ideas? There is no consensus on the answer.

The Federal Copyright Law

The 1976 revised copyright law (17 U.S.C. §§101 et seq.) does not prohibit teachers from duplicating copyrighted material for classroom use, but it does restrict such practices. Specifically, teachers may make a single copy for scholarly use for class preparation, or multiple copies for classroom use, of a chapter from a book, a newspaper or magazine article, a short story or poem, or a chart, graph, diagram, cartoon, picture, and the like if the following conditions are met:

1. The copying is at the instance and inspiration of the teacher.
2. There is not sufficient time prior to use to request permission from the publisher.
3. The copying is only for one course in the school.
4. Each copy includes a notice of copyright as it appears in the book or periodical.

The intent of the copyright law is to allow "fair use" but to avoid wholesale copying of complete works as a substitute for purchase. "Fair use" does not extend to copying of the same item by the same teacher from term to term. If a teacher wishes to use the item again, the best avenue is to write the publisher requesting permission to do so. Some publishers are very accommodating, asking only that the teacher indicate on the copied work that permission has been granted for duplication in the manner requested. Others will charge a fee for use of the work; in some cases, it may be cheaper to purchase the work. Another option is to have the library purchase several copies of the work and assign it as reserve reading.

While the law does not specify any number of words, lines, or illustrations that may be legally copied from printed materials, a committee of educators, authors, and publishers has agreed upon guidelines for copying by not-for-profit educational institutions. In a similar manner, guidelines for educational use of copyrighted music have been developed by music educators and publishers, and guidelines for off-air copying of video programs and copying of computer software have been developed by representatives of educational institutions, copyright proprietors, and creative guilds and unions. Table 4 uses these guidelines to show what and how much may be copied from a variety of sources.

Microcomputer software copying is of particular concern; commentators and vendors alike warn that piracy of software is the biggest threat to its continued development. The 1976 Copyright Act specifies in §117 that computer programs are covered by the law. A computer program is defined as "a set of statements or instructions to be used directly or indirectly in a computer in order to bring about a certain result" (§101). Laws concerning copying of computer software protect both the disk and the manual accompanying it.

Since lawsuits over duplication of copyrighted materials are becoming more common, it is important for school districts to inform employees about the guidelines and monitor compliance. School professionals must pay attention to copyright law matters, since salespersons for commercial companies have been known to inquire about school district practices and report back to their superiors.

Table 4: Complying with Copyright Guidelines

Type of Copyrighted Material	School Personnel May	School Personnel May Not
Books, newspapers, magazines (specific items)	Make single copies for class preparation, or Make multiple copies for classroom use of the following: • 250 words or less from poems • complete prose works if less than 2500 words • excerpts from prose if not more than 1000 words or 10 percent of entire work • one chart, graph, diagram, or illustration from a book or periodical • up to two pages or 10 percent of text from a work of fewer than 2500 words	Copy consumables such as workbooks or standardized tests Copy items for use from term to term Copy more than one poem, article, or essay by the same author, nor more than two excerpts from a collection
Music	Make emergency copies to replace purchased ones Copy excerpts for academic preparation if less than a performable unit or 10 percent of entire work Make single copies for exercises or exams Make single copies of performable units if out of print or unavailable except in a larger work Copy student performances if for evaluation or rehearsals	Edit in a way which distorts the fundamental character of the work Add or alter lyrics Copy complete works Copy consumables
Video programming	Record if off-air copy is used within 10 days and destroyed after 45 days	Make off-air copies routinely Copy in anticipation of requests Alter or combine off-air copies
Software	Make backup copies of purchased software	Make copies (other than backup) unless pursuant to lease or purchase

EXTRACURRICULAR ACTIVITIES AND THE UIL

Here we look at the role of the State Board of Education, the commissioner of education, and the University Interscholastic League in extracurricular activities. We have already discussed the no pass–no play restriction. And in Chapter 8 we discuss the restrictions that removal of students from classrooms by teachers and placement in an alternative education program impose on attending or participation in extracurricular activities.

TEC §33.081 leaves to the State Board of Education the establishment of rules limiting participation in extracurricular activities during the school day and school week, including practice times. While school districts have considerable autonomy in grading matters, final say is now left to the Texas Commissioner of Education. TEC §33.081(g) provides that the decision of the Texas Commissioner of Education or the commissioner's designee in a dispute over student eligibility for extracurricular activities may not be appealed into state court except on the grounds of being arbitrary or capricious.

One of the most contentious issues involves selection of school cheerleaders. As with student grading, the commissioner has opted to defer in most instances to the judgment of the local school board in these matters. In 1991, he was confronted with an appeal involving a student who was not chosen to be a cheerleader. The evidence revealed her score to be thirteen points below that of the lowest-scoring candidate selected. The mother argued that the school district did not investigate and consider her challenge to cheerleader tryout procedures. The commissioner observed that "this is a matter of local control and the determination of the school district should stand, if board policy and procedures were followed." The board had substantial evidence to support its decision not to intervene in the selection process. The commissioner concluded that in the absence of a violation of state law, state regulation, or local policy, he will not substitute his judgment for that of the local board in matters involving cheerleader selection (*Kirchoff v. Silsbee I.S.D.*). In 1992, the commissioner ruled that school districts cannot withhold the identity of evaluators and their reason for low ratings of a cheerleader candidate. He noted, "[T]here is no rational justification for treating a cheerleader evaluation differently from any other student evaluation" (*Amber L. v. Pflugerville I.S.D.*).

In 1995 the Texas Legislature prohibited a school district from holding an extracurricular activity, including practice time, in an athletic club that discriminates on the basis of race, color, religion, creed, national origin, or sex (TEC §33.082). Section 33.085 allows the board to purchase insurance for school athletes as a cost of operating the district's athletic program. Failure to obtain insurance is not to be construed as placing any legal liability on the district or its employees (see the discussion of legal liability in Chapter 10).

In recent years, the Texas Legislature has limited the autonomy of the University Interscholastic League (UIL) by requiring that the UIL submit its rules and procedures to the state board for the latter's approval or modification (TEC §33.083). The legislature has further restricted the autonomy of the UIL by requiring that its funds be deposited with the University of Texas at Austin, its parent organization, and that it file a fiscal report annually with the governor and the legislature. The legislature also required the UIL to establish an advisory council to review the UIL rules and propose recommended changes to the governor, legislature, and State Board of Education (§33.084).

In *Niles v. University Interscholastic League* (1983) the U.S. Court of Appeals for the Fifth Circuit ruled that the UIL one-year residency requirement for eligibility to participate in interscholastic events is rationally related to a legitimate state purpose and does not infringe on any constitutional rights. The Texas Supreme Court struck down a similar rule in 1981 because it allowed no exceptions (*Sullivan v. University Interscholastic League*). The rule has since been changed. Niles was thus ruled ineligible to play football, and the Spring Branch I.S.D. had to forfeit all the games in which he had participated. In deciding this case the Fifth Circuit observed that there is no constitutional right to engage in an extracurricular activity. The Texas Commissioner of Education ruled similarly in *Elder v. Hardin I.S.D.* in 1982.

In other cases, federal courts have upheld the UIL nineteen-year-old eligibility rule (*Blue v. University Interscholastic League,* 1980) and the summer camp rule (*Kite v. Marshall,* 1980), based on essentially the same reasoning as in the *Niles* case. The nineteen-year-old eligibility rule provides that any student who reaches his or her nineteenth birthday on or before the first day of September preceding a league contest is ineligible to participate. The summer camp rule permits students to attend summer athletic camps as long as attendance is in compliance with UIL rules. However, the "over-19" rule cannot be applied automatically to students with disabilities. In 1993, a state appeals court upheld the right of two learning disabled students to play football even though they were ineligible under the rule. Both students had repeated grades early in their schooling because of their disabilities. The court ruled that exclusion of these students would violate their right to be free from discrimination under Section 504 of the Rehabilitation Act of 1973. The court noted that a waiver procedure would provide a means for reasonably accommodating the needs of students with disabilities (*University Interscholastic League v. Buchanan*).

Interestingly, in several cases challenging sanctions imposed by UIL officials, intermediate-level state courts have not accepted the view that UIL is a state agency but have viewed UIL as a private organization. Litigation on UIL matters continues to surface, and the cases demonstrate that this area of the law remains unsettled.

ADDRESSING THE NEEDS OF SPECIAL GROUPS

At-Risk Children

Over the years, the legislature has tried various measures to reduce the dropout rate in Texas schools. At present, the law leaves districts considerable discretion to deal with the problem, holding them responsible for the results through the accountability system.

TEC §29.081 requires each district to develop appropriate compensatory or accelerated programs for students who are not performing well. Accelerated instruction is required for students who are at risk of dropping out of school or have not performed satisfactorily on each section of the secondary exit-level test. The emphasis on accelerated instruction represents an endorsement of the views espoused by Stanford professor Henry M. Levin, the founder of the accelerated schools movement. Levin maintains that at-risk students should be treated in the same manner as gifted students, thus avoiding the stigmatization of "remediation." Districts are required to document the effectiveness of accelerated instruction in reducing the dropout rate and increasing student achievement.

The legislation specifies factors for determining potential dropouts, such as weak academic performance, limited English proficiency, child neglect or abuse, pregnancy, and slow learning. Districts may operate an extended year program for students in kindergarten through grade eight who are identified as unlikely to be promoted to the next grade (TEC §29.082). Each class is limited to not more than sixteen students and must be taught by a specially trained teacher. If a student attends at least 90 percent of the classes, the student must be promoted to the next grade unless the parent or guardian objects. Districts that have an extended year program are required to phase out student retention.

Bilingual Children

In 1974 the U.S. Supreme Court decided in *Lau v. Nichols* that federal guidelines enforcing Title VI of the 1964 Civil Rights Act require school districts to eliminate language deficiencies where school board policies discriminate against minorities, even in the absence of an intent to do so. The case involved Chinese students who were not receiving any instruction in learning English, yet were enrolled in all-English classes. Section 601 of the act at the time banned discrimination based on the grounds of race, color, or national origin in "any Federal program or activity receiving Federal financial assistance." The court noted that California requires English to be the primary language of instruction (as does Texas) and that proficiency in English is a graduation requirement. Concluding that "those who do not understand English are certain to find their classroom experiences wholly incomprehensible and in no way meaningful," the Court also ruled that the school system had to comply with government regulations issued pursuant to the 1964 Civil Rights measure requiring affirmative steps to rectify language deficiencies. As do most districts, San Francisco received substantial federal funds.

Lau had a spillover effect on school districts around the country. The chief problem with the ruling, however, was that the Court did not specify exactly what form bilingual programs are to have in order for school districts to comply with the 1964 act. In providing funds for meeting the needs of limited-English-proficient (LEP) students, the federal government has issued broad guidelines that have been interpreted in various ways by the states and the school districts. Two basic interpretations have resulted in reference to bilingual education programs: (1) providing students with instruction in their primary language and ensuring that English-language instruction be part of the students' daily curriculum until the students can understand enough English to function adequately in an all-English curriculum and (2) immersing students completely in English-as-a-second-language (ESL) programs until the students can function adequately in an all-English curriculum. Variations that resulted from these two basic interpretations have only served to complicate the implementation of the instructional programs geared to meet the needs of the LEP student. Few exemplary programs that meet all the legal requirements exist.

Subchapter B of Chapter 29 of the Texas Education Code sets forth state law with respect to bilingual education. These provisions, which were originally adopted in 1973, were substantially

revised during the 1981 legislative session, as a result of a federal court decision handed down by Judge William Wayne Justice (*United States v. Texas [Bilingual]*). They remain little changed in the present Texas Education Code. TEC §29.051 asserts that English is the primary language of Texas. The provisions require each school district with twenty or more students of limited English proficiency in the same grade to offer bilingual education in kindergarten through the elementary grades; bilingual education, instruction in English as a second language, or other transitional language instruction approved by TEA in postelementary grades through the eighth grade; and instruction in English as a second language in grades nine through twelve. Section 29.055 of the Texas Education Code requires dual-language instruction to be full-time, with basic skills instruction in the primary language of the students and with intensive instruction as well in English-language skills. The program is also to incorporate the cultural aspects of the students' backgrounds. Bilingual classes must be located in regular schools, not separate facilities.

A district that is required to offer bilingual or special language programs must offer a voluntary school program for children of limited English proficiency who will be eligible for kindergarten or first grade at the beginning of the following school year (TEC §29.060). If the district operates on the traditional two-semester system, the program must be offered over the summer and encompass one-half days for eight weeks or a similar schedule approved by the school board. If the district operates on a year-round schedule, then the program must encompass 120 hours of instruction on a schedule approved by the board of trustees. The prekindergarten program must be an intensive bilingual or special language program meeting TEA standards with a student/teacher ratio not exceeding eighteen-to-one.

Under §29.056, TEA is required to develop standardized criteria for identifying, assessing, and classifying bilingual students. This section also provides that parents are to be kept fully informed about placement of their children, and both school district and parents are provided with the right to appeal a placement decision.

Gifted Children

State law requires that school districts be aware of and address the needs of gifted and talented students. A gifted and talented student is defined as one "who performs at or shows the potential for performing at a remarkably high level of accomplishment when compared to others of the same age, experience, or environment and who exhibits high performance capability in an intellectual, creative, or artistic field; possesses an unusual capacity for leadership; or excels in a specific academic field" (TEC §29.121). Using criteria developed by the State Board of Education as part of a state plan for serving these students, each district is required to adopt a process for identifying gifted and talented students and to establish a program for those students in each grade level. Such programs have been in existence in some school districts for years.

Abused and Neglected Children

Section 261.101(a) of the Family Code provides that anyone having cause to believe that a child's physical or mental health or welfare has been or may be adversely affected by abuse or neglect shall immediately make a report to any local or state law enforcement agency or to the Texas Department of Protective and Regulatory Services. A child is defined as a person under the age of eighteen. Definitions of "abuse" and "neglect" are contained in the statute. Generally, abuse includes mental or emotional injury by any person that impairs the child's growth, development, or psychological functioning; physical injury or threat of physical injury by any person against a child; failure to prevent another person from physically injuring a child; sexual contact, sexual intercourse, or sexual conduct; failure to prevent inappropriate sexual behavior with a child; and obscene or pornographic photographing of a child. Neglect encompasses a parent, guardian, or managing or possessory conservator's leaving the child in a dangerous situation where harm could result without providing for the care of the child and without demonstrating an intent to return; failure by any person to protect a child from a situation that could endanger the child; failure by any person to obtain medical attention for a child or to provide food, clothing, or shelter for a child; and failure by the person responsible for the child's care to provide care for a child after the child returns home from an absence. Section 261.101(b) provides that a professional (including a teacher, school nurse, or day-care worker) who has cause to believe that a child has been or may be abused or neglected, has violated the compulsory school law on three or more occasions, or on three or more occasions has been absent from home without parental consent has forty-eight hours to make a report. Anonymous reports are not encouraged but will be received and acted upon in the same manner as those that are not anonymous.

Section 261.109 of the Family Code goes further to state that a person commits a Class B misdemeanor if the person has cause to believe that a child's physical or mental health or welfare has been or may be endangered by abuse or neglect and knowingly fails to report the matter. Thus, the law establishes a duty to inform appropriate agencies, one which is ignored at the risk of fine and imprisonment. A case in point involves the criminal conviction of a teacher in 1992 for failing to report child abuse by two aides. The aides had held the hands of a severely mentally retarded elementary student under hot water as a disciplinary measure, causing severe burns. The teacher was charged with and convicted of failure to report the incident. She was sentenced to 120 days in jail, probated for one year, and fined $1,000. An appeals court affirmed the conviction (*Morris v. State,* 1992). In the past, failure to report suspected child abuse has resulted in the revocation of a teaching or administrator certificate. In the *Morris* decision above, the commissioner revoked her teaching certificate on the ground that the teacher was unworthy to instruct the youth of the state (*Texas Education Agency v. Morris*). Senate Bill 1 leaves the development of new rules relating to the suspension or revocation of certificates to the new State Board for Educator Certification (TEC §21.041(b)).

At the same time, the law expressly shields those who do report in good faith from civil or criminal liability. Section 261.106 of the Family Code stipulates as much, adding that immunity extends as well when one participates in any judicial proceeding resulting from the report. Section 261.108 provides for attorneys' fees and other expenses to persons who report suspected cases of child abuse and then have frivolous lawsuits filed against them for doing so.

According to a 1991 decision of the Texas Commissioner of Education, a school district may not require routing of child abuse reports through school administrators as a condition of employment. Such a requirement violates the reporting provisions of the Family Code. The case involved the nonrenewal of a probationary teacher's contract in part because she didn't follow the principal's directive that all child abuse and neglect reports be channeled through her. The commissioner noted that the district's policy and the principal's directive to follow it interfered with "a superior duty imposed directly on petitioner under [the] penal provisions of the Family Code." The commissioner did note that a school district could require that after an employee follows the reporting requirements in the Family Code, the employee notify the school district (*Pike v. Southwest I.S.D.*).

Under Family Code 261.302(b), child abuse investigations can take place while children are in school. Further, under the Texas Open Records Act, child abuse investigators are allowed access to student records in connection with a child abuse case. In cooperating with child abuse investigators, school officials should retain the interest of the student being questioned so that interviews not take place in a classroom in view of other students and the faculty.

Our society continues to be troubled with the state versus family issue; this makes prompt reporting coupled with documented evidence particularly important. Only under these circumstances are state child protection agencies likely to be successful in intervening before it is too late.

SUMMARY

Significant changes have taken place in recent years in Texas regarding student enrollment. While segregation by law has largely ended, controversy remains over when districts have achieved unitary status and no longer should be subject to court oversight. Given recent U.S. Supreme Court decisions in this area, the long-running statewide desegregation order, *United States v. Texas*, may be nearing an end. While racial and ethnic discrimination issues command less attention today than in the past, sex discrimination and harassment have become major concerns.

Virtually all students, including those who are homeless or have established a residence in a district separate from their parents or guardians, are entitled to a tuition-free education. The emphasis is on student inclusion.

Despite efforts to return more authority to the local district and its employees, significant top-down requirements remain, as the discussion in this chapter regarding the state-mandated curriculum, sex education, student testing, and controls on extracurricular participation demonstrates. At the same time, the Texas Legislature has strengthened school district, campus, and administrator accountability measures. It appears possible that the toughened standards may result in the closure of low-performing schools in the future.

A seminal question is whether legislative efforts to give school districts and campuses greater responsibility for attendance and the instructional program will reduce the dropout rate and improve student achievement. If not, the case for more dramatic reforms such as privatization and school vouchers will be strengthened.

THREE

Special Education

NO AREA of school law has experienced such explosive growth over the past twenty-odd years as special education. Since the early 1970s, the rights of students with disabilities have been increasingly a subject of legislation and litigation. Our purpose in this chapter is to present the legal requirements for identifying and serving children with disabilities in Texas schools. Included will be a discussion of procedures to be followed in disciplining these students. But first, a refresher course on acronyms is in order.

THE JARGON OF SPECIAL EDUCATION

Special educators and their attorneys often seem to have beamed down from another planet where initials and acronyms take the place of words. In order to walk the special education walk you have to talk the special education talk. Here is a quick overview of common terms.

P.L. 94-142: This is the landmark legislation passed by Congress in 1975 guaranteeing every child with a disability a free, appropriate public education. The law was more properly known as The Education for All Handicapped Children Act, and is now known as the Individuals with Disabilities Education Act.

IDEA: The Individuals with Disabilities Education Act.

504: Section 504 of the 1973 Rehabilitation Act, a federal law which prohibits discrimination against persons with disabilities in programs which receive federal funds.

FAPE: Free, appropriate public education. The law mandates that FAPE be available to every child, regardless of the nature or severity of the disability.

IEP:	Individualized education program. This is the basic planning tool for the child's education. It is to be collaboratively developed by school officials and parents.
ARD:	Admission, review, and dismissal. This refers to a committee of school officials and parents who have the responsibility for developing the IEP and placing the child in an appropriate program.
Placement:	This refers to the instructional arrangement in which the child is educated. It can be anything from the regular classroom setting to a special residential school.
LRE:	Least restrictive environment. The placement of the child must be in the LRE which is appropriate for the child. That is, it must enable the child to interact with his or her nondisabled peers as much as is appropriate in light of the nature and severity of the disability.
Related Services:	Special transportation and other noninstructional services that are necessary for the child to obtain benefit from the educational program. These include such things as occupational therapy (OT), physical therapy (PT), counseling, and speech therapy.
Handicapping Condition:	To be eligible to receive federally funded special education services, the child must meet eligibility criteria for one of several handicapping conditions. These include learning disabled (LD), emotionally disturbed (ED), mentally retarded (MR), other health impaired (OHI), visually handicapped (VH), auditorially handicapped (AH), along with others.
EYS:	Extended year services. This refers to services beyond the normal school year.
OSEP:	The Office of Special Education Programs. This is the federal agency with responsibility for the implementation of IDEA.

FEDERAL LEGISLATION

It is difficult to conceive of a piece of legislation with better intentions than IDEA. The idea behind IDEA is that every citizen is entitled to an education appropriate to his or her unique abilities, taking into account his or her disabilities. IDEA also contemplates that each child's program should be individually planned; that the planning should be done by a group of people who know something about education and also know something about the child; that the parents have a unique and very valuable contribution to make and therefore should be significantly involved in the process; that there should be ample procedural safeguards, such as notice to the parents at important times and the opportunity to consent to certain actions of the school; and that children with disabilities should not be segregated from their peers any more than is necessary. We will now examine more closely the components of federal law concerning special education. We will focus our attention on IDEA at this point, leaving the Handicapped Children's Protection Act of 1986 and Section 504 of the 1973 Rehabilitation Act to the end of the chapter.

Identification

School districts cannot sit back and wait for children with disabilities to come to them. They are required by law to take affirmative steps to make sure that every eligible child in the district is "identified, located, and evaluated" (34 C.F.R. §300.128). Referrals can be made by parents, teachers, doctors, psychologists, or others familiar with the child.

Assessment

Years ago a school superintendent discussed with the school district's attorney a situation involving a student who, according to the superintendent, was emotionally disturbed but had never been identified as such by the school. When the attorney asked how the superintendent could know that the student was emotionally disturbed without a proper, formal determination, the superintendent explained, "He's crazy. His whole family is crazy. Everyone around here has known that for years."

It is to avoid such untutored labeling that the law requires the school district to obtain a comprehensive assessment of the student's condition before applying any sort of label and before placing the child in a special education program. Assessment procedures must guarantee that children are assessed in their native language, that measurement instruments are not racially or culturally biased, that tests are validated for the specific purpose they are used, that tests are administered by trained personnel in accordance with their instructions, and that no single criterion (e.g., an IQ score) is used to determine an appropriate program for a child.

Parents who disagree with the school's assessment of their child have the right to obtain an independent educational evaluation (IEE). The IEE must be considered by the school, along with the school's own assessments, and the school may be required to pay for the IEE, unless the school can demonstrate that its assessment was properly done.

However, a parent cannot require the school district to accept an independent assessment in lieu of the district's own assessment. A recent decision from the Fifth Circuit has made this crystal clear. When Wesley Andress was due for an assessment to reconsider his eligibility for special education, his parents objected to the school's conducting the assessment. They argued that Wesley would be psychologically harmed by the assessment process, and offered to provide the school district with assessments they had obtained privately. The school district, however, insisted on its right to conduct its own assessment of Wesley, using the assessment personnel chosen by the school district.

The Fifth Circuit vigorously upheld the school district in this case: "If a student's parents want him to receive special education under IDEA, they must allow the school itself to reevaluate the student and they cannot force the school to rely solely on an independent evaluation" (Andress v. Cleveland I.S.D.).

This case is particularly important because assessment data play such a critical role in the entire process. Assessment data are truly the rudder that steers the ship in special education matters. All decisions concerning the student—the nature of the IEP, the level of inclusion with nondisabled students, the form of discipline to be used, the provision of related services—should reflect the assessment data pertaining to that student.

ARD Committee

Federal law requires a group of knowledgeable people to meet to determine the child's IEP and placement. In Texas, we have designated this group as the ARD committee. The ARD committee must include (1) a representative of the local school district administration, or designee approved by the superintendent; (2) a representative of instruction, typically the teacher; (3) a parent, or the student if he or she is eighteen. This is the minimal membership of an ARD committee. Even when below eighteen years of age, students are welcome at ARD committee meetings at the discretion of the parent.

Other personnel frequently attend, depending on the situation. Someone familiar with the assessment data and having the ability to interpret formalized testing data for the parents and others should be present whenever assessment data are likely to be reviewed. This includes the initial ARD, the three-year reevaluation ARD, and other times as necessary.

At least one ARD committee meeting is necessary for each child each year. The IEP must be reviewed at least as often as annually, thus requiring at least an annual ARD meeting. However, the ARD committee must also meet any time the child's placement is changed. For example, any change in a child's program of more than ten consecutive days is a "change of placement," thus requiring an ARD meeting.

Members of the ARD committee are expected to work collaboratively to develop a program. When they do so and are able to reach consensus, few legal issues arise. When they fail to reach consensus, the school district must give parents the opportunity to recess and reconvene the meeting in ten days or less. If consensus still cannot be reached, then the parents may wish to seek out mediation through the Texas Education Agency or opt for a due process hearing. Most disputes can be resolved through the ARD process. Certainly that is what the law envisions.

Individualized Education Program

If there is any single principle that applies to special education law, it is the principle of individualized decision making. The strengths, weaknesses, and needs of each child are to be considered throughout the decision-making process. Thus the individualized education program (IEP) is crucial. The IEP is a written statement of services to be delivered and goals to be achieved. More specifically, the law requires the IEP to include:

1. Present educational performance levels of the child.
2. Annual goals, including short-term objectives.
3. Specific special education and related services to be provided and the extent to which the child will participate in a regular education program.
4. Projected dates when services are to begin and the expected duration of these services.

5. Appropriate objective criteria and evaluation procedures, along with schedules for determining, at least on an annual basis, whether or not the short-term instructional objectives are being achieved.

Least Restrictive Environment

Federal law expresses a strong preference for placing the child with disabilities in the setting in which that child would be served if there were no disability. This preference goes by various names: least restrictive environment (LRE), mainstreaming, inclusion; all these terms refer to much the same thing. In making placement decisions, the ARD committee is to consider first the regular classroom. If that placement will not afford the student an appropriate education, then the committee should consider supplementing that placement with aids and supplementary services and modifications. If that will not afford the child an appropriate education, then a move to a more restrictive environment is necessary.

The LRE preference in the law is strong but must be considered in light of the primary responsibility of the school district, which is to provide an education that is appropriate. The law mandates LRE, but it also mandates a full continuum of alternative placements, some of them highly restrictive. Obviously it was never the intention of Congress that each and every child be served in a regular classroom all day, every day.

Procedural Safeguards

Much of the federal law is procedural. Congress did not presume to tell educators how to educate children with special needs. Instead, Congress set up a fairly elaborate procedural system for the schools to comply with, assuming that if the schools followed the proper procedure, the end product would be an appropriate education.

Schools are required to give written notice to the parents prior to ARD meetings, prior to assessment of the child, and also at certain times when the school refuses to initiate or change services to a child. Consent is required prior to initial assessment and prior to initial placement in special education. After that initial placement, the school can make changes in placement of a child without consent but must give the parents notice and an opportunity to challenge the ARD's decision.

The law requires some system whereby a parent can challenge the decisions a school district has made in a due process hearing. In

Texas we have independent hearing officers appointed by the Texas
Education Agency who hear such cases. A parent can obtain a hearing concerning virtually anything—the placement, the amount of
related services, the label attached to the child, etc. Like most administrative processes, special education cases must go before a
hearing officer before they go to court. Unlike other administrative
processes, this one does not require the parent first to go before the
superintendent or the school board. The appeal goes directly from
the ARD committee to the hearing officer and then to court. Neither the school board nor the Texas Education Agency can overturn
a hearing officer's decision. Moreover, unlike most administrative
processes, in a special education case the hearing officer comes to
the school district rather than requiring the appealing parties to
come to Austin. In a state the size of Texas, that is no small matter.

Let us now examine how judicial law has affected this system
of special education.

CASE LAW

How Much Student Progress Is Enough?

The U.S. Supreme Court heard its first case pertaining to IDEA
(then known as EAHCA) in 1982. The *Board of Education v. Rowley* case is significant for two reasons. First, it established the principle that school districts are not required to maximize the potential of a child, but rather, to provide some educational benefit to the
child. Since this federal standard is fairly low, advocates for students
with disabilities frequently point to state law in an effort to establish some higher standard. To date, such efforts have not succeeded
in Texas.

Second, the case told us how courts in the future would examine special education disputes. The Supreme Court in *Rowley*
instructed federal courts to ask two questions in special education
cases: (1) did the school district comply with the procedural mandates of the law? and (2) is the IEP reasonably calculated to confer
educational benefit on the child?

The case involved a deaf student, Amy Rowley, and the issue
was whether she was entitled to a sign language interpreter to enable her to secure a free, appropriate public education under the
terms of the act. The lower courts had ruled that while Amy was
progressing from grade to grade and performing above average, she
was not achieving up to her potential because of the absence of the
interpreter and thus was not receiving a free, appropriate education

as spelled out in the law. The Supreme Court, however, ruled that Amy was not entitled to the sign language interpreter. The goal of Congress in enacting the law, wrote Justice William H. Rehnquist for the majority, was not to maximize the potential of handicapped children but rather "to identify and evaluate handicapped children and to provide them with access to a free public education." Since Amy Rowley was progressing from grade to grade and was receiving an adequate education under the program approved by the school administrators to meet her needs, no sign language interpreter was necessary.

While the Rowley case told us how much progress is enough for Amy Rowley and others like her, that same issue is still difficult to deal with in many other cases. Amy was being served in a regular classroom setting. She was able to master the essential elements of the curriculum just as her peers were. She passed from one grade to the next at the same time that they did. Thus it was easy for the Court to conclude that the school district was providing Amy with an education that afforded her some benefit.

The question is much tougher when dealing with students whose cognitive abilities are significantly lower than their peers'. For the severely retarded child, how much progress is enough? For the medically fragile child, how do you define "benefit" or "progress"? This is where the IEP plays a crucial role. If properly written, the IEP should contain measurable annual goals and short-term objectives. If the student has achieved those goals or at least made substantial progress toward achieving them, then a court or hearing officer is likely to determine that reasonable progress has been made. If the goals are so vague as to be unmeasurable, or if the student truly has made little or no progress, then the school has failed in its mission.

Related Services

The second special education dispute to reach the Supreme Court arose right here in Texas. Amber Tatro's parents asked the Irving I.S.D. to provide a service known as clean intermittent catheterization (CIC) for Amber. Amber had spina bifida, a condition that prevented her from voluntarily emptying her bladder. Without someone at the school to provide CIC, Amber would be confined to a homebound program. With CIC, Amber would be able to attend school with her peers. The school district balked at this request, arguing that CIC was a medical service and thus beyond the legal responsibility of a public school (*Irving I.S.D. v. Tatro*).

Recall that related services as defined in IDEA mean "transportation, and such developmental, corrective, and other supportive services (including speech pathology and audiology, psychological services, physical and occupational therapy, recreation, and medical and counseling services, except that such medical services shall be for diagnostic and evaluation purposes only) as may be required to assist a handicapped child to benefit from special education, and includes the early identification and assessment of handicapping conditions in children" (20 U.S.C. §1401(17)). This case focused on the definition of the term "medical services" as used in the law. The school district argued that the only medical services required of a school district are those for diagnostic or evaluative purposes, and that this service went well beyond that. The Supreme Court disagreed.

The Court examined the federal regulations defining "related services," and found that they included "school health services." Noting that school nurses typically provide a variety of services for children and that Amber's CIC could be accomplished by a school nurse or even a layperson, the Court ruled that Irving was required under the law to provide this service to Amber.

In doing so, the Court appeared to take the position that the only "medical services" which a school district is not required to provide are those which must be delivered by a physician or a hospital. Subsequent cases have softened that reading of the Irving case. In drawing the distinction between medical services and related services, the courts look to four key factors:

1. Is the service constant or periodic?
2. Does the service require a health care professional, or can it be done by a trained layperson?
3. Is the service complex or simple?
4. Is the service very expensive, or economically reasonable?

Amber Tatro was successful in her case because the service she requested of the school required periodic attention, could be done by a trained layperson, and was simple and inexpensive. In cases where students have sought the constant attention of a nurse to perform a variety of complex procedures at considerable expense to the school, they have been unsuccessful.

Least Restrictive Environment

The hottest trend in special education circles in the early '90s was "inclusion." The concept is to get away from the notion of "pull-out" programs whereby children with disabilities are taken out of the regular classroom to receive more individualized instruction or special services. Inclusion advocates seek to have more individualized instruction and special services delivered in the regular classroom itself.

However, "inclusion" does not appear anywhere in the law or regulations dealing with special education. Moreover, while the educational theories may change as to what is the best approach in providing for children with special needs, IDEA has not changed since its inception in 1975. It has always expressed a strong preference for as much "inclusion" or "mainstreaming" as the child's ARD committee determines is appropriate for that particular child.

The Supreme Court has not yet handled a case dealing with the LRE component of the law. We can look to the U.S. Court of Appeals for the Fifth Circuit for the leading case on the subject, *Daniel R.R. v. State Board of Education*. Daniel was a six-year-old with Downs Syndrome in El Paso, Texas. Due to his mental retardation and speech impairments, Daniel's developmental age was less than three years and his communication skills were those of a child two years old. Daniel's parents asked the school district to place Daniel in a half-day early childhood program and a half-day in the prekindergarten class. The latter would enable Daniel to interact with his age-appropriate, nonhandicapped peers. The school agreed to give this a try.

By November, the school was ready to pronounce the experiment a failure. The teacher reported that Daniel required almost constant one-to-one attention, that he failed to master any of the skills she was teaching, and that modifying the Pre-K curriculum sufficiently to reach Daniel would have gone well beyond "modification"—it would have been an entirely different curriculum. The school district called for an ARD meeting and proposed moving Daniel out of the prekindergarten program.

After years of litigation (it was the summer of 1989 when the Fifth Circuit passed judgment on the actions of an ARD meeting in November 1986), the Fifth Circuit upheld the school district's proposed change in placement for Daniel. In doing so, the court determined that LRE cases would turn on two critical questions: Can education in the regular classroom, with the use of supplementary aids and services, be achieved satisfactorily? If not, has the school mainstreamed the child to the maximum extent appropriate?

In answering the first inquiry, the Fifth Circuit indicated courts should examine carefully the efforts made by the school district to enable the child to succeed in the regular classroom. Genuine, good-faith efforts are expected. Teachers must modify the curriculum and the methodology for a student with special needs.

The appeals court did not establish a clear litmus test for determining the extent to which efforts should be made to serve children with disabilities in the regular classroom. Rather, three broad generalizations were offered. First, the school does not have to provide "every conceivable supplementary aid or service"; second, "the Act does not require regular education instructors to devote all or most of their time to one handicapped child"; and third, schools are not expected to "modify the regular education program beyond recognition." Applying these standards to a given case is a matter for individualized ARD decision making.

This much is clear. Regular education teachers must be prepared, supported, and trained to handle children with disabilities in the regular classroom. The old attitude of "If he's going to be in my classroom, he's going to have to meet the same expectations, do the same work, comply with the same standards, and achieve the same results as everyone else" is legally obsolete. In the words of the Fifth Circuit:

> States must tolerate educational differences. . . . As a result, the Act accepts the notion that handicapped students will participate in regular education but that some of them will not benefit as much as nonhandicapped students will. The Act requires states to tolerate a wide range of educational abilities in their schools and specifically, in regular education—the EHA's [now IDEA's] preferred educational environment.

The Court's second inquiry arises in those cases where mainstreaming is not appropriate. Even if a child is properly placed in a separate special education program, the school district has the duty to provide as much mainstreaming opportunity as possible. The school should look for opportunities for mainstreaming in art, music, and physical education. The student should have the opportunity to ride the regular school bus, eat with the other students in the cafeteria, attend assemblies, and play on the playground with the other students.

Extended Year Services

Special education's mandates have required educators to shift many a paradigm. For example, every state has a law mandating the number of days of instruction children are to receive. While some schools are experimenting with year-round schooling, the vast majority of children still attend school for approximately nine months, and then take a three-month summer break. But what happens when a student's disability is so severe that the summer break will cause a loss of any progress that may have been achieved?

This has been the issue in several court cases. The most important for us is the Fifth Circuit decision *Alamo Heights I.S.D. v. State Board of Education* (1986). Like every other circuit court that has addressed this issue, the Fifth Circuit determined that for some children an "appropriate" education is one that goes beyond the normal school year. The court stated that "if a child will experience severe or substantial regression during the summer months in the absence of a summer program, the handicapped child may be entitled to year-round services." The court concluded, "The issue is whether the benefits accrued to the child during the regular school year will be significantly jeopardized if he is not provided an educational program during the summer months." The court held in this case that there was sufficient evidence of regression to justify requiring the district to provide summer services to the student.

Thus the paradigm of "Every child gets the same amount of services. That's fair" had to shift under the weight of the law. The new paradigm is "Every child gets an education that is appropriate. For some that requires more than nine months of services. That's fair."

Schools now routinely address extended year services concerns for many children. Again, the key is individualized decision making. A one-size-fits-all summer program does not comply with the legal mandate for individualized consideration. The program should be tailored to the child's needs, rather than the other way around.

Unilateral Placements

In a 1985 case, the Supreme Court opened the door to unilateral parent placements in private school settings. The scenario usually involves a disagreement between school and parent as to the appropriate placement. The school believes the child can be appropriately served by the local school district; the parent believes that only placement in a special, private school, or perhaps in a residential facility, will do the job. As a result of the Court's decision in *School Committee of Burlington v. Department of Education*, it is now possible for parents to recover reimbursement for the costs of such a unilateral placement.

However, parents bear a heavy burden of proof in these cases. First, they must prove that the IEP and/or placement recommended by the school is inappropriate. Second, the parents must prove that the IEP and placement which they have arranged for the child is appropriate. Three factors make this particularly difficult for the parents. First, there is a presumption in the law that the program recommended by the school is appropriate. Second, the law merely requires the school to propose a program which will confer reasonable benefit. Thus the existence of a superior school with a program and placement that will enable the child to reach new educational heights is irrelevant if the school can afford "reasonable benefit." Third, the school's proposed program will almost always be less restrictive than the private placement sought by the parents.

For example, in *Teague I.S.D. v. Todd L.*, the Fifth Circuit denied a parental request for reimbursement of the costs of a unilateral placement at The Oaks, described by the court as "a highly restrictive psychiatric hospital." The school program, according to the court, was conferring and would continue to confer educational benefit on Todd, despite the fact that the IEP called for just two hours of instruction. Todd's condition was such that such a shortened day was educationally appropriate. Moreover, the court was clearly troubled by the restrictiveness of The Oaks, particularly in light of testimony from school district personnel that there were many less restrictive alternatives that could still be tried with Todd. Thus the financial responsibility for The Oaks was the parents' and not the school's.

Even when the parent places the student in a facility which does not meet all of the requirements a public school would have to meet, the parents may be able to obtain reimbursement. This was the situation in *Florence County School District Four v. Carter*. The school district argued that it should not be financially responsible for the private placement of the child since the facility chosen by the parents did not use written IEPs and employed as teachers some staff who were not certified. The Supreme Court unanimously rejected the school's argument. Just because the school could not have placed Shannon Carter in this particular school does not mean the parents cannot do so. Since the school's proposed program for Shannon was determined to be inappropriate, and the parents' chosen placement was conferring educational benefit, the public school was stuck with the tab.

After the *Burlington* and *Carter* decisions, schools only have one surefire defense to a claim for reimbursement of a unilateral placement. That defense is that the school district was then, and is now, ready, willing, and able to provide FAPE.

Private School Children

One of the conditions that comes with the federal special education money is that schools must make special education services available to students who are enrolled in private schools by parental choice. This provision is increasingly a source of contention between parents and schools. The public school is clearly required to make an effort to ensure that the parents of private school children are aware of the availability of special education services. Moreover, any referral of a child who is attending a private school is to be handled just as if the child were in the public school. The school should conduct an assessment and make a determination as to the student's eligibility for special education. If the student is eligible, the school should propose an IEP, including special education and related services appropriate for the child.

The parents then have three options. They can enroll the child full-time in the public school, in which case the school's proposed IEP would go into effect. They can completely reject the IEP and stay in the private school at their own expense. Or the parents may choose to "dually enroll" the child. Under this alternative, the student is enrolled in both the private and the public school, receiving the special education and related services from the public school.

In one of the few Texas cases dealing with dual enrollment, a hearing officer ruled that the amount of attendance required of the private school child who wishes to dually enroll is determined individually by the IEP. If the IEP calls for three hours per day of special education instruction, then the child must attend the public school for three hours per day in order to be "dually enrolled." On the other hand, if the IEP calls for very limited services, such as speech therapy once a week, then the child should be considered dually enrolled if the child merely comes to the public school for speech therapy once a week as required by the IEP (*Patrick H. v. Austin I.S.D.*, 1994).

When it is impossible to implement the IEP by dual enrollment, the parent must choose between the free public school program and the private school at parental expense. Such is the lesson of *Riqui M. v. College Station I.S.D.* In this case, the student's needs were so extensive that a partial enrollment in the public school would not have afforded the child an appropriate education. Thus the hearing officer ruled that the school was not required to provide special education or related services to the student. Since he was not enrolled in the public school, and since dual enrollment would not be appropriate, the school had no further legal responsibility for the child.

Service to private school children sometimes raises issues about church-state separation. Can the public school provide services to the child enrolled in a private religious school? Can the public school do so at the private school site? In *Zobrest v. Catalina Foothills School District*, the U.S. Supreme Court ruled that the public school could provide a sign language interpreter for a student at a Catholic school. The school had argued that such an arrangement violated the establishment clause, discussed in more detail in Chapter 7. The Court rejected that notion. The Court did not say that IDEA required such services for private school students, but ruled that the Constitution did not forbid the arrangement.

Subsequent to *Zobrest,* most school districts have provided a wide variety of services to private school children who dually enroll and can come to the public school to receive educational services. But what if the parents request the public school to provide the services at the private school?

Litigation on this issue after *Zobrest* is mixed. However, the highest-level court to tackle the issue has answered in the negative. In *Goodall by Goodall v. Stafford County School Bd.* the Fourth Circuit Court of Appeals held that IDEA does not require a public school to provide special education services at the private school. Subsequently, however, four federal district courts have ruled that public schools must serve private school students on the site of the private school. All four cases are now on appeal to the circuit court level. Though none of these cases are from the Fifth Circuit, we can still look forward to more clarification of this thorny issue in 1996 and 1997.

DISCIPLINE OF CHILDREN WITH DISABILITIES

In Chapter 8 we describe the most common forms of student discipline and their legal implications. In dealing with a student with disabilities, there are some additional considerations. We discuss them here, beginning with two important federal court decisions and concluding with a review of discipline procedures under Texas law.

S-1 v. Turlington, a decision handed down by the U.S. Court of Appeals for the Fifth Circuit in 1981, arose when school officials in

Florida, which was then included in the Fifth Circuit, expelled several disabled students for almost two years. This was the maximum penalty available under state law. The behavior of the students was certainly serious: masturbation, sexual acts against fellow students, willful defiance of authority, insubordination, vandalism, and profane language. The students were each classified as mentally retarded. None was classified as emotionally disturbed.

The parties to the suit agreed that it would be illegal for the school officials to expel a student for behavior that directly resulted from a student's disability. The school asserted that it had taken that factor into account with regard to the only student who had raised the issue—S-1. Both the school superintendent and the school board determined that S-1 was not emotionally disturbed, and, therefore, his inappropriate behavior could not have arisen from his disability.

The Fifth Circuit found fault with that analysis in several respects. First, the school officials should have made a determination as to whether or not there was a link between handicap and behavior with regard to each of the students, not just the student who had raised the issue. Second, the court rejected the idea that the determination hinges on whether or not the student is emotionally disturbed. The school was required to have such a determination for any child with a disability. Third, the court found fault with the superintendent and board for making the determination. Rather, the determination should have been made by the knowledgeable group trained to make such decisions—in Texas that means the ARD committee.

Perhaps the most confusing aspect of the Turlington case, however, was its treatment of the issue of whether or not expulsion can be imposed on a student with disabilities. The Fifth Circuit chided the trial court for dodging the issue, stating that "we cannot ignore the gray areas that may result if we do not decide this question." The court then proceeded to create a considerable gray area itself, by observing:

> We therefore find that expulsion is still a proper disciplinary tool under the EHA [now IDEA] and section 504 when proper procedures are utilized and under proper circumstances. We cannot, however, authorize the complete cessation of educational services during the expulsion period.

Most educators find this to be the functional equivalent of saying you can go swimming—just don't get wet. How Texas has dealt with this will be reviewed below.

In 1988, the Supreme Court spoke to the issue of special education and discipline in the case of *Honig v. Doe*. John Doe and Jack Smith were suspended from school for behavior that was believed to be dangerous. John had attempted to choke another student, leaving abrasions on the victim's neck. Jack had made lewd comments and on previous occasions had stolen, extorted money, and made sexual comments to female classmates. It was undisputed that these behaviors were related to the students' handicapping conditions.

While it is unclear exactly how long Jack was suspended, John's suspension lasted five-and-one-half weeks (twenty-four school days). The suspensions probably would have lasted much longer had the lower court not issued an injunction forbidding the school from taking such disciplinary actions against Jack and John. Although the lower courts addressed several issues and made a number of findings, only one issue addressed by the Supreme Court is crucial to this discussion. This issue concerns the so-called "stay put" provision of IDEA, which states in relevant part: "During the pendency of any proceedings conducted pursuant [to IDEA], unless the State or local educational agency and the parent or guardian otherwise agree, the child shall remain in the then current educational placement of such child" (20 U.S.C. §1415(e)(3)). The "then current placement" of the handicapped student refers to the child's placement prior to the expulsion or other change of placement. The "stay put" provision is triggered by an appeal before a special education hearing officer under the IDEA. Once the parents disagree and appeal the matter, the student must "stay put" in his or her current placement while the appeal is pending.

In the Honig case, San Francisco school officials argued that Jack and John were dangerous. Invocation of the "stay put" provision would put them right back in school, where they had endangered other students. The "stay put" provision, school officials asserted, was not applicable to situations where students presented a clear and present danger to others. However, the Supreme Court could find no support for that argument in the statute. There is no stated exception in the "stay put" provision for situations in which the student's behavior is determined to be dangerous to the student or to others. In addressing this issue the Supreme Court held in *Honig* that the "stay put" provision is unequivocal and is not subject to an exception for dangerous students. The Court concluded that when a suspension of a handicapped student for more than ten days is proposed and the student's parents do not agree to the suspension and appeal the matter pursuant to IDEA, thus triggering the "stay put" provision, the school district must seek the aid of a court if the school officials consider it necessary that a particularly dangerous student be enjoined from attending school. In such circumstances, the Supreme Court ruled, the school will have to overcome the presumption in favor of the student's current educational placement by showing a court "that maintaining the child in his or her current placement is substantially likely to result in injury either to himself or herself, or to others."

Some Texas schools have had to resort to court protection in dealing with dangerous students. One reported case is *Texas City I.S.D. v. Jorstad*. In that case the school sought an injunction to keep an emotionally disturbed middle school student out of regular classes pending the resolution of a due process hearing. The school did not seek to bar the student from school altogether. Instead, it proposed temporary placement in the Behavioral Management Class at the middle school. Testimony from Mr. Carter, the principal, was summarized by the court as follows:

> Mr. Carter testified that John has been manifestly disruptive on innumerable occasions. He has received numerous complaints from parents, teachers, and others, regarding John's conduct. He has been called to assist teachers, on several occasions, regarding disruptions, and where John has been physically aggressive. John has frequently struck other students, and has run away from his individual aide. He has entered the classrooms of other teachers, and has locked himself in another teacher's classroom. He has twice tried to jump out of second floor windows, and on a third occasion, successfully exited a window, on the second floor, some twenty feet above some concrete steps, at considerable peril to himself. . . . John's propensity for extremely loud and wide ranging profanity is significant, and frequently disruptive. This profanity is used throughout both classroom and hallway settings. He has, on several occasions, threatened to kill himself, and others. Mr. Carter further testified that John has caused substantial physical damage to school property, including the virtual destruction of a "time out" room. . . . Mr. Carter testified that John has been involved in approximately thirty physical assaults on teachers, staff, his individual aide, and other students, and innumerable verbal assaults.

Citing similar testimony from teachers and staff, the judge gave the school district the injunction. However, the judge noted that only in such cases where the need is clear and the evidence is strong will such injunctions be granted.

More recently the Eighth Circuit Court of Appeals has addressed the standards a school must establish in order to justify the issuance of an injunction to override the stay put rule. The Court held that schools must prove two points: first, that without the injunction the student is substantially likely to cause injury to someone; and second, that the school has done all that it reasonably could do to reduce the risk of injury (*Light v. Parkway School District*, 1994).

There is one situation in which Congress has created an exception to the stay put rule. If the student is disciplined for bringing a firearm to school, the school is authorized by IDEA to place the student in a temporary alternative placement for up to forty-five days. If the parent challenges this placement, the student is to stay in the alternative placement during the pendency of the subsequent hearing. This amendment to IDEA is known as the Jeffords Amendment, and may be the subject of further revision as IDEA goes through Congressional reauthorization in 1995–1996.

With these decisions in mind, let us examine some Texas rules regarding discipline of students with disabilities. (Note: for those unfamiliar with the student discipline system in Texas, it may be useful to review the material in Chapter 8 before reading the next section.)

Students with disabilities can be suspended, or otherwise removed from school on a short-term basis just as other students are. The same rules and timelines apply. However, with the student with disabilities, the school must also count these days toward application of what is known as the sixteen-day rule. State Board of Education (SBOE) rules require an ARD meeting whenever the days of emergency removal, alternative education program (AEP) placement, or suspension add up to sixteen in a single school year. The idea behind the rule is to prevent a school from undermining an IEP and placement through constant short-term disciplinary sanctions. If the student is removed from the normal academic setting (i.e., the setting called for by the IEP) sixteen days in a single school year, the principal should notify the parents of the need for an ARD meeting to review the situation.

Students with disabilities can be removed to an alternative education program for disciplinary reasons, just as other students can. Short-term (ten days or less) removal to an alternative education program can be done administratively, subject to the sixteen-day rule. However, if the removal is for more than ten consecutive days, it constitutes a change of placement, thus requiring ARD committee action. Keep in mind that when the ARD committee makes such a move, it must guarantee that the student's IEP can be implemented in the alternative setting.

Students with disabilities can be suspended for a short term for disciplinary reasons, just as other students can. Since a suspension under Texas law must be for three days or less, no ARD committee action is necessary. However, the school must count these days in connection with the sixteen-day rule.

In response to the Fifth Circuit decision in *S-1 v. Turlington*, the State Board of Education has adopted rules that require an ARD meeting prior to a proposed expulsion. The ARD committee must determine whether the assessment data on the student is current, whether the behavior of the student is substantially connected with the disability, whether the student's placement is so inappropriate that it brought about the inappropriate behavior, and what services are to be provided to the student after expulsion.

Recall the Fifth Circuit's confusing ruling that expulsion was permissible but a complete cessation of services was not. Texas responded with a rule requiring the ARD committee to devise an IEP for the period of expulsion. However, unlike the typical IEP, which must confer educational benefit, the post-expulsion IEP, according to SBOE rules, must merely prevent significant regression and assist the student upon returning to school. It should be noted that OSEP takes the position that FAPE is still required after expulsion. That position is under attack in litigation filed by the State of Virginia. Stay tuned for further developments. But whatever the result of that litigation, it is clear that schools must produce a post-expulsion IEP, outlining the services the school will provide during the student's expulsion.

The express intent of Congress in enacting IDEA was, in part, to prevent school districts from unilaterally taking action to exclude handicapped students from school. The *Honig* decision and the state board rules prohibit unilateral long-term actions by school districts excluding handicapped students from school—even in the case of dangerous students—unless parental agreement is secured or court relief is sought by the district when its action is appealed. The rules are complex and can be a trap for the unwary school official. School districts should ensure that the appropriate personnel are aware of the rules and follow them.

HANDICAPPED CHILDREN'S PROTECTION ACT OF 1986 (HCPA)

One of the most significant developments in special education law was the passage of the Handicapped Children's Protection Act of 1986. Congress enacted this act in order to nullify certain interpre-

tations previously set forth by the Supreme Court in a case called
Smith v. Robinson (1984). The act provides that a court, in its discretion, may award reasonable attorneys' fees as part of the costs to
the parents or guardian of a handicapped child or youth who is the
prevailing party in an administrative hearing or court action. To be
a "prevailing party," a parent does not have to "win" in the sense of
total vindication. To prevail means essentially that the legal relationship between the parties has been altered. Thus a parent can be
a prevailing party as the result of a settlement rather than a final decision of a hearing officer or court (*Shelly C. v. Venus I.S.D.*).

A provision in the HCPA provides that parents may not be
awarded attorneys' fees and related costs subsequent to the time
of a written offer of settlement by the school district to the parent if
(1) the offer is made more than ten days before an administrative
hearing begins, (2) the offer is not accepted by the parent within ten
days of the hearing, and (3) the relief finally obtained by the parent
is not more favorable to the parent than the offer of settlement. The
purpose of this provision is to encourage settlement of these disputes and to provide a mechanism to that end.

Apparently, a prevailing parent may recover attorneys' fees and
costs in either of two ways. If a parent is unhappy with the decision
of the hearing officer in the administrative hearing, the parent may
appeal to a state or federal court and include in the lawsuit a request
that the court award attorneys' fees and costs in the event that the
parent is the prevailing party in the litigation. If, on the other hand,
the parent prevails in the administrative hearing and does not wish
to appeal to a court, the parent may file an "application" for fees and
costs with the court. The sole object of this proceeding is the court's
determination regarding the issue of fees and costs. This was the
issue in *Kristi W. v. Graham I.S.D.* (1987). The U.S. District Court
in Amarillo determined that the parent would be entitled to fees
and costs on the basis of having prevailed in the administrative
hearing although no appeal on the merits had been presented to the
court. The Fifth Circuit supported this view in its 1988 holding in
Duane M. v. Orleans Parish School Board.

In general, it is safe to say that the courts are fairly liberal in
applying these standards. A good illustration arose in the Pasadena
I.S.D. There, the ARD committee initially found a child to be
speech-impaired and specified provision of speech therapy services.
Disturbed at their daughter's continuing poor performance, the parents sought an independent assessment. The assessment revealed
the child to be mildly retarded. The parents then requested the
school district's ARD committee to reconsider their request for ad-

ditional services. The ARD committee refused to do so until after the parents' attorney filed a due process hearing request with TEA. At that point, the school district and the parents reached a settlement in which the district agreed to provide everything the parents had requested except a declaration that the child was mentally retarded or suffered any handicapping condition other than speech impairment. The parents requested that the school district pay their attorneys' fees. The district refused to consider the parents a prevailing party under the Handicapped Children's Protection Act, pointing out that the services were not related to the child's speech impairment. Further, the services were not related to special education but were available to any parent who requested them.

The Fifth Circuit upheld the trial court's award of attorneys' fees. The appeals court noted that the individualized instruction and special therapy obtained through the settlement clearly altered the relationship between the district and the child, and were designed to improve the child's education. This much is required in order to be a prevailing party for attorneys' fees purposes. The fact that there was no nexus between the child's speech impairment and the remedies she received pursuant to the settlement was irrelevant. "The school district's arguments reflect a preoccupation with *labels* that the EHA [now IDEA] and HCPA do not share. While Angela was not *labeled* under the settlement as mentally retarded, she *obtained* in the settlement agreement educational services designed to reverse her educational deficiencies. For all practical purposes, Angela received every remedy her parents requested other than the mentally retarded classification." The district could not rely upon the formalistic exclusion of the mentally retarded classification from the settlement as the basis for denial of attorneys' fees (*Angela L. v. Pasadena I.S.D.*, 1990).

Another significant provision of the Handicapped Children's Protection Act is the guarantee that rights established by the U.S. Constitution, Section 504 of the Rehabilitation Act of 1973, and other federal civil rights statutes are not limited by any of the rights or remedies available under the IDEA. The effect of this provision is to guarantee to the parent the broadest possible basis for seeking relief. Let us now turn to Section 504.

SECTION 504 OF THE 1973 REHABILITATION ACT

Section 504, which prohibits discrimination on the basis of disability in programs receiving federal financial assistance, is increasingly being used to broaden the rights of students with disabilities. Section 504 applies throughout a school district if one or more programs within the district receive federal funds. The definition of "handicapping condition" in §504 is more broad than in IDEA. A handicapped student is one who has a physical or mental impairment that substantially limits one or more life activities, has a record of such impairment, or is regarded as having such an impairment. Thus, the Office of Civil Rights, which oversees enforcement of the statute, has determined that handicapping conditions may include drug and alcohol addiction, attention deficit disorder, obesity, AIDS, lengthy hospitalization due to depression, etc. As with IDEA, program modifications may be necessary for students who have or are regarded as having these or similar conditions.

Further, §504 protects these students from various types of discrimination and requires school districts to meet their unique needs even though they are not within the ambit of IDEA. Thus, they are entitled to identification, evaluation, and reevaluation; to a free, appropriate education that includes the provision of regular or special education and related aids and services designed to meet their individual needs; and to some of the procedural safeguards accorded handicapped students and their parents under IDEA. However, IDEA funds cannot be used to comply with §504 requirements. For an excellent discussion of §504 requirements and their implications for school districts, see "Section 504's Prohibition against Discrimination Due to Handicap: Applicability to Students in School" by Elena Gallegos and Laurie Rodriguez, which appeared in the May 1991 issue of the *Texas School Administrators' Legal Digest*, pp. 1–6.

Section 504 does not so much lower the threshold of eligibility as it does broaden it. Students are not eligible under 504 unless they demonstrate two conditions: a physical or mental impairment, and a substantial limitation of a major life activity. Students who have a disability with no substantial impairment are not eligible. Thus the student with an ADD diagnosis who is doing just fine in school without any special assistance, does not qualify under 504. So, too, the student who is doing poorly in school is not automatically eligible unless the student's problems are attributable to a physical or mental impairment. Thus an LEP (limited-English-proficient) student who comes to the school from a dysfunctional family or a condition of extreme poverty may experience great difficulty in school. Unless the student has a physical or mental impairment, however, the student is not a candidate for 504 eligibility. Section 504 and the district's "at-risk" program are not supposed to be synonymous.

Careful readers will observe that the 504 definition of persons with disabilities contains three prongs. Persons are eligible under 504 if:

1. They have a physical or mental impairment which substantially limits a major life activity;
2. They have a record of such an impairment; or
3. They are regarded as having such an impairment.

However, it is only the first group that is entitled to special treatment. Only the first group is entitled to an evaluation, an individualized program, decisions by committee, etc. The second and third groups are entitled only to be free from discrimination. In other words, a student who has a record of impairment, such as a record of treatment for alcohol abuse, should not be kept out of the band or the basketball team as a result of that record. But the school has no duty to refer, evaluate, individually accommodate, and place that student. So, too, with the student who is regarded by some as retarded because of an unusual physical appearance. The school should assure that individual of nondiscrimination. But unless the student actually suffers from a physical or mental impairment, the school should not refer, test, individually accommodate, or place that student. In short, the second and third prongs of the 504 definition come up much more often in the employment context than they do in public school services.

SUMMARY

Commentators on the American scene who decry the "litigation explosion" of the late twentieth century have a case in point regarding children with disabilities. There is no question that litigation has increased dramatically in special education, and it appears to be here for the long run. The litigation has had at least two effects. On the one hand it has certainly made the schooling process more adversarial and stressful for many. Decisions sometimes seem to turn on attorneys' advice as often as on what is best for the child. But on the other hand the litigation has moved a forgotten minority to the forefront of our consciousness. Americans can be proud of the fact that our schools have a "zero reject" philosophy. Services that had been denied to students with disabilities for decades are now routinely provided. This wouldn't have happened in the absence of lawsuits challenging the way we used to do things.

FOUR

Employment

IN THIS chapter we will describe in general terms the conditions of employment in Texas public schools. It is not possible to include coverage of individual school policies or contracts. Readers are advised to review them in conjunction with this material. We will first look at the hiring process and then examine the types of employment contracts available in Texas public schools. The latter half of the chapter focuses on employee entitlement to Fourteenth Amendment due process rights when negative personnel decisions are made.

THE HIRING PROCESS

Certification

Senate Bill 1 has created a new entity to govern teacher certification. The legislature has directed the State Board for Educator Certification to "regulate and oversee all aspects of the certification, continuing education, and standards of conduct of public school educators" (TEC §21.031). In particular, the new board will have the power to adopt rules to specify the various classes of educator certification, the period for which each certificate is valid, the requirements for issuance and renewal of certificates, the rules for out-of-state educators, and the disciplinary provisions whereby a certificate may be suspended or revoked. Moreover, the new board will have the power to establish training requirements for obtaining a certificate, entering an internship or induction-year program, and the minimum academic qualifications required for certification.

There are two restrictions on this broad grant of authority. First, the board must appoint an advisory committee with respect to each class of educator certificates. The advisory committee, composed of members of that class, will make recommendations for standards for the class. Second, rules adopted by the board must be submitted to the State Board of Education (SBOE) for review. However, it will take a two-thirds vote of the SBOE to reject any proposed rule. The power of the SBOE is further limited by a provision that specifies that the SBOE "may not modify a rule proposed by the State Board for Educator Certification." The SBOE must either accept or reject, and can only reject by a two-thirds vote. It is clear, then, that the State Board for Educator Certification will be the key entity in the certification business.

The board will consist of fifteen members, but only twelve of them will have voting status. The nonvoting members are to be one TEA employee appointed by the commissioner, one employee of the Texas Higher Education Coordinating Board appointed by the commissioner of higher education, and one dean of a college of education to be appointed by the governor. The twelve voting members are all gubernatorial appointees. Four must be public school teachers, two must be public school administrators, one must be a public school counselor, and five must be citizens who have never been employed by a public school or by a teacher preparation program in a college or university.

Not everyone who works for a public school district has to be certified. The new law requires certification for teachers, teacher interns, teacher trainees, librarians, educational aides, administrators, and counselors. There are many other professional employees working for Texas public schools. What credentials must they possess? According to Senate Bill 1, persons hired as audiologists, occupational therapists, physical therapists, physicians, nurses, school psychologists, associate school psychologists, social workers, and speech language pathologists must be licensed by the state agency that licenses that profession.

The State Board for Educator Certification is likely to have a significant impact on teacher preparation programs in colleges and universities. The legislature has given the board the power to adopt rules to govern the approval and continuing accountability of all such programs. Among other things, the board is to "annually review the accreditation status of each educator preparation program" (TEC §21.045). All such programs must meet the accreditation standards no later than September 1, 1998.

Testing will continue to play a part in certification. The board is to propose rules prescribing comprehensive examinations for each class of certificate issued.

Finally, there are now two nontraditional routes to employment as a teacher in Texas public schools. The first such route is alternative certification. This process, authorized in previous legislative sessions, is alive and well in Texas, and will continue to provide an avenue into the profession for those who have not gone through a formal teacher preparation program. The legislative scheme for alternative certification is pared down so as to leave all of the details to the State Board for Educator Certification.

The second nontraditional route is completely new, and sure to be controversial. It authorizes a school district to issue a "teaching permit" to a person who is not certified. Unless the individual is to be employed in career or technology education, he or she must possess a baccalaureate degree. Beyond that, there are no specific requirements for issuance of a permit. The district that employs a teacher by permit must inform the commissioner of the person's name, qualifications, and the subject matter to be taught. The commissioner has thirty days to review the information submitted, and, if appropriate, may determine that the individual is "not qualified to teach." The legislature has given the commissioner no guidance as to what makes a person "not qualified to teach." If the commissioner fails to act within thirty days, the permit is approved. Once that occurs, the permit remains valid unless revoked for cause by the district that issued it.

A teaching permit is not as flexible as a certificate obtained through alternative certification. The alternatively certified teacher can teach in any Texas public school district. The permitted teacher can only teach in the district that issued the permit. If the teacher wishes to move to another district, the new district would have to issue a permit and submit it to the commissioner, just as the original district did.

Advertising

Neither state nor federal law requires that employers, including schools, must advertise position vacancies. However, the posting of vacancies is a good way for a school district to demonstrate that it does not discriminate in the hiring process. Failure to advertise for vacancies can have the effect of perpetuating the infamous "good ole boy network" to the detriment of minority groups.

Pre-Employment Inquiries

Since race, sex, religion, national origin, and disability are not to be taken into account in making employment decisions, they should not be inquired about in the pre-employment process. When a complaint is filed with the Equal Employment Opportunity Commission (EEOC) or Texas Commission on Human Rights, the school district is sure to be asked about its employee-selection process. The EEOC looks unkindly on the asking of certain questions. For example:

1. Those that focus on a person's race, color, religion, or lineage, including whether or not a person is an alien. The U.S. Court of Appeals for the Fifth Circuit has ruled that employers cannot discriminate against a legally admitted alien solely on the basis of citizenship (*Guerra v. Manchester Terminal Corp.*, 1974).
2. Those that ask about pregnancy.
3. Those that ask about a disability.

A number of other inquiries may or may not violate the law, depending on the framework within which they are asked. Thus, questions about military discharge, arrest record, and financial status are out-of-bounds unless the employer can show some relationship to job performance. The same is true of questions about military status, height, weight, children and their care, and personal appearance. Tests may be used as employment screening devices as long as they are related to job requirements and are not discriminatory.

Selecting Staff

In the process of revising the Education Code, one of the key issues legislators had to confront involved the hiring process. Early drafts of the new law proposed that the school board be effectively taken out of the loop—that all hiring and firing decisions be made by the superintendent. There also was sentiment for moving hiring decisions to the campus level as much as possible. What ultimately emerged in Senate Bill 1 is an interesting set of checks and balances. Because of the hiring process now mandated by law, it is all the more important that all players, from the campus to the school board presidency, understand who is to do what.

The law requires school boards to adopt policies regarding the employment and duties of personnel. But the law goes on to dictate two key provisions of that policy. The first deals with the relationship between the board and the superintendent. The policy must provide that the superintendent has the "sole authority" to make recommendations to the board regarding the selection of all personnel. The board can accept or reject any of the superintendent's recommendations, but it cannot simply choose someone who has not been recommended. If the board rejects the recommended person, the superintendent is to recommend someone else. Ultimately, then, the board cannot force the superintendent to hire a person the superintendent would not recommend.

Although the legislature chose not to take school boards out of the hiring loop, it permits boards to take themselves out of it. The law specifically allows the board to delegate final hiring authority to the superintendent. If the board does not do so, then all personnel will be recommended by the superintendent and approved by the board. Presumably a district could delegate final authority to the superintendent for certain categories of employees, such as nonprofessional personnel, while retaining the superintendent-board arrangement for others. This is the practice today in many districts.

The second provision that must be included in local policy addresses the relationship between the campus principal and the central office. It requires local policy to call for each principal to approve each teacher or staff appointment to the principal's campus, in accordance with Section 11.202 of the Code. That section reads, in part:

(b) Each principal shall:
(1) except as provided by Subsection (d), approve all teacher and staff appointments for that principal's campus from a pool of applicants selected by the district or of applicants who meet the hiring requirements established by the district, based on criteria developed by the principal after informal consultation with the faculty. . . .

The Subsection (d) exception relates to necessary teacher transfers due to enrollment shifts or program changes. In those instances, the superintendent has "final placement authority for a teacher."

While principals do not actually hire staff, it should be clear that the principal plays a key role in the selection of staff for the campus. Challenges to hiring decisions in the future are likely to focus on the principal's role. If the principal asks an improper question (e.g., "do you plan to have children anytime soon?"), the rejected applicant could seize on that as evidence of discrimination. Moreover, the principal's approval authority is not limited to the initial hiring decision. Reassignments from one campus to another also require approval of the principal (Att'y. Gen. Op. DM-27, 1991).

In all of the above, the law is subject to constant reinterpretation as situations arise. As a result, the ins and outs of the hiring process grow progressively more complex. Basically, the aim of both federal and state nondiscrimination statutes is to eliminate those practices that clearly discriminate against a prospective employee for reasons unrelated to the job.

Criminal History Checks

Senate Bill 1 requires that the State Board for Educator Certification obtain criminal history record information on all holders of and applicants for educator certification. With this requirement in place, the legislature no longer requires such a background check by each school district, with one exception noted below. However, schools are authorized to conduct criminal history record checks, and will likely continue to do so, at least for noncertified employees and for volunteers, since the State Board will have no information on those persons. Furthermore, the law allows schools to obtain criminal history information relating to volunteers or employees of other organizations which contract with schools, if the person in question will have continuing duties to be performed at the school or at any other location where students will be regularly present. In other words, if IBM regularly sends Ms. Adams to the school as a volunteer pursuant to the "adopt-a-school" program, the school is authorized to obtain criminal history information on Ms. Adams.

The exception to the general rule involves contracted transportation services. When a school district contracts with another entity for transportation, it must obtain criminal history information regarding bus drivers. If the records check turns up information that the driver has been convicted of a felony, or a misdemeanor involving moral turpitude, the individual may not, without the school's permission, drive a bus on which students are transported.

What if an employee is hired, and then the school obtains information pertaining to an earlier conviction? Schools are authorized to discharge an employee in those situations provided that (1) the conviction is for a felony or a misdemeanor involving moral turpitude and (2) the employee failed to disclose the conviction.

RESTRICTIONS ON EMPLOYMENT

Four restrictions on employment in Texas public schools are worth our attention. First, public school employees under state law may not hold two legally incompatible offices—for example, being a teacher and also a trustee of the same school district. However, a teacher may serve without pay as a trustee in another school district or as a member of the governing board of a local government unit, such as a city or a town. Under a provision of the Texas Constitution, teachers have been ruled eligible to serve as justice of the peace, county commissioner, notary public, or postmaster and receive a salary (Texas Constitution, Art. XVI, §40, as interpreted in *Ruiz v. State,* Texas Court of Appeals–Corpus Christi, 1976).

A second restriction is set forth in the Texas nepotism statutes, contained in Chapter 573 of the Government Code, which prevents school districts from employing persons related within the prohibited degree by blood or by marriage to a board member. The effect of the law is not changed by a trustee's abstaining from voting on the employment of the relative. The statutes, however, permit the continued employment of an employee who, before his or her relative became a school board member, was continuously employed by the district for (1) at least thirty days, if his or her relative was appointed to the board, or (2) at least six months if his or her relative was elected to the board. (The one-year continuous employment period that remains in the statute now only applies to governing bodies whose members are elected in November; it does not apply to school districts that use a January, May, or August election date.) A person who has served continuously for the required time prior to the relative's becoming a board member may be reappointed for subsequent school years and even promoted. In any such decision, however, the related board member must not participate in the deliberation or vote.

Employees who have not served continuously for the required period prior to the relative's becoming a board member may finish out their contracts but may not be rehired (*Att'y. Gen. Op. M-862,* 1971). The same rules apply when the employee's status changes by virtue of marrying a relative of a board member. If the employee had not been employed by the district for the required period of time prior to the date of the marriage, the contract may not be renewed. Nor does the fact that the employee is paid out of federal, not state, funds alter the thrust of the nepotism statute (*Att'y. Gen. Op. LA-80,* 1974).

Do the nepotism restrictions apply to relatives of the superintendent? What about relatives of the principal? Prior to 1981, there was some question regarding a board's hiring of a superintendent's spouse. In that year a Texas court of appeals clarified the matter. The court observed that a superintendent is not an officer, but rather an agent of the school board, which has the exclusive authority to employ teachers. Therefore, it is not a violation of the nepotism statute for a school board to hire a superintendent's spouse

(Pena v. Rio Grande City C.I.S.D.). In 1992 the attorney general issued an opinion applying the same logic to cases involving relatives of a campus principal. Although campus principals must now approve all appointments to their campuses, this does not amount to the power to actually hire the employee. Thus the nepotism laws impact relatives of board members, but not the relatives of administrators *(Att'y. Gen. Op. DM-132, 1992)*.

A final nepotism issue concerns the coverage of this law. In 1992, the attorney general reversed an earlier opinion, and decided that the nepotism restrictions apply to independent contractors as well as employees *(Att'y. Gen. Op. DM-76, 1992)*. Thus the school must be careful in choosing outside consultants and contractors, as well as regular employees.

In 1988 the Texas Attorney General issued an opinion to the effect that a substitute teacher is not "continuously employed" and thus may not be appointed to work for a district after the election of a relative to the board, no matter how long the person may have been serving as a substitute. Subsequent legislation softened the blow of this ruling by allowing a school district to hire a board member's relative to work as a bus driver or a substitute teacher if the district is located in a county with a population of less than thirty-five thousand. Then in 1995 the legislature completely overturned the 1988 A.G.'s opinion insofar as substitute teachers were concerned. Henceforth, substitutes are not covered by nepotism laws, and thus may be employed by districts irrespective of their relatives. Thus as the law now stands, the board president's spouse can be hired as a substitute teacher in any district; can be hired as a bus driver in schools located in counties of less than thirty-five thousand population; but cannot be hired in any other capacity.

A third restriction involves outside employment. A school district has the authority to prohibit all outside employment, though most do allow professional employees to engage in part-time employment. A district may not, however, make a practice of allowing some employees to engage in outside employment, but not others. A Fifth Circuit decision makes this clear *(Gosney v. Sonora I.S.D., 1979)*. *Gosney* involved a junior high school principal who also operated a cattle ranch and then purchased a retail dry goods store. The school had a policy against any full- or part-time outside employment. When Billy Gosney's contract was not renewed despite assertions that his school employment would not be adversely affected, he sued. The Fifth Circuit Court of Appeals agreed that Gosney's contract had been nonrenewed unfairly. Emphasizing that school districts can regulate, even prohibit, outside employment, the court noted that in this instance many school employees were involved in outside employment but were not held accountable to the rule. Even Gosney, in apparent contradiction to the rule, had run a cattle ranch for many years previous to the nonrenewal. Because the rule was selectively enforced, it denied Gosney his Fourteenth Amendment right to equal protection of the laws.

Finally, employees sometimes ask if it is legal for a school district to require employees to live within the district. The answer is yes. Several circuit courts have upheld such restrictions with regard to school employees. The Fifth Circuit case on point deals with municipal employees, but the answer is the same. In *Wright v. City of Jackson,* the Fifth Circuit upheld a municipal ordinance requiring city employees to have their principal place of residence within city limits. Given the mobility of Texans, few districts require all employees to live within the district. More often, this restriction is applied only to selected high-level administrators.

Such was the case in Dallas I.S.D., which terminated the employment of an administrator who failed to comply with district policy requiring certain high-level executive and administrative employees to reside in the district. The commissioner of education affirmed the man's termination, noting that it did not violate his constitutional right to travel (*Davis v. Dallas I.S.D.,* 1994).

NONDISCRIMINATION

Both federal and state laws prohibit most forms of discrimination in the employment process on the basis of race, color, religion, sex, national origin, age, or disability. These protections apply to all school employees—not just those with contracts. The at-will custodian is protected from discrimination to the same degree as the principal with a two-year contract.

What follows is a review of the most prominent types of discrimination and the legal implications.

Racial Discrimination

Most cases alleging discrimination are brought under Title VII of the Civil Rights Act of 1964. This is perhaps the most prominent federal law involving discrimination, as it covers discrimination in both public and private employment, and it prohibits discrimination on the basis of race, color, religion, sex, or national origin. Title VII does allow exceptions in areas other than race or color for "bona fide occupational qualifications." For example, a religious school is permitted to give preference to a person of its faith in hiring for most positions.

Persons are required under Title VII to seek redress under state law before pursuing federal remedies. In Texas that redress is provided by the Texas Commission on Human Rights Act, Article 5221k, Texas Civil Statutes, which outlaws discrimination by public and private employers with fifteen or more employees on the basis of race, religion, color, sex, national origin, age, and mental or physical disability. Exemptions are provided in the case of religious private schools for employment preference for those of the same religious faith and for public schools for personnel transactions designed to comply with court-ordered or voluntary desegregation plans.

In a 1993 ruling, the Supreme Court reaffirmed the principle that a person alleging racial discrimination under Title VII bears the ultimate burden of proving that race was the motivating factor in the adverse decision (*St. Mary's Honor Center v. Hicks*). Under the Supreme Court's interpretation of Title VII, discharged employees are entitled to a presumption of discriminatory treatment by the employer if they can show that they: (1) are a member of a protected class, (2) were qualified for the position in question, (3) were demoted or discharged, and (4) that the position remained open or was filled by someone not of a protected class (*McDonnell Douglas Corp. v. Green*, U.S. Supreme Court, 1973). The Supreme Court made it clear in *St. Mary's Honor Center v. Hicks* that this presumption does not shift the ultimate burden of proof, which at all times remains with the employee charging the unlawful discriminatory treatment.

Allegations of racial discrimination are frequently made when statewide standards impact minority groups more than Anglos. For example, in 1978 the U.S. Supreme Court affirmed a state's use of the National Teacher Examination. The Court determined that the test was a rational means to certify public school teachers under the Fourteenth Amendment and Title VII even though it resulted in the disqualification of a greater proportion of black applicants, and the placement of black teachers in lower-paying positions (*National Education Association v. South Carolina*). For example, the test score requirements disqualified 85 percent of black applicants in 1976 but only 17.5 percent of white applicants. The lower court determined that a state study showing that the test correlates with teacher training programs was sufficiently trustworthy to sustain South Carolina's burden under Title VII. One important factor in the outcome of such cases is the ability of the state to validate the tests in the employment context when they have a disproportionate impact on minority groups. Doing so serves to undermine the argument that the tests carry a racially discriminatory purpose.

Predictably, Texas has been through similar litigation. When House Bill 72 imposed the TECAT (Texas Examination of Current Administrators and Teachers) in 1984, a suit was filed alleging that the test discriminated against blacks. In the suit, teachers argued both that the TECAT had a disparate impact on blacks, and that the use of the TECAT amounted to disparate treatment on the basis of race. As to the disparate impact theory, the Fifth Circuit ruled that the proof offered by the teachers fell short. In particular, the passage rate of blacks was 95.58 percent compared to a white passage rate of 99.75 percent. This, in the opinion of the court, was not a significant statistical discrepancy. To succeed on the disparate treatment theory, the teachers were required to prove intentional discrimination. This they could not do. The TECAT was administered to all teachers of all races with no intent to cause harm to any particular group. Thus the TECAT survived the challenge (*Frazier v. Garrison I.S.D.*, 1993).

Sex Discrimination

Title VII is also frequently used in lawsuits alleging sex discrimination in public employment. Under Title VII, when plaintiffs prove by a preponderance of the evidence that defendants discriminated against them contrary to law in an employment decision, school administrators must be prepared to show a legitimate, nondiscriminatory reason to refuse to employ a person when his or her qualifications match those of other applicants. As the U.S. District Court for the Western District of Texas noted in connection with a sex discrimination charge against El Paso Community College, "the defendant is not required to prove that the person chosen was *more* qualified than the plaintiff; employers are *free* to choose among equally qualified applicants so long as illegal criteria are not used" (*Elias v. El Paso Community College District*, 1982).

Perhaps the most common allegation of sexual discrimination in the schools today involves sexual harassment. Federal law does not prohibit sexual harassment per se. Rather, it defines sexual harassment as a form of sex discrimination. Federal guidelines define sexual harassment as "unwelcome sexual advances, requests for sexual favors, and other verbal or physical conduct of a sexual nature" where "such conduct has the purpose or effect of unreasonably interfering with an individual's work performance or creating an intimidating, hostile, or offensive working environment" (29 C.F.R. §1604.11(a)).

Judicial decisions have divided sexual harassment cases into two categories: quid pro quo harassment and hostile environment cases. In a quid pro quo case there is an actual tradeoff—submission to unwelcome sexual advances leads to promotion or advancement, or refusal of sexual advances leads to demotion, loss of privileges, or termination. While a "hostile environment" case is usually less blatant, it is every bit as illegal. A hostile environment exists when unwelcome sexual advances, comments, and other verbal or physical conduct create a hostile, abusive, or offensive environment that is sufficiently severe or pervasive as to alter the conditions of employment.

While sexual harassment constitutes sex discrimination under federal law, it can also lead to criminal penalties under state law. Texas Penal Code §39.02 contains a provision subjecting persons acting within the scope of employment to criminal penalties for intentionally subjecting another to mistreatment that they know is unlawful (termed "official oppression"). In 1991 the Texas Court of Criminal Appeals, the highest state court dealing with criminal matters, addressed a case involving a police chief convicted of official oppression for placing his hand on a female subordinate's buttocks and engaging in other acts of sexual mistreatment, e.g., telling her he didn't want her to wear a bullet-proof vest because he would not be able to touch and feel her breasts. The employee filed a complaint with the city manager, who found her allegations without foundation. The employee was later terminated. She filed a criminal action under §39.02. The police chief was found guilty at the trial court level and so appealed to the Court of Criminal Appeals. The Texas Court of Criminal Appeals rejected the police chief's claims that he was acting as a private individual when the incidents took place. The high court also rejected his assertion that the statute applies only when the victims are not employees. "The language of the statute is unambiguous and clearly intends to prosecute a public servant who acts under color of his office or employment whether the oppressed person is a private individual or an employee of the public servant's office" (*Bryson v. State*).

Charges of sex discrimination can also be brought under the Equal Pay Act of 1963. This law prohibits wage discrimination among employees on the basis of sex when they perform substantially the same work. It applies to both professional and nonprofessional workers. Exceptions are allowed for seniority, merit, productivity, or any other factor not related to sex. The Equal Pay Act has come up in cases involving female teachers, coaches, and administrators who perform substantially the same duties as their male counterparts.

Still another avenue to complain of sex discrimination is Title IX of the Education Amendments of 1972. Title IX provides that no person shall be discriminated against on the basis of sex in any education program or activity receiving federal funds. If sex discrimination in violation of Title IX is proven, federal funding could be terminated. (See the discussion of the *Franklin v. Gwinnett* case in Chapter 2.) Ever since its enactment, Title IX has been the subject of considerable controversy and confusion. At first, it was argued that the law applied only to students, not employees. But in 1982 the U.S. Supreme Court ruled in *North Haven Board of Education v. Bell* that the law could apply to employees as well.

Later, in *Grove City College v. Bell* (1984), the Court trimmed the wings of Title IX by ruling that it applies only to educational programs that themselves receive federal aid. The *Grove City* decision caused considerable controversy and led to the passage, over President Reagan's veto, of the Civil Rights Restoration Act of 1987. The act covers four major civil rights statutes and provides that, when an institution such as a college or school district receives any federal funds, the provisions of the statutes apply throughout the entire institution, not just to a particular program within the institution. The four statutes are Title IX of the Education Amendments of 1972, §504 of the Rehabilitation Act of 1973, the Age Discrimination Act of 1975, and Title VI of the Civil Rights Act of 1964, which prohibits discrimination on the basis of race. The *Grove City* decision and the subsequent Civil Rights Restoration Act of 1987 provide a good example of the possible interplay among the judicial, legislative, and executive branches of government.

Though Title IX applies to employees, it may not be used as an avenue for the recovery of damages. In *Lakoski v. James* the Fifth Circuit ruled that employees who seek money damages for intentional sex discrimination in federally funded educational institutions must assert their claims through Title VII, rather than Title IX. This ruling will mean that such claims will have to be subjected to the administrative process required under Title VII before suit can be filed.

Besides all these avenues of recourse under federal law, a person can also complain of sex discrimination under the Texas Constitution, which expressly prohibits it. A volleyball coach in the Harlingen C.I.S.D. recently persuaded the commissioner that the school district's schedule of coaching stipends discriminated against her on the basis of sex, in violation of the Texas Constitution. The coach asserted and proved that her duties as volleyball coach were substantially similar to those of higher-paid male coaches in other sports. Since the district was unable to justify its pay scale for coaches on the basis of legitimate, gender-neutral criteria, the commissioner concluded that the volleyball coach was the victim of sex discrimination (*Schultz v. Harlingen C.I.S.D.*).

Age Discrimination

Another important federal law affecting employment is the Age Discrimination in Employment Act of 1967 (ADEA), which prohibits discrimination against individuals over the age of forty. While an employer always has the right to terminate an employee who is not performing satisfactorily, there is no longer a permissible mandatory retirement age. In 1983 the U.S. Supreme Court ruled that the ADEA applies to state and local governments (*EEOC v. Wyoming*). Thus, it is illegal to discriminate against an employee because of age unless age is a bona fide qualification reasonably necessary to carry out job responsibilities.

Religious Discrimination

Title VII of the Civil Rights Act of 1964 forbids discrimination in employment on the basis of religion. In addition to this prohibition on discrimination, employers must provide reasonable accommodation for the religious practices of their employees. This issue is discussed further in Chapter 7.

Discrimination on the Basis of Disability

Hailed as the most sweeping civil rights legislation since 1964, the Americans with Disabilities Act (ADA) is sure to have a major impact on school districts. Although public schools that receive federal funds have been operating under a similar mandate since the passage of the Rehabilitation Act of 1973, the ADA sweeps broader, reaches further, and perhaps most importantly, has moved this particular form of discrimination to the forefront of public awareness. Under the ADA, both public and private employers with twenty-five or more employees are prohibited from discriminating against individuals with disabilities in hiring, advancement, discharge, and other terms and conditions of employment. Key features of the law include:

1. A disability is broadly defined to include a number of physical or mental impairments that substantially limit one or more of the major life activities such as walking, learning, or working. The law encompasses persons having an impairment, having a record of impairment, or being regarded as having an impairment.
2. Drug users are not considered individuals with disabilities, but those who have successfully completed a drug rehabilitation program and are no longer using drugs are protected.
3. Compulsive gambling, homosexuality, bisexuality, and a number of sexual behavior disorders are not classified as disabilities.
4. The law requires employers to make "reasonable accommodation" for persons protected by ADA. An employee is "qualified" for a job if the employee can perform the "essential functions" of the job with or without "reasonable accommodation." Thus an employer cannot simply turn away an applicant with a disability. The employer must determine if reasonable accommodations will enable the employee to perform the essential functions of the job. The term "reasonable accommodation" is just one of many terms which will require further definition through litigation. We know from the regulations that it may include such things as making existing facilities accessible, job restructuring, modified work schedules, acquisition of special equipment, and the provision of readers, interpreters, etc.
5. Employers are not required to endure "undue hardship." Like "reasonable accommodation," this term needs some fleshing out. Unfortunately, this will have to take place on an expensive, case-by-case basis.
6. Pre-employment medical exams and inquiries through job application forms or interviews regarding the disability and its severity are strictly prohibited. Pre-employment inquiries are to be limited to those concerning ability of the person to perform the job. A medical exam may be required only after the job is offered, and only if all employees in that particular category are required to undergo such an exam.

ADA is complex and will require careful study and training. Personnel administrators and school principals, who now are intimately involved in campus staff selection, must become familiar with such terms as "reasonable accommodation," "undue hardship," and "essential functions of the job." The statute is codified as 42 U.S.C. §§12.101 et seq.

The predecessor of the ADA was §504 of the 1973 Rehabilitation Act. Much of the terminology and substance of the ADA is borrowed from §504, which applies only to institutions which receive federal funds. In a significant decision, the U.S. Supreme Court ruled that under §504, recipients of federal money may not discriminate against persons who are or are perceived to be physically or mentally impaired by contagious diseases unless they pose a real risk of infection to others or cannot perform their duties. The case involved a teacher with tuberculosis, but it could be relevant to decisions concerning teachers with AIDS. In the decision, Justice Brennan noted for the majority that the basic purpose of §504 is "to insure that handicapped individuals are not denied jobs or other benefits because of the prejudiced attitudes or the ignorance of others" (*School Board of Nassau County v. Arline*). The Texas Attorney General has interpreted relevant provisions of the Texas Commission on Human Rights Act, Article 5221k, in a similar fashion and concluded, "Persons discriminated against on the basis of handicaps perceived by their employers have standing to complain under the act, even if the person in fact is not handicapped" (*Att'y. Gen. Op. JM-648*, 1987).

Affirmative Action

An extensive discussion of the concept of affirmative action is beyond the scope of this book. Suffice it to say that if a court determines that a governmental employer has engaged in discriminatory practices, the court can impose certain requirements on the employer to remedy past discrimination through affirmative measures. It is less clear whether public school districts can voluntarily adopt preferential hiring programs. In this context the term "affirmative action" has many meanings. It is most often used to mean those activities undertaken to make sure that persons and groups previously excluded from the employment marketplace are notified of job openings and given assistance in making application. It does not usually mean preferential treatment in hiring, though it can have this meaning where court-ordered or voluntary preferential employment programs are instituted.

In 1991 Congress enacted and President Bush signed the Civil Rights Act of 1991. This legislation had the effect of reversing or modifying a number of recent U.S. Supreme Court employment decisions watering down affirmative action. Key provisions of the statute include:

1. Extension of a prohibition on racial and ethnic discrimination in the making of contracts to the performance, modification, and termination of contracts in public and private organizations. The prohibition extends beyond the employment context. Thus, a minority child subject to discrimination after being admitted to a private school would have a cause of action. The modifications serve to broaden the application of a post–Civil War statute, 42 U.S.C. §1981, by reversing the U.S. Supreme Court's holding in *Patterson v. McLean Credit Union* (1989).

2. Authorization of compensatory and punitive damages against an employer in cases of intentional discrimination under Title VII of the 1964 Civil Rights Act and the new Americans with Disabilities Act. Punitive damages, however, are available only against a private employer and are capped at certain amounts depending upon the size of the employer's workforce. To obtain punitive damages, the individual must establish that the employer acted with malice or reckless indifference.

3. Restoration of the burden of proof on the employer to establish that a challenged practice having a disparate impact on racial minorities was justified by business necessity. The U.S. Supreme Court had modified this burden in *Wards Cove Packing Co. v. Atonio* (1989), by requiring the plaintiff to prove absence of business necessity—a very difficult task. The change restores the thrust of a 1971 ruling (*Griggs v. Duke Power Co.*).

4. Broadening employer liability in a "mixed motive" employment decision—one where both illegitimate discrimination and legitimate reasons are present. The employer cannot avoid liability by relying on the legitimate reasons. However, if the employer can establish that it would have made the same decision absent consideration of the illegitimate discrimination, the employee's remedies are limited and do not extend to reinstatement, back pay, or damages. This provision reverses the Supreme Court's decision in *Price Waterhouse v. Hopkins* (1989).

The statute adds to the complexity of personnel decision making and broadens the liability of employers. It is thus important for personnel officers and principals to become familiar with its terms.

While other federal laws affect employment, these are the most notable regarding discrimination. Interpretations regarding their coverage are frequently changing, as administrative agencies and courts struggle to apply their provisions to a diverse set of circumstances. As a result, many questions regarding discrimination in employment remain unanswered. Future litigation may well involve greater reference to Texas's civil rights law and also to the Texas Constitution, which to date has not been utilized very much in employment litigation.

Wage and Hour Requirements

In 1985 the U.S. Supreme Court ruled that the minimum wage and maximum hour provisions of the Fair Labor Standards Act apply to local government functions. The Court overruled a 1976 decision to the contrary, thus restoring the application of FLSA to nonprofessional employees in local governmental activities, including public schools (*Garcia v. San Antonio Metropolitan Transit Authority*). The FLSA provisions apply only to nonprofessional employees, such as maintenance workers. Teachers who spend over 50 percent of their time in teaching but engage in certain nonprofessional tasks, such as bus driving, ticket taking, and so on, are not subject to the FLSA requirements in the latter activities. Paraprofessionals and students may be covered by the law, although students working directly for schools are exempt from coverage if their work is an integral part of the regular education program.

Professional employees are exempt from the FLSA with regard to overtime, and thus are not entitled to receive overtime pay. Furthermore, professional employees have not been successful in efforts to be compensated at their regular rate for services beyond the normal school day. As long as these requests are reasonable, they usually raise no legal questions. Thus, a teacher who filed a grievance seeking additional pay and reimbursement for child care costs when she was required to be a ticket taker at a night football game was unsuccessful at both the district and commissioner levels. The commissioner noted that the teacher had agreed in her contract to perform "such additional duties as may be assigned." The 8 A.M. to 3:45 P.M. attendance requirement specified in local policy simply established minimum working hours and did not preclude additional assignments (*Watson v. Lampasas*, 1989).

The most interesting illustration of the FLSA in the school context arose when cafeteria workers in Greenwood I.S.D. were required to serve meals after hours for the monthly school board meetings. The school district did not pay the workers for this, contending that the workers had volunteered to provide this service. When the workers became vocal in their complaints, they were terminated, thus leading to allegations of violations of the Whistle Blower Act, discussed in Chapter 6. The court determined that the workers were not volunteers, and should have been compensated. The point, for purposes of our discussion of the FLSA, is that school districts should assume that school employees serving a school function are doing so as employees, and should be compensated (*Knowlton v. Greenwood I.S.D.*).

EMPLOYMENT OF SCHOOL PERSONNEL

Most employees of Texas public schools have a contract. However, many employees are not given a contract, but work on an at-will basis. In this section we will examine the legal ramifications of at-will employment as well as the various contractual arrangements.

At-Will Employment

An at-will employment arrangement is one in which there is no contractual commitment to a specified period of employment. Most noncertified employees in Texas public schools have no written contract. School policy typically declares such employees to be at-will, meaning that either employer or employee can terminate the relationship at any time.

It is often assumed that an at-will employee is one who does not have a written contract. However, this is not always the case. The absence of a written contract does not, in and of itself, indicate that the employment relationship is at-will. Statements in school policy, employee handbooks, correspondence, and even verbal assurances have been determined to create a legitimate and reasonable expectation of employment for a specific period of time.

By the same token, the existence of a written contract does not necessarily preclude an at-will relationship. The essence of the at-will relationship is the right of either party to terminate the employment relationship at any time, for any legally permissible reason. An employee could have a formal, signed, written contract, complete with notary seals, and still be at-will if the language of the contract gives the employer the right to terminate the relationship at any time, without notice or hearing, and for any legally permissible reason.

It has often been said that the at-will employee can be terminated "for good reasons, bad reasons, or no reasons at all." This is not true. However, the widespread currency of this statement has created a false sense of security in school officials when dealing with the at-will employee.

An at-will employee enjoys every protection afforded by the law to all other employees, except for those that directly arise from the contract or from teacher certification. Thus provisions in the Education Code which deal with contract renewal and nonrenewal do not apply to the at-will employee. However, all of the federal and state mandates prohibiting discrimination apply with equal force to the custodian and to the superintendent. The constitutional requirement of due process does not apply to the at-will employee, since there is no property interest in his or her continued employment. But the constitutional rights of expression, association, and the right to petition for redress of grievances apply. Therefore, the at-will employee can charge that his or her termination was in retaliation for constitutionally protected conduct.

Thus the terminated at-will employee is not without legal recourse. Such an individual can complain that the decision was discriminatory on the basis of race, sex, religion, age, national origin, or disability. The terminated at-will employee can file suit, alleging that his discharge was in retaliation for his exercise of constitutional rights or that it was in response to her "blowing the whistle" on wrongdoing or that it resulted from his refusal to carry out an illegal order (*Sabine Pilots Services Inc. v. Hauck*, Texas Supreme Court, 1985).

Can at-will employees be terminated for "no reasons at all," as is commonly said? The fact of the matter is that no employee is ever terminated for no reason. There is always a reason.

Well, then, can they be terminated for "bad reasons"? Not if those reasons are so bad that they violate state or federal law. The reason may be "bad" in the sense that it does not amount to "good cause." It may be "bad" in the sense that a reviewing body (court or EEOC) may not agree with the wisdom of the decision. But if the decision is so "bad" that it violates state or federal law, then it is a wrongful discharge. So it is not safe to say that at-will employees can be terminated for "bad reasons."

The more appropriate statement is this: at-will employees can be terminated for any legally permissible reason. They can be terminated at any time, and there is no constitutional requirement of pre-termination due process. The employee may, however, file a griev- ance or a lawsuit asserting that the termination was impermissibly motivated.

Educator Contracts: An Introduction

Senate Bill 1 brought about substantial changes in the law pertain- ing to contracts between school districts and teachers. Before we discuss those changes, a brief historical overview is in order. In the past, Texas had a unique system whereby each school district would choose whether it would offer its teachers *term* contracts or *continuing* contracts. The procedures for renewal and nonrenewal, the timelines, the reasons for possible termination or nonrenewal, and the rules of probation were different under the two systems. The conventional wisdom was that continuing contracts provided teach- ers with greater job security. But after enactment of the Term Con- tract Nonrenewal Act (TCNA) in 1981, differences between the two systems were less pronounced. Now, under Senate Bill 1, the two systems have been brought even closer together.

Probationary Contracts

For starters, Senate Bill 1 creates a unified probationary period. Those new to the profession may not appreciate the significance of this, but it represents a major simplification of a confusing situ- ation. In the past, Texas not only had two different types of teacher contracts, but also two very different types of probationary periods. Thus there were really four classifications of teacher contracts: (1) probationary contracts in a term contract district; (2) term con- tracts; (3) probationary contracts in a continuing contract district; and (4) continuing contracts.

Senate Bill 1 has unified the term and continuing contract sys- tems for purposes of the probationary period. In other words, when a teacher first goes to work for a school district, the teacher will serve a probationary period which is basically the same in all school dis- tricts throughout the state. After the probationary period, districts will still split into term contract districts and continuing contract districts. But in the beginning, all teachers will be under the same system.

Probationary contracts are governed by Sections 21.101 et seq. of the Education Code. Key features are as follows.

Probationary contracts go to teachers, principals, supervisors, counselors, nurses, and all other full-time professional employees who are required to hold educator certification. However, a probationary contract is not to be given to a superintendent. In the discussion that follows, we will use the term "teacher" to cover the wide range of employees defined by the law. Decisions of the commissioner have made it clear, however, that that broad definition of "teacher" has its limits. Merely holding a position that requires a bachelor's degree does not qualify (*Hightower v. Mount Pleasant I.S.D.*, 1986). Moreover, that a particular employee has a valid certificate or teaching permit is not the crucial factor; the *position* must require such a certificate or permit. For example, a former administrator who served as a director of transportation was not covered, because the position did not require a certificate or permit (*Richardson v. Refugio I.S.D.*, 1986; *Hightower v. State Commissioner of Education*, 1989). If the state does not require certification for the job, but the local district does, the employee is a "teacher" within the meaning of the statute. The district would then be obligated to follow statutory nonrenewal policies (*Rodriguez v. Eagle Pass I.S.D.*).

The probationary period can be as long as three years, except for teachers coming to the district after having been employed in public education for five of the eight preceding years. For those experienced educators, the probationary period is just one year. During the probationary period, the teacher will be employed on a contract that cannot exceed one year in length. Thus in the typical situation, the teacher will serve under three consecutive one-year contracts.

There is nothing in the law that requires a probationary contract to be for a full school year. The district could contract with its probationary staff for shorter periods of time—for example, for a semester rather than a full year. However, this would present some practical problems in cases of contract nonrenewal. As noted below, the notice of nonrenewal of the contract must be given at least forty-five days before the last day of instruction. Thus if the contract is only for one semester, by the time the notice of nonrenewal is due, the district will have had very limited experience with the probationary employee.

The school district can extend a probationary period for a fourth year if "the board of trustees determines that it is doubtful whether the teacher should be given a continuing contract or a term contract." So in some situations a teacher will be serving a probationary period that lasts four years. If the board decides to extend probation for a fourth year no hearing is required, but according to earlier versions of the law the board of trustees must actually "determine" and "recite" that it is in doubt whether the educator should be given a continuing contract. Failure to make this recitation on the record during an open meeting of the board can lead to a reversal of the decision, and an award of a nonprobationary contract (*Turley v. Schertz–Cibolo–Universal City I.S.D.*, 1992).

Senate Bill 1 makes it easy to terminate the relationship between the probationary teacher and the school district if the termination is to take effect as of the end of the teacher's contract. This has traditionally been referred to as a nonrenewal, but Senate Bill 1 uses the expression "termination." Whatever the terminology, the process is simple. The board simply gives notice to the teacher of its intention to terminate the teacher's employment. Notice must be given by the forty-fifth day before the last day of instruction required under the contract. If the district fails to give this notice in a timely fashion, the contract is automatically renewed. No specific reason for termination is required. The board can make this decision "if in the board's judgment the best interests of the district will be served by terminating the employment." The law does not require the district to afford the teacher a hearing, although the district could choose to do so. Whatever decision the board makes is "final and may not be appealed." Keep in mind, though, that this statement of finality does not prevent the terminated teacher from filing suit alleging a wrongful discharge.

Suppose a district is so dissatisfied with a probationary teacher's performance that the district wants to terminate the relationship immediately, rather than waiting for the contract to run out. In that case, the school must provide the teacher with formal due process and must demonstrate a good reason for ending the employment relationship earlier than expected. State law permits early termination of a probationary contract, or suspension without pay for the rest of the school year, "for good cause as determined by the board of trustees, good cause being the failure to meet the accepted standards of conduct for the profession as generally recognized and applied in similarly situated school districts in this state."

The process to be followed would be the independent hearing system, described below. For present purposes, suffice it to say that the teacher is entitled to a full-blown due process hearing, including the right to present evidence, to cross-examine witnesses, to be represented by counsel, and so on.

Probationary teachers can resign without penalty up to forty-five days before the first day of instruction. With school starting in mid-August in most districts these days, this means the teacher must resign or honor the contract by approximately July 1. Teachers who wish to resign after the "no penalty" date must get the consent of the board or its designee. Teachers who leave without consent and thus fail to honor the contract are subject to sanctions imposed by the State Board for Educator Certification.

Teachers with either a term or continuing contract can be returned to probationary status, but only after the school has given the teacher notice of proposed nonrenewal or termination. Even then, the return to probation requires teacher consent. In effect, this new provision in the law amounts to a one-year buyout of a contract. By agreeing to a return to probation the teacher must surely realize that the district can easily terminate the teacher's employment with the district as of the end of the probationary contract. But the teacher might agree to this, in lieu of possible termination immediately.

Teachers do not have to return to probationary status when they move to a new position within the district. For example, assume that a teacher has served as a classroom teacher for seven years, then is promoted to an administrative position such as assistant principal. The teacher does not go back on probation. Her service with the district is continuous, albeit in two different positions.

Suppose a teacher works for a school district for six years, then leaves for two years, and then returns to the district. Does the teacher have to serve a second probationary period? No. This issue was decided by the case of *Meno v. Kitchens*, 1994. The court ruled that the TCNA did not permit a second probationary period under these circumstances. This seems even clearer under Senate Bill 1, which specifically says that probationary contracts are to go to those teachers employed by a school district "for the first time, or who ha[ve] not been employed by the district for two consecutive school years subsequent to August 28, 1967" (TEC §21.102).

Term Contracts

After the probationary period, the teacher must receive either a continuing or a term contract. It is up to the local school board to determine which type of contract to issue. What follows is a brief introduction to the vocabulary, history, and legal requirements pertinent to term contracts.

Schools can take one of three actions regarding a term contract teacher's contract. The school can (1) renew the contract; (2) nonrenew the contract; (3) terminate the contract. The expression "termination" refers *only* to the action of the district to end the contract prior to its normal expiration date. This deprives the teacher of a property interest, and thus requires good cause and procedural due process.

School law makes quite a distinction between "termination" and "nonrenewal" of a term contract. To the employee, it makes little difference—he or she is unemployed. But the legal analysis does change significantly depending on whether the school's action is a termination or nonrenewal. A nonrenewal of contract refers to the decision of the school district to let the term contract expire. When an employee is nonrenewed she is permitted to fulfill the terms of her existing contract. But the district offers no new contract to continue the employment relationship.

The situation is slightly more complex if the employee has a multiyear term contract. In those cases, the common practice is for the school district to extend the contract each year. Assume, for example, that Mr. Hudson has a two-year contract, covering the 1995–1996 and 1996–1997 school years. In most school districts, the custom would be to consider the extension of the contract in the spring of 1996. At that time the board would consider extending Mr. Hudson's contract for the 1997–1998 school year. However, if the board chooses not to extend the contract, Mr. Hudson still has a valid contract for the 1996–1997 school year. The board has not "nonrenewed" Mr. Hudson, it has merely "nonextended" him. Mr. Hudson could file a grievance over this nonextension, but otherwise has no legal recourse. The decision to renew or nonrenew the multiyear contract can only be made in the final year of the contract.

The Term Contract Nonrenewal Act was adopted by the legislature in 1981. Prior to 1981, a school district could lawfully inform a term contract employee at the end of the contract of the fact of nonrenewal with no further ado. A teacher's procedural rights at the end of the twentieth one-year term contract were no greater than his or her rights at the end of the first one-year term contract. The TCNA significantly narrowed the differences between term and continuing contracts. Senate Bill 1 further narrowed those differences. Key features of term contracts under Senate Bill 1 are as follows.

Term contracts can be issued to "teachers" as that term is defined in Section 21.201. That section defines "teachers" to include "a superintendent, principal, supervisor, classroom teacher, counselor, or other full-time professional employee who is required to hold a certificate issued under Subchapter B or a nurse" (TEC §21.201).

A term contract is any nonprobationary contract for a fixed term. The length of the contract can be up to five school years.

There is nothing in the law that prevents a school district from offering longer contracts to certain classes of employees as opposed to
others. Typically, administrators have multiyear contracts whereas
teachers are employed year-to-year.

There is no longer a specific set of statutes referred to as "The
Term Contract Nonrenewal Act." However, many of the requirements of the TCNA are still in place. For example, the board must
give notice of proposed renewal or nonrenewal by the forty-fifth day
before the last day of instruction in the school year. If the board fails
to give the notice in timely fashion, the district, as a matter of law,
has elected to "employ the teacher in the same professional capacity for the following school year." However, if the contract is a multiyear contract, this notice requirement only applies during the last
year of the contract.

Prior to Senate Bill 1, the TCNA required the notice of proposed nonrenewal to include a statement of all the reasons for the
proposed action. Those reasons had to have been included in district
policy. Senate Bill 1 still requires that school board policy contain a
statement of all of the reasons why a teacher's contract might be
nonrenewed. But there is no longer a requirement that the notice of
proposed nonrenewal that is sent to a particular teacher contain a
list of the reasons for the nonrenewal of that teacher.

One of the reasons for nonrenewal, reduction in force, merits
special comment. Reduction in force is clearly a valid reason for the
nonrenewal of a term contract. In a line of cases reaching from
Strauch v. Acquilla I.S.D. (1983) to *Wasserman v. Nederland I.S.D.*
(1988), and including challenges under the Term Contract Nonrenewal Act, the commissioner has adhered to the proposition that, before an employee covered by a term contract can be nonrenewed on
the basis of reduction in force, the district must give the employee
an opportunity to apply for any position that is available at the time
of the hearing and for which the employee is qualified. The *Wasserman* case involved an athletic director who was reassigned to a new
position as athletic coordinator/business manager because a majority of the board no longer wanted him to continue in the previous
position. Later, the man's contract was nonrenewed for reasons of
loss of enrollment and loss of funding. The commissioner held that
"reduction in force does not constitute a valid reason for nonrenewal, if on the date of nonrenewal, there is another position for
which the teacher is qualified, unless the district has a valid reason,
supported by substantial evidence at the local hearing for not reas-
signing the teacher." In the hearing, the superintendent acknowl-

edged that vacancies existed for which the employee was qualified. The commissioner granted the employee's appeal.

This rule was further refined in the case of *Parr v. Waco I.S.D.* (1991). In that case the commissioner overturned the nonrenewal of an administrator based on reduction in force. At the time of the nonrenewal, the position of vocational coordinator was open. The administrator was certified for the position but was not considered by the selection committee to be qualified. However, no evidence was produced establishing qualifications for the position or the reasons why the selection committee judged the administrator not to be qualified. The commissioner observed that "once an open position is established and Petitioner has shown that she is certified and at least minimally qualified for the position, Respondent has the burden to prove that Petitioner was not qualified for the open position." Had the qualifications and standards of the position been introduced into evidence at the local hearing and had the rationale of the committee been established, "the outcome would have been different." The employee was entitled to reinstatement in the same professional capacity for the ensuing school year. For a detailed discussion of the technicalities of reductions in force, see "Reductions in Force of Texas Public School Professional Staff" by John Aldridge in the August 1991 issue of the *Texas School Administrators' Legal Digest*, pp. 1–6, 20.

The role of the teacher's evaluation in the nonrenewal process has been changed also. The TCNA required that the board consider the teacher's evaluation prior to any decision not to renew the contract. Much litigation ensued over this apparently simple requirement. Did the board have to consider the evaluation from this year, or is last year's acceptable? Must the evaluation be complete at the time of review? Does the board have to review the evaluation at the time of the nonrenewal, or at the time of the proposed nonrenewal? What if the nonrenewal has nothing to do with performance in the classroom—does the board still have to review the evaluation? The new provisions in Senate Bill 1 simply say that districts must evaluate teachers at least once a year, and that "The board must consider the most recent evaluations before making a decision not to renew a teacher's contract if the evaluations are relevant to the reason for the board's action." Whether this will put an end to the wrangling over these issues is doubtful.

A term contract teacher is entitled to a hearing prior to nonrenewal. When the teacher receives notice of the proposed nonrenewal, the teacher has fifteen days in which to request a hearing. The board may either conduct the hearing itself, under rules adopted by the board, or the board may choose to use the independent hearing system described below. However, if the board chooses to conduct the hearing itself, it must allow the teacher to be represented, to hear the evidence, to cross-examine adverse witnesses, and to present evidence. Furthermore, the hearing must be closed to the public unless the teacher requests an open hearing.

If the teacher is nonrenewed, the teacher may appeal to the commissioner of education. The commissioner's review will be, as it was under the Term Contract Nonrenewal Act, a "substantial evidence" review. This means that the commissioner may not substitute his judgment for that of the board of trustees unless the board's decision was arbitrary, capricious, unlawful, or not supported by substantial evidence. In conducting the review, the commissioner will simply review the transcript of the hearing before the local board, rather than re-hear the evidence at the Texas Education Agency.

Districts still retain the power to terminate a term contract teacher prior to the end of the contract, but only for "good cause," or due to a financial exigency that requires a reduction in personnel. Boards of trustees will have the opportunity to define the term "good cause," there being no definition of that term in the relevant section of state law. Later in this chapter, we will provide some examples of what constitutes "good cause." Whatever the reason for a termination, since it involves a deprivation of a property interest, the teacher is entitled to a full due process hearing. State law now mandates that such a hearing be conducted pursuant to the state's new independent hearing process, described below.

A term contract teacher can be suspended without pay for good cause as determined by the school board. The suspension cannot extend beyond the end of the school year. The district is required to give notice to the teacher, who is then entitled to request an independent hearing, as outlined below.

If a school district fails to give the teacher timely written notice of proposed nonrenewal, then it has, by law, renewed the teacher "in the same professional capacity." The key to determining an employee's "professional capacity" is the contract. The Tarkington I.S.D. issued a two-year contract to an employee in 1990, stating that the employee was hired as "a professional employee." The contract contained the usual reassignment clause, stating that the man could be reassigned to other positions. The man's initial assignment was as athletic director. But after the first year of the contract, the district moved him to a teacher/assistant principal assignment. The man complained that the district had changed his professional capacity without complying with the TCNA. The man's appeal was denied by the commissioner. Noting the broad language of the contract, the commissioner ruled that the man did not have a property interest in serving as athletic director. His professional capacity was as a "professional employee." He was still a professional employee. His salary had not been cut. Therefore, the district did not change his professional capacity and did not have to comply with the TCNA (*Keith v. Tarkington I.S.D.*, 1991). Although the TCNA no longer exists, the Texas Education Code still contains the same language pertaining to "same professional capacity." Thus the interpretation of the TCNA, as in the Tarkington case, will likely still be followed under Senate Bill 1.

A closely related issue concerns the handling of employees who have dual assignments, the most common of which is "Teacher/ Coach." If the district wants to terminate the coaching duties, but renew the person as a teacher, must it comply with the statutory nonrenewal scheme? Again, the key appears to be the language of the individual's contract. In a 1985 decision, the Texas Commissioner of Education observed that a school district can hire a person to serve as teacher and coach in one of two ways—either with a single "Teacher/Coach" contract, or with two contracts, one for teaching and the other for coaching. Under the two-contract arrangement, it might be possible to terminate the coaching contract without adhering to statutory nonrenewal provisions, while retaining the person as a teacher. Under the unified contract, however, nonrenewal of either portion of the contract means that the employee is not coming back "in the same professional capacity," and thus nonrenewal procedures are necessary. Moreover, under the unified contract, nonperformance of any of the duties could lead to nonrenewal of the entire employment relationship, provided the district complies with the statutory scheme for nonrenewal (*Hester v. Canadian I.S.D.*).

These principles came into play in a 1988 decision involving a unified "teacher/coach" contract. The district wanted to retain the man as a teacher only without coaching duties. Since the man would not be renewed "in the same professional capacity," the district fully complied with the TCNA by providing notice and a nonrenewal hearing. The commissioner concluded that the district had presented substantial evidence to support nonrenewal of the "teacher/coach" contract. The district was then free to offer the man a new contract as a teacher only (*Barizon v. Midland I.S.D.*). In another 1988 case, a continuing contract teacher with a supplemental coaching contract argued that his supplemental coaching contract was covered by the TCNA and could not be nonrenewed without the protections of the Act. The commissioner held that such supplemental coaching contracts are not covered by the Act, because the position of coach does not meet the definition of "teacher" as set forth in the TCNA (*Schomber and Doyle v. North Forest I.S.D.*).

In yet another example, five persons employed as teacher/deans appealed to the commissioner when they were "reassigned" to positions as teachers only. The commissioner, consistent with earlier decisions, ruled that these people could not simply be "reassigned" out of the deanships. Instead, the district would have to follow the TCNA to nonrenew the existing "teacher/dean" contracts, and bring the employees back as teachers only (*Abbott et al. v. Ector County I.S.D.*, 1991).

These cases involving employees who serve as teachers and coaches indicate that *Hester* was well-settled law under the TCNA. Since Senate Bill 1's language regarding "the same professional capacity" is the same as in the TCNA, these interpretations should continue in full force. If a district uses a unified "Teacher/Coach" contract, it may nonrenew the employee in both capacities provided it complies with Senate Bill 1's provisions concerning such nonrenewals. If, on the other hand, a district hires a person as a "teacher," with a separate, supplemental contract as a coach, it may terminate or nonrenew the coaching contract without meeting Senate Bill 1's requirements. However, termination or nonrenewal of the supplemental coaching contract would have no bearing on the employee's rights under the teaching contract.

So let's get to the nub of the matter: can a coach be nonrenewed because of a lousy win-loss record? In a case involving the nonrenewal of a teacher/assistant coach, the commissioner found a win-loss record insufficient evidence under the substantial evidence standard for nonrenewal under the TCNA. The commissioner noted that while a win-loss record is relevant to assessment of a coach's performance, "when considered in a vacuum, a poor record does not constitute even a scintilla of evidence that bad coaching was responsible for that record. Too many other factors influence a won-loss [*sic*] record over which the coach has no control." Here, the coach's contract was nonrenewed for "significant lack of student progress." His team failed to make the playoffs, a goal set by the school district. However, there was considerable evidence that the students had progressed during the evaluation period. The commissioner added that, even if it were appropriate to consider a win-loss record in a vacuum for assessing a head coach's performance, such a standard cannot apply to assistant coaches: "This philosophy—i.e., 'We win as a team and lose as a team'— . . . cannot stand as a reason for nonrenewing an assistant coach who is doing his job competently and in accordance with district policy. Nonrenewal must be based on personal accountability" (*Hester v. Canadian I.S.D.*).

Suppose a school district wrongfully nonrenews a contract. What remedy is the employee entitled to? In an unpublished decision, a Texas court of appeals suggests that the employee can obtain reinstatement in the same professional capacity as well as monetary damages for breach of contract. The court held that the law concerning contract nonrenewal which existed at the time of the making of the contract forms a part of the contract. Therefore, if the school breaks the law, it also breaches the contract (*Wilmer-Hutchins I.S.D. v. Meno*).

This analysis may be impacted by a very interesting section of Senate Bill 1 dealing with appeals to the commissioner. Section 21.304 of the Texas Education Code says that the commissioner may reverse the decision of the school board to nonrenew or terminate a teacher. In that event, the commissioner is authorized to reinstate the teacher, along with an order for back pay and employment benefits from the time of discharge to reinstatement. However, the law goes on to give school districts an avenue to avoid reinstatement: "Instead of reinstating a teacher under Subsection (e), the school district may pay the teacher one year's salary to which the teacher would have been entitled from the date on which the teacher would have been reinstated."

The argument will likely be made that these provisions preclude any further remedy, such as for breach of contract damages. But future litigation will decide the outcome of that argument.

Continuing Contracts

Recall that if a school district continues to employ a teacher after the completion of a probationary period, the school district must give the teacher either a term contract or a continuing contract. The key distinguishing feature of a continuing contract is that it automatically rolls over from one year to the next, without the necessity of board action. Under prior law, there were many other distinctions between the term and continuing contracts, but many of those have been eliminated or at least narrowed by Senate Bill 1. The law pertaining to continuing contracts is found in Texas Education Code

Sections 21.151 et seq. Key features of continuing contracts are as follows.

Under prior law, continuing contracts could not be issued to administrators. Senate Bill 1 is ambiguous on this point. The new law authorizes issuance of a continuing contract to any person who is a "teacher" as that term is defined in Section 21.101. That section defines "teacher" as including principals, supervisors, counselors, and nurses, none of whom was eligible for continuing contract status in the past. However, Section 21.155 of the Code confuses the issue. It states that a district may grant an administrator a continuing contract as a teacher "at the completion" of the person's service as an administrator. This implies that continuing contracts cannot be granted to administrators, but may be issued to former administrators who move into teaching positions. No clear answer to this ambiguity exists at this time.

As noted, there is no specific length of time for a continuing contract. Once entered into, the contract remains in effect until the teacher resigns, retires, is terminated, or returned to probationary status.

In the continuing contract system, there is no such thing as a "nonrenewal." Since the contract does not require renewal, but rather, automatically continues from one year to the next, it would not make sense for the school district to "nonrenew" the contract. This means that districts need not give notice of proposed termination as of a specific date, as they must do with term and probationary contracts. Recall that both term and probationary contracts automatically renew if the district fails to give notice of possible nonrenewal by the forty-fifth day before the last day of instruction. No such notice requirement exists with continuing contracts. However, there is one provision in the Code which only applies if the district wishes to break off the contract at the end of a school year. Section 21.157 authorizes such action due to a "necessary reduction of personnel," provided that the reductions are made "in the reverse order of seniority in the specific teaching fields."

Continuing contract teachers may be terminated at any time "for good cause as determined by the board of trustees, good cause being the failure to meet the accepted standards of conduct for the profession as generally recognized and applied in similarly situated school districts in this state" (TEC §21.156).

What about teachers who are still employed under a continuing contract that predates Senate Bill 1? Section 21.154 effectively incorporates those contracts by saying that continuing contract teachers can be terminated "for a reason stated in the teacher's contract that existed on or before September 1, 1995."

Regardless of the reason for termination of the continuing contract, the procedure to be followed for such a termination must be in accordance with Senate Bill 1—meaning the independent hearing system described below. This is the case even with those terminations based on pre–Senate Bill 1 contracts. In lieu of discharge, schools can suspend a continuing contract teacher without pay for a period of time not to exceed the current school year. However, such action must be done through notice to the teacher, who then is entitled to an independent hearing, just as if the school were proposing termination.

Keep in mind that the continuing contract teacher can be returned to probationary status, as outlined above, provided that the teacher consents to the move.

The case of *James v. Hitchcock I.S.D.*, decided by a Houston court of appeals in 1987, illustrates the importance of the wording of a continuing contract. James served the district under a continuing contract that specified 203 days of service. State law guaranteed James 183 days of employment, and the extra 20 days were in addition to that guarantee and locally funded. In 1981, the district informed James that beginning with the 1981–1982 school year, the district would begin to reduce her locally funded days. In doing so, the district maintained that since James's contract contained a clause accepting rules and regulations then in existence or added at a later time, the reduction in her locally funded days was authorized by the clause and the policy of reduction. James disagreed and eventually filed suit over the matter. The court held that the continuing contract entitled James to 203 days of employment. The court stated: "When those 20 days became part of the contract, they acquired tenure protection . . . to hold otherwise would seriously undermine economic security for public school teachers—a goal of the continuing contract law."

However, in a 1994 dispute, the commissioner distinguished the James case and upheld a school district's decision to reduce a continuing contract teacher from 202 days to 188. The commissioner placed emphasis on the fact that the change was made at a time when the teacher could have resigned from the district without penalty, and was accompanied by notice and an opportunity for a hearing (*Sanford v. La Porte I.S.D.*).

The court's decision in *James v. Hitchcock* holds that if a continuing contract specifies a certain number of days of service, that term becomes part of the continuing contract and cannot be modified unilaterally. What if the number of days is *not* specified in the continuing contract? In that case the school district retains the right to modify the duty schedule for the upcoming school year prior to the commencement of the contract. This is the ruling of the Texas Commissioner of Education in *Kinnaird v. Houston I.S.D.* (1991), in which teachers complained in part that their duty schedules had been illegally changed from 260 days per year to 183 days per year. The commissioner noted that the teachers had received timely notice of the change and could have resigned, which they chose not to do. Such was not the case in *Bacon v. Galveston I.S.D.* (1991), where the continuing contract teacher was not given notice of a reduction by the administration in the number of days of assignment prior to beginning performance. The commissioner granted the teacher's appeal.

Putting these cases together, we should realize that the terms of the written continuing contract must be carefully examined. If the particular terms stated in any given continuing contract are "tenured," modification of these terms would appear to require mutual agreement, or action by the board to terminate the existing contract.

Since Texas has long had a dual system for teacher contracts, questions have arisen as to the power of the school district to move from one system to another. Can the board rescind its adoption of the continuing contract system and switch to the term contract system? In 1980 the attorney general issued an advisory opinion indicating that school districts could do so. However, the continuing contracts in force at the time of rescission continue in force. In other words, the rescission cannot deprive existing teachers of their rights under the contracts they hold (*Att'y. Gen. Op. MW-238*, 1980).This may be less of an issue after Senate Bill 1 than it was beforehand. Senate Bill 1 does not appear to require a district to choose one system over another. It appears that districts can combine the two systems to some degree. In fact, in a Question and Answer document promulgated by the Texas Education Agency after the enactment of Senate Bill 1, this exchange is included:

Q. May a continuing contract district, by local policy, offer a teacher new to the district, who has been in employment in public education for at least the last five of the preceding eight years two one-year term contracts following a one-year probationary contract prior to employment under a continuing contract?

A. Yes. Prior law required a district to elect continuing contract status for its employees. Subchapter D of Chapter 21 does not contain the requirement, so a district could have a mix of continuing and term contract teachers, if it desired.

Regardless of the type of contract used by a school district, contracts with teachers must be in writing. In *Delgado v. Eagle Pass I.S.D.* (1989), a teacher had worked for a district for two months, was paid for his work, and had accepted the position by relinquishing a job in another district. The school board had not given the teacher a written contract, however, and, after approximately two months, terminated the teacher. The commissioner of education held that the teacher had been an at-will employee since only the school board is empowered with the authority to hire teachers and "no representative of a district has the power to create a binding teaching contract. No person may reasonably rely upon appearances to the contrary."

Furthermore, the general rule is that terms of the contract must be approved by the school board. In the 1987–1988 school year, the Katy I.S.D. employed its teachers with a contract stating that "the Board agrees to pay the employee an annual salary in accordance with the District's salary schedule as adopted by the Board." The Katy administration then issued "salary notification letters" to inform the teachers of the actual salary each would receive. The district began the school year paying each teacher pursuant to the salary notification letter. Midway through the year the district discovered that a number of the salary notification letters were erroneous. The district then reduced payments to those teachers who were receiving more than they were supposed to receive pursuant to the board-adopted salary schedule. The district did not take away any overpayment that had already been paid—it merely dropped the teachers down to the proper schedule for the remainder of the school year. The commissioner of education denied the appeal of the teachers: "The established rule is that salary statements unauthorized by a school district's board of trustees and unsigned by the parties do not form a part of the employment contract" (*Sones v. Katy I.S.D.*, 1992).

Indeed, teachers should be on notice that verbal commitments from school administrators may not be legally binding when it comes to employment contracts. In *Brown v. Georgetown I.S.D.* (1987), the commissioner of education held that representations concerning salary made by school administrators during employment negotiations are not binding on the district's board of trustees.

In the case, the assistant superintendent told the teacher that she would receive a larger salary if she completed her master's degree. The teacher completed her master's degree over the summer and did not receive the higher salary. The commissioner denied any relief sought by the teacher, stating " . . . prospective teachers must be aware that they are dealing with a public body which is bound only by officially adopted actions."

The terms and conditions of a contract are always important. But it can safely be said that they are more important in a private school setting than in the public school setting. The relationship between employer and employee in the public schools is determined, in large part, by constitutional restrictions and statutory provisions in the Education Code and other legislation. Generally speaking, however, the constitutional restrictions do not apply to the private school; and there are far fewer statutory provisions applicable to the private schools. Most of the Education Code, for example, applies only to public schools, not private schools. Thus the relationship between employer and employee in the private school setting is almost entirely determined by the terms and conditions of the contract between the parties. With fewer legal restrictions, private schools retain more flexibility in their employment relationships, but need to be particularly careful as to what they say in those contracts.

Special Rules for Superintendents

Superintendents must be employed under a term contract. A district cannot issue a superintendent a probationary or a continuing contract. A special section of the Code, 21.212, spells out two special rules that apply to superintendents. First, the timeline for notice of proposed nonrenewal of a superintendent differs from the typical term contract nonrenewal timeline. The superintendent is entitled to notice "not later than the 30th day before the last day of the contract term."

Second, the superintendent is entitled to "reasonable notice of the reason for the proposed nonrenewal." No such requirement applies to the teacher holding a term contract, although it is likely that school districts will give notice of the reasons so that teachers can adequately prepare for a hearing.

Perhaps the most important distinction regarding superintendents, though, concerns the cost to the district in buying out the superintendent's contract. Superintendents typically have multiyear contracts. School board members who are unhappy with the super-

intendent face a dilemma: either produce sufficient evidence to justify firing the superintendent (thus likely embroiling the district in
costly litigation); wait for the contract to run out (which still requires legal proceedings to nonrenew the contract); or negotiate
a buyout. Superintendent buyouts have become commonplace.

However, Senate Bill 1 has significantly raised the stakes in
cases of superintendent buyouts. Section 11.201 now says that any
buyout of a superintendent's contract must be reported to the Texas
Education Agency. TEA will then deduct from the district's funding
for the next school year a sum equal to the amount of the buyout.
Thus local taxpayers will pay twice for a buyout. For example, if the
board agrees to pay the superintendent $75,000 in exchange for an
immediate resignation, it will actually cost the district $150,000.
No doubt this will cause local school boards to look more favorably
on the other options.

PROPERTY RIGHTS AND DUE PROCESS

No discussion of the rights of public school employees would be
complete without a discussion of the concept of due process. A term
that is overworked and often misapplied, "due process" is, nevertheless, a key concept in the arena of public employment.

The Fourteenth Amendment provides that no state shall deprive a person of life, liberty, or property without due process of law.
(The Fifth Amendment contains a similar limitation on actions by
the federal government.) As noted in Chapter 1, we can restate this
proposition to mean that rights can be regulated or even taken away
altogether if due process of law is provided.

The concept of due process of law is a means of assuring that
decisions made by government officials affecting people's essential
rights are made fairly. (Since the Fourteenth Amendment pertains
only to states and their political subdivisions, nonpublic schools
and colleges are not subject to its strictures. As noted previously,
the rights of nonpublic school personnel are almost exclusively a
matter of contractual terms and institutional policies and are not
protected by the federal constitution.)

Judges view due process in two ways: substantive due process
and procedural due process. *Substantive due process* means that
the content (or substance) of rules and decisions must be fair. Substantive due process is regarded as having been denied in instances
where a reasonable person could only conclude that fairness had not
been afforded. However, courts usually defer to school officials on

the merits of personnel decisions and only in the rarest of instances will intervene on the basis of substantive due process. *Procedural due process* means that decisions are to be reached in accordance with a procedural process that will satisfy the requirements of the Fourteenth Amendment as applied by the federal courts to the facts of a particular situation. A board policy stipulating a set of predetermined procedures meeting at least the minimal requirements of due process as discussed later in the chapter will suffice in most cases. The assumption is that, if certain procedures are followed, fairness will be assured. In essence, substantive due process focuses on the outcome of the decision process, while procedural due process focuses on how the decision is made.

Whether we are talking about substantive or procedural due process under the Fourteenth Amendment, a necessary prerequisite is that a recognized liberty or property right must be implicated. Courts are unlikely to intervene in a challenged personnel decision without this threshold requirement. The U.S. Court of Appeals for the Fifth Circuit included this quotation from Supreme Court Justice John Paul Stevens in one of its decisions on the nonrenewal of a public school teacher:

> The federal court is not the appropriate forum in which to review the multitude of personnel decisions that are made daily by public agencies. We must accept the harsh fact that numerous individual mistakes are inevitable in the day-to-day administration of our affairs. The United States Constitution cannot feasibly be construed to require federal judicial review for every such error. In the absence of any claim that the public employer was motivated by a desire to curtail or to penalize the exercise of an employee's constitutionally protected rights, we must presume that official action was regular and, if erroneous, can best be corrected in other ways. The Due Process Clause of the Fourteenth Amendment is not a guarantee against incorrect or ill-advised personnel decisions. (*Russell v. El Paso I.S.D.*, 1976, p. 565)

Thus, an important initial inquiry in any proposed termination is whether the teacher or other professional employee is to be deprived of "property" within the meaning of the Fourteenth Amendment guarantee that property may not be taken without due process of law. In 1972 the U.S. Supreme Court ruled that teachers have a protectible Fourteenth Amendment property right in continued employment if state law gives them a "legitimate claim of entitlement" to it (*Board of Regents v. Roth*). In a companion case, *Perry v. Sindermann*, the Supreme Court noted that in rare instances a nontenured teacher might be able to show that a public educational institution had a de facto tenure system. Under such circumstances, the teacher would be entitled to procedural due process if the contract were not renewed. The case involved a teacher at Odessa Junior College who, after being employed for four one-year contracts, was nonrenewed. No notice or hearing was provided. The Court remanded the case to a lower court for determination of whether through policies and practice Odessa Junior College had a de facto tenure system.

Both the courts and the commissioner of education have ruled, however, that de facto tenure is not a legal possibility in Texas public schools. *Steelman v. Red Water I.S.D.* (1982) dealt with a nonrenewed teacher who had received favorable evaluations and assurances of reemployment, and claimed that the district had a de facto tenure policy because of an open letter from the board stating "as long as a teacher does his or her job effectively, that person's job is secure and is in no way in jeopardy." The commissioner rejected this claim. According to the commissioner, the only way an employee can enjoy tenure is if the district has formally adopted the continuing contract law, discussed earlier. Redwater I.S.D. had not done so. The commissioner observed that even if the district had considered the letter to be a written tenure policy it would be invalid. Similarly, the commissioner rejected the claim of a junior high school principal that a district can, through custom and practice, create an expectation of continuing appointment for administrators (*Austin v. Houston I.S.D.*, 1983).

To summarize, the U.S. Supreme Court has ruled that states and their political subdivisions can create property rights protected by the Fourteenth Amendment. Public employment may give rise to such a right; whether it does depends upon state law, local policies, and contractual provisions. Once a governmental entity has created a property right protected by the Fourteenth Amendment, it may not take that right away without providing the employee due process of law.

When Do Texas Educators Have Property Rights?

An at-will employee has no property right in the job. Much of the litigation involving at-will employees concerns whether or not they truly are "at-will." Employees without formal written contracts frequently point to employee policies, manuals, and even verbal promises in an effort to establish that there was a contractual relationship of sorts. Only if a contractual relationship of some sort can be

established is the employee entitled to due process prior to termination. Why? Because absent such a contractual relationship there is
no property right. Absent a property right, no process is due.

The contractual employee clearly has a property right in the job
during the term of the contract. Any effort of the school district to
terminate the contract prior to its stated date of expiration is a deprivation of property. Thus, some amount of process is due.

In each of the following instances, the school district is seeking
to terminate the contract prior to its normal expiration date, and,
therefore, must afford due process:

Case One: the employee has a contract for the 1996–1997
school year. In November 1996, the school district seeks to terminate the contract immediately, due to alleged theft of school property.

Case Two: the employee has a contract for the 1996–1997
and 1997–1998 school years. The school district
seeks to terminate the contract in February
1997 due to alleged violation of school policies.

Case Three: the employee has a contract for the 1996–1997
and 1997–1998 school years. The school district
seeks to "nonrenew" the contract after the
1996–1997 school year due to excessive absences. The school district considers this a
"nonrenewal" since it is occurring as of the end
of one school year, and prior to the start of the
next. In fact, however, it is a termination of a
contract that has another full year to run. The
employee has a property interest in the job for
the entire length of the contract, and thus, is entitled to due process.

If the school seeks to terminate a contract prior to its normal
expiration date, it is depriving the employee of property and must
afford the employee due process. Note that the nature of the contract, in this context, does not matter. Whether the employee is a
continuing contract teacher with twenty years on the job, or a first-
year probationary teacher, the *constitutional* analysis and the *constitutional* right to due process is the same.

What of the due process rights of teachers facing nonrenewal of
a term contract? Suppose the district proposes to nonrenew a teacher's term contract, and the teacher requests a hearing. Make the further supposition that the district, required to give a hearing, fails to

do so. Clearly the district has violated state law and the employee can obtain any remedy available to the employee under state law. But can the employee pursue a claim of violation of his or her constitutional rights to due process?

The question has an interesting history. Until 1993 the answer was "no." The leading legal authority on the subject was the case of *English v. Hairston* (1989). In that case, the Fifth Circuit ruled that term contract employees covered by the Term Contract Nonrenewal Act have no property rights at the end of their contracts but are entitled only to the procedural protections of the TCNA in the event of proposed nonrenewal of their contracts.

So the matter stood until June 23, 1993, when the Texas Supreme Court came to the opposite conclusion on the same question. The case arose when the Tolar I.S.D. nonrenewed teacher/coach Gary Grounds in 1984. Believing that Grounds was probationary, the district refused to give him a statement of reasons for the nonrenewal or a hearing. When the commissioner ruled that Grounds was not probationary, and thus ordered the district to renew the contract, the district still refused. Grounds sued. More than nine years after the initial nonrenewal decision, the Texas Supreme Court ruled that Gary Grounds had a property interest entitled to due process protection. In a footnote, the court explained the conflict with the earlier Fifth Circuit decision:

We therefore disagree with the Fifth Circuit's decision in *English v. Hairston*, which held to the contrary. [Cite omitted]. *English* relied on *Hix* which correctly stated the law prior to the TCNA's enactment but no longer accurately reflects a term-contract teacher's interest in renewal. (*Grounds v. Tolar I.S.D.*)

What teachers won through the courts, however, they may have lost in the legislature. For the final turn in the road is Senate Bill 1, which includes this simple declaration: "A teacher does not have a property interest in a contract beyond its term" (TEC §21.404(e)). Since the courts have always recognized that property interests are created, defined, and limited by state law, this clear-cut expression of state law may resolve the issue: no property interest means that constitutional due process is not required in the case of a term contract nonrenewal.

As a footnote to this discussion, we should point out that it is not at all clear just what the significance of the debate is. Mr. Grounds, for example, after winning his case at the Texas Supreme Court, had to go back to the Court of Appeals for determination of just what he was entitled to now that it was established that his constitutional rights were involved. The Court concluded that whatever injuries and injustices the man had suffered, they were not attributable to the deprivation of his constitutional rights. Among other things, the Court noted that Mr. Grounds was making more as a truck driver and insurance salesman than he had as a teacher/ coach. After reviewing the situation, the Court awarded him the grand sum of $1.00. We hope he did not have to split this with his attorney.

How Much Process Is Due?

Understanding when process is due is only the beginning of a due process analysis. The next question is: How much process is due? Courts regularly intone that due process is not an absolute and that it varies according to the deprivation of property in question. In the case of dismissal of an educator with a property right, however, the concept of due process is reasonably well defined.

Due Process in General. One principle applies regardless of the legal framework under which an educator's property right arises: due process must precede the taking. The U.S. Supreme Court made this point abundantly clear in *Cleveland Board of Education v. Loudermill* (1985). Thus it is no longer permissible to fire an employee who has a property right and then "cure" any due process defect by providing notice of reasons and a hearing after the fact (*Wells v. Dallas I.S.D.,* 1983).

As for the level of formality of due process in a typical employee termination case, the essentials are timely notice of why dismissal is being sought, a fair hearing where the employee can present a defense and question the evidence against him or her, and sufficient evidence to establish good cause for dismissal. An early and important case is *Ferguson v. Thomas,* a 1970 Fifth Circuit Court of Appeals ruling. In *Ferguson,* the court stated that in a dismissal for cause action a teacher must at a minimum:

1. Be advised of the cause or causes of the termination in sufficient detail to fairly enable him or her to show any error that may exist.
2. Be advised of the names and the nature of the testimony of witnesses against her or him.
3. At a reasonable time after such advice, be given a meaningful opportunity to be heard in his or her own defense.

4. Be given an opportunity for a hearing before a tribunal that both possesses some academic expertise and has an apparent impartiality toward the charges.

At the same time, the court noted that "standards of procedural due process are not wooden absolutes" (p. 856). What happens if a school district adopts additional due process procedures beyond the *Ferguson* requirements and then fails to follow them? Is this a violation of constitutional law? The U.S. Court of Appeals for the Fifth Circuit answered in the negative in a 1985 ruling, *Levitt v. University of Texas at El Paso.* The case involved a college professor who complained that not all of the procedures set forth in university policies were followed in connection with his termination, hence he was denied due process. The Fifth Circuit wrote: "There is not a violation of due process every time a university or other government entity violates its own rules. Such action may constitute a breach of contract or violation of state law, but unless the conduct trespasses on federal constitutional safeguards, there is no constitutional deprivation." Here, the court found that all the requirements set forth in *Ferguson* had been met.

The issues of the nature of the hearing and the weight of the evidence are frequently of concern. Can a school board, which makes final personnel decisions, be impartial? This question was raised in an important 1976 U.S. Supreme Court case. The case, *Hortonville Joint School District No. 1 v. Hortonville Educational Association,* involved striking teachers who were dismissed by the Hortonville, Wisconsin, school board when they refused to return to work. Instead, they continued their strike in direct violation of Wisconsin's no-strike law. The teachers were given a hearing before the board prior to their dismissals. They argued that the hearing they received was unfair because their employer, the board, was involved in the labor dispute and thus could not be impartial. Chief Justice Warren Burger for the majority ruled against the teachers, pointing out that the mere fact the board "was 'involved' in the events preceding this decision, in light of the important interest in leaving with the Board the power given by the state legislature, is not enough to overcome the presumption of honesty and integrity in policymakers with decision-making power" (p. 497). In short, for employees to succeed in charging members of the board with partiality, they must produce clear evidence that such is the case.

One employee successfully did so in the case of *Thompson v. Rockwall I.S.D.* This case arose from the termination of an athletic director. The commissioner eventually upheld the termination, which was based on repeated failure to comply with directives and school policy, much of it involving inappropriate language and possession of alcohol. The commissioner agreed with the local board that the contract should be terminated. However, the commissioner charged the board with violating the athletic director's due process rights in the manner in which the termination was handled. Specifically, the commissioner noted that the superintendent repeatedly and prematurely participated in deliberations with the board pertaining to this situation to the point that the board was prejudiced by the time they conducted the actual hearing. The remedy to which the employee was entitled was another hearing. Since he had already had another hearing before the commissioner, the ultimate ruling was in favor of the school district.

But this case points out the fine line local boards must walk in dealing with matters that may come before them in the future. Board members are not expected to be completely ignorant, but they must not be so involved in pre-termination discussions that they lose their impartiality.

Good Cause. Even if a school district follows all the right procedures at all the right times, its decision to terminate an employee is subject to attack pursuant to the notion of substantive due process. In this case, the employee argues that the procedures may have been correct, but the decision was based on evidence that failed to establish "good cause" for the school to terminate the contract.

What constitutes good cause for dismissal? No mechanical test can be applied. Basically, good cause means that convincing evidence supports one or more reasons listed in board policies for employee termination. For example, in 1975 the Fifth Circuit awarded a Texas school superintendent his salary for the balance of his contract when the board fired him after a falling-out. Expressing reluctance to intervene in school district decision making, the court nevertheless noted that "the record suggests that the post-hoc list of administrative deficiencies presented to Roane was an effort to rationalize a decision stemming from different views on classroom construction" (*Roane v. Callisburg I.S.D.*). Mere disagreement over school business does not constitute good cause. By contrast, the dismissal of a special education teacher in the Beaumont I.S.D. was upheld based on evidence produced at the school board hearing that the teacher failed to attend a scheduled in-service meeting, failed to complete a form for Southern Association accreditation of the school, left the campus without permission during a preparation period, and failed to complete and sign her staff evaluation form. The federal district court found the evidence sufficient to support the charge of "repeated failure to comply with official directives and established school board policies" and "repeated and continuing neglect of duties" (*Heins v. Beaumont I.S.D.*, 1981).

A few general principles apply in determining what constitutes good cause for terminating a term contract employee during the term of the contract. Conduct that is potentially harmful to students can justify termination. Sexual misconduct with students, of course, justifies termination. A vice-principal who engaged in sexual intercourse with a student and fondled four others was terminated for good cause (*Taplin v. Fort Worth I.S.D.*, 1989). An employee who assaults another person and engages in violent conduct at school may be justifiably terminated for such conduct. A teacher's aide who was employed under contract was properly terminated for slapping a teacher (*Martinez v. Crosbyton I.S.D.*, 1985). Insubordination or refusal to comply with directives or policy may justify dismissal during the term of a contract. A counselor sought permission to be excused from attending an end-of-school Counselor Work Week so that she instead could attend a university seminar. She was denied permission, she ignored the directive given to her to participate in the Counselor Work Week, and her calculated insubordination in doing so and in failing to comply with the directive justified her termination (*Jones v. Northside I.S.D.*, 1987). An employee's misappropriation of public funds is, of course, a criminal violation that justifies termination. A superintendent who used his official capacity to obtain the services of school employees for the personal benefit of himself and his political allies was justifiably terminated (*Brosette v. Wilmer-Hutchins I.S.D.*, 1984). Finally, an educator may be terminated for violating the Code of Ethics and Standard Practices for Texas Educators (*Green v. Irving I.S.D.*, 1988).

Mid-contract terminations are not to be undertaken lightly. Often, to justify such action, the employee must have been given an explicit directive to change or improve his or her conduct or to cease certain behaviors, and must have had an opportunity to comply, before termination will be justified. Isolated instances of misconduct often can and should be handled by less drastic means than termination. In fact, decisions of the commissioner appear to require "remediation" in most cases.

The requirement to provide for remediation means that the employee be advised of deficiencies and likely consequences, be given a corrective plan, be given assistance in complying with the plan, and be given a reasonable time in which to improve. The Texas Com-

missioner of Education has required that, absent acts involving ir-
remediable behavior, such as violence or significant emotional or
physical harm to students, remediation must be given prior to
termination of a continuing contract teacher or placement of the
teacher back on a probationary contract (*McRuiz v. Cleburne I.S.D.*,
1990). The commissioner has also required a corrective plan prior to
termination of a term contract employee (*Peck v. Texas School for
the Blind*, 1990). While the decisions are less consistent regarding
nonrenewal of a term contract, offering remediation prior to nonrenewal helps demonstrate that the employee is being treated fairly.

Although this requirement to permit remediation may delay
the school's efforts to terminate a weak teacher, it also may make
the case much easier when it is presented. It is normally considerably easier to establish failure to follow the requirements listed in a
remediation plan than to prove "incompetency."

Conduct that poses the potential for significant harm to students is only one type justifying termination upon a single occurrence. All factors and circumstances surrounding the employee's
conduct must be considered. The district must be able to present
evidence that will support its charges. As the decisions make clear,
however, school districts in Texas are able to terminate an employment relationship in mid-contract where the conduct of the employee provides good cause for doing so. No doubt the most celebrated "good cause" case in Texas over the past few years is the
infamous "pig castration" case. In that case a teacher was terminated for allowing a student to orally castrate a pig in a vocational
agricultural course. The teacher celebrated the incident by photographing the student, pig blood on his mouth and shirt, pig testicles
held over his head. Not surprisingly, the commissioner found this to
be good cause for termination (*Pirkey v. Harmony I.S.D.*).

Finally, "good cause" cannot involve any form of impermissible
discrimination. The same federal and state laws that prohibit discrimination on the basis of race, color, religion, sex, national origin,
age, or disabilities in hiring practices apply to termination practices
as well. Racial discrimination charges are particularly sensitive.
The dismissal of a teacher in the Richardson I.S.D. affords a good
illustration.

The case involved a black fifth-grade teacher who, in an alter-
cation with a white student, struck him with her hand, causing
a small cut. The teacher claimed self-defense, since the student
had become abusive. As an employee on a continuing contract, the
teacher was entitled to a full due process hearing before she could

be dismissed. After both a fact-finding hearing and an open meeting before the school board, she was dismissed for violating board policy on the administering of corporal punishment.

The teacher sued the school district in federal court, advancing four arguments against her dismissal. Pointing out that the school district was operating under a court desegregation order, the judge reviewed her arguments in some detail. Her first argument was that the action had violated the so-called *Singleton* rule, a requirement imposed by a Fifth Circuit Court of Appeals ruling that any teacher "dismissed or demoted" as part of an overall reduction in staff resulting from court-ordered conversion to a unitary school system must be chosen on the basis of "objective and reasonable nondiscriminatory standards" (*Singleton v. Jackson Municipal Separate School District*, 1970, p. 1218). The replacement for the dismissed teacher was white. The court rejected this argument, since her dismissal involved no desegregation-related reduction in force.

Second, the teacher argued that her procedural due process rights had been violated. The court also rejected this argument, since the district had complied with statutory and case law requirements throughout all the relevant proceedings. But the court did agree with her third argument that the district had denied her substantive due process. Noting that the teacher had a fifteen-year unblemished record in the school district, the court concluded that her dismissal, "based on such an unusual, one-time event" and on a policy provision "largely if not completely unenforced prior to this event," was arbitrary and capricious (p. 86). The court also agreed with her fourth argument that the action denied her equal protection of the laws under the Fourteenth Amendment because previous violations of the school board's policy on corporal punishment by white teachers had not resulted in their dismissal. Thus, the teacher's dismissal "was an intentional act of racial discrimination violating the Equal Protection Clause" (*United States v. Richardson I.S.D.*, 1979, p. 87).

Constructive Discharge

A significant footnote to the discussion of termination of property rights involves the concept of "constructive" discharge. This is the situation in which an employee resigns and then claims that the resignation was not voluntary. The employee contends, instead, that the actions of the employer forced him or her into an involuntary resignation. The focus of a constructive discharge case is twofold. First, were the employee's working conditions "intolerable" and, second, was there "illegal conduct" on the part of the employer (*Young v. Southwestern Savings and Loan Assn.*, 1975)? A constructive discharge results when job conditions are so difficult or so unpleasant that a reasonable person in the employee's place would have felt compelled to resign (*Junior v. Texaco, Inc.*, 1982). Moreover, in the case of a constructive discharge, the employer is liable for illegal conduct leading to the discharge, just as he or she would be in the case of formal discharge (*Kline v. North Texas State University*, 1986). The fact that an employee resigns does not prevent him or her from filing a federal lawsuit claiming that the resignation was forced due to intolerable conditions created by the employer. While the employee's legal burden in such a case is demanding, school administrators should be aware of constructive discharge as an issue that increasingly is being litigated in federal court.

Educator Reputational Rights

In addition to specific guarantees in the Bill of Rights, such as freedom of speech and association, the U.S. Supreme Court has recognized certain other rights to be implicit in the word "liberty" of the Fourteenth Amendment. Among them are the right of the parent to select a nonpublic school; the right to privacy, which will be discussed in Chapter 9; and the right to a good reputation. With regard to reputation, the Supreme Court recognized in a 1971 case that, "where a person's name, reputation, honor, or integrity is at stake because of what the government is doing to him, notice and an opportunity to be heard are essential" (*Wisconsin v. Constantineau*, p. 437).

In the education context, the implications are that a school district cannot stigmatize an employee's reputation in the context of an adverse employment decision. The relevant case for Texas is *Dennis v. S & S Consolidated Rural High School District* (U.S. Court of Appeals for the Fifth Circuit, 1978). The case involved a public school teacher whose term contract was not renewed. The court noted that the school board did not have to accord Dennis a hearing or give him the reasons for the nonrenewal under the law at the time. However, the school did grant his request for a hearing, and at the hearing one of the board members told Dennis that a reason for the nonrenewal was his "drinking problem." Denying the allegation, Dennis sued in federal court. The Fifth Circuit agreed that Dennis's reputation had been tarnished, but it did not order his reinstatement. It rather ordered the school district to give him another hearing so that he would have the opportunity to clear his name. Whether the court would have ordered his reinstatement in his old job along with back pay had he not gotten another teaching job is not known.

Several later developments have increased concerns regarding damage to reputation. In *In re Selcraig*, a 1983 Fifth Circuit ruling, a Dallas I.S.D. administrator brought suit against the district and several of its administrators for allegedly stigmatizing his reputation in connection with the loss of his position in the district. To pursue his case, he argued that he needed to know who in the district had passed information about him to the press. The administrator, Dr. Paul Trautman, was not successful, because it was not clear to the court whether he had waived his right to a name-clearing hearing under the *Dennis* ruling. What is important about the case is a comment by Circuit Judge Alvin Rubin that school administrators may properly reply to inquiries from the press. But, having done so, "they are obligated thereafter to afford procedural due process to the person charged." This means informing the employee who has suffered some injury to his employment or employment opportunities of his right to a name-clearing hearing. If the employee denies the accusations and is not given a name-clearing hearing, he may be entitled to compensatory and even punitive damages if he shows the charges were false and made maliciously.

A later Supreme Court case emphasizes that the stigmatizing statements create a right to a name-clearing hearing only if they arise in conjunction with termination or nonrenewal of employment. The case involved a clinical psychologist at a government hospital who resigned rather than go through a termination action that might damage his reputation. When he sought employment at another government hospital, he signed a form allowing his previous employer to release all information about him. When contacted, his former supervisor responded by speaking critically of the psychologist's job performance. He noted that the psychologist was "both inept and unethical, perhaps the least trustworthy individual I have supervised in my thirteen years. . . ." As a result, the psychologist was not credentialed and his employment in federal service was terminated. He sued his previous supervisor. The high court noted that although the psychologist might have a claim for defamation under state law, he could not claim deprivation of his reputational liberty rights under the Fourteenth Amendment, because he had voluntarily resigned. Stigmatization by itself is insufficient to constitute a liberty-right violation. Stigmatization must occur in conjunction with a contract nonrenewal or termination (*Siegert v. Gilley*, 1991). Three justices dissented, noting in part that Siegert's future loss of government employment should have been sufficient to constitute a liberty-right deprivation.

Furthermore, an individual cannot "bootstrap" himself into a name-clearing hearing. When the employee himself is the one who publicizes the defamatory remarks, there is no right to a name-clearing hearing (*Jones v. Comal I.S.D.*). Similarly, the U.S. Court of Appeals for the Fifth Circuit rejected a teacher's claim that the reading of a letter from teachers in his department at an open board meeting violated his constitutional rights. The court noted that, "for us to hold that a member of the Board was not entitled to confront Burris and challenge his conclusions without fear of being sued for depriving him of his liberty would tie the hands of the school boards and prevent them from fulfilling their vital role in the community" (p. 1092). The Fifth Circuit also rejected the teacher's claim that allegedly defamatory information about him in a file maintained by the school principal deprived him of a liberty right to a good reputation. As long as the information is kept confidential, there is no constitutional violation (*Burris v. Willis I.S.D.*).

Reassignment

Most Texas teacher and administrator contracts contain a clause to the effect that the employee may be assigned and reassigned at the discretion of the superintendent. In spite of such contractual language, reassignments frequently lead to litigation. The leading recent case on this issue is *Jett v. Dallas I.S.D.* (1989). The case arose when the athletic director and head coach at South Oak Cliff High School in Dallas was reassigned to another school as a teacher with no coaching duties. There was no reduction in salary or supplemental pay. Jett came out even financially, but he complained that he was unfairly deprived of a "property right" in the position of athletic director and head coach.

Jett served under a typical "teacher contract," which indicated that he was employed "subject to assignment." The reassignment was done without any formal notice or hearing—in short, without due process. The Fifth Circuit focused on the exact extent of Jett's property interest. Did he have a property interest in being head coach and athletic director? Or did he merely have a property right in the financial aspects of the contract? The court ruled that Jett's property right included only the economic benefits of the contract.

Since he received all of those economic benefits, even after the reassignment, he was not deprived of any property right. Therefore, he was not entitled to notice and a hearing or any of the other aspects of due process. After the *Jett* case, reassignment clauses should be understood to mean what they say.

The whole question of reassignment calls forth a ghost of reassignments past in the case of *Briggs v. Crystal City I.S.D.* (1972). Crystal City I.S.D. hired Briggs to be its superintendent and, shortly thereafter, attempted to reassign him to a teaching position. Briggs sued, and a Texas court of appeals held that a superintendent occupies a unique position and that any reassignment would be a material change in the contract. In other words, a superintendent is one of a kind.

THE NEW INDEPENDENT HEARING SYSTEM

Beginning January 1, 1996, Texas had a new system for handling hearings concerning teacher termination. Previously, local school boards had conducted hearings concerning teacher termination, pursuant to local policy and local rules. Teachers could then appeal to the Texas Education Agency, where a second hearing was held.

Senate Bill 1 imposes a new system on each district in the state. Hearings are now conducted by independent hearing examiners appointed by the state. The role of the local school board is significantly reduced. The role of the commissioner is also reduced. Key features of the new system are as follows.

Teachers and other contractual personnel are entitled to a hearing concerning a termination of contract, or a suspension without pay. Note that the type of contract does not matter—probationary, continuing, or term. A teacher is entitled to a hearing concerning any termination, as opposed to a nonrenewal, of a contract. Keep in mind that a nonrenewal of a probationary contract requires no hearing at all. As for nonrenewal of a term contract, the local board can decide to conduct its own hearing, or to use the independent hearing process.

The commissioner is required to certify hearing examiners according to criteria developed by the State Board of Education, in consultation with the State Office of Administrative Hearings. State law only requires that the hearing examiners be licensed to practice law in Texas, and not serve as agents or representatives of a school district, a teacher in a dispute with a school district, or an organization of school employees, administrators, or school boards. Furthermore, a hearing officer may not be associated with a law firm that serves as representative or agent of any of these entities. Thus the lawyers and law firms which have represented schools and school employees, as well as the lawyers at the Texas Association of School Boards, are disqualified. However, the law does not prevent the appointment of a lawyer who formerly represented schools or school employees.

A teacher must make a written request for a hearing to the commissioner, with a copy to the local district. The request must be made within fifteen days after receipt of written notice of the proposed action. The commissioner then has ten days to appoint one of the certified hearing examiners to the case.

Either party can reject the assigned examiner for cause. The rejection must be in writing, and must be filed with the commissioner within three days after notification of the assignment. The commissioner must then decide if good cause for rejection exists. If so, the commissioner is to appoint the next person on the list.

Rather than taking pot luck with the next person on the list, the parties are authorized to agree on a noncertified hearing examiner, provided that the individual chosen is licensed to practice law in Texas. It does not appear that the parties can agree to use an examiner who is certified. Certified hearing examiners are to wait their turn.

The parties are also authorized to agree that the decision of the hearing examiner will be final and nonappealable on all or some of the issues.

The teacher has the right to be represented at the hearing, to hear the evidence on which the charges are based, to present evidence, and to cross-examine adverse witnesses. Rules of Civil Evidence apply, and a court reporter must be employed to record the hearing. In general, the hearing is to be conducted just as a nonjury trial, with the school district bearing the burden of proof.

The hearing examiner has extensive powers to control the process. The examiner can issue subpoenas, rule on motions and admissibility of evidence, and maintain decorum at the hearing. In this connection, it should be noted that the hearing will be private unless the teacher requests that it be open. Even then the hearing examiner can close the hearing to maintain decorum. Finally, the hearing examiner has the power to protect the privacy of a witness who is a child by closing the hearing to receive the child's testimony or issuing other orders consistent with practices in criminal cases in which children are the victims.

The hearing examiner and the court reporter are to be paid for by the school district. The commissioner is to establish hourly rates for hearing examiners, along with a per-case maximum.

The hearing examiner must issue a written recommendation no later than forty-five days after the date when the commissioner received the request for a hearing. This puts the hearing on a fast track, but again, the parties can agree to waive this timeline. The recommendation must include findings of fact and conclusions of law. It may include a proposal for granting relief, including rein-statement, back pay, or employee benefits. The hearing examiner may not propose recovery of attorneys' fees or other costs as relief. Copies of the recommendation are to go to the parties, the president of the school board, and the commissioner.

The matter then goes to the board. At this meeting, the board must consider the recommendation and allow each party to present an oral argument. In effect, the board is acting as an appellate body. The board can limit the amount of time each side has, provided that each side has an equal amount of time.

The board can adopt, reject, or change the hearing examiner's conclusions of law or proposal for relief, provided that the board states in writing the reason and the legal basis for a change or rejec-tion of the recommendation. With regard to the findings of fact, however, boards are even more restrained. They can reject or change a finding of fact "only after reviewing the record of the proceedings before the hearing examiner and only if the finding of fact is not supported by substantial evidence." Again, such a change must be accompanied by a written statement as to the reason and the legal basis for the change.

Boards will probably want some legal advice in handling these matters, and are authorized to get advice "from an attorney who has not been involved in the proceedings." Thus the attorney who rep-resented the district before the hearing examiner should not be the attorney advising the board as to what to do with the hearing exam-iner's recommendation.

Finally, boards can delegate all of these responsibilities to a committee of the board, thus keeping some members of the board out of the process altogether.

A teacher can appeal the board's decision to the commissioner by filing a "petition for review" within twenty days. The commis-sioner is then required to review the record and the oral argument before the local board. In most instances the commissioner will base his decision on the record review without hearing any new evidence.

With regard to nonrenewals of term contracts, the commissioner may not substitute his judgment for that of the board of
trustees unless the decision was arbitrary, capricious, unlawful, or
not supported by substantial evidence.

The same standard applies in termination cases, but only if the
board accepted the hearing examiner's recommended findings of
fact without modification. Boards that change the findings of fact
can be reversed if the commissioner determines that their decision
was arbitrary, capricious, unlawful, or if "the hearing examiner's
original findings of fact are not supported by substantial evidence"
(TEC §21.303(b)(2)). This is a curious provision. Why should the validity of the decision turn on fact findings that were reversed by the
local board? Some attorneys are arguing that this is a simple case of
legislative error. We shall have to wait and see how this curious provision is interpreted in actual cases.

The commissioner must issue a decision thirty days after the
last day on which a response to the petition for review could have
been filed. If the commissioner fails to act, the decision of the local
board is affirmed. This fast track will be a relief to all parties. In the
past, nonrenewal disputes at the Texas Education Agency have
dragged on for years. With the new law, a final decision from the
commissioner will be issued no later than seventy days after the local board's decision (twenty days for teacher appeal; twenty days for
school response; thirty days for commissioner decision).

If the commissioner reverses the board's decision, he must order the district to reinstate the teacher and to pay any back pay and
employment benefits from the time of discharge or suspension.
However, the district is not required to accept the teacher back. In
lieu of reinstatement, the district can pay the teacher one year's
salary. Thus the worst situation for the school district would involve back pay for seventy days (unless the parties agreed to waive
timelines), plus one year's salary.

Either party can appeal the commissioner's decision to the district court in the county in which the district's administrative offices are located. This is a significant change from prior law, which
required all appeals to go to Travis County. The parties can still take
an appeal to Travis County, but only with agreement of all parties.
School districts which are light years, geographically and politically,
from Travis County, are not likely to agree.

The appeal involves a "substantial evidence" review of the record, meaning that the court can reverse the decision only if it finds
that the decision was not supported by substantial evidence, or

that the commissioner's conclusions of law were erroneous. Just as with the commissioner, the court cannot reverse the decision on the basis of a procedural irregularity unless it finds that the error likely led to an erroneous decison by the commissioner.

In sum, the use of independent hearings for teacher terminations is truly one of the most significant changes enacted by Senate Bill 1. How it will play out remains to be seen. The legislature hopes that this process will save money, and be perceived as a more equitable method of resolving disputes. School administrators and board members are wary. Teachers are hopeful. Lawyers figure they'll come out all right. We will have to wait and see.

COMPENSATION DISPUTES

Due to recent litigation, school districts are now much more aware of the "no penalty resignation date" faced by teachers. In the San Elizario I.S.D., the board set salaries for the upcoming year on July 10th. However, the teachers were locked into the contract as of July 1. Any resignation after that date required board approval. When the new salary schedule actually lowered the salaries of some of the teachers, they took the matter to the commissioner, who ruled that the district was obligated to compensate the teachers pursuant to the previous year's salary schedule (*San Elizario Educators Association v. San Elizario I.S.D.*).

Occasionally, a district erroneously makes an overpayment to a teacher, a situation that has given rise to litigation on at least two occasions. The commissioner of education decided in a 1985 case that, while districts theoretically can recover an erroneous overpayment, they may not do so if such recovery would be inequitable. The situation in *Lee v. Alief I.S.D.* arose after a computer error caused the district to overpay a teacher some $2,500. To recover the money, the district cut the teacher's salary 44 percent over the remainder of the teaching year. This caused the teacher, a single parent, to obtain a loan to support her family. Because the amount was relatively small and because the teacher had incurred a liability (the loan), the commissioner sided with the teacher and ordered the district to restore the deducted funds. In an earlier decision, a Texas court of appeals ruled against the district when it tried to recoup sick leave overpayments made the *previous* year by impounding funds due teachers on their *current* contracts (*Benton v. Wilmer-Hutchins I.S.D.*, 1983). The court held that the dispute over the previous year's overpayments was unrelated to and could not generate deductions from the teachers' paychecks. The current salaries were amounts lawfully due, reasoned the court, and were not subject to the proposed unilateral deduction by the district.

TEACHER APPRAISAL

Teacher evaluation is a subject that has received considerable legislative attention over the past several years. Prior to passage of the Term Contract Nonrenewal Act in 1981 there was no state law requiring any kind of teacher evaluation in Texas. Some districts devised their own systems, others did not. The TCNA required that those teachers serving under a term contract be evaluated in writing at least once a year. All other decisions about evaluation were left to the local district.

In 1984, H.B. 72 imposed the Texas Teacher Appraisal System (TTAS), the first effort to adopt a uniform system of teacher evaluation throughout Texas. The TTAS was necessary to implement the career ladder, another major 1984 reform. The career ladder provided financial incentives to induce good teachers to keep teaching, rather than moving into administration. TTAS was intended to be the instrument that measured the difference between the average classroom teacher and the instructional star. High scores on TTAS were to be clear evidence of outstanding classroom performance, meriting additional compensation. That was the theory.

It did not work out that way. If the legislature expected Texas teachers to fall into a neat bell curve on the TTAS, they were sadly mistaken. The vast majority of teachers were rated "clearly outstanding" or "exceeds expectations." It became quite an insult for a teacher to fall into the satisfactory category. Such a teacher would most likely be among the lowest-rated teachers in the district. Many members of the public blamed appraisers for being too soft, but the appraisers blamed TTAS. Since teachers usually knew when they would be observed; since TTAS called for identification of certain specific behaviors, which most teachers could readily do; since the appraisal depended entirely on performance in a single forty-five-minute time frame, appraisers charged that the proverbial "trained monkey" could score "exceeds expectations."

Perhaps the weakness of TTAS was best illustrated by the fact that teachers rated "satisfactory" under TTAS could still be nonrenewed for inadequate classroom performance. The commissioner of education made this clear in a 1988 decision. Among the reasons supporting the nonrenewal under consideration were disorganized classes, inadequate discipline, insufficient structure to learning activities, and students wasting time. A conference was held in November regarding these matters. At the conference, the teacher was advised to remove the deficiencies. The problems continued. Later, his contract was not renewed. The commissioner found the decision was supported by substantial evidence and rejected the teacher's arguments that satisfactory appraisal ratings should insulate the teacher from contract nonrenewal: "Even if it is assumed that Petitioner's teaching performance was satisfactory to his appraisers, he was clearly on notice of specific problems which required correction. While statutory appraisal scores may be some evidence of the overall level of teaching performance, they are not conclusive on the issue of whether a teaching contract should be renewed" (*Magouryk v. Bloomburg I.S.D.*).

Despite a huge state investment in the development of TTAS and the training of the appraisers, by 1993 the conventional wisdom was that the system did not work well. Thus it was not surprising when the 1993 legislature dismantled the career ladder, and made significant changes in the appraisal system as well. Further changes were made in 1995. Here is a summary of current law.

The commissioner is to recommend an appraisal system and a set of criteria for rating teacher performance, but the local district can use a system devised locally. If the district chooses to use a locally devised system, it must develop the system through district and campus-level site-based decision-making committees. Any locally devised system must reflect the teachers' implementation of discipline management procedures, and the performance of students. A locally devised system must be approved by the board, but the board's hands are restricted on this matter. In order to insure that the site-based decision-making committees are real players in this system, the law requires that the local board accept or reject the plan in toto. The board cannot modify the plan.

The commissioner is to adopt a "recommended appraisal process and criteria on which to appraise the performance of teachers." The commissioner's appraisal system must use criteria which are observable, job-related behaviors, including implementation of discipline management procedures and the performance of students under the teacher's supervision. In developing the appraisal system, the commissioner is to solicit and consider the advice of teachers. Note, however, that the commissioner's process is merely recommended, not required.

Whether a local district adopts the commissioner's plan or uses its own, the criteria for teacher evaluation must include the performance of students. For the first time, a teacher's evaluation will depend to some degree on the performance of students. Exactly how this will work remains to be seen, and is sure to be one of the most controversial features of any system of teacher evaluation.

All that is required in the new system is a single appraisal by a single appraiser. This is a considerable reduction from the original TTAS system, which required two appraisals per year by two appraisers (four observations). The teacher can demand a second appraisal by a different appraiser. The teacher is also specifically permitted to file a written rebuttal to the appraisal. If the teacher does so, the rebuttal must be kept in the personnel file along with the appraisal. As to whether or not a teacher is given advance notice of the date and time of the appraisal, this is a local matter. The law says that the teacher "may" be given such advance notice. The process must guarantee a diagnostic and prescriptive conference between the appraiser and the teacher. A teacher who also directs extracurricular activities is to be appraised only on the basis of classroom performance—not on performance in connection with extracurricular activities.

In what may be a significant change, schools are now specifically authorized to send copies of a teacher's evaluation (along with any rebuttals) to a district in which the teacher has applied for employment if the new district requests such information. Time will tell if this becomes a common practice or not. As to the general public, however, teacher evaluations are not accessible. Senate Bill 1 includes Section 21.355, which states that "A document evaluating the performance of a teacher or administrator is confidential."

The rules for administrator appraisal are very similar to those for teachers. The local district is to use its own locally developed system, or the commissioner's recommended system. The law does not specifically require an annual appraisal of every administrator, but it prohibits use of school funds to pay any administrator who has not been appraised within the preceding fifteen months.

Some special rules exist for the appraisal of principals. First, their appraisal is to include consideration of the performance of the campus with regard to the academic excellence indicators and campus objectives which are a part of the campus improvement plan. Second, principals have the opportunity to earn performance incentives. The commissioner is to design an objective system to evaluate principals based on information derived from PEIMS (Public Education Information Management System). The system is to focus on gains on the principal's campus, and is specifically required not to include subjective items. The commissioner may award performance incentives to high-achieving principals through this system. Awards of up to $5,000 for those principals in the top quartile are possible.

Finally, the commissioner is to develop both a job description and an evaluation form to be used by school districts in evaluating counselors.

OTHER EMPLOYMENT BENEFITS

Planning and Preparation Period

Exactly what benefits an employee is entitled to depends to a great extent on the actual wording of the employment contract and the policies of the school district. State law does, however, set forth some demarcations on benefits with which school districts must comply. For example, each classroom teacher is to have at least 450 minutes within each two-week period for instructional preparation, parent-teacher conferences, evaluating students' work, and planning. Each planning and preparation period must be at least 45 minutes long, and must be scheduled during the school day. During the planning and preparation period, the teacher may not be required to participate in any other activity (TEC §21.404). The commissioner has ruled that a district may not require a teacher to attend an in-service meeting during the 45-minute period (*Strater v. Houston I.S.D.*, 1986).

Duty-Free Lunch

Classroom teachers and full-time librarians are also entitled to at least a 30-minute lunch period free from all duties and responsibilities connected with the instruction or supervision of students, unless the district is faced with such dire situations as personnel shortage, extreme economic conditions, or unavoidable or unforeseen circumstances. In any event a teacher may not be required to supervise students during the duty-free lunch more than one time per week (TEC §21.405).

Personal Leave

The state sick leave program for school employees was scrapped by Senate Bill 1. In its place is a statute guaranteeing every school district employee five days of personal leave per year. There is no limit on the accumulation of personal leave, and it moves with the employee from one district to another. Over a long career, therefore, employees who are able to accumulate these personal leave days will have a great job benefit. The school board is authorized to develop policies governing the use of personal leave. It is likely that restrictions on the use of personal leave days will be challenged by school employees.

This could turn out to be one of the greatest gains for school employees arising from Senate Bill 1. Under prior law, employees could accumulate sick leave, but could not use it unless they were sick. Many longtime school employees had over one hundred days of sick leave, but they were never able to use them. With the switch to personal leave, however, this may change. Presumably a person can use personal leave for virtually any reason. Thus twenty years from now, if an employee has accumulated one hundred days of personal leave, will that employee be able to take a one-hundred-day paid vacation? It would appear so. And after twenty years of service without taking a day off, that vacation would no doubt be well deserved!

What about those employees who currently have a large accumulation of sick leave days—can they convert these to personal leave? No such luck. Accumulated sick leave will continue to be governed by prior law, which limited its use to sickness or death in the immediate family.

Of course a district can adopt a local sick leave plan or local personal leave plan to supplement what the state provides. Absent some abuse of discretion, a school district's interpretation of its local leave policies will be affirmed if challenged. For example, the mother of a quadriplegic son sought to use seven days of sick leave to assist him in enrolling in college and to locate an attendant to provide for his personal needs. The school district advised the mother that sick leave could not be used for this purpose. The principal advised her that two days of hardship leave could be used instead, with her salary docked for additional days. The mother subsequently filed a grievance asking that all seven days of her absence be taken from accumulated sick leave. The Texas Commissioner of Education noted that both state law and local policy limited sick leave to illness and to family emergencies. Neither applied in this case. "The district reasonably interpreted the provisions of its own sick leave policy as it related to the Petitioner's circumstances and such interpretation complies with state law and agency regulation" (*Waligura v. El Campo I.S.D.*, 1991).

Health Insurance

TEC §22.004 requires each school district to offer its employees health insurance. The insurance can be provided by a risk pool involving one or more districts, by an insurance company, or by a health maintenance organization (HMO). The insurance plan must be comparable to the insurance program the state offers its employees. Costs may be shared by employees and the district. Before a district contracts with an insurer or HMO, the latter must provide an audited financial statement showing its financial condition. Alternatively, a school district can opt to participate in the state health insurance program, subject to certain conditions. School districts must certify annually to the executive director of the Employees Retirement System that the district's coverage meets the requirements of the statute.

Districts with twenty or more employees are also subject to the provisions of a federal statute known by the cheerful acronym COBRA (Consolidated Omnibus Budget Reconciliation Act of 1985). COBRA requires that the district offer health insurance continuation to (1) the employee for eighteen months after a termination (other than for gross misconduct) or reduction in hours, (2) dependents of the covered employee for thirty-six months after the employee becomes eligible for Medicare benefits, (3) dependents of the covered employee for thirty-six months after the employee's death or the divorce or legal separation of the employee from a spouse, and (4) a dependent child for thirty-six months after the child ceases to be a dependent under the terms of the plan. The district may require premium payments of not more than 102 percent of the usual cost of the plan for the period of continuation coverage (42 U.S.C. §§300bb-1 et seq.). The purpose of COBRA is to guarantee coverage to some of the people who routinely fall through the cracks of the nation's health care system.

Assault Leave

The legislature has provided additional protection for school employees who are physically assaulted during the performance of their duties. Such employees are entitled to take "the number of days of leave necessary to recuperate from all physical injuries sustained as a result of the assault." This paid leave can continue, if necessary, up to two full years. Leave taken as a result of an assault may not be deducted from accrued sick leave. In other words, this is paid leave on top of other sick leave available to the employee. Furthermore, the employee is to be placed on assault leave status immediately upon request. Upon investigation of the claim, the district may change the assault leave status and charge the leave, first against accumulated personal leave, and then, if necessary, against the employee's pay (TEC §22.003(b)).

Social Security and Annuities

School districts are not required to participate in the federal Social Security System and most do not. However, Government Code §822.001 requires every employee of Texas public school districts to belong to the Teacher Retirement System of Texas. In addition, school districts may establish their own supplementary annuity programs. School districts may also provide various insurance programs for their employees paid for out of local funds.

Temporary Disability Leave

Section 21.409 of the Texas Education Code provides that each full-time educator employed by a school district is entitled to a leave of absence for temporary disability without fear of termination. Pregnancy is specifically listed as a temporary disability. Requests must be made to the superintendent and include a physician's statement confirming the inability to work and indicating the date the employee wishes to begin the leave and the probable date of return. Insofar as pregnancy is concerned, teachers are allowed to take a leave of absence only for the period a physician certifies they are unable to work. This precludes taking a leave of absence under §21.409 for infant-nurturing purposes. Such a leave will be available, however, under the federal Family and Medical Leave Act.

Temporary disability leave is unpaid. The primary purpose of the leave is to assure the employee that he or she will have a job upon returning to good health. The district cannot terminate an employee while he or she is on temporary disability. The employee is required to notify the superintendent at least thirty days prior to the expected date of return and include a physician's statement indicating the employee's physical fitness for resumption of regular duties. Section 21.409(e) provides that an employee who returns to work "is entitled to an assignment at the school where the employee formerly taught, subject to the availability of an appropriate teaching position. In any event, the educator must be placed on active duty not later than the beginning of the next term."

In 1992 the attorney general was asked about the effect of site-based decision making on this guarantee. As already noted, TEC §11.202 gives campus principals the power to approve all appointments to the campus. The attorney general concluded that an employee returning from disability leave must be placed on his or her former campus unless another principal voluntarily accepts the employee. The returning employee is to go to the former campus if a position is available there. However, if no such position is available, the school cannot force some other principal to accept the employee. As of the beginning of the next school year, however, the school district has the duty to make sure a position is available. Again, if no other principal will take the employee, the principal of the campus where the teacher formerly taught must do so (*Att'y. Gen. Op. DM-177*, 1992). In cases involving enrollment shifts or program changes, however, the superintendent has the final word on employee assignments.

Section 21.409(f) leaves the length of leave of absence up to the superintendent but provides that the school board may establish a maximum length for a leave of absence for temporary disability of not less than 180 calendar days.

The school board has the right under §21.409(c) to establish a policy providing for placing an educator on involuntary leave of absence "for temporary disability if, in the board's judgment and in consultation with a physician who has performed a thorough medical examination of the educator, the educator's condition interferes with the performance of regular duties." The policy must allow the employee the right to present testimony and/or other information to the board relevant to such determination. The Texas Commissioner of Education's position on involuntary leaves was revealed in a 1983 decision, *Moore v. Dallas I.S.D.* The ruling involved a teacher who was placed on involuntary leave of absence without pay until she submitted a psychological evaluation pronouncing her fit to teach. She was denied a hearing when she protested this administrative decision. While agreeing that school districts inherently possess the power to require teachers to submit to a psychological examination, the commissioner noted that, in his opinion, "an administrative order to that effect is itself appealable to the Board of Trustees and the Commissioner of Education." Here, there was a clear violation of the predecessor to the existing §21.409 and of the teacher's due process rights because she was denied compensation and employment without being afforded a hearing.

Family and Medical Leave Act

The Family and Medical Leave Act was one of the first major legislative enactments of the Clinton administration. It went into effect

August 5, 1993. Under the Act, eligible employees will be entitled
to up to twelve weeks of unpaid leave per year (1) to care for new-
born, adopted, or foster children; (2) to care for a spouse, child, or
parent with a serious health condition; (3) when a serious health
condition prevents the employee from performing the essential
functions of the job. To be "eligible" an employee must have been
with the district for at least twelve months, and must have worked
at least 1,250 hours. Since this is unpaid leave, its primary purpose
is to assure the employee of a job upon his or her return. The district will be obligated to restore the returning employee to his or
her former position or an equivalent position with equivalent pay,
benefits, and terms and conditions of employment. Family and
Medical Leave runs concurrently with other leave available to the
employee. In other words, if the employee already has twelve
weeks of sick leave accumulated, the employee is entitled under
this law only to those twelve weeks, and not twelve paid weeks
(sick leave) followed by twelve unpaid weeks (Family and Medical
Leave).

Miscellaneous Leave Policies

School districts may offer local leave programs for a variety of purposes—for example, local sick leave, death leave, professional leave,
maternity leave. The policies governing local leave programs are developed by local school districts. The only restriction is that local
leave must not be used to benefit a private organization or individuals contrary to a provision of the Texas Constitution.

Other types of leave allowed by state law include military leave
and developmental leave. Under Texas Civil Statute §5765, employees who are members of the state militia or the U.S. reserve forces
must be granted up to fifteen days per year of leave without loss of
salary for participation in authorized duty. Teachers on military
leave cannot be required to pay the cost of a substitute (*Att'y. Gen.
Op. MW-240*, 1980). Under TEC §21.452, boards of trustees may
grant certified teachers who have served at least five consecutive
years in the district a developmental leave of absence for study, research, travel, or other suitable purpose. Such leave is limited to one
school year at one-half salary or one-half school year at full salary.
While on developmental leave, the teacher is entitled to the same
employee benefits available to employees of the district. Note that
developmental leaves are discretionary with school districts; districts may, but do not have to, offer this benefit.

WORKERS' COMPENSATION
AND UNEMPLOYMENT COMPENSATION

Two subjects of increasing financial significance to public education in Texas are workers' compensation and unemployment compensation. Although a detailed discussion of these matters is beyond the scope of this book, no discussion of employment matters would be complete without some attention to both.

In the matter of workers' compensation, state law provides that a school district shall extend such benefits to its employees by one of the following options: becoming a self-insurer, providing insurance under workers' compensation insurance contracts or policies, or entering into interlocal agreements with other political subdivisions providing for self-insurance. In practice, almost all Texas school districts have chosen to meet their obligations through the option involving entering into interlocal agreements with each other.

One very important provision in the workers' compensation statute prohibits an employer from retaliating against an employee because the employee has filed a workers' compensation claim. In 1995, the Texas Supreme Court held that cities (and therefore, presumably, school districts) could be held liable for such retaliation despite the immunity generally enjoyed by governmental entities. Two cities had argued that they were immune from liability even if they had fired an employee for filing a workers' comp claim. The Court disagreed. However, the Court did limit the liability of the cities to the amounts set out in the workers' comp statute. Thus the $1,000,000 award against one of the cities was reduced (*City of LaPorte v. Barfield* and *City of LaPorte v. Prince*).

Districts frequently are perplexed about whether they must hold positions open for employees who are on sick leave and drawing workers' compensation, or create new positions for employees who want to return to work but cannot perform their normal duties. There is no legal obligation to hold positions open indefinitely or to create limited-duty jobs for employees who cannot return to their former jobs. However, with the advent of the Americans with Disabilities Act, districts will have to "reasonably accommodate" injured workers whose injuries cause them to be classified as having a disability. Thus districts will have to demonstrate creativity and flexibility in responding to individual situations.

Unemployment compensation is the state's effort to help people over the rough spots and is intended to provide compensation for a specified number of weeks to people who are unemployed through no fault of their own. As in the case of workers' compensation, most Texas school districts meet their obligations by entering a joint group account with other political subdivisions.

There are two situations in which an employee should not receive unemployment compensation benefits: if the employee is dismissed for misconduct or if the employee voluntarily quits. These matters are presided over by the Texas Employment Commission, a three-member body composed, theoretically, of a representative of employers, a representative of employees, and a representative of the public. While the individual commissioners no doubt have attempted to fulfill their respective roles, the commission as an institution has had a tendency during much of the decade of the 1980s to be generous with the funds it dispenses.

SUMMARY

No area of school law generates more legal disputes than personnel. This is not surprising, since school districts employ so many people and have to comply with so many federal and state mandates. If nothing else, this chapter should have made clear that personnel administration is no simple task. With the push toward site-based decision making, it is all the more important that knowledge of the basics of the law move from the central office to each campus. The director of personnel for the district needs to be an expert on the matters discussed in this chapter. But the principal needs to have a good grasp on the subject as well.

FIVE

Grievances and the Role of Employee Organizations

DURING THE 1980s and 1990s, a number of developments in public education combined to create a greatly expanded role for employee organizations: the Term Contract Nonrenewal Act, the career ladder, the state-mandated appraisal system, site-based decision making, and, most important, a wide-open grievance process. Senate Bill 1's expansion of due process rights for teachers is sure to continue the trend toward greater influence of professional organizations.

This chapter will deal with the role of professional organizations, particularly with regard to grievances. We will begin with a brief description of collective bargaining as it exists on the national scene and then proceed to a discussion of the Texas system. Finally, we will consider the current state of Texas law in the area of employee grievances.

COLLECTIVE BARGAINING ON THE NATIONAL SCENE

Public sector collective bargaining did not begin until 1959 when Wisconsin passed the first collective bargaining law. However, collective bargaining has been allowed in the private sector since 1935 when Congress passed the National Labor Relations Act (NLRA), sometimes called the Wagner Act. Its passage followed years of labor strife in major industries.

Where unionization has occurred in the private educational sector, it has been conducted under the terms of the NLRA. However, two U.S. Supreme Court decisions have dramatically curtailed union activities in private schools and colleges. The first, *NLRB v. Catholic Bishop of Chicago*, was a 1979 ruling holding that the NLRA does not extend to labor matters in church-operated schools. Since over 85 percent of private schools are church related, the ruling has virtually stopped collective bargaining in the nonpublic elementary-secondary sector. Then in 1980 the U.S. Supreme Court ruled in *NLRB v. Yeshiva University* that the faculty at Yeshiva are in effect "managerial employees" and thus excluded under the act from bargaining. Since the faculty at many other, if not most, private colleges and universities function in the same manner as do the Yeshiva faculty, the future of collective bargaining in that sector seems dim.

Another feature of the federal labor law is important for us in Texas, for it allows states to pass "right-to-work laws." Right-to-work laws do not ban unions or collective bargaining; rather, they prevent unions from negotiating so-called union security agreements. Union security agreements are designed to eliminate "free riders"—those who enjoy the fruits of bargaining but, because they choose not to belong to the union, do not share in the costs. The most common union security agreements are the union shop and the agency shop. The union shop specifies that every employee must join the union within a specified time. Failure to do so will result in termination of employment. The agency shop requires the payment of a so-called representation fee to the union by nonunion members equal to the costs of negotiating and administering the contract. The agency shop fee approximates that of union initiation fees and dues.

Federal law is particularly important in the area of labor relations because it has served as a model for state legislation. The NLRA does not apply to public sector employees. But since 1959, over half the states in the country have adopted some type of collective bargaining law for public employees. To varying degrees, the states have incorporated into their laws the NLRA's concept of full bargaining rights. Basically, full bargaining rights encompass:

1. The right to organize collectively or to refrain from doing so.
2. The right to be represented by a single bargaining agent.
3. The right to democratic internal union organization (one person has one vote; usually, only union members are allowed to vote).
4. The right to bilateral negotiations over conditions of employment.
5. The right to a binding contract between the employer and the union (individual employee rights are surrendered to the bargaining agent).
6. The right to strike or to negotiate binding arbitration of both grievance and contract term disputes.

Few states have come close to granting employees all of these statutory rights, believing that there exists a very real difference between the private industrial sector and government service. Thus, for example, most states that allow collective bargaining do not allow public employees to strike.

THE LAW IN TEXAS

With the exception of police and fire fighters, Texas does not allow public employees to engage in collective bargaining. The relevant law is contained in Chapter 617 of the Government Code. Section 617.002 prohibits political subdivisions of the state from recognizing a labor organization as the bargaining agent for a group of public employees and from entering into collective bargaining agreements with labor organizations. It specifies that any such contracts are void. Section 617.003 prohibits strikes by public employees and provides that employees who do so shall forfeit all civil service rights, reemployment rights, and any other rights, benefits, or privileges.

While Texas law outlaws collective negotiation, it does not prohibit unions from existing, nor public employees from joining them. In fact, Texas law repeats itself in an effort to make sure that employees are not forced into membership of any particular group. Section 617.004 proclaims that an individual may not be denied employment because of the individual's membership or nonmembership in a labor organization. TEC §21.407 requires that no school district, board, or administrator directly or indirectly require or coerce any teacher to join any group, club, committee, organization, or association. TEC §21.408 affirmatively states that educators have the right to join or refuse to join any professional association or organization. School administrators are well advised to be circumspect about these provisions. Subtle endorsements by an administrator may be seen by some as "coercion." In *Att'y. Gen. Op. LO-95-047*, the attorney general opined that "mere words of encouragement to join a particular teacher organization or association, when uttered by a high-level administrator in a particular context," could be construed to be coercive. Thus the beginning of the year recruitment drives of the various organizations should be conducted exclusively by teachers.

To facilitate membership in professional organizations, the legislature has added §21.001 to the Texas Education Code, requiring

school districts to deduct from an employee's salary an amount
equivalent to membership fees or dues in a professional association
if the employee so requests. The district may charge an administrative fee for doing so.

Perhaps the most litigated portion of Texas law dealing with
employer-employee relations is Government Code Section 617.005,
which states that public employees have the right to present grievances concerning their wages, hours of work, or conditions of work
either individually or through a representative "that does not claim
the right to strike." The grievance provision has taken on new significance in recent years as teachers have sought to grieve subjects
that once were not considered grievable under the policies of many
districts. We will look more carefully at public school grievances in
the next section of this chapter.

Prior to Senate Bill 1, the Education Code included a provision
that authorized "consultation" between school boards and professional organizations regarding "matters of educational policy and
conditions of employment." Consultation is not to be confused
with collective bargaining, for the two are significantly different.
Nevertheless, consultation was seen by some as a first step toward
collective bargaining.

Senate Bill 1, however, scrapped consultation altogether. Texas
no longer has a statute authorizing official consultation between
teacher organizations and school boards.

Does this preclude a school board from "consulting" with various professional organizations? No. School boards are free to consult with whomever they choose in formulating school policy and
budgetary decisions. But boards who choose to engage in consultation should be careful not to do so in a way that effectively "co-
erces" teachers to join a particular organization. Such was the underlying concern behind the case of *San Antonio Federation of
Teachers v. San Antonio I.S.D.*

In that case the San Antonio Federation of Teachers challenged
the school board's agreement with the San Antonio Teacher's Council because the agreement recognized the Teacher's Council as the
sole agent for consultation. The Federation argued that this "exclu-
sivity" provision was coercive, since the only way teachers could
participate in consultation would be through the favored organization. The commissioner agreed. In a 1980 ruling the commissioner
declared that such an exclusive agreement violated the provision in
the Code which prohibits coercing teachers to join groups, clubs,
committees, or organizations.

Just as school boards must be careful to avoid an appearance of favoritism toward a particular group, so must administrators. An interesting illustration concerns an assistant principal in Ysleta I.S.D. The assistant principal stated at a faculty meeting that he was a member of the Association of Texas Professional Educators (ATPE) and would be available to talk with interested teachers about the organization. A faculty member objected to his statement, considering it a subtle form of coercion and thus a violation of the Code. Later, the school board approved a resolution stating that, since solicitation of membership by administrators can be construed as coercive, "administrators should not participate in the recruitment of members of professional organizations to which teaching personnel are eligible to belong." The resolution went on to specify that such presentations should be made by other teachers rather than administrators. Excluded from the board resolution were other organizations, such as PTA and booster clubs. ATPE appealed the resolution to the Texas Commissioner of Education, who ruled that the resolution was overly broad, and, therefore, unenforceable. As the commissioner noted, the resolution as written prohibited administrators under *any* circumstances from recruiting members for professional organizations. The commissioner noted that a narrowly worded resolution would be valid "if specifically restricted to apply to administrators only at those times when the administrators are performing their duties of employment." The commissioner added that even in the absence of a policy "any administrator would be well advised to avoid soliciting membership in a professional organization at any time when a teacher might reasonably perceive that the administrator is acting in his or her capacity as a superior addressing his or her subordinate" (*Association of Texas Professional Educators v. Ysleta I.S.D.*).

What Is Grievable: The Changing Landscape

Texas public school employee organizations have one significant thing in common with traditional labor unions: the right to represent their members in grievance proceedings. Indeed, the brave new world of expansive grievance procedures has been a tremendous boon to employee organizations. In a legal world devoid of collective bargaining and strikes, grievances have given the organizations a whole new service to offer their members.

Any discussion of grievances immediately implicates both a provision of the Texas Constitution and Section 617.005 of the Government Code, which, as we have seen, allows employees to present grievances. The constitutional provision is Article I, §27, which in one form or another has been part of the Texas Constitution since 1845. It provides that "the citizens shall have the right, in a peaceable manner, to . . . apply to those invested with the powers of government for redress of grievances . . . by petition, address, or remonstrance."

Two significant things happened with regard to employee grievances in the public sector in the 1980s. First, the scope of what is "grievable" expanded tremendously. Second, the responsibility of school administrators and board members to hear grievances was spelled out in some detail for the first time.

Most school districts have had some form of grievance process for decades. But for many years the process was virtually unusable. A bold teacher would occasionally inquire about filing a grievance over a reassignment, or language in the teacher's contract, or perhaps teaching load, only to be informed that "that's not grievable." What was "grievable" appeared to many to be a moving target, diminishing in size. It was understood that teachers could grieve over "wages, hours, and conditions of work," but those terms were narrowly construed. Many "conditions of work" were considered management prerogatives, or features of the board's exclusive authority, and thus not a proper subject for a grievance.

All that changed with an attorney general's opinion and a series of decisions from the commissioner. In 1984, Attorney General Jim Mattox was asked about the scope of employee grievances under Texas law. Specifically, the attorney general was asked to outline "conditions of work" which were the proper subject of a grievance. Mattox opined that the term "conditions of work" could not be construed to "restrict, limit, narrow, or exclude" any aspect of the employment relationship from the grievance process. Mattox concluded his opinion [*Att'y. Gen. Op. JM-177*]:

> the term "conditions of work" should be construed broadly to include any area of wages, hours, or conditions of employment, and any other matter which is appropriate for communications from employees to employer concerning an aspect of their relationship.

Thus the door opened wide. It is now clear that employees have the right to grieve virtually anything. Grievances are routinely filed over assignments and reassignments, appointments to extra duty, salary and merit pay, the wording of reprimands or other written communications. If an employee is terminated and has no other means of complaining of the decision, a grievance can be filed. Thus an at-will employee can grieve the termination. A probationary teacher whose contract is nonrenewed cannot invoke the independent hearing process, but he can file a grievance.

The last bastion of the old "not grievable" defense had to do with personnel evaluations. Administrators argued that the evaluation process was highly subjective and dependent on personal observation by a skilled and trained observer. Although they conceded that the Texas Teacher Appraisal System allowed a teacher to grieve a procedurally marred evaluation (e.g., the evaluator failed to observe the classroom for the forty-five-minute period required by law), administrators argued that teachers should not be permitted to complain of the actual, substantive content of the evaluation.

For almost two years, despite intense pressure, the commissioner avoided the subject of grievances over the content of evaluations. In December 1987, however, the commissioner issued two decisions that answer various questions concerning appraisal complaints and grievance procedures. In the first, *Etzel v. Galveston I.S.D.*, the commissioner held that the content of an evaluation was grievable as a "condition of work." In *Etzel*, a teacher grieved a procedural violation of the appraisal processes as well as the rating received. The commissioner concluded that the complaint concerning the evaluation *procedure* should have been allowed to be presented to the board under the district's policy. He also concluded that the complaint regarding the evaluation *content* could appropriately "be concluded" at the level of the district superintendent. The commissioner noted that a board, not trained in the Texas Teacher Appraisal System, was not qualified to substitute its judgment for that of a trained evaluator on a professional matter of judgment on appraisal scores *unless* there was some evidence of a procedural defect that resulted in an incorrect rating. The commissioner then hedged on those statements about concluding grievances at the level of the superintendent, however, by observing that an opportunity to address concerns to the board (presumably including those about the content of an evaluation) in an open forum would satisfy both the requirements of Article I, §27 of the Texas Constitution, which allows persons to present complaints to governmental entities, and Texas statutory law.

The second case, *Falvey v. Alief I.S.D.*, also dealt with grievances over the content of evaluations. A teacher demanded a hearing before the board to formally grieve her evaluation, but the board refused. The district had an open-forum policy, but the teacher did not request to be heard through that channel. Following the same reasoning as in *Etzel*, the commissioner concluded that the teacher was entitled to present her grievance by meeting informally with her evaluator and, ultimately, her superintendent. According to the commissioner, both are in a "position of authority" to address grievances over the content of evaluations under state law. The commissioner concluded by again noting that in most circumstances a board of trustees is not an appropriate entity to consider grievances concerning content of evaluations. However, he noted that a district's allotment of a forum wherein employees have the opportunity to present grievances to the board satisfies the statutory requirements of Article 5154c, §6, and the constitutional requirements of Article I, §27.

The message was reasonably clear. Teachers had to be permitted to file grievances over the content of an evaluation. Those grievances were "heard" as long as they were heard by the superintendent, or some other administrator empowered to take action. And as long as the school board permits an "open forum" for hearing complaints (see the discussion below), it has carried out its duty to the employee.

But what happens if the board insists on hearing and *granting* the grievance? Can a board, neither trained nor certified in the appraisal process, reverse the substantive decision of the appraiser? That interesting situation came before the commissioner in 1991. A teacher filed a grievance with the board of trustees over the contents of her appraisal. The assistant principal who conducted the appraisal denied credit to the teacher on two of the seventy-two indicators on the TTAS. The school board granted the grievance, thus awarding the teacher credit for the two indicators. Then it was the assistant principal's turn to grieve. Noting that she was certified and trained to conduct TTAS appraisals, whereas the members of the school board were not, the assistant principal asked the board to reverse itself, and deny credit for the two indicators. Not surprisingly, the board refused to do so. So the assistant principal appealed to the Texas Commissioner of Education. Following his previous admonitions to school board members not to substitute their judgment for that of trained evaluators, the commissioner granted the assistant principal's grievance (*Navarro v. Ysleta I.S.D.*). This appeared to send a loud and clear message to school boards—don't change appraisal ratings for a teacher.

However, that was not the end of the story. The teacher took the case to Travis County District Court, where the judge took a slightly different approach. The judge ruled that the school board does have the authority to review the educational judgment of an appraiser, and may award credit if the appraiser's judgment "was clearly erroneous or an abuse of discretion." Moreover, the judge ruled that the commissioner also had the authority to overrule the appraiser. "The Commissioner," according to the court's ruling, "must make an independent decision as to whether the appraiser's educational judgment was clearly erroneous or an abuse of discretion" (*Heredia v. Central Education Agency*, 1992).

This case then went back to the Texas Education Agency for a second time, where the commissioner again ruled in favor of the assistant principal. Applying the district court's criteria, the commissioner ruled that the decision of the assistant principal was neither clearly erroneous nor an abuse of discretion. The commissioner observed that "the abuse of discretion standard is not met simply because a disagreement exists as to who is correct" (*Navarro v. Ysleta I.S.D.*, 1994).

Keen observers will note that this is an extraordinary amount of legal and administrative energy over the denial of credit on two indicators on a single appraisal. Such is the world of grievances. No doubt both sides felt there were larger issues at stake. The final lesson of this saga is that teachers can grieve over the contents of an evaluation, and can get the evaluation changed if they can persuade someone higher up that the evaluation was an abuse of discretion or clearly erroneous. Those are two historically slippery terms.

Hearing Employee Grievances

While the "grievable" door swung wide open in the 1980s, we also learned just what it means to present a grievance and what the employer must do to "hear" the grievance. In a nutshell, the case law has made it clear that a grievance significantly differs from a situation in which a due process hearing is necessary. The common operative term is "stop, look, and listen."

The first significant case on the subject was *Professional Association of College Educators v. El Paso County Community College District* (hereafter referred to as *"PACE"*). In *PACE*, the appeals court held that Article I, §27 of the Texas Constitution does not require school boards to negotiate or even respond to grievances and complaints filed by those being governed, "but surely they must stop, look, and listen." The constitution simply requires school boards to "consider" the grievances addressed to them by citizens, including the district's employees.

According to *PACE*, whether a board appropriately considers a grievance (or remonstrance) under the "stop, look, and listen" standard will be determined as follows. A board which, when presented with a remonstrance, immediately files it in a waste basket can hardly be said to have "considered" it. A board which delays action upon a remonstrance in order to study and deliberate on the issues presented will quite clearly have "considered" a remonstrance, particularly if it modifies or changes its decision upon the issue confronting it. In between these extremes, the board may "consider" the remonstrance by reading it, perhaps on occasion having discussions, and then proceeding to act contrary to the contentions raised in the remonstrance.

Thus, "consideration" of grievances is the measure required of school boards by the Texas Constitution. One pundit has suggested that boards purchase a "Consid-O-Meter," to be attached by electrodes to the brain cells of each board member. Until such a device is invented, schools will have to go through a more cumbersome method of proving that they gave the matter "consideration."

The consideration issue arose in the public school context in *Corpus Christi I.S.D. v. Padilla* (1986). In *Padilla*, two employees claimed that the school district denied them their constitutional and statutory rights when it refused to give them a grievance hearing before the board of trustees. While the employees could have presented their grievances to the board during the "open-forum" portion of the board's meetings, the employees refused to do so.

Speaking first to the constitutional claim, the court held that Article I, §27 of the Texas Constitution only guarantees citizens "access to the government's ear." The "government" of a school district is its school board. According to the court, although a school board does not have a duty to provide formal procedures for citizens to vent their complaints, it must "consider" petitions or grievances. An open forum at each board meeting suffices to provide the constitutionally required access to the school board.

The court *then* addressed the relevant state statute (at that time Article 5154c, §6, now found at Government Code Section 617.005). Unlike the constitutional provision, the statute does not require that employees be afforded the opportunity to present grievances to the school board. The statutory right of employees to present grievances over conditions of work simply requires access to someone "in a position of authority" who could rectify the grievance if he or she found it to be valid. In *Padilla*, the court concluded that the superintendent was a "person in authority" over the work assignments that the employees were grieving in that case. He had heard and denied the employees' grievances. Since the statutory right of the employees to present their grievances to a person in authority was not violated, and since the employees chose not to exercise their constitutional right as citizens to present their grievances in the open forum section of a school board meeting, the court in *Padilla* granted a summary judgment against the employees on both their statutory and constitutional claims.

The Texas Commissioner of Education clarified the responsibilities of school officials in hearing grievances in *Malone v. Houston I.S.D.* (1987). The case involved a coach's grievance concerning his reassignment from the position of head basketball coach. The district had refused to permit him to grieve the reassignment through the grievance process. The commissioner concluded that the district erred. A district has three options in hearing a grievance, according to the commissioner: "It may consider the substance of the grievance; that is, stop, look, and listen, and not respond. It may consider the grievance and act upon it. The district may consider the grievance and deny it. But in no event can a district fail to consider a grievance concerning a condition of work."

In *Malone* the commissioner clearly set out the dichotomy between employee grievances to the superintendent as the "person in authority" and the constitutional presentment of concerns to the board under Article I, §27: "The superintendent, in most board policies, is the chief executive officer of the district and the administrative head of the school system. As such, the superintendent is in a position of authority able to remedy employee grievances. Thus, presenting a grievance to the superintendent meets the 'presentment' requirements of Art. 5154c, Sec. 6 [now Government Code 617.005]. Should an employee wish to present his concern to the board of trustees, he or she may do so pursuant to the constitutional right set forth in Art. I, §27, regardless of any limitation contained in local board policy."

Suppose a school board gets tired of hearing teacher grievances and citizen complaints. Can it adopt a policy limiting employees to written complaints, thus saving the board the time involved in actually hearing verbal presentations? According to the commissioner, the board can do so. In a 1993 decision the commissioner ruled that such a school board policy did not violate a person's right of presentment under the Texas Constitution (*Beaumont Teachers Association v. Beaumont I.S.D.*).

One other case gives significant guidance in understanding the grievance procedures required by state law. Employee grievances may be presented individually or combined for a group presentation, according to the court of appeals decision in *Lubbock Professional Firefighters v. City of Lubbock* (1987). Like many school districts, the city of Lubbock prohibited its employees from filing "group grievances." The city's practice was held to violate state law. The

court held the employees have the right either to present their grievances individually or to combine them together for a group presentation. These are not "class action" grievances, however, since the
court held that the grievance must name the individual employees
bringing any group grievance. Although the case deals with firefighters rather than teachers, it is applicable to all political subdivisions, including school districts.

However, if a school district fails to challenge the right of an
employee organization to file a grievance, it may waive the possibility of complaining of it later. Such was the case in *Josh v. Beaumont
I.S.D.*, a 1993 decision of the Texas Commissioner of Education. In
a dispute over salaries of a large group of employees, the Beaumont
Teachers Association (BTA) filed the grievance on behalf of many of
its members. The school district asked that BTA be removed from
the case. But since the district had heard and acted on the BTA's
grievance at the local level, the commissioner refused to do so.

In summary, public employees in Texas are entitled to grieve
just about anything, so long as they understand that the powers-
that-be are required only to listen to those grievances. A public-
forum presentation to the school board will suffice, as will a written
presentation. This should not unduly burden school administrators
or boards.

However, school administrators sometimes feel burdened by
teachers who will not meet with their supervisors unless a professional representative is present. Can a teacher do this? Suppose a
principal wants to meet with a teacher to discuss complaints which
have been made concerning the teacher. The teacher refuses to meet
with the principal until her TSTA (Texas State Teachers Association) representative can be present. Does the principal have to post-
pone the meeting until the teacher's spokesperson can participate?
No. According to *Arce v. Ysleta I.S.D.*, a public employee does not
have a right to representation during a supervisory conference, even
when disciplinary measures may be taken as a result of the conference. The commissioner discussed the application of the statute
then found at Article 5154c, Section 6 to this situation:

> Although Art. 5154c Sec. 6 is broad in scope, this section governs the pre-
> sentment of grievances to an employer. This is a situation in which the
> public employee is approaching the public employer with concerns about
> conditions of work, wages or hours. This situation differs from the case at
> hand, in which the employer is making inquiries with regard to [the em-
> ployee's] work and actions. This provision does not extend to employer-

employee conferences, nor has it been interpreted by the courts to extend to such conferences.

A similar dispute arose in a 1991 case, after a parent requested a conference with the teacher over problems the student was experiencing in the teacher's class. The counselor set up the conference. When the conversation focused on the student's relationship with the teacher, the teacher walked out. Concerned about possible disciplinary action, the teacher maintained she was entitled to legal representation. The principal later placed a letter of reprimand in the teacher's file. The teacher complained of the reprimand, and carried the matter to the Texas Education Agency. The Texas Commissioner of Education denied the teacher's grievance. Parent-teacher conferences in the district were found to be informal, noninvestigatory proceedings used as administrative tools. No disciplinary action stemmed from participating in them. Thus, the teacher had no need for representation. The commissioner noted that the conference involved confidential information about the student. Having a third-party representative present would undermine the confidentiality. The commissioner noted that "a teacher has no right to representation outside a formal grievance proceeding" (*Thrower v. Arlington I.S.D.*).

Though the *Arlington* case may seem to imply that teachers are entitled to representation in conferences which could lead to disciplinary action, the *Ysleta* decision clearly rejects that implication. It appears, then, that an employee is entitled to representation when the employee initiates the conference to complain of wages, hours, or conditions of work. When the employer initiates the conference to discuss concerns or complaints, the employee cannot insist upon representation.

It is important to note, however, that the employee's right of representation applies at the first stage of the grievance proceedings, as well as the presentment to the superintendent and school board. This issue was addressed in the Lubbock Firefighters case. As in many school district grievance policies, the Lubbock policy provided an informal first level for employee grievances from which employee representatives were prohibited. The court struck down this practice, holding that the employee has the right to legal representation at any level, including the informal stage of a grievance.

Finally, school administrators should be particularly careful about protecting the rights of employees to file grievances after the commissioner's decision in the case of *Sitzler v. Babers* (1992). In that case a teacher filed a complaint with the now-abolished Teachers' Professional Practices Commission, asserting that her former principal had, among other things, told prospective employers that the teacher had filed three grievances and had caused chaos on the campus. The PPC considered this retaliatory action and recommended an official reprimand of the principal. But when the case came before the commissioner for final action, he felt that "a more severe sanction" was called for. The commissioner revoked the principal's mid-management certificate.

SUMMARY

While Texas law does not allow public school personnel to engage in collective bargaining activities, teachers may join professional associations, which act much like unions. In recent years, employees' right to present grievances has taken on a broad new dimension. Employees may grieve virtually anything, either individually or through a representative. Moreover, they are entitled to representation throughout the entire grievance process, from the first level through an appeal to the board. All this has created an important new role for employee organizations in Texas public education. The law has clarified the duty of the school to "hear" and "consider" the grievance all the way through the system.

SIX

Expression and Associational Rights

IN A DEMOCRATIC society, rights of expression are especially valued. Included in the term "rights of expression" are freedom of speech, freedom of the press, and freedom of assembly and association—in short, the key provisions of the First Amendment in the Bill of Rights. The First Amendment reads: "Congress shall make no law respecting an establishment of religion, or prohibiting the free exercise thereof; or abridging the freedom of speech, or of the press, or the right of the people peaceably to assemble, and to petition the Government for a redress of grievances." The religion components of the First Amendment will be discussed in the next chapter. By virtue of the Fourteenth Amendment, the provisions of the First Amendment apply to public school districts.

The counterpart to the First Amendment in the Texas Constitution is Article I, §8, which states in part, "Every person shall be at liberty to speak, write or publish his opinions on any subject, being responsible for the abuse of that privilege; and no law shall ever be passed curtailing the liberty of speech or of the press." While plaintiff's attorneys rarely have used the Texas free speech clause in the past, they are utilizing it more now because of the expansive interpretation given it by the Texas Supreme Court in a 1992 decision (*Davenport v. Garcia*). The decision is instructive in describing the development of the free speech clause in the Texas Constitution. The court noted that Article I, §8 affords greater protection to free speech than the First Amendment, adding that "it has been and remains the preference of this court to sanction a speaker after, rather than before, speech occurs." In 1995 the U.S. Court of Appeals for the Fifth Circuit noted that the drafters of the Texas Constitution rejected the language of the First Amendment, preferring instead broader support for free speech. Thus, a claim under Article I, §8 is not the equivalent of a claim under the First Amendment (*Carpenter v. Wichita Falls I.S.D.*). At the same time, it is important to note that the remedies available under the state provision are less extensive than under the First Amendment. The Texas Supreme Court ruled in 1995 that, unlike federal law and the First Amendment, state law does not allow damages for a violation of free speech and assembly under Article I of the Texas Constitution. Remedies are limited to declaratory and injunctive relief and to such actions as re-instatement and back pay (*City of Beaumont v. Boullion*).

Expression issues often surface in disputes over employee non-renewal or termination and student discipline. Employees and students often argue, sometimes with good reason, that the actions taken against them were in retaliation for the exercise of free speech. Exactly what rights of expression and association Texas public employees and students are entitled to is the focus of this chapter. Since private school employees and students cannot assert a cause of action under either the federal or state constitutions in their schools (see Chapter 1 for a general discussion), the extent to which these rights are protected in that setting depends upon the policies of the institution with which they are affiliated.

EDUCATOR RIGHTS OF EXPRESSION

Expression outside the School

Frequently, it is asserted that public school teachers and administrators have the same civil rights outside school as do any other citizens. While this claim has some truth, it is also true that the educator's job may be in jeopardy if the exercise of a right undermines job effectiveness. A brief review of key U.S. Supreme Court decisions in this area will make this point clear.

The most important case insofar as educator rights of expression are concerned is *Pickering v. Board of Education* (U.S. Supreme Court, 1968). *Pickering* involved a teacher who was dismissed from his job for sending a letter critical of the school board to a local newspaper. Both the school board and the lower courts concluded that the letter, which contained some false statements, was detrimental to the interests of the school system and that the interests of the school should take precedence over the teacher's claim to freedom of expression. But the U.S. Supreme Court ruled unanimously that the school board was wrong in firing the teacher. Justice Thurgood Marshall, who wrote the opinion in *Pickering*, sought to balance the teacher's rights of expression on public issues outside school with the legitimate interests of the school board in assuring an efficient and orderly learning environment in school. Since the statements in the letter were not aimed at any person with whom the teacher would come in contact in carrying out his duties, and the falsehoods were not carelessly made nor did they impede school operations, the Supreme Court concluded that the teacher should not have been dismissed. In a later case, the U.S. Supreme Court extended the *Pickering* principle in a unanimous decision upholding a teacher's right to speak out at a school board meeting about employment matters (*City of Madison v. Wisconsin Employment Relations Commission*, 1976).

What is interesting about *Pickering* is that, while it does convey substantial support for teacher expression outside school, it also contains some caveats. The Court did not state that educators have an unrestricted, absolute right to freedom of expression outside school. In fact, Justice Marshall openly acknowledged that the government "has interests as an employer in regulating the speech of its employees that differ significantly from those it possesses in connection with regulation of the speech of the citizenry in general" (p. 568). If it can be shown that the statements are made recklessly or with knowledge of their falsity, that school functioning or the teacher's performance is impaired, or that the superior-subordinate relationship is undermined, then sanctions, including dismissal, might appropriately be brought against the employee. For example, in a 1990 decision by the U.S. Court of Appeals for the Fifth Circuit, Frank Nieto, a school maintenance supervisor, was discharged after he complained that the school's basketball coach was abusing students. Nieto had conducted his own investigation, which included pulling students out of class for questioning. Teachers complained that his actions were highly disruptive. The court held that Nieto's speech was of public concern, but the public interest was outweighed by the district's interest in "promoting the public services it performs" (*Nieto v. San Perlita I.S.D.*).

Pickering is an important case, for it recognizes that educators— and, by implication, all public employees—do have a substantial right to freedom of expression as citizens in the community. It is also important because it conveys to administrators the burden of documentation they must shoulder to take adverse action against an employee who they believe has abused the right. For example, in *Alaniz v. San Isidro I.S.D.*, the Fifth Circuit upheld a lower court ruling in favor of the school district's deputy tax assessor-collector, who was fired after an opposition political party won control of the board. Romula Alaniz had actively supported the policies and candidates of the incumbent party, headed by her brother-in-law. She maintained that she would not have been fired but for her First Amendment political activities. She was awarded $51,000 in back pay and $40,000 in compensatory damages for mental anguish and emotional distress and was ordered to be reinstated to her position.

The extent of free speech rights under the *Pickering* ruling is more limited for public employees who occupy policy-making or confidential positions. This is clear from a 1992 ruling of the U.S. Court of Appeals for the Fifth Circuit involving the removal of the superintendent in the Salado I.S.D. The superintendent, Nolan Kinsey, had supported a losing slate of candidates in a school board election. While he had not openly campaigned or made financial contributions, he had voiced support for his choices in conversations with Salado citizens and expressed concerns about the opposition. When the opposition won and became a majority on the school board, the relationship between Kinsey and the board deteriorated. Eventually, he was removed from his position. Kinsey filed suit, claiming that his removal was in retaliation for his exercise of First Amendment rights in connection with the school board election. The litigation involved several trips to the courthouse, the last of which was in 1992 when the Fifth Circuit, sitting *en banc*, upheld his removal by a thirteen-to-two vote (*Kinsey v. Salado I.S.D.*). The majority noted that the *Pickering* balancing test favored the public employer in this case, given the close working relationship between the superintendent and the school board. "[I]n light of his high-level policymaker and confidential position, Kinsey stepped over the line . . . in so doing, he abandoned any shelter otherwise provided him by the First Amendment" (p. 996).

In a 1995 decision related to the election process, the U.S. Supreme Court ruled seven-to-two that the distribution of anonymous fliers is a form of core political speech protected by the First Amendment. The case involved the circulation of anonymous leaflets protesting a proposed school tax levy in an Ohio school district. School officials filed a complaint with the Ohio Elections Commission, which fined the person $100 for violating an election law that required a name and address on every piece of campaign literature, including homemade handbills. Writing for the Court, Justice John Paul Stevens held the law unconstitutional, pointing out that "Anonymity is a shield from the tyranny of the majority" (*McIntyre v. Ohio Elections Commission*).

In 1977, the Supreme Court again addressed the issue of employee expression rights outside school. In *Mt. Healthy City School District Board of Education v. Doyle*, a marginally qualified teacher on a probationary contract made comments critical of the school over a local radio station. The teacher was not given a continuing contract. He asserted that the primary reason was his radio presentation and argued that such expression is a constitutionally protected right. The Court agreed that it is but also was concerned that a marginal candidate not take unfair advantage of the *Pickering* decision by exercising protected expression rights just before an adverse employment decision is to be made. Thus, the Court ruled that the employee first has the burden of proving that the adverse employment decision was substantially based on the exercise of the right. Subsequent case law has established that the person bringing the suit must show at least some circumstantial evidence to prove illegitimate intent. Mere allegations will not suffice (*Thompkins v. Vickers*). This burden was not difficult for Fred Doyle in the *Mt. Healthy* case because the superintendent had sent him a memo in which he listed the radio talk show remarks as a factor in the nonrenewal decision. The lesson for administrators, of course, is not to inform employees that legally impermissible reasons played a substantial role in a negative employment decision.

If the employee is successful in sustaining his burden, the school district then must be given the opportunity of showing that there are other valid reasons, unrelated to the exercise of the right, to support its decision. Where there is a long history of inadequate employee performance, the exercise of expression rights is not likely to make any difference, assuming that the employee's evaluations document the deficiencies and that efforts at remediation have been to no avail. The Supreme Court sent the *Mt. Healthy* case back to the trial court to make this determination, since Doyle had been involved in a number of employment-related incidents. The district court later upheld his termination, a decision affirmed by the Sixth Circuit in 1982.

The so-called *Mt. Healthy* test is often used in employment cases. For example, a white cafeteria worker protested her dismissal several years ago from a predominantly black public school in Mississippi, one of the states within the jurisdiction of the U.S. Court of Appeals for the Fifth Circuit. The worker alleged that the only reason she was released was because she had decided to send her son to a private school, which was largely segregated. As noted in Chapter 2, parents have a constitutional right to select a private school for their children. Since a constitutional right was involved, the burden of justification shifted to the school district to show that she was fired for reasons having nothing to do with the exercise of the right. The school was unable to shoulder this burden, and the court awarded the employee damages, including back pay, attorneys' fees, and reinstatement to her position (*Brantley v. Surles*, 1985).

The outcome was different in a 1989 decision involving the Longview I.S.D. Despite evidence that racial discrimination and retaliation for the exercise of First Amendment rights had played a substantial role in the nonrenewal of an African-American teacher's contract, administrators were successful in convincing William Wayne Justice, a civil rights–oriented federal judge in East Texas, that the nonrenewal was justified. The judge noted that the school district had carefully evaluated the teacher, even to the point of having scripted her classroom performance. The evaluations, he wrote, "form a compelling record of plaintiff's primary weaknesses." On the strength of the evidence, Justice concluded that the school district had established that even in the absence of racial bias and retaliation, it would have decided not to renew the plaintiff's contract (*Johnson v. Longview I.S.D.*). It helped that the district had replaced the teacher with another African-American. The lesson for school administrators is clear: document *job-related deficiencies* carefully and thoroughly so that the *Mt. Healthy* test can be met.

One of the more interesting applications of the *Mt. Healthy* test involves a newspaper's claim of retaliation by a county board of supervisors for critical articles it published about the board. The newspaper argued that the county board became so upset over the articles that the board shifted most of its legal announcements to a competing paper. The newspaper maintained that the switch violated its right to freedom of the press. The Fifth Circuit agreed and sent the case back to the trial court to determine if the county board could advance other reasons unrelated to the First Amendment to justify the switch. The appeals court added that in order to escape any legal liability the supervisors would have to show that "each and every one" of the legal notices had been placed in the competing paper for legitimate reasons (*North Mississippi Communications, Inc. v. Jones*). The important lesson for Texas school boards is not to retaliate against newspapers for critical stories about the school district.

Ordinarily, reassignments are within the discretion of school officials, and most contracts contain a statement that the employee may be reassigned. However, even a reassignment cannot be made in retaliation for an employee's exercise of expression rights. It makes no difference whether the employee has a contract of employment or is employed on an at-will basis. A case in point is a 1987 decision by the Fifth Circuit. The case involved Odessa Reeves, a school administrator of long standing. Reeves was reassigned from being a Chapter I coordinator to director of reading after she had testified on behalf of several teaching assistants who were suing the district over their terminations. She was moved from the central office to the kitchen of a home economics class in a junior high school. She supervised no employees in her new position and for some time did not have a job description. She was required to stay in her office until 5 P.M. while other administrators left at 4 P.M. Previous perquisites, such as reimbursement for attending conferences, were withdrawn. The appeals court agreed with the trial court that the reassignment was an unconstitutional retaliation for her previous trial testimony, a protected form of expression. "To allow a government employer to retaliate via demotion, transfer, or reassignment against an employee's unfavorable trial testimony would undermine the ability of the witness to speak truthfully without fear of reprisal" (p. 31). Since there were no other reasons to support the reassignment, the court, following *Mt. Healthy*, ordered Reeves reinstated to the Chapter I position. While she had voluntarily accepted the lower pay that went with the reassignment, she was entitled to the difference between her former and present pay rate (*Reeves v. Claiborne County Board of Education*).

Expression within the School

Expression within the school has three important dimensions. The first relates to expression outside the classroom but on the school grounds, the second concerns itself with classroom academic freedom, and the third relates to retaliation for speaking out about suspected wrongdoing under the Texas Whistle Blower statute. The first is discussed in this section, and the next two in the following sections.

In 1979 the U.S. Supreme Court ruled that the First and Fourteenth amendments to the U.S. Constitution can under certain circumstances protect private communication between a public school teacher and a school principal (*Givhan v. Western Line Consolidated School District*). At the same time, the Court stated that, since subordinate-superior relations are particularly sensitive, the content of what is said, as well as the time, place, and manner in which it is said, can be taken into account in deciding what is and is not constitutionally protected. This employer-employee relationship factor, while briefly mentioned in *Pickering*, was not particularly stressed in that case.

Following the *Givhan* decision, the U.S. Supreme Court issued two important rulings pertaining to teacher expression within the workplace, the first involving mailboxes and the second involving teacher complaints over working conditions. Both are indicative of a trend toward giving public officials greater control over employee expression on the job.

The first is a 1983 ruling, *Perry Education Association v. Perry Local Educators' Association*. In *Perry*, the Court decided in a narrow five-to-four ruling that school mailboxes are not automatically "public forums" available to teachers, their associations, and others to disseminate information. A public forum is a place where persons and groups can come together for expressive purposes free from government control except in extreme situations, e.g., imminent threat of lawless action. Street corners and public parks are examples of public forums. At the opposite end of the spectrum from the public forum is the closed forum—government property which is traditionally not a place for public communication. A good example is the operating room of a public hospital. The Supreme Court viewed the school mail system to be a closed forum under the school's control and reserved for its use so long as officials are not suppressing expression because they disagree with the message.

The Supreme Court recognized that a school, as part of its control over the mail system, may decide to open up the mail system to certain types of communication but limit it regarding others—in effect, to create a "limited public forum" where certain categories of expression but not others are allowed. A limited public forum can be considered to be midway between a public forum and a closed forum. In the *Perry* case the school permitted its faculty collective bargaining agent to use the internal mail system pursuant to a contract provision but denied access to other employee organizations. It also granted access to certain community groups, such as the YMCA, Cub Scouts, and church organizations. "This type of selective access does not transform government property into a public forum," wrote Justice Byron White.

It is doubtful whether Texas public school systems could grant exclusive use of the mail system to a teacher organization, since Texas does not have a state law allowing schools to grant exclusive recognition rights to one organization. This conclusion is supported by the Fifth Circuit in a 1985 decision involving Garland I.S.D. (*Texas State Teachers Association v. Garland I.S.D.*). The Fifth Circuit also ruled in the *Garland* case that, since the campus itself is not a public forum, the school district could deny all employee organizations access during school hours yet allow other, unrelated groups, such as civic and charitable organizations, to meet with students and faculty during nonclass school hours. However, Garland could not prohibit its teachers from talking among themselves

about TSTA or about labor relations matters on campus unless material and substantial interference with school activity could be
shown, since such speech is protected expression. The decision was
later affirmed by the U.S. Supreme Court.

It is important to note that school district control over the mail
system is not absolute. In *Ysleta Federation of Teachers v. Ysleta
I.S.D.*, the Fifth Circuit applied the *Perry* ruling to a school policy
limiting teacher organizations to a one-time-only use of the school
mail system. The district had opened the mail system to all employee organizations and required prior administrative approval of
the material to be circulated. Failure to secure approval would result in suspension of access to all means of in-school communication, including the mail system. The appeals court returned the case
to the lower court to see if the Ysleta I.S.D. could justify its one-
time-only rule as narrowly drawn and furthering a compelling state
interest, a heavy burden of justification. In the *Garland* case, the
Fifth Circuit observed that Garland I.S.D. could not allow teachers
use of the mail system for internal communication, then restrict
the use to nonlabor matters.

The Ysleta I.S.D. case is also instructive because it sheds light
on the legality of a policy giving the superintendent complete discretion to review all material prior to its distribution by employees
and their organizations. Since the superintendent could deny access
not only to the mail system but also to school bulletin boards and
similar communication vehicles if he determined the intended
communication to be not in conformity with school board policy,
the Fifth Circuit declared the regulation a clear violation of the First
Amendment. The court noted that the *Perry* case involved only the
mail system and that the Supreme Court explicitly denied school
authorities the right to suppress expression through the mail system
because they oppose the speaker's views. The Fifth Circuit agreed
with the lower court that the prior-review policy was constitutionally unacceptable because it did not limit the discretion of the superintendent. The court referred to its 1982 ruling in *Hall v. Board
of School Commissioners*, in which it required prior-review policies
involving teacher expression to have sufficient guidance through
clearly articulated prior-submission procedures and approval standards to prohibit "the unbridled discretion that is proscribed by the
Constitution." The general format of these procedures and standards is discussed later in the chapter in connection with non-
school-sponsored student publications.

Taken together, the *Perry* decision and the later Fifth Circuit
rulings suggest that administrators must be sensitive to employee

First Amendment rights when making decisions about school mailboxes and similar types of communication systems, even when the
decision is to make these school-sponsored channels of communication closed forums.

The second important decision of the U.S. Supreme Court in
the context of in-school employee speech is *Connick v. Myers*,
handed down in April of 1983. That decision involved the issue of
whether employee expression concerning on-the-job complaints is
constitutionally protected and thus cannot be used in a negative
employment decision. By another five-to-four vote, the Court ruled
that such expression is *not* protected and thus *can* serve as grounds
for dismissal. The case involved an assistant district attorney in
New Orleans who constructed a questionnaire dealing with internal
employment matters after an unpleasant run-in with her superior
over a job transfer. Sheila Myers circulated the questionnaire to her
colleagues, asking them to complete it voluntarily. The questionnaire dealt with internal working conditions. When Harry Connick,
Sr., heard about the questionnaire, he fired her. At the time, she was
an at-will employee. (Harry Connick, Sr., is the father of the popular
singer of the same name.)

Reversing a decision of the Fifth Circuit, the high court held
that an employee's speech is protected only when the employee
speaks as a citizen on *matters of public concern* but not when he or
she speaks on matters only of personal interest. Referring repeatedly
to the decision in *Pickering v. Board of Education*, the Court drew a
distinction between expression involving the public interest and expression involving working conditions. Writing for the majority,
Justice Byron White observed that, "when close working relationships are essential to fulfilling public responsibilities, a wide degree
of deference to the employer's judgment is appropriate. Furthermore, we do not see the necessity for an employer to allow events to
unfold to the extent that the disruption of the office and the de-
struction of working relationships is manifest before taking action"
(p. 1692). Justice White added, "We caution that a stronger showing
may be necessary if the employee's speech more substantially involved matters of public concern."

The implications of the *Connick* decision for public school
principals are important. The administrator must determine if the
expression is protected by the First Amendment before recommend-
ing a negative employment decision on this basis. According to a
1994 U.S. Supreme Court decision, this requires that the employer
must "tread with a certain amount of care" by conducting a reasonable investigation to determine what the person said (*Waters v.*

Churchill). Does the expression involve community interests? If the answer is no, it probably is not protected. For example, a teacher who refers to himself as a perfect "10" and to other personnel as "witches" or "bug-eyed troublemakers" is not engaging in protected expression, according to a 1983 decision of the Texas Commissioner of Education (*Bowen v. Channelview I.S.D.*). The teacher, according to the commissioner, "was clearly speaking out as a disgruntled employee with private complaints rather than as a private citizen on a matter of public concern." Similarly, a teacher who spoke out against her principal in a crowded school cafeteria over her evaluation results was not engaging in protected expression, according to another decision of the commissioner of education (*McDaniel v. Vidor I.S.D.*). Nor is a coach who, contrary to the wishes of the athletic director, addressed the school board on the organization of the school district summer recreation program (*Salinas v. Lyford C.I.S.D.*). In the *Salinas* case, the coach argued that the nonrenewal of his supplemental coaching contract was in retaliation for the exercise of his speech rights under Article I, §8 of the Texas Constitution, the counterpart to the First Amendment in the U.S. Constitution. Applying the same community interest/working condition dichotomy used in federal law to the state constitution, the commissioner of education found no evidence that the coach sought to discuss a failure of the district to discharge its duty, expose potential wrongdoing, evaluate district conduct, or voice dissatisfaction with the proposed summer recreation program.

On the other hand, a teacher who complains about the religious components of a school holiday observance program or about sexual harassment of female teachers may well be speaking out on matters of public interest. In *Wells v. Hico I.S.D.*, the Fifth Circuit in 1984 found sufficient evidence to support a jury verdict in favor of two teachers who complained about the school's handling of a federally funded reading program. The program had been the subject of debate in the community. Debate intensified when one of the teachers spoke out at a school board meeting about the program. The contracts of the two teachers were subsequently not renewed. They sued, arguing in part that their nonrenewals were in retaliation for their speaking out. The Fifth Circuit noted that after the school board meeting the two teachers received poor evaluations and that the evaluations included negative comments by the school principal regarding their appearance before the school board. The school was unsuccessful in arguing that the pair would have been nonrenewed even had the expression not occurred—an attempt to meet the conditions set forth in the *Mt. Healthy v. Doyle* ruling.

In recent years, the Fifth Circuit has rejected efforts by public employees to get around the *Connick* decision. One case involved a state junior college professor who tried to claim that her contract nonrenewal was in retaliation for her comments about nepotism, favoritism, and misallocation of funds. The evidence, however, showed that she was mostly concerned with her own job security and had not implicated broader community interests until after the contract nonrenewal. Such "retrospective embellishment" cannot be used to transform unprotected private job complaints into constitutionally protected speech (*Dodds v. Childers*). In another case, the Fifth Circuit rejected an English teacher's claim that the filing of a grievance over her performance evaluation was a substantial reason for the nonrenewal of her contract and thus violated her First Amendment right to petition the government for a redress of grievances (*Day v. South Park I.S.D.*). While there was evidence of retaliation for filing the grievance, the appeals court observed that "An employee's complaint to her superior on a personal matter is no more a matter of public concern when embodied in a letter to him requesting a hearing than it is when spoken to him. . . . [W]e are hesitant to elevate such an employee's complaint to the level of constitutional protection merely because she has asserted it in the form of a grievance" (p. 703).

However, public employees in Texas have a statutory right to present grievances to their employers under Chapter 617 of the Government Code. They also have a right to present a complaint to the school board under Article I, §27 of the Texas Constitution, which allows citizens to "apply to those invested with the powers of government for redress of grievances or other purposes, by petition, address, or remonstrance." In both instances, retaliation is impermissible. Thus, while the action taken against the teacher in the *Day v. South Park I.S.D.* case may not be a violation of free speech, it would still be unlawful under state law.

In one 1991 decision, the Fifth Circuit expressed frustration with cases involving retaliation claims over expression inside the school. The case involved a college professor who alleged that he had been unfairly denied summer employment and salary increases, and that he had suffered other miscellaneous harassments because he had spoken out on the lowering of academic standards and challenged department decisions. The appeals court found that the expression was not constitutionally protected, because it involved complaints about working conditions. However, in the process of deciding the case, the judges observed, "In public schools and universities across this nation, interfaculty disputes arise daily over teaching assignments, room assignments, administrative duties, classroom equipment, teacher recognition, and a host of other relatively trivial matters. A federal court is simply not the appropriate forum in which to seek redress for such harms." The court added, "We have neither the competency nor the resources to undertake to micromanage the administration of thousands of state educational institutions" (*Dorsett v. Board of Trustees for State Colleges and Universities*).

While most of the cases discussed in this section concern teachers, they apply as well to administrators. For example, the Texas Commissioner of Education has upheld an administrator's right to communicate his views regarding professional organizations to members of the teaching staff. The commissioner noted in the 1983 decision: "Certainly a careful administrator can promote his or her professional association to teachers without being coercive. A policy which automatically equates 'recruiting' with 'coercion,' and which does not allow for the consideration of the particular facts and circumstances of each case, represents a substantial infringement on the First Amendment rights of the administrator" (*Association of Texas Professional Educators v. Ysleta I.S.D.*). However, the expression rights of administrators may not be coextensive with those of teachers. The same reasoning used in the *Kinsey* decision discussed above regarding the school superintendent–board relationship may apply to some extent to lower-level administrators as well.

In sum, while a public employee cannot suffer a negative employment decision for exercising free speech rights, the latter are protected only under certain circumstances. In a 1995 decision, the Fifth Circuit identified a three-part test for determining when particular speech by a public employee is protected. Elements of the *Pickering, Connick*, and *Mt. Healthy* U.S. Supreme Court decisions are clearly evident in the test:

> First, the speech must have involved a matter of public concern. Second, the public employee's interest in commenting on matters of public concern must outweigh the employer's interest in promoting efficiency. The third prong of the test is based on causation; the employee's speech must have motivated the decision to discharge the employee. (*Fowler v. Smith*)

In the *Fowler* case, a director of maintenance operations for the Angleton I.S.D. argued that he was terminated because he spoke out against privatizing the district's maintenance, custodial, and food service departments. The Fifth Circuit upheld the district court's ruling that Fowler failed to pass the third test: he could not establish that his protected speech was the basis for the termination. Rather, the school district established that it took the action because the maintenance director admitted using a school truck to pull his boat, kept a pool table in the maintenance building, stored his boat on school property, drove the school vehicle to pool halls, and sent school employees on personal errands.

Academic Freedom

Expression in the classroom is one of the most sensitive areas of education law, for it involves four sometimes clashing interests: the interest of the state and the local school board in seeing that the curriculum reflects the collective will of the community, the interest of the student in having access to knowledge and ideas, the interest of the teacher as a professional in controlling class discussion and choosing instructional methodologies, and the interest of parents in controlling their children's education. Traditionally, legislatures and courts have accorded states and school boards broad authority to determine the curriculum and to control teacher classroom behavior in the kindergarten through twelfth-grade classroom. For example, in a 1968 landmark decision, *Epperson v. Arkansas,* the U.S. Supreme Court struck down an Arkansas statute forbidding the teaching of evolution in the public schools because of its conflict with the constitutional mandate separating church and state. But at the same time, the Court acknowledged that, "by and large, public education in our Nation is committed to the control of state and local authorities" (p. 104). In 1974 the U.S. Supreme Court affirmed a lower court ruling that a state has a right to prohibit discussion of birth control in its public schools (*Mercer v. State*). However, since the Court did not write an opinion in the case, the contours of its decision remain undefined.

In a number of cases, the federal courts, including the Supreme Court, have clearly supported the claim of public college and university professors to a constitutionally protected right of academic freedom in the classroom. The entitlement of public school teachers to the same right has received less judicial attention.

While the U.S. Supreme Court has not yet directly decided a case involving teacher academic freedom in the classroom, individual justices have on occasion expressed at least some support for its existence as a constitutional right. For example, in the *Epperson* case referred to above, Justice Abe Fortas, who wrote the majority opinion, observed that "our courts . . . have not failed to apply the

First Amendment's mandate in our educational system where essential to safeguard the fundamental values of freedom of speech and inquiry and belief" (p. 104). He went on to comment that "it is much too late to argue that the State may impose upon the teachers in its schools any conditions it chooses" (p. 107). In his concurring opinion in that case, Justice Potter Stewart agreed that a state could decide that only one foreign language shall be taught in the public school system, but he doubted that a state could punish a teacher for asserting in the classroom that other languages exist. And in a 1979 ruling upholding New York State's right to deny public school teaching certificates to aliens, Justice Lewis F. Powell noted that, "in shaping the students' experience to achieve educational goals, teachers by necessity have wide discretion over the way the course material is communicated to students" (*Ambach v. Norwick*, p. 78).

While we cannot be sure how the U.S. Supreme Court would rule on the issue of teacher academic freedom in the classroom, we do know the view of the U.S. Court of Appeals for the Fifth Circuit, at least insofar as classroom *discussion* is concerned. In 1980, the Fifth Circuit ruled that public school teachers do have a First and Fourteenth Amendment liberty right to engage in classroom discussion (*Kingsville I.S.D. v. Cooper*, 1980). The case involved a teacher of American history in the Kingsville, Texas, school system. The teacher, Janet Cooper, had taught on one-year term contracts for several years, her contract being renewed annually. In the fall of 1971, Cooper employed a simulation exercise to introduce her students to the characteristics of rural life during the post-Civil-War Reconstruction era. The role-playing triggered controversy in the classroom and in the community. In a subsequent consultation with her principal and the district personnel director, Cooper was admonished "not to discuss Blacks" in class and that "nothing controversial should be discussed in the classroom." However, she was not advised to discontinue the simulation exercise, and hence she completed the project with her class. In the spring Cooper was again recommended for reemployment by the principal and superintendent. But, contrary to their recommendation, the board of trustees declined to issue her a contract.

The appeals court upheld the lower court's finding that Cooper's constitutional rights had been violated, declaring that "we thus join the First and Sixth Circuits in holding that classroom discussion is protected activity" (p. 1113). The court went on to declare that the proper test to determine if a teacher has abused the right is "not whether substantial disruption occurs but whether such disruption overbalances the teacher's usefulness as an instructor."

Here there was no evidence that Cooper's usefulness as a teacher had been impaired. Indeed, school administrators had recommended that her contract be renewed. The appeals court affirmed the trial court's order of reinstatement and asked the lower court to reevaluate the amount of back pay and attorneys' fees due her.

Nearly a decade later, the Fifth Circuit refused to extend academic freedom to encompass a teacher's selection of an unapproved supplemental reading list (*Kirkland v. Northside I.S.D.*, 1989). Noting that Timothy Kirkland had not availed himself of school guidelines for compiling history materials, the appeals court took particular offense at the teacher's testimony that he alone had the authority to control the content of his world history class, even to the point of using sexually explicit magazines in classroom discussion. The court likewise took offense at the comments of Kirkland's attorney, who stated that a teacher could limit discussion to subject matter consistent with his own political views. The appeals court summarized its position: "Our decision should not be misconstrued as suggesting that a teacher's creativity is incompatible with the First Amendment, nor is it intended to suggest that public school teachers foster free debate in their classrooms only at their own risk or that their classrooms must be 'cast with a pall of orthodoxy.' We hold only that public school teachers are not free, under the First Amendment, to arrogate control of curricula" (pp. 801–802). The court affirmed the nonrenewal of the teacher's contract.

Kirkland's case was weakened by the fact that he had not made an issue of the supplemental reading list until after his contract was nonrenewed. It is possible that a more direct challenge involving a teacher's use of supplemental reading materials under a different set of facts could lead to a different result. For example, in a decision predating the Fifth Circuit's *Kirkland* decision, a Texas federal district court ruled that in the absence of school directives on the use of supplemental materials, "a teacher has a constitutional right protected by the First Amendment to engage in a teaching method of his or her own choosing, even though the subject matter may be controversial or sensitive" (*Dean v. Timpson I.S.D.*, p. 307). The case involved the termination of a teacher who introduced a sex-role survey printed in *Psychology Today* into her psychology and speech classes.

The Texas Commissioner of Education has also viewed the authority of the school board over the curriculum broadly. Recall that §11.151(b) of the Texas Education Code states that the trustees "have the exclusive power and duty to govern and oversee the management of the public schools of the district." In a 1980 decision, the commissioner of education cited the predecessor to this provision in striking down a teacher challenge to school board authority to specify the materials and techniques for teaching sex education (*Vawter v. Bandera I.S.D.*). The teachers argued that the board resolution severely and unduly restricted their ability to properly teach sex education. In his ruling, the commissioner observed that "it is difficult to imagine an area over which the Respondent's Board of Trustees may more appropriately exercise its broad managerial powers than that of determining which teaching resources and techniques are to be approved for a given course of study. As the Respondent undoubtedly possesses the authority in its schools to cease the teaching in its schools of sex education altogether, how can it be argued that Respondent lacks authority to determine how and by what means and techniques the subject will be taught?"

In *Villa v. Marathon I.S.D.* (1984), the commissioner decided against a teacher who claimed his right to academic freedom was violated when he was ordered not to show a movie to his science class. Though there was no district policy governing use of movies, the commissioner noted that the movie, entitled *The Prejudice Film*, had been approved by the administration for showing to the teacher's health class but had been deemed inappropriate for his science class. Noting that "a school district must have the right to require its teachers to teach science during science class," the commissioner rejected the man's claim. He upheld the nonrenewal of the teacher's contract for failure to follow the film directive, as well as other directives relating to the teacher's performance as a coach.

While teacher discussion rights in the classroom—as contrasted with the right to control teaching methodology—are protected under the weight of judicial authority, they can be abused and lose their protection. A 1985 decision of the Texas Commissioner of Education makes this clear. The decision, *Whalen v. Rocksprings I.S.D.*, involved a seventh-grade science teacher who became involved in an extended question-and-answer session with her class that encompassed matters related to sex education. In the course of responding to questions about AIDS, contraceptives, and the development of sperm, the teacher engaged in what school officials considered unnecessarily graphic description harmful to the emotional well-being of students of that age and grade level in the largely rural community. For example, with regard to learning more about sperm, the teacher advised male students in her class to go home, lock the bathroom door, and masturbate. The teacher was dismissed in midyear following a due process hearing, a dismissal the commissioner of education upheld, though with some reservations. He noted that what might not be appropriate in a rural community could very well be acceptable in an urban setting. The commissioner stated that, for a teacher to show that his or her comments were protected by academic freedom, the teacher has to show that the comments were reasonably relevant to the subject matter of the class, had a demonstrated educational purpose, and were not proscribed by a school regulation. The last condition is interesting in light of the *Kingsville* decision, where the Fifth Circuit found such a proscription unconstitutional. In any case, it is clear that at some point a teacher's classroom discussion will lose its protected status and could serve as grounds for contract nonrenewal or termination.

In 1995 the commissioner declared that "instructing students is part of the school's curriculum and therefore constitutes matters of private concern" (*Hammonds v. Mt. Pleasant I.S.D.*). This statement seems at odds with the Fifth Circuit's *Kingsville* ruling that classroom discussion is protected expression, even in the face of a directive not to discuss controversial topics. The *Hammonds* decision involved the nonrenewal of a teacher who used sexually explicit plays in her drama class and had students read portions of books containing sexually explicit language, despite directives to the contrary from the principal. The commissioner noted that when classroom expression is related to the school curriculum, "a district may impose restrictions on the expression so long as they are 'reasonably related to legitimate pedagogical concerns.' " The two decisions might be reconciled in that the expression in *Kingsville* involved expression on social and political issues (race relations), while the expression in *Hammonds* involved sexually explicit language deemed inappropriate for high school students.

One type of expression in the classroom that clearly has no constitutional protection is profanity. The U.S. Court of Appeals for the Fifth Circuit concluded in *Martin v. Parrish* in 1986 that use of profanity in a college classroom to "motivate" students is not related to any matter of public concern and is not protected by the First Amendment. The instructor in the case had exhorted his class with words like *hell, damn,* and *bullshit.* He continued to do so after a warning and was terminated. The court found that, since profanity was not germane to the subject matter of the course and had no educational function, it was not necessary to consider the instructor's claim of academic freedom.

In another decision, the Fifth Circuit ruled that academic freedom does not include the right to award a grade. The case involved a professor who contested the request by his department chairman that he award a "B" to a student in his class (*Hillis v. Stephen F.*

Austin State University). The court noted that academic freedom is a murky concept whose "perimeters are ill-defined and the case law defining it inconsistent." The court did not choose to include a teacher's right to award a grade within it. In a 1987 decision, the Texas Commissioner of Education cited the *Hillis* ruling in a case involving a teacher who was told to regrade a paper based on a parent's complaint but delayed doing so. After repeated conferences, the teacher was told to assign the paper a specific grade. Continued delay resulted in termination of his contract. Holding that the teacher had no right to award a grade as a matter of academic freedom, the commissioner noted that the local school board guidelines on grading did not support the teacher's contention that his grading system had to encompass matters of form—for example, neatness, legibility, accuracy. Thus, the teacher was insubordinate in failing to follow the directives of his superiors to award a specific grade based only on content (*Cooke v. Ector County I.S.D.*). In a 1992 decision, the commissioner rejected a teacher's assertion of a contractual right to award a grade. The commissioner added that when a school district grading policy lacks clarity, the principal has the authority to establish directives for its interpretation (*Fleming v. San Marcos I.S.D.*). In a 1994 decision, the commissioner extended the principal's authority to include assignments as well as grading (*Rendon v. Edgewood I.S.D.*).

Given the tenuous nature of the teacher's claim to classroom academic freedom, the following guidelines should be observed:

1. Teachers should be careful not to use their freedom of expression rights within the school in such a way as seriously to erode their ability to work with school administrators and colleagues.
2. Before teachers make any determination for themselves about what they can or cannot do in the classroom, they should endeavor to ascertain what school policy is with respect to curriculum practices and the role of the teacher.
3. While teachers do have a constitutional right in Texas by virtue of the Fifth Circuit decision in *Kingsville* to engage in classroom discussion, the right has not been accorded much support by the Texas Commissioner of Education. Teachers should make sure that the discussion is germane to their subject-matter area, is balanced, and has not undermined their effectiveness.
4. Teachers should proceed with caution when it comes to selecting materials and teaching methodology, as well as awarding

grades. It is always best to check with board policy and administrative directives before proceeding.

Texas Whistle Blower Act

In 1983, the legislature passed a law known as "The Whistle Blower Act" prohibiting a governmental body from retaliating against an employee who reports a violation of law to the appropriate law enforcement authority if the report is made in good faith (Texas Government Code, Chapter 554). An employee or appointed officer who is fired or otherwise penalized for reporting may sue for injunctive relief, money damages, court costs, and attorneys' fees. Prior to an amendment in 1995, damages available to an employee could be extensive. The legislature in 1995 capped the amount of damages available under the act. Compensatory damages that can be awarded for such injury as future pecuniary loss, emotional pain, and mental anguish are now capped at $50,000 for governmental organizations with less than 101 employees, $100,000 for organizations with 101 to 200 employees, $200,000 for organizations with 201 to 500 employees, and $250,000 for organizations with more than 500 employees. Exemplary damages are no longer available. Supervisors can be liable for taking adverse personnel actions against whistle blowers up to a maximum of $15,000. A civil penalty against a supervisor cannot be paid by the employing governmental entity.

The employee has the burden of proving that the adverse personnel action was in retaliation for reporting a violation of the law, though the law presumes this to be the case if the termination occurs within ninety days of making a report. The governmental entity is not liable if it can show that it would have made the same negative employment decision in the absence of the employee's reporting. Before filing suit, the employee must exhaust local administrative remedies, such as a grievance procedure. The law further requires each governmental body to post a sign in a prominent place informing employees of their rights under this statute.

The term "appropriate law enforcement authority" means either law enforcement personnel or someone within the organization that the employee believes is responsible for enforcing the law allegedly violated. Thus, the statute would protect an employee who reports a violation of law to the school board. In one recent case, the superintendent was held to be an appropriate law enforcement authority to whom cafeteria workers could complain about violations of the Fair Labor Standards Act (*Knowlton v. Greenwood I.S.D.*, 1992).

While Texas school districts are generally immune from damage suits, the Whistle Blower Act creates an exception. Thus, the district can bear a heavy burden of responsibility if it upholds retaliatory action against an employee who reports in good faith an alleged violation of the law. The Texas Supreme Court has defined "good faith" to mean an honest belief that the conduct is a violation of the law, a belief that is reasonable in light of the employee's training and experience. The court noted that the act would protect a public employee from retaliation even if the report was erroneous and even if the employee had a malicious motive (*Wichita County, Texas v. Williams*, 1996).

EDUCATOR FREEDOM OF ASSOCIATION

Closely related to the right of expression is the right to assemble and, by implication, to associate. The First Amendment as applied to the states through the Fourteenth Amendment has been construed to guarantee the public school teacher the freedom to associate. A key ruling is *Shelton v. Tucker* (U.S. Supreme Court, 1960). There the Supreme Court struck down an Arkansas statute requiring teachers to file affidavits listing their membership in organizations for the previous five years. Justice Stewart wrote in his majority opinion that "the vigilant protection of constitutional freedoms is nowhere more vital than in the community of American schools" (p. 487). He concluded that "the statute's comprehensive interference with associational freedom goes far beyond what might be justified in the exercise of the State's legitimate inquiry into the fitness and competency of its teachers" (p. 490).

In *Burris v. Willis I.S.D.*, a 1983 decision, the U.S. Court of Appeals for the Fifth Circuit emphasized that a teacher's freedom of association "is closely akin to free speech" and that in a small community like Willis issues affecting local school matters can become matters of great importance. Thus, the Fifth Circuit found sufficient evidence that a vocational director's association with former school board members in a dispute over teacher use of school vehicles went beyond mere friendship and may have triggered the nonrenewal of his contract by a realigned school board. The case was remanded to the trial court to see if the board could show that it was not retaliating against the employee when it nonrenewed his employment. In *Guerra v. Roma I.S.D.*, 1977, a Texas federal district court found that the three-year contracts of four public school teachers with long service in the district were nonrenewed primarily because of their support of and association with an unsuccessful candidate for the school board. While the board advanced reasons for its action, the court found them unconvincing in this pointed statement: "The court finds these reasons an incredible basis for unfavorable action upon the employment contracts of four demonstrably able and praise-worthy teachers whose records were without blemish and who enjoyed the full support of their principal and superintendent. There are too many fish in this milk for me to believe it has not been watered. I find the reasons given pretexts, and their insubstantiality adds weight to the allegations that these teachers suffered political retaliation" (p. 820). The court ordered that the teachers be offered reinstatement and be awarded monetary damages, as well as attorneys' fees.

Also instructive with regard to associational rights is a 1984 decision of the Fifth Circuit involving El Paso Community College. The case involved an association of faculty members and a sister organization of administrators, both of which alleged that the college and its officials discriminated against them by denying them access to the campus mail service while granting the right to others. The groups also alleged that the college and its officials intimidated and discriminated against their members, including the college dean, who was fired. A jury found for two of the five plaintiffs, including the dean, and awarded damages, including attorneys' fees. However, the trial judge did not reinstate the dean to his position. The associations appealed.

The Fifth Circuit explicitly endorsed the right of association and applied it to the right to form, join, and participate in the affairs of unions: " . . . the First Amendment is violated by state action whose purpose is either to intimidate public employees from joining a union or from taking an active part in its affairs or to retaliate against those who do. Such 'protected First Amendment rights flow to unions as well as to their members and organizers' " (*Professional Association of College Educators, TSTA/NEA v. El Paso County Community College District*, p. 262). The court went on to note that, even if the college had not made its mail system a public forum, it could not discriminatorily grant or deny access as a means for advancing or discouraging particular points of view. It cited its *Ysleta* ruling discussed earlier in the chapter in support of this assertion. It also applied its no-discrimination rationale to use of a campus grievance system. The court likewise concluded that the jury had sufficient evidence to find that the dismissal of the dean was in retaliation for his involvement in union activities and to award him damages against the college president. It did not accept the college's argument that the dean got all the due process to which he was entitled. "When presented with a claim that a faculty member was discharged in retaliation for exercising First Amendment rights, a federal court does not sit simply to review administrative findings or to measure the procedural regularity of the process" (p. 1055). However, the court did not order the dean reinstated, noting that, while this would normally be done in a First Amendment case, there might be extenuating circumstances precluding reinstatement. The majority emphasized that where First Amendment matters are concerned a court should deny reinstatement "only in exceptional circumstances." The case was sent back to the lower court for further proceedings.

The type of damages that can result from denial of associational and expression rights is well illustrated by an unreported decision of the Federal District Court for the Western District of Texas involving alleged discrimination against the San Antonio Teacher's Council (SATC) by San Antonio I.S.D. A war of words erupted in 1980 between the organization and the school district over the election of trustees to the school board. The brouhaha escalated. The district then changed some of its policies with respect to teacher associations. SATC found its privileges, such as payroll deductions and use of mailboxes and campus facilities, revoked. The association sued, claiming retaliation for the exercise of protected rights of expression and association.

The court ruled in favor of SATC (*SATC/TSTA v. San Antonio I.S.D.*, 1984). Asserting that retaliation was clearly the motivating factor for the board's actions, the judge ordered the district to pay $21,135 in compensatory and punitive damages to SATC and its officers, plus attorneys' fees and court costs in the amount of $188,281. The school district was also ordered to reinstate all the organization's privileges and to recognize TSTA as the exclusive representative of its teachers, a decision seemingly at odds with Texas state law (see Chapter 5).

Texas statutory law protects the right of association as well. While school districts are precluded by state law from recognizing teacher unions as bargaining agents and from engaging in collective negotiation, Chapter 617 of the Texas Government Code recognizes that "no person shall be denied public employment by reason of membership or nonmembership in a labor organization." (An expanded discussion of the legal framework regarding teacher associations and collective bargaining activities will be found in the previous chapter.) Further, TEC §21.407 prohibits a school district from directly or indirectly coercing a teacher to join any group, club, committee, organization, or association or to refrain from participating in political affairs in the teacher's community. TEC §21.408 provides that professional employees have a right to join or not join any professional association or organization.

STUDENT RIGHTS OF EXPRESSION

Until the mid-1960s, students had few rights in the public school setting. Traditionally, young people were under the control of their parents at home and under the control of teachers and administrators at school. What rights they had within the school depended on the policies of the school district and the practices of its employees. The legal doctrine of *in loco parentis* described the relationship of school personnel to students. Meaning "in place of a parent," it cloaked school personnel with the authority of a parent in supervising students at school. State courts rarely (and federal courts almost never) intervened in the student-school relationship; it would take an extreme case of abuse of *in loco parentis* authority to involve them, much as is the case today with the parent-child relationship.

The 1960s saw dramatic expansion of student constitutional rights, especially in the context of expression and association. There are many reasons—the pressures of minorities for civil rights protection, the liberalism of the Warren Court, the lowering of the age of majority from twenty-one to eighteen, abuses of *in loco parentis* authority in the schools, and student radicalism triggered by the Vietnam War. These and other forces resulted in the U.S. Supreme Court's declaration in the momentous *Tinker v. Des Moines School District* decision in 1969 that "it can hardly be argued that either students or teachers shed their constitutional rights to freedom of speech or expression at the schoolhouse gate" (p. 506).

The student rights movement was short-lived. By the mid-1970s federal courts began to accord greater deference to school district decision making. By the 1980s, the expansion of student rights ended; indeed, some retreat became evident. In the remainder of this chapter we will review some of the important developments pertaining to student constitutional rights of expression and association in the public school.

Communication among Students on Campus

The *Tinker* case involved several high school and junior high students who wore armbands in school signifying their opposition to the war in Vietnam. School officials had learned that something like this might happen and, as a result, had developed a rule that any student who wore an armband to school would be asked to remove it and, if compliance were not forthcoming, would be suspended until the armband was removed. The students, who according to the evidence were sincere in their beliefs, wore the armbands despite the rule and were suspended. Through their parents, they sued the school, claiming the regulation and its enforcement infringed their constitutional right of free speech. In essence, they asked the Supreme Court to grant freedom of expression rights to public school students.

The Supreme Court agreed with the students, noting that the public schools cannot be "enclaves of totalitarianism." "School officials do not possess absolute authority over their students. Students in school as well as out of school are 'persons' under the Constitution. They are possessed of fundamental rights which the State must respect, just as they themselves must respect their obligations to the State. In our system, students may not be regarded as closed-circuit recipients of only that which the State chooses to communicate. They may not be confined to the expression of those sentiments that are officially approved" (p. 511). Supporters regard *Tinker* as the seminal case for opening the school to a variety of ideas.

But the Court did not adopt an "anything goes" viewpoint. At several points, the majority opinion emphasized that student expression in or out of class that "materially disrupts classwork or involves substantial disorder or invasion of the rights of others is, of course, not immunized by the constitutional guarantee of freedom of speech" (p. 513). Since the wearing of the armbands in the public schools of Des Moines had generated no sigificant disturbance within the school, the Court decided for the students.

In a pointed dissent, Justice Hugo Black asserted that the armband-wearing had indeed been disruptive to learning in the school by taking the minds of the students off their schoolwork. "One does not need to be a prophet or the son of a prophet," he wrote, "to know that after the Court's ruling today some students in Iowa schools and indeed in all schools will be ready, able, and willing to defy their teachers on practically all orders" (p. 525). Some commentators believe that Justice Black's prophecy has come true.

What is material disruption and substantial invasion of the rights of others? A riotous situation that prevents students from getting to classes and prevents teachers from teaching certainly falls into this category. For example, in a 1966 case that the U.S. Supreme Court cited with approval in *Tinker*, the U.S. Court of Appeals for the Fifth Circuit upheld a school board regulation prohibiting students from wearing "freedom buttons" when students not wearing them were harassed and disturbances occurred in the halls (*Blackwell v. Issaquena County Board of Education*). Less clear are situations which *might* lead to disruption or invasion of the rights of others if allowed to continue. Consider, for example, the wearing of a *Tinker*-like armband that signifies a day of mourning for the slain leader of a neighborhood gang or that signifies minority student opposition to the school district's use of "Dixie" as its fight song. In these instances, if a suit is brought, the burden is upon school officials to make a convincing showing that their actions in prohibiting expression, or curtailing it once begun, were appropriate under the circumstances. A good illustration is a 1993 California federal court decision involving a school dress code prohibition on the wearing of clothing identifying any college or professional sports team. The school had developed the code as an anti-gang measure. The court ruled that the provision denied elementary and middle school students their *Tinker* right to express support of a college or university or a professional sport team, because there was no evidence of gang activity at their schools. While the court was not supportive of enforcement of the dress code at the elementary and middle schools, it did find that the school district had established a presence of gang activity at the high school and thus could enforce the dress code against such attire in that setting. However, the court added, "[W]e assume that in carrying out their duties defendants will recognize and from time to time review their encroachments on First Amendment rights of their student population and revise any restrictions to conform to the existing situation" (*Jeglin v. San Jacinto Unified School District*). The decision is also noteworthy for its support of protected speech in the context of personal attire and for its conclusion that elementary students, like older students, are entitled to First Amendment protection under *Tinker*. There is a dearth of case law on both points. It should be pointed out that in Texas, school districts have a right to promulgate dress codes under a Fifth Circuit Court ruling (*Karr v. Schmidt*, 1972) and a Texas Supreme Court ruling (*Barber v. Colorado I.S.D.*, 1995). However, it is doubtful that a dress code regulation could prevent students from conveying nondisruptive messages on their attire, e.g., the slogan "Jesus loves me" on a pair of tennis shoes or "You can force me to go to school, but you can't force me to learn" on a sweatshirt.

It is important to note that the *Tinker* case involved symbolic expression that was meaningful to the students and to other persons in the school and the community. By contrast, a male student who dons Mickey Mouse ears at his high school graduation ceremony, walks backwards through the school library, or wears earrings is not engaging in cognitive expression of the type protected in *Tinker*. To claim First Amendment protection, a student has to demonstrate that his conduct conveys a particularized message and to show a strong likelihood that the message will be understood by those who view it. Thus, an Illinois court rejected a student's claim that his First Amendment rights were violated when he was suspended for violating a school rule prohibiting the wearing of earrings. The ban was part of an effort by the school to control gang activity. The court found the student's message was one of "individuality" and a willingness to break school rules to convey it (*Olesen v. Board of Education*). Compare the *Jeglin* decision discussed above on this point.

Further, not all forms of meaningful expression are constitutionally protected. In 1985 the U.S. Supreme Court ruled that indecent expression is entitled to no constitutional protection. *Bethel School District No. 403 v. Fraser* involved a high school senior who used sexual innuendo in a nominating speech during a voluntary school assembly for electing student body officers. The short speech evoked a lively and noisy response from students, including sexually suggestive movements by a few. However, no riotous situation occurred, and the assembly continued on schedule. School officials suspended Matthew Fraser for three days and denied him permission to speak at the graduation ceremony, though he had been elected to do so by his peers. Fraser claimed he used sexual innuendo as a speech technique to gain audience attention. In addition to being an honor student, Fraser was a member of the debate team and the recipient of the top speaker award in statewide debate championships for two consecutive years.

The Supreme Court upheld the sanctions against Fraser. Writing for the seven in the majority, Chief Justice Warren Burger noted that the school has an interest in having students express themselves in an acceptable manner. While *Tinker* protects political speech, there is no constitutional protection for lewd, sexually explicit speech in the educational setting, though such expression might be protected outside school. This ruling gives school officials the authority to restrict the wearing of T-shirts and other apparel emblazoned with slogans and diagrams deemed indecent or in bad taste. Some school districts have developed speech codes to prevent verbal abuse such as racial harassment, obscenity, and profanity. While cases like *Tinker* and *Fraser* give school officials considerable authority over student expression, speech codes need to be carefully developed to avoid intruding upon protected rights. A poorly drafted speech code could run afoul of a 1992 U.S. Supreme Court ruling striking down a St. Paul, Minnesota, ordinance outlawing acts that arouse anger or alarm based on race, color, creed, religion, or gender (*R.A.V. v. St. Paul*). The law was judged unconstitutional because it restricted only a certain form of hate speech, not all hate speech, and thus was not content-neutral.

To sum up, public school students have a constitutional right to express themselves on controversial topics on school grounds so long as they do so without causing material disruption or substantial invasion of the rights of others. Under *Tinker*, students' commentary can pertain to matters involving themselves, the school, or the community. In this sense, their speech rights are broader than those of school employees, who are not protected when they speak out on internal working conditions. However, the *Fraser* ruling denies constitutional protection for student expression that school officials deem to be lewd, profane, or indecent. And, of course, school officials are relatively free to discipline students for engaging in conduct that enjoys no constitutional or statutory protection at all. Hair length, matters of dress, running in the halls, and many other kinds of student conduct fall into this category.

School-Sponsored Student Publications

In 1988 the U.S. Supreme Court ruled in *Hazelwood School District v. Kuhlmeier* that school administrators have broad censorship powers over student newspapers produced under the auspices of the school as long as their actions are based on "legitimate pedagogical concerns" and as long as the school has not by policy or practice converted the school-sponsored student newspaper into a public forum where controversial views can be freely expressed. Justice Byron White differentiated interstudent communication from communication by students through channels maintained by the school. The former is personal in character and protected by the Court's decision in *Tinker v. Des Moines School District*. The school has broad control over the latter, the five-person majority held, because it is part of the school curriculum. Channels of communication maintained by the school include not only school-sponsored publications, such as newspapers and yearbooks, but also theatrical productions and "other expressive activities that students, parents, and members of the public might reasonably perceive to bear the imprimatur of the school" (p. 569). For an activity to fall into the school-sponsored category, the Court noted, it must be supervised by a faculty member and be designed to impart particular knowledge or skills. Thus, a school literary magazine produced under the supervision of a faculty member would likely be a school-sponsored channel of communication, while an assembly program or commencement might not be. To what degree students may have *Tinker* rights of expression in the latter has yet to be determined.

In the words of the Court, educators are entitled to exercise greater control over student expression through school-sponsored channels of communication "to assure that participants learn whatever lessons the activity is designed to teach, that readers or listeners are not exposed to material that may be inappropriate for their level of maturity, and that the views of the individual speaker are not erroneously attributed to the school" (p. 570). The Court thus recognized that, as publisher of a school newspaper or producer of a school play, a school may delete material that the school considers potentially disruptive, ungrammatical, poorly written, inadequately researched, biased or prejudiced, vulgar or profane, or unsuitable for immature audiences.

The dissenters, led by Justice William J. Brennan, Jr., asserted that there was no justification for carving out an exception to *Tinker*-protected student speech. "Instead of 'teaching children to respect the diversity of ideas that is fundamental to the American system,' and 'that our Constitution is a living reality, not parchment preserved under glass,' the Court today teaches youth to discount important principles of our government as mere platitudes" (p. 580).

The decision drew a storm of protest from press associations, civil rights groups, many educators, and students. It was feared that heavy-handed censorship by school officials could result in a resumption of student-produced "underground" newspapers, prevalent in the late 1960s and early 1970s, as students turn away from bland and irrelevant publications controlled by the school. The impact of the law was felt in other ways, too. Along with more authority to control school-sponsored publications came increased responsibility for what is published. News stories surfaced of lawsuits filed by parents against school districts and officials for failure to screen out offensive material. One lawsuit involved the McAllen I.S.D. over insertion of the word "slut" in connection with the yearbook photo of a high school freshman. By the early 1990s, four states had passed laws barring most forms of censorship of student-produced newspapers, and many school districts did so through their own policies.

Some courts have applied the *Hazelwood* rationale to the public school classroom. One of the earliest cases involved a challenge by Florida students and their parents to the discontinuation of a humanities textbook in an elective high school literature course after school officials received complaints from a clergyman about sexually explicit passages in such optional readings as *The Miller's Tale* and *Lysistrata*. The Court of Appeals for the Eleventh Circuit upheld the removal as a curricular decision based upon legitimate pedagogical reasons (*Virgil v. School Board of Columbia County, Florida*, 1989). The appeals court was not comfortable with its decision: "Like the district court, we seriously question how young persons just below the age of majority can be harmed by these masterpieces of Western literature." But the court concluded that it should not second-guess the wisdom of the board's action. Similarly, the Sixth Circuit affirmed a Michigan federal district count ruling that there was no violation of a second grader's free speech rights when the teacher refused to allow the student to show a videotape of herself singing a proselytizing religious song to her class during show and tell (*DeNooyer v. Livonia Public Schools*, 1993). The district court determined that *Kuhlmeier*, not *Tinker*, provided the proper rationale for deciding the case. Thus, the court observed that the teacher had not converted the classroom into a public forum and that the purpose of show and tell was to develop self-esteem through oral presentation, not provide an opportunity for indiscriminate public expression. These decisions raise questions about the extent to which the *Tinker* ruling continues to protect student classroom expression.

Non-School-Sponsored Student Publications

Suppose students wish to circulate literature of their own making on campus. To what extent can school officials regulate this material? The Supreme Court refused to say in the *Hazelwood* case what standards would be appropriate for regulating non-school-sponsored publications. While such student-produced communications fall into the *Tinker*-protected expression category because they are interstudent in character, lower courts in the past have recognized that student rights must be balanced against the school's legitimate interest in an orderly educational environment.

A recent illustration of the problem is afforded by a case involving the Dallas I.S.D. A number of students at Skyline High School challenged a school policy that prevented them from meeting periodically outside the school cafeteria to engage in prayer and reading of the Bible and from distributing religious tracts in front of the school building as students exited from the school buses. The school advanced several arguments in defense of its position. First, the Equal Access Act (to be discussed below and in some detail in the next chapter) provides the exclusive means for students to engage in religious expression on school property. Second, students do not have free speech rights to preach, proselytize, and distribute religious material in large groups on school property. Third, if school officials allow students to engage in these activities, they will be breaching the wall of separation between church and state.

The federal district court rejected all three arguments in a 1992 decision (*Clark v. Dallas I.S.D.*). Basing his decision on *Tinker*, the judge ruled that students have a right to engage in religious speech on campus, as well as to distribute religious materials peacefully. He found neither the *Hazelwood* ruling nor the Equal Access Act germane to the dispute. No school-sponsored publications were involved, and no religious meetings of the type contemplated under the Equal Access Act were being held. "This case involves suppression of a student's personal expression that happens to occur on school premises. . . . The conduct at issue was voluntary, student-initiated, and free from the imprimatur of school involvement" (p. 120).

To balance the interests at stake in cases like this where non-school-sponsored materials are to be distributed on campus, courts in the past have approved a system of prior review, that is, a procedure whereby school officials can review the materials intended for distribution on campus during school hours and screen out that which is deemed inappropriate. Most Texas school districts have adopted a prior-review policy with these components:

1. Criteria that spell out what is forbidden, e.g., materials that constitute hate literature or are obscene, sexually inappropriate, libelous, or disruptive of school operations.
2. Procedures by which students submit proposed materials to be reviewed.
3. A brief period of time during which the principal or other school official must make a decision.
4. An appeal procedure.
5. A reasonable time during which the appeal is to be decided.

Prior-review systems must be carefully worded and applied to withstand constitutional scrutiny. Thus, prior-review policies that screen out material proselytizing a particular religion, that do not contain brief timelines, or place the burden of proving speech to be lawful on the would-be speaker rather than burdening the censor to prove speech unlawful have been struck down in several jurisdictions outside of Texas (*Rivera v. East Otero School District,* 1989; *Slotterback v. Interboro School District,* 1991).

In addition to a prior-review system, school officials also have the right to determine the time, place, and manner of distribution of non-school-sponsored materials. Thus, for example, an Illinois federal district court ruled that a school could limit distribution of *Issues and Answers,* a newspaper published by Student Action for Christ, to exits before and after school and to a place near the cafeteria. The court agreed with the school that hallways and classrooms are not public forums and may be off-limits to distribution (*Nelson v. Moline School District No. 40,* 1989).

The leading Texas case on non-school-sponsored publications dates back to 1972. *Shanley v. Northeast I.S.D.* involved a school effort to ban an underground newspaper produced by students from distribution near and on the school campus. *Shanley* is important for what it says about the limits of school authority. The case involved several seniors at MacArthur High School in the Northeast I.S.D. of San Antonio who were suspended for distributing a student-produced newspaper called the *Awakening* on a sidewalk across from the school one afternoon after school hours and one morning before school opened. The paper had been produced by the students outside school without using any school materials or facilities. The distribution of the paper created no disruption at the time it was handed out or during school hours. The court described the nonschool publication as "one of the most vanilla-flavored ever to reach a federal court" (p. 964).

The students were suspended pursuant to a board policy that "any attempt to avoid the school's established procedure for administrative approval of activities such as the production for distribution and/or distribution of petitions or printed documents of any kind, sort, or type without the specific approval of the principal shall be cause for suspension and, if in the judgment of the principal, there is justification, for referral to the office of the Superintendent with a recommendation for expulsion." In trenchant terms, Circuit Judge Irving Goldberg scolded the school board for exceeding the bounds of its authority: "It should have come as a shock to the parents of five high school seniors in the Northeast Independent School District of San Antonio, Texas, that their elected school board had assumed suzerainty over their children before and after school, off school grounds, and with regard to their children's rights of expressing their thoughts. We trust it will come as no shock whatsoever to the school board that their assumption of authority is an unconstitutional usurpation of the First Amendment" (p. 964).

While the court did not say a school may never discipline students for off-campus behavior unrelated to a school activity, it did note that geographical location is an important determinant in deciding who has jurisdiction—school, parent, police. Thus, "the width of a street might very well determine the breadth of the school board's authority" (p. 974). The court pointed out that students, like everyone else, are subject to disturbing the peace, inciting to riot, and littering laws. In this instance, the school board had clearly overstepped its authority, for the off-campus distribution of the student-produced newspaper had created no disruption or interference with the rights of others on campus. In short, the school board could not justify either the rule or its enforcement—a burden that school officials must assume when disciplining students or teachers for exercising constitutional rights.

STUDENT FREEDOM OF ASSOCIATION

High school students have a right to assemble peacefully for expressive purposes in the vicinity of the public school, and students at the collegiate level have a relatively unfettered right to assemble and to associate. The U.S. Supreme Court ruled as much in two 1972 cases (*Grayned v. Rockford* and *Healy v. James*). In *Healy*, the Court struck down all efforts by a public college to avoid recognizing the 1960s activist group Students for a Democratic Society (SDS), except one. Would they agree to observe college rules? If so, they must be recognized as a campus organization. "Among the rights protected by the First Amendment is the right of individuals to associate to further their personal beliefs. While the freedom of association is not explicitly set out in the Amendment, it has long been held to be implicit in the freedoms of speech, assembly, and petition. There can be no doubt that denial of official recognition, without justification, to college organizations burdens or abridges that associational right" (p. 181).

The support given the right of association coupled with the recognition of student free speech rights in *Tinker v. Des Moines School District* indicates that students at the secondary level also have a right to come together for expressive purposes on the public school campus as long as no material disruption or invasion of the rights of others occurs. Because the public school is not a public forum, however, the right of association does not automatically extend to nonstudents. Provisions of the Texas Education Code make this clear. Thus, TEC §37.105 allows the board of trustees or its representatives to refuse to allow persons having no legitimate business to enter school property. Undesirable persons may be ejected upon refusal to leave peaceably. TEC §37.107 makes trespass on school property a crime.

Does the right to associate restrict school officials in deciding which student groups may and which may not function as school-recognized organizations? The answer appears to depend upon the type of group and the legitimacy of the school's reasons in denying status as a campus organization to a student group. For example, a federal district court in Michigan ruled in the early 1970s that it "is patently unconstitutional" to deny recognition in the absence of disorder to student groups because they advocate controversial ideas or take one side of an issue (*Dixon v. Beresh*, U.S. District Court, Michigan, 1973). As noted in the next chapter, the federal Equal Access Act precludes discriminating on the basis of speech content against non-curriculum-related student groups that meet on school grounds during noninstructional time.

State law makes it a crime for a student or nonstudent to be a member of, pledge membership in, or recruit others to join fraternities, sororities, secret societies, and gangs in public elementary and secondary schools (TEC §37.121). In addition to being charged with a Class C misdemeanor, a student who violates this provision may be placed in an alternative education program (see Chapter 8). According to a subsection of the statute, a fraternity, sorority, secret society, or gang is defined as one that "seeks to perpetuate itself by taking in additional members from the pupils enrolled in school on the basis of the decision of its membership rather than upon the free choice of any pupil in the school who is qualified by the rules of the school to fill the special aims of the organization." Specifically exempted are organizations for public welfare such as Boy Scouts, Hi-Y, Girl Reserves, DeMolay, Rainbow Girls, Pan-American Clubs, scholarship societies, and other similar educational organizations sponsored by the state or national education authorities. What impact this provision may have on the constitutional right of students to associate awaits future litigation.

There are other student organizations which are in the gray area. Can a school district refuse to recognize a controversial student organization such as a gay student rights club if the students obtain a faculty sponsor and meet other criteria for school recognition? The answer remains unclear. On the one hand, school officials may seek to refuse recognition on grounds that the existence of such a school-sanctioned organization would have a detrimental impact on younger students. Or, in the case of an extremist group, the school might argue that its presence would likely trigger disruption. These arguments would be most persuasive in certain settings—the junior-senior high school or an ethnically mixed school experiencing considerable racial tension. On the other hand, students interested in the formation of such clubs would argue that they seek only to explore the issue intellectually, not to take an advocacy role or to engage in illegal activity. However, it needs to be emphasized that if the secondary school has a "limited open forum" under the Equal Access Act, the school cannot deny access of these groups to the campus during noninstructional time.

The U.S. Supreme Court has not yet dealt directly with student organizations. However, in a 1989 decision, the Court ruled that the right of association protected by the First Amendment relates to expressive activities and not to those that are strictly social. The case involved a Dallas city ordinance that restricted admission to certain dance halls to persons between the ages of fourteen and eighteen. The Court rejected the assertion that the ordinance violated a right to associate for recreational purposes (*City of Dallas v. Stanglin*).

SUMMARY

While the U.S. Supreme Court has extended expression rights under the First and Fourteenth amendments to the U.S. Constitution to teachers and students, in neither case are these rights absolute. Teachers and administrators have a right to expression on public issues and to association in the community and within the school as long as their effectiveness as employees is not jeopardized and as long as the educational environment is not disrupted. Teacher classroom academic freedom rights are much less extensive. In the Fifth Circuit, teachers have a right to engage in classroom discussion as long as any resulting disruption does not overbalance the teacher's usefulness as an instructor. Teachers in Texas generally do not have the right to select teaching materials and methodology unless given this right by the school officials.

Students have considerable entitlement to freedom of speech, assembly, and association in the public school as long as there is no material disruption of classwork or of school activity and as long as there is no substantial interference with the rights of others. At the same time, school officials retain considerable control over the contents of school-sponsored channels of communication, such as newspapers, yearbooks, literary magazines, and school plays. The extent of their authority to exercise similar control over the contents of non-school-sponsored materials that either students or teachers wish to distribute on campus appears more limited. Following an announced system of prior review will lessen the chances that authority will be inappropriately exercised. School officials are empowered by state law to limit student association with fraternities, sororities, secret societies, and gangs while on campus.

Underlying the cases in the expression area for both teachers and students is the complex and controversial issue of the purpose of schools. Are schools to be places where community values are inculcated and respect for authority instilled? Or are they to be marketplaces of ideas where students shed the trappings of the past and seek their own identity? There appears to be no consensus on the answer among either educators or judges, and this fact largely accounts for the disputatious character of the law of speech, press, and association in the public school arena.

SEVEN

Religion in the Schools

FEELINGS ABOUT the appropriate role that religion should play in public education run deep and often are conflicting. This is particularly apparent when shifting population patterns increase the diversity of family backgrounds in school communities. Increasingly, court battles are being waged between those who demand that schools and religion be kept separate and those who demand greater accommodation of religion in public education. School officials are often caught in the middle and must navigate a narrow channel between what is legally permissible and what is not.

The first part of this chapter looks at the legal framework within which these battles take place. The rest of the chapter is devoted to an in-depth examination of contemporary religious issues in Texas schools.

LEGAL FRAMEWORK

Separation of Church and State

The First Amendment to the U.S. Constitution begins not with a statement about free speech or press rights but with a statement about religion: "Congress shall make no law respecting an establishment of religion, or prohibiting the free exercise thereof . . ." Since the sentence comes first in the amendment, it is apparent that the writers of the Bill of Rights felt very strongly about the relationship between government and religion.

This statement, which applies to state governments and public schools through provisions of the Fourteenth Amendment, has two distinct components: *the establishment clause* ("Congress shall make no law respecting an establishment of religion") and *the free exercise clause* ("or prohibiting the free exercise thereof"). In this first section we will discuss the establishment clause.

Note that the word *an* appears before the word *establishment*. The U.S. Supreme Court has construed this to mean that not only is government not to set up a state church, but it is also not to aid any particular religion. In short—the Jeffersonian principle of separation of church and state.

Beginning with *Everson v. Board of Education* (1947), the first major case involving the establishment clause and education, the U.S. Supreme Court struggled to find a consistent way of deciding establishment-clause cases. *Everson* involved a New Jersey plan to reimburse the transportation expenses of parents who sent their children to parochial and other private schools. The Court in a five-to-four decision ruled that the plan did not violate the "wall of separation" between state and church because its purpose was to enable both public and private school students to get to school safely.

A year later in *McCollum v. Board of Education*, the Court ruled that a release-time program whereby religious instruction was given to students on a voluntary basis in the public schools did breach the wall of separation. But four years later in *Zorach v. Clauson*, the Court upheld a New York program that allowed students interested in religious instruction to leave school early so they could receive religious instruction at off-campus centers.

By what rationale were these decisions being made? It was difficult to tell, in part because the justices did not agree and sometimes switched sides. For example, Justice Hugo Black wrote the *Everson* and *McCollum* decisions but dissented from the ruling in the *Zorach* case. Considerable criticism greeted the Supreme Court decisions, and much of it continues. Given the close traditional linkage among church, home, and school, the criticism is understandable. Indeed, the first federal act to aid education, the 1787 Northwest Ordinance, stated that "religion, morality, and knowledge being essential to good government and the happiness of mankind, schools and the means of education shall forever be encouraged." By the early 1970s the justices had developed a set of guidelines to use in resolving complex church-state issues. The guidelines were:

1. The purpose of a challenged law or practice must be secular (as opposed to sectarian).
2. The primary effect of the law or practice must be one that neither advances nor inhibits religion (and thus does not impair the practice of one's religious beliefs).
3. The law or practice must not involve excessive entanglement between state and church (this guideline is most often related to state efforts to aid religiously affiliated private schools).

For a law or practice to be constitutional, it had to pass all three of the so-called *Lemon* tests, named after the 1971 *Lemon v. Kurtz-*

man decision in which they were advanced. To withstand an establishment clause challenge, according to the Supreme Court, a law or
practice must be neutral regarding religion—neither promoting nor
retarding it. Such was not the case with the posting of the Ten Commandments in public schools, a case reaching the U.S. Supreme
Court in 1980. The Court struck down the classroom posting as
lacking a secular purpose since "the Ten Commandments is un-
deniably a sacred text in the Jewish and Christian faiths" (*Stone v.
Graham*).

More recently, some members of the Court have urged amend-
ing the *Lemon* guidelines or abolishing them altogether in favor of a
more flexible approach to resolving establishment clause issues. It
is widely presumed that any modification would make it easier to
include manifestations of religion in public schools. However, in a
1993 ruling to be discussed below, Justice Byron White appeared
to reaffirm the *Lemon* precedent on behalf of the Court majority in
the face of a pointed attack by Justice Antonin Scalia. In dissent,
Scalia had written that a majority of the current sitting justices—
including Justice White—had "personally driven pencils through
[*Lemon*'s] heart," yet, "Like some ghoul in a late-night horror movie
that repeatedly sits up in its grave and shuffles abroad, after being repeatedly killed and buried, *Lemon* stalks our Establishment Clause
jurisprudence once again, frightening the little children and school
attorneys . . ." (*Lamb's Chapel v. Center Moriches School District*,
pp. 2149–2150). White responded, "While we are somewhat di-
verted by Justice Scalia's evening at the cinema, we return to the reality that there is a proper way to inter an established decision and
Lemon, however frightening it might be to some, has not been overruled" (p. 2148, n. 7). In decisions in 1994 and 1995, the Court did
not use the *Lemon* guidelines nor specifically overrule them. The
1994 decision struck down the creation of a public school district to
provide special education to the children of a group of Hasidic Jews,
since the action benefited only one religious sect and was thus not
neutral regarding religion (*Board of Education of Kiryas Joel Village
School District v. Grumet*). In 1995 the Court ruled that the University of Virginia could not deny student activity funds to a student
religious magazine, because to do so would constitute impermissible viewpoint censorship in violation of the First Amendment free
speech clause (*Rosenberger v. University of Virginia*).

Provisions of the Texas Constitution similarly reflect a desire
to separate church and state. Prior to the revolution of 1836, Texans
had been forced to observe the state religion of Mexico, Roman Ca-
tholicism. To preclude a similar situation from ever arising again,

the authors of the 1845 state constitution made it clear in Article I, §6 that "no man shall be compelled to attend, erect, or support any place of worship, or to maintain any ministry against his consent." Section 6 also states that "no preference shall ever be given by law to any religious society or mode of worship." Interestingly, the Supreme Court of Texas ruled in 1908 in *Church v. Bullock* that the recitation of the Lord's Prayer in public schools did not violate these provisions. Justice Thomas J. Brown noted that "Christianity is so interwoven with the web and woof of the state government that to sustain the contention that the [state] constitution prohibits reading the Bible, offering prayers, or singing songs of a religious character in any public building of the government, would produce a condition bordering upon moral anarchy" (p. 118). Justice Brown's premise would be questioned today, given the increasing variety of religious denominations among us. The value of this ancient decision as legal precedent is questionable in light of modern legal developments in the state-church relationship.

Article I, §7 of the Texas Constitution is very specific in prohibiting the expenditure of public dollars for sectarian purposes. It reads, "No money shall be appropriated, or drawn from the Treasury for the benefit of any sect, religious society, theological or religious seminary; nor shall property belonging to the State be appropriated for any such purposes." While there is no relevant case law to convey its meaning in practice, a common assumption is that it is even more strict than the First Amendment establishment clause.

What happens if these state and federal constitutional provisions are in conflict? Suppose that the U.S. Supreme Court were to rule that a state-funded voucher program encompassing private sectarian schooling does not violate the First Amendment establishment clause. Would Article I, §7 of the Texas Constitution still prohibit the expenditure of public money for this purpose? The decision would be left to the Texas courts. An analogous situation arose in Washington State in 1986. The U.S. Supreme Court ruled unanimously that the establishment clause does not prevent the provision of state vocational rehabilitation services to aid a blind student to pursue studies at a Christian college to become a minister (*Witters v. Washington Department of Services*). Significantly, the Court noted that it was considering only the First Amendment issue and that, on remand, the Washington State Supreme Court was free to consider the "far stricter" dictates of the Washington state constitution. The Washington high court later did so and denied the aid as violative of a state constitutional provision (*Witters v. State Commission for the Blind*).

However, if the voucher program were federally funded, the outcome likely would be different. The Federal Supremacy Clause of the U.S. Constitution, Article VI, §2, provides that federal law takes precedence over state law. Recently, a federal appeals court ruled that the Washington State Constitution could not bar student religious clubs from the campus when they had a right to be there under the terms of the federal Equal Access Act (to be discussed later in this chapter). The court observed that while state constitutions can be more protective of individual rights than the federal constitution, they cannot abridge rights granted by federal law (*Garnett v. Renton School District No. 403*). Thus, a federally funded voucher system that enfranchises parents with the means to choose a private sectarian school likely would take precedence over a state constitutional provision that bars the use of public money for religous purposes unless Congress specified to the contrary in the legislation. In recent years voucher bills have been introduced into the U.S. Congress, and it is possible that a conservative majority could pass such a measure.

Free Exercise of Religion

The second component of the First Amendment in the U.S. Constitution is the free exercise clause: "or prohibiting the free exercise thereof." This clause assures that people shall be free to exercise their religious beliefs without government restraint or persecution. Like the establishment clause, the free exercise clause applies to states and their political subdivisions, including public school districts, under the Fourteenth Amendment. When coupled with the protection accorded speech, press, and assembly in the First Amendment, the free exercise clause provides extensive protection for religious expression and exercise.

Article I, §6 of the Texas Constitution expresses much the same concern about religious freedom: "All men have a natural and indefeasible right to worship Almighty God according to the dictates of their own consciences. . . . No human authority ought, in any case whatever, to control or interfere with the rights of conscience in matters of religion. . . . [I]t shall be the duty of the Legislature to pass such laws as may be necessary to protect equally every religious denomination in the peaceable enjoyment of its own mode of public worship."

Even though there is wide latitude accorded freedom of religion in the U.S. Constitution and in the Texas Constitution, the exercise of the right is not absolute. There are limits to what courts will allow under the free exercise clause. Thus, while the Supreme Court has never permitted the government to punish individuals for purely religious belief, religious belief when accompanied by action is another story.

The problem is highlighted when the exercise of one's religious beliefs is accompanied by action that clashes with otherwise legitimate governmental authority. For example, the U.S. Supreme Court decided in *Reynolds v. United States* in 1878 that, while Mormons have a right to believe in polygamy, Congress has a right to prohibit its practice. In the course of his opinion, Chief Justice Morrison R. Waite made the interesting observation that "Congress was deprived of all legislative power over mere opinion, but was left free to reach actions which were in violation of social duties or subversive of good order" (p. 164). "Suppose one believed that human sacrifices were a necessary part of religious worship," he added. "Would it be seriously contended that the civil government under which he lived could not interfere to prevent a sacrifice?" (p. 166). Of course, by preventing the practice of polygamy, Congress did interfere with the Mormons' religious freedom.

A more recent illustration of the clash between religious practice and governmental authority is the 1990 Supreme Court ruling upholding denial of unemployment benefits to a worker who was terminated for using peyote, an illegal hallucinogen, in a Native American religious ceremony (*Employment Division of Oregon Dept. of Human Resources v. Smith*). The *Smith* decision prompted Congress to enact legislation in 1993 protecting religious rights. The Religious Freedom Restoration Act (RFRA) provides that government shall not substantially burden a person's exercise of religion. If government does so, it must demonstrate that the burden "is in furtherance of a compelling governmental interest" and "is the least restrictive means of furthering that compelling governmental interest." Under the act, the plaintiff must first show that his religious exercise rights have been substantially burdened. While the meaning of "substantially burdened" remains unclear, all U.S. Supreme Court justices agreed in the *Smith* decision that the First Amendment free exercise clause does not require courts to ask whether conduct at issue is "central" to the individual's religion; rather, sincerity of belief is sufficient.

An initial concern to greet the passage of RFRA was whether the act itself is constitutional. In 1995 a Texas federal district court judge became the first to strike the act down in a dispute over a historic preservation ordinance that officials of the town of Boerne used to halt expansion of a Catholic church. The church argued that

the restriction was illegal under RFRA. The judge ruled that in enacting the law, Congress had sought to impose its view of the meaning of the First Amendment over that of the U.S. Supreme Court and
thus violated the separation of powers between the branches of gov-
erment. His decision was later reversed by the Fifth Circuit (*Flores
v. City of Boerne*).

Early rulings involving RFRA have not yet established a clear
view of how the act will apply to public schools. In a 1995 decision,
the Ninth Circuit Court of Appeals ruled that a California school
district's no-knives policy was inappropriately applied to Sikhs who
wore long ceremonial knives called "krpans" to school. The court
acknowledged the compelling purpose of the school district in protecting student safety but noted the district's duty under RFRA to
achieve that interest in the least restrictive manner regarding the
Sikhs' religious rights. The appeals court upheld a district court
plan whereby the children kept their krpans sheathed and shielded
from public view (*Cheema v. Thompson*). By contrast, a federal district court in New York ruled in 1995 that RFRA does not require a
public school to exempt a non-curriculum-related student Bible
club that meets during noninstructional time from the school's
nondiscrimination policy. The club sought to restrict leadership
roles to Christian students. The court characterized the school's
policy of preventing religious discrimination on campus as both
compelling and the least restrictive way of accomplishing that goal
(*Hsu v. Roslyn Union Free School District*). In 1993 a Texas federal
judge found that in-school suspension of Native American students
for wearing their hair long violated their sincerely held religious beliefs under the free exercise clause regarding the spirituality of long
hair, as well as their right to symbolic expression regarding their
tribal heritage and traditions (*Alabama and Coushatta Tribes of
Texas v. Big Sandy I.S.D.*). The ruling was appealed to the Fifth
Circuit, which returned it to the lower court for a determination
whether the long-hair restriction violated the students' rights under
RFRA. The case was settled when the school district agreed to allow
the students to sign an exemption form indicating that their long
hair was attributable to religious belief or expression.

Closely related to the belief-action issue is the definition to be
accorded religion. Does "religion" refer to established denominational churches only or does it extend to a strictly personal belief
system? For First Amendment establishment clause purposes,
courts generally define religion as deity based, one generally recognized as a bona fide religion. But for free exercise clause purposes,
the definition is often more relaxed and can extend to a belief sys-

tem that is philosophically rather than religiously based. Yet there are limits even under the free exercise clause. For example, in an involved Texas federal court case, *Theriault v. Silber* (1978), the federal district court refused to accord a prisoner's asserted new religion, the Church of the New Song, protected status under the First Amendment. After considerable investigation, the judge concluded that the Church of the New Song was really "a sham designed and calculated to obtain favored treatment for its members incarcerated in various prisons" (p. 264).

There is inherent tension in both the federal and state constitutions between the principle of separation of church and state and the principle of religious freedom. Too much of one may interfere with the other. For example, public school officials are concerned that if they allow students and teachers to proselytize their religious views on campus, they will be promoting religion and thus breaching the separation of church and state. Conversely, if school officials deny them the opportunity to do so, students and teachers will argue that their free exercise rights are being violated. How courts have responded to this concern will be discussed later in the chapter.

In addition to these constitutional provisions, there are also federal and state statutes which protect religious freedom. For example, Title VII of the 1964 Civil Rights Act outlaws discrimination on the basis of race, color, religion, sex, and national origin in public and private employment. The statute does allow religious preference by sectarian private schools. The Texas Commission on Human Rights Act, Article 5221k, Texas Civil Statutes, has similar provisions. The state has a general antidiscrimination law, §106.001 of Title 5 of the Civil Practices and Remedies Code, which prohibits officers and employees of state and local government from discriminating in a variety of contexts on the basis of race, religion, color, sex, national origin, age, and mental or physical handicap. Together with a 1993 unanimous U.S. Supreme Court ruling (*Lamb's Chapel v. Center Moriches School District*), this law prohibits school officials from denying religious groups the same access to school facilities afforded to other community organizations. The *Lamb's Chapel* case was decided on the grounds of free speech. Since the Long Island school district had created a "limited public forum" by allowing use of its facilities after hours for social, civic, and recreational purposes, it could not grant access to all but religious groups. The evangelical Christian church in the *Lamb's Chapel* ruling had asked permission to use a room at the school to show a six-part film series presenting a Christian perspective on family life and child rearing.

The decision left open the question whether school districts can permit religious worship to take place on school property.

TEC §25.901 tracks U.S. Supreme Court rulings in declaring that a public school student has an absolute right to pray or meditate voluntarily and individually in school so long as there is no disruption of instructional or other activities. The provision also provides that no person may require, encourage, or coerce a student to engage in or to refrain from prayer and meditation. TEC §22.901 prohibits asking about the religious affiliation of anyone applying for public school employment. The prohibition extends to persons or organizations used to obtain positions for public school employees. It tracks the prohibition against religious tests for public office contained in Article I, §4 of the Texas Constitution, except that the constitutional provision allows asking an applicant whether or not the applicant believes in the existence of a Supreme Being. That provision was struck down in an unreported decision of a U.S. district court in Houston in 1982 as a violation of the individual's religious freedom (*Roe v. Klein I.S.D.*). In 1961 the U.S. Supreme Court ruled that requiring public officers to declare a belief in God constitutes a religious test for public office that invades the individual's right to religious freedom (*Torcaso v. Watkins*). As we have noted, federal law takes precedence over state law, so the Texas constitutional provision is null and void.

This, then, is the general legal framework surrounding the role of religion in public education. It is important to note that two constitutions are involved: federal and state. In the past, virtually all of the litigation has involved the religion clauses of the federal constitution. However, recently, plaintiff's attorneys have discovered the state constitution, and more litigation has been based on its provisions. These constitutional provisions, coupled with federal and state statutes, provide ample opportunity for litigation, as the rest of the chapter attests.

CONTEMPORARY ISSUES

Concerns about the role of religion in Texas public schools have surfaced over a variety of issues. Included among them are:

• State-sponsored school prayer and silent meditation
• Teaching creation-science
• Religion in classrooms and holiday programs

- Distributing Bibles in schools
- Promoting secular humanism
- Granting access to student religious clubs and organizations
- Giving religious exemptions to parents and students
- State assistance to private sectarian schools

Each will be discussed in turn.

State-Sponsored School Prayer and Silent Meditation

There are two major U.S. Supreme Court prayer decisions. The first, *Engel v. Vitale* (1962), involved a denominationally neutral prayer composed by the New York State Board of Regents: "Almighty God, we acknowledge our dependence upon Thee, and we beg Thy blessings upon us, our parents, our teachers, and our Country." The second case, *School District of Abington v. Schempp* (1963), decided together with *Murray v. Curlett*, involved state laws requiring selection and reading of passages from the Bible and recitation of the Lord's Prayer.

The Court ruled against the state-endorsed prayers in both cases. Since the state had in effect made a law respecting an establishment of religion in these cases, the Court ruled that the Constitution was violated. Writing the majority opinion in the *Engel* case, Justice Black noted, ". . . we think that the constitutional prohibition against laws respecting an establishment of religion must at least mean that in this country it is no part of the business of government to compose official prayers for any group of the American people to recite as a part of the religious program carried on by government" (p. 425). Certainly, the U.S. Supreme Court's school prayer decisions leave no doubt that officially prescribed school prayers with or without student exemptions are illegal in Texas public schools.

In 1978 and again in 1981, before the circuit was split into two parts, the U.S. Court of Appeals for the Fifth Circuit struck down statutes enacted by Florida and Louisiana, respectively, that tried to place school-endorsed prayer back in the classroom (*Meltzer v. Board of Public Instruction* and *Karen B. v. Treen*). In the latter case, the state argued that the purpose of the daily prayer and silent meditation program was to increase religious tolerance by exposing students to beliefs different from their own and to assist them in developing a greater awareness of the spiritual dimensions of human nature. The school district where the challenge originated established guidelines that provided, first, the teacher must ask if any student wishes to volunteer a prayer and, if none does, then the teacher may offer a prayer. If the teacher decides not to do so, then silent meditation would begin immediately. The silent meditation component was not involved in the lawsuit. Students who did not wish to participate in the prayer portion of the program could either remain seated or stand outside the classroom. A letter was sent home to parents indicating that parental permission and a verbal request by the student were necessary for participation in the prayer program. Despite the precautions, the Fifth Circuit ruled that the prayer section of the statute and the school district guidelines violated the establishment clause of the First Amendment. In 1983 a Texas federal court prohibited a school district from having its school song recited or sung at extracurricular activities (*Doe v. Aldine I.S.D.*). The court found the school song essentially to be a Christian prayer, noted its pervasive presence at school events and activities, and observed that school officials frequently led its recitation or singing. The court also ordered that the posting of the prayer over the entrance to the school gymnasium be removed.

Would the legal outcome be different if the prayer program were initiated not by the school but by students? Given the Fifth Circuit ruling in *Hall v. Board of School Commissioners of Conecuh County* in 1981, the answer is no, though more recent rulings have renewed interest in the question. In *Hall* the court noted that all parties to the lawsuit, as well as the trial court, agreed that a high school's permitting students to conduct morning devotional readings over the school's public address system was unconstitutional. The appeals court noted as well that the school district had allowed such activity to take place up until the filing of the lawsuit in 1979. Because of the laxity in following established law, the Fifth Circuit concluded that the plaintiffs were entitled to have the school district pay their legal fees as well as to an injunction prohibiting continuation of the practice.

Nor would the outcome likely be different if a student group, such as the student council, were to sponsor the program. In 1981 the U.S. Court of Appeals for the Ninth Circuit affirmed a lower court ruling striking down a program whereby the student council opened optional school assemblies with a prayer (*Collins v. Chandler Unified School District*). As to the assertion that student free expression rights would be violated by prohibiting the prayers, the appeals court observed that the establishment clause takes precedence.

It is important to point out, however, that while these rulings clearly establish that school-sponsored prayer is unconstitutional, nothing prohibits students from praying privately or from assem-

bling in groups for religious speech or prayer on campus. As we
noted in the previous chapter, only if the praying becomes disruptive can it be grounds for student discipline (*Clark v. Dallas I.S.D.*).
Thus, if students use bullhorns, block access to classes, or create
unruly crowds, disciplinary measures may be warranted.

In 1985 the U.S. Supreme Court was confronted with an Alabama statute authorizing public schools to set aside time for silent
meditation or prayer (*Wallace v. Jaffree*). The Court concluded that
the "or prayer" addition to an earlier statute authorizing silent
meditation amounted to an unconstitutional attempt to restore
prayer to public schools. However, in his opinion for the six-justice
majority in the *Jaffree* case, Justice John Paul Stevens wrote, "The
legislative intent to return prayer to the public schools is, of course,
quite different from merely protecting every student's right to engage in voluntary prayer during an appropriate moment of silence
during the school day" (p. 2491). It would thus appear that a moment for silent meditation would pass constitutional muster. In
1995 the Texas Legislature gave school districts the option of starting the school day with a period of silence during which students
"may reflect or meditate" (TEC §25.082). At the same time, the provision in the Code that recognizes a student's right to pray or meditate individually in a nondisruptive manner also recognizes that a
student may not be required, encouraged, or coerced to engage in or
not engage in prayer or meditation (TEC §25.901). Thus, a student
who does not want to meditate during a period for silent meditation
cannot be compelled to do so.

Arguments have been advanced that prohibiting state-mandated
prayer programs in public schools inhibits the religious freedom of
those who wish to say such prayers. In *School District of Abington
v. Schempp*, the U.S. Supreme Court's 1963 school prayer decision,
Justice Potter Stewart put it this way in his dissenting opinion:

[A] compulsory state educational system so structures a child's life that if
religious exercises are held to be an impermissible activity in schools, religion is placed at an artificial and state-created disadvantage. Viewed in
this light, permission of such exercises for those who want them is necessary if the schools are truly to be neutral in the matter of religion. And
a refusal to permit religious exercises thus is seen, not as the realization
of state neutrality, but rather as the establishment of a religion of secularism, or at the least, as government support of the beliefs of those who
think that religious exercises should be conducted only in private.
(P. 1619)

Two responses to this criticism have been advanced. First, religious exercise generally means the right to worship. Keeping the school neutral with respect to religion has little impact on one's right to worship, since accessibility to churches remains undiminished. Second, a state-mandated religious program would likely have a coercive effect on those whose religious beliefs are not in accord with the program. When school communities become diverse in family religious background, religious factions in the community often raise objections to various expressions of religion in schools.

More recently the Supreme Court has allowed greater government accommodation of religious freedom by approving chaplain-led prayers before the convening of the Nebraska Legislature (*Marsh v. Chambers*, 1983) and allowing a city's inclusion of a nativity scene as part of an annual Christmas display (*Lynch v. Donnelly*, 1984). But the justices were closely divided. Further disagreement among the justices about the wall of separation was apparent in a 1989 decision, in which a slim majority of the Court upheld the display of a menorah together with a Christmas tree at one location but struck down the display of a creche standing alone at another location (*County of Allegheny v. American Civil Liberties Union*). In 1995 a majority of the Court agreed that the state does not promote religion by allowing the Ku Klux Klan to erect an unattended cross during the Christmas season in a public plaza adjacent to a government building. The justices, however, were divided on determining at what point government accommodation might amount to unconstitutional endorsement of religion (*Capitol Square Review Board v. Pinette*).

Given these divided rulings and indications of a shift among some of the justices toward greater recognition of free exercise rights, many commentators expected that the Court would approve the inclusion of invocations and benedictions at school commencement ceremonies in a 1992 decision, *Lee v. Weisman*. In the *Engel* prayer decision, Justice Black recognized that not all expressions of religion in public life violate the Constitution:

There is of course nothing in the decision reached here that is inconsistent with the fact that school children and others are officially encouraged to express love for our country by reciting historical documents such as the Declaration of Independence which contain references to the Deity or by singing officially espoused anthems which include the composer's professions of faith in a Supreme Being, or with the fact that there are many manifestations in our public life of belief in God. Such patriotic or ceremonial occasions bear no true resemblance to the unquestioned religious exercise that the State of New York has sponsored in this instance. (P. 435, n. 21)

But the Court did not consider prayer at commencement to be ceremonial. In a five-to-four ruling in the *Lee* case, the Court declared that school-sponsored sectarian and nonsectarian invocations and benedictions at school graduation ceremonies where the school selects the clergy and advises them what kind of prayers to give violate the establishment clause. The majority based its decision on two points. First, the state in the person of the school principal is pervasively involved in directing the religious exercise to the point of "creating a state-sponsored and state-directed religious exercise in a public school." And second, the practice exerts undue psychological pressure on the objecting student to participate. The majority observed that graduation is a seminal event in the life of a student and, this being so, it could not be said that attendance was truly voluntary. Thus, the majority viewed commencement prayer differently from the legislative prayer it had upheld in *Marsh*. The majority did not employ the *Lemon* establishment clause guidelines to decide the case, thus leading Justice Antonin Scalia, writing for the four dissenters, to conclude that the Court was ready to abandon them.

When it decided the *Lee* case, the Supreme Court returned a somewhat similar case to the Fifth Circuit. In that case the Fifth Circuit had upheld the Clear Creek I.S.D. school board's resolution leaving the inclusion of invocation and benediction at graduation exercises to the discretion of the senior class. After reconsidering its ruling in light of *Lee*, the Fifth Circuit once again upheld the Clear Creek plan (*Jones v. Clear Creek I.S.D.*). Under the resolution, if the senior class votes in the affirmative, then an invocation and benediction can be given by a student volunteer. The message must be nonsectarian and nonproselytizing. The Fifth Circuit pointed out that, unlike the disfavored *Lee* practice, the Clear Creek prayer program did not implicate school officials in prayer decision making and did not have the same psychologically coercive effect on objecting students. The ruling was appealed to the U.S. Supreme Court, which refused to hear it in June of 1993, thus leaving the Fifth Circuit decision standing. Many commentators, however, found it difficult to distinguish the two rulings and expected that litigation would continue. Indeed, in 1994 the Ninth Circuit ruled that student-led prayers at an Idaho school graduation ceremony were unconstitutional, observing that it did not find the Fifth Circuit's ruling persuasive (*Harris v. Joint School District No. 241*). Though later vacated by the U.S. Supreme Court on grounds of mootness, the decision represents disagreement among the federal courts on the matter. Continuing inconsistency could lead the U.S. Supreme Court to take up the issue in the future. In the meantime, the Fifth Circuit's *Jones* ruling governs practice in Texas.

Under the rationale of the Supreme Court's *Lee v. Weisman* decision, baccalaureate ceremonies that are pervasively religious, school-sponsored, and held on campus violate the establishment clause. To avoid constitutional problems, a religiously oriented baccalaureate service should be held off school grounds and without school sponsorship. Alternatively, the service could be held on campus if the school is not the sponsor and if the facility is rented to nonschool sponsors pursuant to a neutral school rental policy. As noted earlier, the U.S. Supreme Court has upheld the rental of school facilities to religious organizations. A Wyoming federal court has ruled that accommodating baccalaureate services in this manner does not violate the establishment clause (*Shumay v. Albany County School District*).

The *Lee v. Weisman* decision called into question prayer at other school functions such as extracurricular activities, athletic events, and school board meetings. In 1995 the Fifth Circiut ruled in a long-running case involving the Duncanville I.S.D. that school districts and their employees may not lead, encourage, promote, or participate in prayers with or among students during curricular or extracurricular activities, including before, during, or after school-related sporting events (*Doe v. Duncanville I.S.D.*). The appeals court rejected the contention that such restriction denies school employees a constitutional right to join students in prayer activities. Participation by coaches and other school employees would "signal an unconstitutional endorsement of religion," the court noted, since they are representatives of the school. However, employees are not required to leave the room when students pray or otherwise treat student religious beliefs with disrespect. By a two-to-one margin, the appeals court upheld use of "The Lord Bless You and Keep You" as the Duncanville I.S.D. choir's theme song because of its widely recognized musical value.

In 1996 the Fifth Circuit affirmed a federal district court decision that halted enforcement of a Mississippi statute allowing nonproselytizing student-initiated voluntary prayer at compulsory and noncompulsory school assemblies, sporting events, and other school-related student events (*Ingebretsen v. Jackson Public School District*). The appeals court noted that the statute had been enacted following the termination of a school principal who allowed students to begin each school day with a prayer over the intercom system. The clear intent of the law, according to the court, was to return prayer to the public schools contrary to the secular purpose requirement of the *Lemon* tests. The court noted that the statute permitted school teachers and administrators to participate in prayer, lead prayer, and punish students who leave class or assemblies to avoid listening to prayer. Further, the statute "will inevitably involve school officials in determining which prayers are 'nonsectarian and nonproselytizing' and in determining who gets to say the prayer at each event." For these reasons, the statute unconstitutionally advanced religion in the schools and excessively entangled the government with religion. The court noted that the statute also had a greater coercive effect on students than the graduation prayer at issue in *Lee v. Weisman* because many of the activities where prayer would take place are compulsory. Finally, the court held that the statute represented an unconstitutional government endorsement of religion. The *Ingebretsen* decision clearly limits the application of the Fifth Circuit's earlier *Jones v. Clear Creek I.S.D.* decision to the graduation context.

In sum, until the U.S. Supreme Court decides otherwise, prayer is illegal when school personnel organize, encourage, or participate in prayer on campus or at school extracurricular and athletic events. While nonproselytizing student-initiated prayer is permissible at school graduation ceremonies, it is unconstitutional in other contexts such as extracurricular activities, sporting events, and school assemblies. Students themselves have a constitutional right to engage in nondisruptive voluntary prayer individually or in groups on campus so long as it is not done under the auspices of the school.

Teaching Creation-Science

In another famous case, *Epperson v. Arkansas* (1968), the U.S. Supreme Court had little trouble finding the absence of a secular purpose and neutral effect in a state law prohibiting the teaching of evolution in the public schools. Noted the Court, "The law's effort was confined to an attempt to blot out a particular theory because of its supposed conflict with the Biblical account, literally read" (p. 109). But could the state pass a law prohibiting a teacher from mentioning the biblical view of creation in a lesson plan on the origin of humans? A good case could be made that such a law has the reverse effect of the Arkansas law—it discriminates against religion, thus jeopardizing state neutrality with respect to religion, and may interfere as well with the teacher's right to freedom of speech in the classroom.

After a number of lower court decisions involving creation-science, the U.S. Supreme Court settled the matter with its 1987 decision in *Edwards v. Aguillard*. The case concerned a challenge to a statute passed by the Louisiana Legislature requiring Louisiana schools to give equal treatment to creation-science. The statute, entitled the Balanced Treatment for Creation-Science and Evolution-Science Act, required that, if either evolution or creation-science was taught, the other theory also had to be taught. The law also required each school board to prepare curriculum guides and to make available teaching aids and resource materials on creation-science and prohibited a school board from discriminating against anyone who taught creation-science.

Applying the first of the *Lemon* guidelines, the majority of the Court found that the act's primary purpose was to restructure the science curriculum to conform to a particular religious viewpoint. The Court rejected the state's argument that the statute's purpose was to promote academic freedom. Teachers had ample freedom before the law was enacted to add other scientific theories about the origin of humans to the curriculum. By limiting them to only two views and requiring that both be taught, the Louisiana statute resulted in precisely the opposite of academic freedom.

The decision is important because it adds the U.S. Supreme Court's finality to earlier lower court decisions rejecting the mandatory teaching of creation-science in public schools. But, at the same time, it is important to note that a school district is not left with the option of teaching only evolution. Justice Brennan noted, in a key sentence, "teaching a variety of scientific theories about the origins of humankind to school children might be validly done with the clear secular intent of enhancing the effectiveness of science instruction" (p. 2583). Thus, it would appear to be legal under the *Edwards* ruling for a school district to include in its curriculum the scientific evidence associated with creation-science, as long as the scientific evidence associated with a variety of other theories is also included and the material is presented objectively. The religious underpinnings of any of the theories should not be stressed.

Case law in other jurisdictions indicates that courts do not look kindly upon school personnel who take it upon themselves to supplement the science curriculum by inserting their religious views. For example, in a 1994 ruling, the Ninth Circuit was confronted with a California science teacher who asserted a First Amendment

right to teach his students creationism as expounded in the Book of
Genesis. School officials directed the teacher to confine his teaching
to evolution, as required by the approved curriculum, and to cease
attempting to influence students to his personal religious beliefs.
The appeals court upheld a lower court ruling in favor of the school
district (*Peloza v. Capistrano Unified School District*). The court
noted that evolution is not a religion and thus rejected the teacher's
claim that teaching it violated the establishment clause. The appeals court also upheld the school district's directive prohibiting the
teacher from having any religious discussions with students during
the school day, given his penchant for proselytizing. "The school
district's interest in avoiding an Establishment Clause violation
trumps [the teacher's] right to free speech." In another case, *Webster
v. New Lenox School District No. 12*, a social studies teacher claimed
a right to teach creation-science in order to balance views in the
textbook that he disagreed with, e.g., the world is over four billion
years old. The superintendent directed Ray Webster to avoid advocacy of a Christian viewpoint, though he could discuss objectively
the historical relationship between church and state when appropriate to the curriculum. The Seventh Circuit upheld the trial court
ruling that the teacher did not have a First Amendment right to
teach creation-science. The judges noted, "Clearly, the school board
had the authority and the responsibility to ensure that Mr. Webster
did not stray from the established curriculum by injecting religious
advocacy into the classroom" (p. 1007).

Religion in Classrooms and Holiday Programs

The U.S. Supreme Court has commented in several decisions that
nothing precludes public schools from teaching *about* religion. For
example, in the *Schempp* prayer decision, Justice Tom C. Clark
wrote that "one's education is not complete without a study of comparative religion or the history of religion and its relationship to the
advancement of civilization. It certainly may be said that the Bible
is worthy of study for its literary and historic qualities" (p. 225).

   Thus, the curriculum need not be sanitized of any mention of
religion. In fact, if this were to occur, a strong argument could be
made that the school has become hostile, rather than neutral, toward religion. There are strong pedagogical reasons for including religion in the curriculum. Given that we are a religious people, it
would be difficult to teach social studies and history classes without reference to religion. Works of literature with religious significance are often read in English classes. Involvement of religion in

the curriculum in this manner raises few legal questions as long as it is done objectively as part of an otherwise secular program of study. But when teachers stray beyond objective inclusion to promoting religion, then the wall of separation between church and state may be breached. A case in point concerns a teacher in Denver, Colorado. The teacher's principal directed the teacher to remove two books on Christianity from his personal library in the classroom and not to display a Bible on his desk nor read from it during the silent reading period. The teacher also had displayed a religious poster in the classroom. The trial court found that the teacher's motive was to endorse religion by his actions and backed the principal. The U.S. Court of Appeals for the Tenth Circuit affirmed the decision in a two-to-one decision, noting that the school's principal was acting to assure the school's neutrality regarding religion in light of the impressionable age of the fifth grade students (*Roberts v. Madigan*).

In 1988, a coalition of fourteen organizations advanced the following six guidelines for teaching about religion in the public school:

1. The school's approach to religion must be academic, not devotional.
2. The school may strive for student awareness of religion but should not press for student acceptance of any one religion.
3. The school may sponsor study about religion but may not sponsor the practice of religion.
4. The school may expose students to a diversity of religious views but may not impose any particular view.
5. The school may educate about all religions but may not promote or denigrate any religion.
6. The school may inform the student about various beliefs but should not seek to confine him or her to any particular belief.

If these guidelines are followed, the potential for a damaging lawsuit will be minimized.

To what extent do students have a right to engage in religious discussion and proselytizing in the classroom? While the case law is not well developed, courts seem to view the classroom as a closed forum to such activity. The only U.S. court of appeals opinion on the issue to date involves the refusal of a junior high school teacher in Tennessee to allow a ninth grader to submit a research paper on the life of Jesus. The teacher contended that the student's strong Christian beliefs might lead to misunderstandings about any negative comments the teacher might make in grading the paper. She also didn't believe the student would have to do much new research on the topic, contrary to the purpose of the exercise. The U.S. Court of Appeals for the Sixth Circuit ruled that teachers deserve wide latitude in giving student assignments and that while students do not shed their constitutional rights in school, "Learning is more vital in the classroom than free speech." The court added, "Papers on the transfiguration of Jesus and similar topics may display more faith than rational analysis in the hands of a young student with strong religious heritage—at least the teacher is entitled to make such a judgment in the classroom" (*Settle v. Dickson County School Board*). The ruling was appealed to the U.S. Supreme Court. Lawyers for the Settles planned to argue that the Sixth Circuit decision ran counter to guidelines issued in August 1995 by U.S. Education Secretary Richard W. Riley for handling religious matters in the public schools. The guidelines track the case law as described in this chapter. One of the guidelines states that "Students may express their beliefs about religion in the form of homework, artwork, and other written and oral assignments free of discrimination based on the religious content of their submissions. Such home and classroom work should be judged by ordinary academic standards of substance and relevance, and against other legitimate pedagogical concerns identified by the school." The lawyers never got to make the argument because the high court declined to hear the case.

In *DeNooyer v. Livonia Public Schools*, a Michigan federal district court ruled that there was no violation of a second grader's free speech rights when the teacher refused to allow the student to show a videotape of herself singing a proselytizing religious song to her class during show and tell. The teacher had not converted the classroom into a public forum; the purpose of show and tell was to develop self-esteem through oral presentations, not provide an opportunity for indiscriminate public expression. These cases are troubling in the sense that they appear to discriminate against religious speech in the classroom.

Another sensitive curriculum issue concerns Bible study classes. While offering such courses may be legally possible, a review of lower court decisions indicates that most such classes do not pass judicial muster. A case in point relevant to Texas is *Hall v. Board of School Commissioners*, a 1981 Fifth Circuit decision. The Bible literature course at issue in the case used a state-approved textbook entitled *The Bible for Youthful Patriots, Parts I and II*. The textbook was found to approach the subject from a fundamentalist Christian perspective, and Bibles were distributed to students who did not have them. The course was taught by an ordained Baptist minister, who also was a teacher at the high school and who, according to expert testimony, taught essentially a fundamentalist, evangelical doctrine. The appeals court concluded that, even assuming the school's purpose was to restrict the course to secular study, the primary effect was the advancement of religion. Use of the state-approved textbook was prohibited. The appeals court directed the lower court to fashion an appropriate remedy "to ensure that any future course is taught within a secular framework focusing on the literary or historical aspects of the Bible, not the religious aspects" (p. 1003).

Thus, Bible study courses at the elementary and secondary levels must be carefully constructed to withstand legal challenge. If the intent is to teach religion, rather than to teach about religion, the courses are best taught off school grounds and without school involvement. As noted at the start of the chapter, while the school may not allow outsiders to give religious instruction on school premises, the U.S. Supreme Court has upheld released time programs whereby schools have the discretion to dismiss students for off-campus religious instruction (*Zorach v. Clauson*, 1952).

Is it an unconstitutional advancement of religion to include religious symbolism, Christmas carols, and the like during the Christmas season in classroom programs and school assemblies? The leading decision in this area comes from the U.S. Court of Appeals for the Eighth Circuit, which has jurisdiction for a number of Midwestern states. In *Florey v. Sioux Falls School District* (1980), the Eighth Circuit ruled that a school policy allowing teachers to observe holidays that have both a religious and a secular basis is constitutional. Included among the holidays were Christmas, Easter, Passover, Hanukkah, St. Valentine's Day, St. Patrick's Day, and Halloween. The school policy allowed explanation of the nature of the holidays in an unbiased and objective manner without sectarian indoctrination, together with references to music, art, literature, and the use of religious symbols. One of the three judges in the case dissented from the ruling. He maintained that the policy was sectarian in purpose, suggesting that, if the goal was purely instructional, "the observance of the holidays of religions less familiar to most American public school children than either the Christian or Jewish holidays would seem more likely to increase student knowledge and promote religious tolerance" (p. 1324). In a number of Texas school districts, this is what is done. The *Florey* decision has been generally followed in the years since it was handed down. The most recent example involves a federal district court's citing *Florey* in upholding inclusion of religious songs in a school choir program (*Bauchman v. West High School*). The case first arose when a Jewish choir student objected to the singing of "May the Lord Bless You and Keep You" and "Friends" at high school graduation. The trial judge refused to halt the songs, a decision the U.S. Court of Appeals for the Tenth Circuit reversed. However, students and parents skirted the order by singing one of the songs anyway. The student continued her lawsuit, protesting the inclusion of religious songs in the choir repertoire and the requirement that the choir sing at Mormon temples. The trial judge ruled that the inclusion of the songs was not the equivalent of prayer. "Public schools are not required to delete from the curriculum all materials that may offend any religious sensibility," he wrote. The decision has been appealed once again to the Tenth Circuit.

Distribution of Religious Literature

It is impermissible for school personnel or outside organizations to distribute Bibles and other religious material to public school students on school grounds. This is the teaching of *Meltzer v. Board of Public Instruction*, the 1978 Fifth Circuit ruling referred to in the context of the school prayer discussion. While it is impermissible to allow school personnel and religious officials to distribute religious material, it is permissible to provide a place in a public school where adherents of any faith may deposit religious literature for voluntary student pickup. However, to remain neutral, schools must accommodate requests from any religious denomination to have their materials available for student pickup. It thus may be preferable to have persons from the community wanting to distribute religious literature to students do so off school grounds.

    While school officials and outside groups may not distribute religious literature on campus, such is not the case with students. As discussed in the previous chapter, a federal judge ruled in *Clark v. Dallas I.S.D.* that student distribution of religious material is within the ambit of the First Amendment free speech clause.

Secular Humanism

Some accuse the public schools of fostering an anti-God "religion of secular humanism" by not according religion a greater role in the curriculum. To date, the concept of secular humanism as a religion under the establishment clause has not been accepted by the judiciary. As the U.S. Court of Appeals for the Ninth Circuit recently observed, "Both the dictionary definition of religion and the clear weight of caselaw are to the contrary" (*Peloza v. Capistrano Unified School District*). Parents in the Houston I.S.D. argued in 1972 that the teaching of evolution in the public schools without critical analysis and without the inclusion of other theories in the lesson plan violated the establishment clause because it constituted state promotion of a "religion of secularism." Plaintiffs also asserted that their religious freedoms were compromised because the teaching of evolution constituted a direct attack on their religion. The district court rejected both contentions. District policy did not prohibit discussing the biblical view of creation, and the judge considered classroom materials discussing Darwinian evolution "peripheral to the matter of religion." Nor did the judge find any substantial interference with the right of plaintiffs to exercise their religious beliefs (*Wright v. Houston I.S.D.*). The *Wright* decision is noteworthy because it reconfirms the historic power of the school over the curriculum. The Fifth Circuit noted in affirming the district court's decision, "To require the teaching of every theory of human origin, as alternatively suggested by plaintiffs, would be an unwarranted intrusion into the authority of public school systems to control the academic curriculum" (p. 138).

A more recent decision involving the secular humanism issue occurred in Alabama in 1987. In *Smith v. Board of School Commissioners of Mobile County*, fundamentalist Christians alleged that textbooks used in the public schools unconstitutionally established the religion of secular humanism. In an extraordinary decision, the trial judge found that secular humanism constituted a religion for establishment clause purposes. It was the first time any court had so ruled. He then found that forty-four of the forty-five textbooks at issue in the case unconstitutionally advanced the religion of secular humanism. The books included elementary school social studies texts, high school history texts, and high school home economics texts. The trial judge forbade the public schools from using the forty-four books for any purpose other than as a resource in a comparative religion class.

Given the novelty of the trial judge's thinking, most legal commentators were not surprised when the Eleventh Circuit reversed the decision. The appeals court simply assumed for the sake of argument, without deciding, that secular humanism is a religion. The school district had not breached the establishment clause, the appeals court reasoned, merely because some of the content of the books happened to coincide with secular humanist views. In an apt analogy, the court noted that, simply because religious commandments prohibit murder and theft, governmental action making those actions crimes is not an advancement of religion. In order for governmental conduct to constitute an impermissible advancement of religion, the governmental action must amount to an endorsement of religion. The books at issue were not hostile to religion, the court noted. "The message conveyed by these textbooks is one of neutrality: the textbooks neither endorse theistic religion as a system of belief, nor discredit it" (p. 692).

The *Smith* decision is currently the leading decision on the issue of secular humanism. An important question left unresolved is whether secular humanism is a religion under the establishment clause. The Supreme Court has not settled the issue, mainly because no case has yet reached it involving an alleged establishment of anything other than Protestant Christianity.

An issue somewhat related to secular humanism arose recently when parents in two separate actions accused school officials of unconstitutionally promoting a pagan religion by utilizing an elementary school supplemental reading series called "Impressions." The series consists of some ten thousand literary selections and suggested classroom activities. The parents primarily objected to thirty-two readings that they contended promoted the practice of witchcraft, a religion they call "Wicca." Most of the challenged selections ask children to discuss witches or sorcerers. Some selections also ask students to pretend that they are witches or sorcerers and role-play these characters. The parents argued that the readings and activities constitute impermissible advancement of religion contrary to the establishment clause and also evince hostility to the Christian religion by indoctrinating students in non-Christian values and denigrating Christian symbols and holidays.

In one of the cases, the U.S. Court of Appeals for the Seventh Circuit had trouble understanding what religion was being promoted. "[W]e have before us a party claiming that the use of a collection of stories, a very few of which resonate with beliefs held by some people, somewhere, of some religion, has established this religion in a public school. This allegation of some amorphous religion becomes so much speculation as to what some people might think" (*Fleischfresser v. Directors of School District 200*, p. 688). The court went on to find no violation of the *Lemon* guidelines. Nor did the court find the reading program substantially burdened the parents' free exercise rights, noting they remain free to teach their children religion. Further, the court observed that the government has a compelling purpose in using the series to "build and enhance students' reading skills and develop their senses of imagination and creativity." A Florida court of appeals drew from the *Fleischfresser* reasoning in rejecting a similar challenge to the observance of Halloween in an elementary school. The court concluded that Halloween decorations portraying witches, cauldrons, and brooms "make Halloween a fun day for students and serve an educational purpose by enriching their educational background and cultural awareness" (*Guyer v. School Board of Alachua County*, p. 808). Both the Florida Supreme Court and the U.S. Supreme Court refused to hear the *Guyer* case.

In the other decision involving the "Impressions" reading series, the U.S. Court of Appeals for the Ninth Circuit assumed, without deciding, that Wicca was a religion for establishment clause purposes. While the court ruled similarly to the Seventh Circuit, they did note that having students perform religious rituals could constitute a violation of the establishment clause. However, in this instance, the court noted that the rituals were not religious in nature. "[T]he activities in the Challenged Selections are fantasy activities, drawn from a secular source and used for a secular purpose, that happen to resume religious practices. They are *not* 'overt religious exercises' that raise Establishment Clause concerns" (*Brown v. Woodland Joint Unified School District*, p. 1382). The activities thus could be differentiated from having students perform a baptism, take communion, or chant a rosary. In a footnote, the court cautiously observed that some student participatory activities of a religious nature might even be permissible in school if used for secular purposes. The judges cited as examples having students act out a ceremonial American Indian dance, reenact the Last Supper, or conduct a Passover dinner if presented for historical or cultural purposes.

Student Religious Clubs

In 1981 in *Widmar v. Vincent*, the U.S. Supreme Court upheld the right of student groups to hold religious services in buildings on a public university campus. The majority ruled that the use of buildings for this purpose does not confer state endorsement of religious activities when other, nonreligious groups have access to the buildings. Rather, such a policy of accommodation advances the free expression rights of the university students.

Congress followed up on the *Widmar* decision in 1984 by passing the Equal Access Act, which gives non-curriculum-related student groups access to public secondary schools during noninstructional time to engage in religious, political, philosophical, or other types of expression. The law applies only to secondary school campuses in districts receiving federal financial assistance and only if school officials have converted the campus into a "limited open forum" by allowing one or more non-curriculum-related student groups to meet on school premises for expressive purposes (20 U.S.C. §4071(a)). "Noninstructional time" means the time when no instruction is taking place, i.e., before and after school or during a student activities period.

The U.S. Supreme Court ruled in 1990 that the Equal Access Act does not violate the Constitution (*Westside Community Schools v. Mergens*). The case involved a Christian club that wanted to use the high school campus before and after school for religious discussion and worship. The school argued that since it allowed only curriculum-related student clubs to use the campus, it did not have to grant access to Bridget Mergens's Christian club. Mergens argued that some of the student clubs were not curriculum-related. She pointed to the chess club, a surfers' group, and a service organization.

The Court interpreted a curriculum-related group to mean one that meets any of the following requirements: (1) the subject matter of the group is taught, e.g., French Club; (2) the subject matter of the group concerns the body of courses as a whole, e.g., student government; (3) participation in the group is required for a course, e.g., band; and (4) participation in the group results in academic credit, e.g., orchestra. Since the chess club, surfers' group, and service organization did not fit into any of these categories, they were non-curriculum-related. Thus, the school had a limited open forum and had to grant the same access to the Christian club as to the other non-curriculum-related clubs, i.e., the right to meet on campus before and after school and the right to school bulletin boards, the PA system, and similar facilities to announce its meetings.

The school had also argued that if it allowed the Christian club to use the campus, it would be breaching the wall of separation between church and state. The Court rejected the argument, noting that the Equal Access Act does not violate the establishment clause of the First Amendment but rather represents a reasonable accommodation to the free speech and associational rights of public secondary students. In a key passage, the justices observed that secondary students are sufficiently mature to recognize that the school is not endorsing religion by allowing students themselves to engage in religious communication on campus during noninstructional time.

While the Equal Access Act thus allows a student religious group to discuss religion and engage in prayer on campus before and after school if the secondary school maintains a limited public forum, the law specifies that school personnel may only be present at these religious meetings in a *nonparticipatory* capacity.

It is important to note that the Equal Access Act applies to non-school-sponsored student religious organizations. The statute does not limit the First Amendment rights of individual students to come together voluntarily during the school day for religious expression on school grounds, including prayer and the distribution of religious literature, so long as it is done in a nondisruptive manner (*Clark v. Dallas I.S.D.*).

Religious Exemptions

In education, the most celebrated free exercise case is *West Virginia State Board of Education v. Barnette*, a 1943 U.S. Supreme Court ruling. There the Court ruled that the school board could not compel Jehovah's Witnesses to salute the flag. The students and their parents objected that under their religion saluting the flag was a violation of a tenet against worshipping a graven image (Exodus 20: 4–5). The case is especially important because it asserts that the government may never compel a person to profess a belief.

Writing for the majority, Justice Robert H. Jackson emphasized that the First Amendment was especially designed to protect freedom of spirit and intellect. "If there is any fixed star in our constitutional constellation, it is that no official, high or petty, can prescribe what shall be orthodox in politics, nationalism, religion, or other matters of opinion or force citizens to confess by word or act their faith therein" (p. 642). Jackson added that the ruling was not just confined to those who assert a religious basis for their refusal. "While religion supplies appellees' motive for enduring the discomforts of making the issue in this case, many citizens who do not share these religious views hold such a compulsory rite to infringe constitutional liberty of the individual" (p. 283). Thus a student who refuses to salute the flag for philosophical reasons is entitled to the same exemption as a student who asserts a religious reason for not doing so.

While Justice Jackson was speaking in sweeping terms about the First Amendment, it must be remembered that the decision was announced in the midst of World War II. The excesses of Nazi Germany in promoting nationalism among the youth of that country undoubtedly played a part in the justice's choice of wording. The West Virginia decision has been confined to the flag-salute context and by no means has been read to allow students and their parents a general First Amendment right to seek exemptions from compulsory school or curriculum requirements (however, as noted in Chapter 1, the Texas Education Code does give parents the right to request exemptions from school activities to which they object on religious or moral grounds).

Another U.S. Supreme Court decision of great importance is *Wisconsin v. Yoder* (1972), involving the religious objections of the Old Order Amish to compulsory schooling beyond the eighth grade. The Court ruled for the Amish in this instance but cautioned that it would be extremely reluctant to extend the ruling to other religions. To date, no other religion has been given as broad an exemption as the Old Order Amish.

A number of recent cases have dealt with the objections of parents and teachers alike to various school practices, based on claims of interference with religious beliefs. For example, in *Davis v. Page* (1974), parents of the Apostolic Lutheran faith objected to the exposure of their children to audiovisual equipment. In *Davis*, a New Hampshire federal district court noted that the state has a legitimate interest in providing uniform education for all its youngsters and that "it is impossible for the state to provide an educational program which is totally acceptable to all religious faiths" (p. 405). However, the court did agree that excusing the children from participating in noneducational activities where audiovisual equipment is used does not violate the establishment clause and represents an agreeable accommodation with the plaintiffs' religious beliefs under the free exercise clause.

A similar issue arose in the early 1980s in Tennessee. There, fundamentalist Christians asserted that they were entitled to an exemption from reading the Holt, Rinehart, and Winston reading series because of their religious beliefs. When the school board mandated that all children must read the series, objecting students refused to do so. Several were suspended, and a lawsuit ensued.

The U.S. Court of Appeals for the Sixth Circuit in a widely reported decision ordered that the parents' complaint be dismissed (*Mozert v. Hawkins County Board of Education*, 1987). To violate the free exercise clause, the government must have compelled or coerced a person either to affirm/disavow beliefs or to do/not do acts that are forbidden or required by the person's religion. Mere exposure to religiously objectionable material did not constitute an infringement on the students' right to freely exercise their religion. "There was no evidence that the conduct required of the students was forbidden by their religion. Rather, the witnesses testified that reading the Holt series 'could' or 'might' lead the students to come to conclusions that were contrary to teachings of their and their parents' religious beliefs. This is not sufficient to establish an unconstitutional burden" (p. 1070).

The *Mozert* decision, however, may have been undermined to some extent by two developments. First, the U.S. Supreme Court justices in *Employment Division of Oregon Dept. of Human Resources v. Smith* agreed that centrality of faith is not a prerequisite to finding a free exercise violation; sincerity of belief is sufficient. Second, Congress enacted the Religious Freedom Restoration Act in 1993, which, as noted earlier in the chapter, requires a school district to show a compelling purpose when a person's religion is substantially burdened. How these developments might affect the outcome of a case involving facts similar to those in *Mozert* are not known.

The Texas Education Code has several provisions granting exemptions for religious reasons to school-related requirements. TEC §26.010 gives parents the right to request an exemption from classroom and other school activities that conflict with a parent's religious or moral beliefs, provided the parent presents a written request and the purpose is not to avoid a test or prevent a child from taking a subject for an entire semester. TEC §25.087 requires school districts to excuse a student from school for religious observances based on a written request from a parent or guardian. Excusal includes travel days to and from the observance. TEC §38.001 grants an exemption from immunization requirements for students entering elementary or secondary school or an institution of higher education upon presentation of an affidavit "stating that the immunization conflicts with the tenets and practice of a recognized church or religious denomination of which the [student] is an adherent or member, except that this exemption does not apply in times of emergency or epidemic declared by the commissioner of health."

TEC §21.406 provides that a school district may not deny a teacher a salary bonus because a teacher is absent from school for observance of a religious holy day. The law, however, applies only to pay supplements. Thus, a teacher can still be required to supply a substitute or give up regular wages for observing a religious holy day.

Administrative guidelines under Title VII of the 1964 Civil Rights Act require employers to make "reasonable accommodation" to the religious practices of employees and job applicants. A refusal to accommodate is justified only by a demonstration that an undue hardship would result. A Texas federal district court decision sheds some light on what "reasonable accommodation" amounts to (*Padon v. White*, 1979). *Padon* involved a Seventh Day Adventist who refused to perform anything other than emergency work on Saturday at the Richmond State School. The employee, Emmit Padon, claimed that his religion required him to refrain from routine work from sundown on Friday to sundown on Saturday. Friction developed with his employers over the building of a bathhouse on Saturdays, and Padon was eventually discharged. The court ordered his reinstatement, noting that the employer could easily have accommodated his bona fide religious practice and, indeed, had done so for a number of years. Noting that an employer has an affirmative duty under Title VII to attempt accommodation, the court relied on a U.S. Supreme Court decision to conclude that "an employer need not accommodate religious practices which would cause the employer to incur more than de minimis costs" (p. 608). Here, the employer's costs were minimal.

Such was not the case in a decision involving the religious beliefs of a Chicago public school teacher. In *Palmer v. Board of Education*, the U.S. Court of Appeals for the Seventh Circuit agreed in 1979 with the trial court that the teacher could be dismissed from her job for refusing to lead children in the Pledge of Allegiance to the flag and teach them patriotic songs. The teacher, a Jehovah's Witness, refused to do so for religious reasons. The district court noted that the school had made a reasonable but unsuccessful effort to accommodate her beliefs and concluded that, given continual complaints from parents and curricular disorder, the school's compelling interest in regulating the curriculum justified the teacher's dismissal. The district court judge observed that the school would have dismissed anyone who refused to follow curriculum requirements. The state therefore was neutral with respect to religion. The case was distinguished from two earlier federal rulings upholding the right of teachers to be exempt from the flag salute in the absence of disorder.

The U.S. Supreme Court elaborated a bit on accommodating an employee's religious practices in *Ansonia Board of Education v. Philbrook* in 1986. In that case, board policy required the employee to take unpaid leave for holy day observance after the three days of paid leave for this purpose were used up. The board did allow an additional three paid leave days for personal leave, but these days could not be used for religious purposes. Ronald Philbrook wanted to use the additional personal leave days for religious purposes or, alternatively, to pay the cost of a substitute while still receiving full pay. The school board rejected both proposals. The Court ruled that the board's position was sufficient under the law unless it could be shown that the three days for personal leave could be used for any purpose other than religion, in which case it would constitute unlawful religious discrimination.

In 1984 the Texas Commissioner of Education upheld the contract nonrenewal of a teacher who refused to conduct Halloween activities in her fourth-grade classroom because she found Halloween to be synonymous with "anti-Christian, pagan worship" (*King v. Whiteface C.I.S.D.*). The teacher said she would conduct instead autumn art and "food-a-rama" projects. The principal directed her by memo to submit a plan for Halloween observance, but she refused to change her intentions. Later, the principal evaluated her performance as unsatisfactory but noted that he would change the evaluation if she would follow his directive regarding the Halloween program. She refused, and her contract was subsequently nonrenewed. The commissioner noted that the principal had tried to accommodate her religious beliefs by stating in his memorandum that she need not participate in the Halloween activities herself and that the plans could be directed by another teacher or by himself. The teacher did not accept the offer of accommodation. The commissioner held that the school had done all it was required to do under the civil rights laws and that the nonrenewal did not penalize her free exercise rights. "The fact that petitioner has a right to practice her religious beliefs free from school district interference does not mean that she may prohibit her students from engaging in activities she finds morally offensive." He added that "the school district has the right to insist that its employees comply with reasonable directives and cooperate with their superiors, even in matters that would ordinarily be considered relatively minor."

Assistance to Sectarian Private Schools

Many states, particularly in the northeastern part of the country, have long had substantial numbers of children attending private schools. It must be remembered that before there were public schools, education was the province of the private sector. Efforts to have all students attend public schools were thwarted by an important U.S. Supreme Court decision, *Pierce v. Society of Sisters* (1925). The Court ruled unanimously that a state law requiring all students to attend public schools would undermine the Fourteenth Amendment property right of private school operators to operate schools. The Court also noted that such a law would diminish the Fourteenth Amendment liberty right of the parent to control the upbringing of children. In short, the state could not monopolize the educational process. At the same time, the Court recognized the right of the state "reasonably to regulate" private schools.

Despite the rise of the public school, many states have long sought ways of aiding private schools directly or, more recently, of providing low- and middle-income parents with tuition tax credits or tuition vouchers so that they can enroll their children in private schools. Efforts in these directions have been stimulated by concerns about the diminished quality of public education. At the moment, about 11 percent of the total U.S. school enrollment attends private schools.

Because most of the private schools are religiously affiliated (over half of the total are Roman Catholic), efforts to aid the private sector quickly run into the establishment clause. As noted at the start of the chapter, the U.S. Supreme Court ruled in 1947, in the first major case involving the establishment clause and education, that it is not a breach of the wall of separation between church and state for the government to underwrite the bus transportation costs of pupils attending religious schools. The Court ruled in a 1968 case that a state could loan secular textbooks to religious schools (*Board of Education v. Allen*) and later upheld state-supported standardized testing, diagnostic service, and counseling programs for private schools (*Wolman v. Walter*, 1977). However, in other cases the Court has struck down efforts to aid private schools. In *Grand Rapids v. Ball* (1985) the Court decided against a program that sent public school teachers into private schools to conduct remedial and enrichment classes during the day and extracurricular activities after school hours. In *Aguilar v. Felton* (1985), the Court disallowed the use of Title I money for remedial courses taught by public school teachers in New York City private schools.

In 1993, the Supreme Court ruled in a narrow five-to-four decision that it is not a violation of the establishment clause for a public school district to pay the costs of a sign language interpreter for a deaf student who attends a private religious school (*Zobrest v. Catalina Foothills School District*). The decision was based in part on a 1986 ruling that allowed a blind student to use a state vocational education grant to attend a seminary (*Witters v. Washington Dept. of Services*). The majority likened the assistance to pupil benefit programs such as bus transportation reimbursement that have only an incidental effect of benefiting religious institutions. The four dissenters argued that the publicly funded sign-language interpreter's "every gesture would be infused with religious significance," thus involving the state in impermissibly inculcating religion. The Court did not rule whether the school district was legally obliged to provide the related service under the Individuals with Disabilities Education Act, a matter for the lower courts to decide.

Supporters of tuition tax credits and vouchers to parents were given a boost in 1983 when the U.S. Supreme Court in a five-to-four decision upheld a Minnesota plan of tax deductions for educational expenses at both public and private schools (*Mueller v. Allen*). In an earlier case, the Court had struck down tuition grants and tax benefits for low-income families who send their children to private schools (*Committee for Public Education v. Nyquist*). The majority distinguished the *Nyquist* decision in that under the Minnesota plan, the money flowed to parents, not schools, and both public and private schools were included. In a key passage, Justice William Rehnquist, who wrote the opinion, observed that "The historic purposes of the [establishment] Clause simply do not encompass the sort of attenuated financial benefit, ultimately controlled by the private choice of individual parents, that eventually flows to parochial schools from the neutrally available tax benefit at issue in this case" (p. 3069). The *Mueller* decision has led many commentators to predict that the U.S. Supreme Court will uphold a voucher program whereby parents use public funds to send their children to any public or private sectarian or nonsectarian school of their choice.

Lacking the long tradition of private education, Texas has not been in the forefront of efforts to aid the nonpublic educational sector, though in recent legislative sessions increasing interest has been expressed in voucher plans. In 1995 the Texas Legislature narrowly rejected a pilot voucher program that would have provided low-income families with state-funded scholarships to send their children to sectarian and nonsectarian private schools. There is little doubt that such a program, if enacted, would be challenged under provisions of the Texas Constitution. As noted at the beginning of the chapter, Article I, §7 of the Texas Constitution states that "no money shall be appropriated or drawn from the Treasury for the benefit of any sect, or religious society, theological, or religious seminary; nor shall property belonging to the State be appropriated for any such purposes." This provision was added in 1896 and represented a victory for public school advocates. Article VII, §5 of the Texas Constitution provides in part that "no law shall ever be enacted appropriating any part of the permanent or available school fund to any other purpose whatever [than support of the public free schools]; nor shall the same, or any part thereof ever be appropriated or used for the support of any sectarian school."

Taken together, these two provisions of the state constitution suggest a stricter adherence to separation of church and state in Texas than under the federal constitution and the constitutions of many states. A review of Texas Attorney General advisory opinions over the years illustrates this point. For example, on several occasions in the early 1940s the attorney general cited both clauses of the Texas Constitution in advising that parochial students may not be transported by public school bus (*Att'y. Gen. Op. 0-4220*, 1941; *Att'y. Gen. Op. 0-7128*, 1946). In 1993 the attorney general advised that prekindergarten programs created pursuant to the Texas Education Code must be part of the public schooling system because prekindergarten students are entitled to the benefits of the available school fund. He added, "under Article VII, Section 5, the available school fund can be used only for the support of the public free schools" (*Att'y. Gen. Op. DM-200*). These opinions demonstrate strong endorsement of a wall of separation between church and state in Texas. How Texas courts would apply state constitutional provisions to a voucher program channeling public money to parents who then choose from among a variety of public and private religious and nonreligious schools is not known. In the case of higher education, the Texas Attorney General has advised that tuition equalization grants do not violate state constitutional strictures (*Att'y. Gen. Op. M-861*, 1971). The presumption under both state and federal constitutions seems to be that since college students are less impressionable than younger students, this form of indirect aid does not violate strict adherence to separation of church and state.

Parents choosing a sectarian private school for their children's education and the operators of these schools occasionally complain that state and federal legislation interferes with their religious freedom. The U.S. Supreme Court had ruled in the important 1925 *Pierce* case, which upheld the right of private schools to operate, that states nevertheless could "reasonably regulate" private schools: "No question is raised concerning the power of the State reasonably to regulate all schools, to inspect, supervise, and examine them, their teachers, and pupils; to require that all children of proper age attend some school, that teachers shall be of good moral character and patriotic disposition, that certain studies plainly essential to good citizenship must be taught, and that nothing be taught which is manifestly inimical to the public welfare" (p. 534).

The problem is that some parents and private school operators
believe that such governmental regulation serves to undermine
their schools' religious character. In many states, lawsuits over state
regulation of private schools, especially those with a fundamentalist
religious philosophy, proliferate. Such is not the case in Texas. Private schools need not be accredited by the state. While the Texas
Education Code contains an elaborate chapter providing for the certification and regulation of private schools, §132.002(a)(2) grants an
exemption to "nonprofit schools owned, controlled, operated, and
conducted by bona fide religious, denominational, eleemosynary
[charitable], or similar public institutions exempt from property
taxation. . . ." The clause goes on to say that such schools may
choose to apply for certification and, in such event, are subject to
the provisions of the chapter.

Certification of private schools is no longer a responsibility of
the Texas Education Agency. The Texas Legislature shifted that responsibility to the Texas Employment Commission in 1995. Prior
to the change, TEA granted state certification to private schools approved by a coalition of private school associations. Many private
schools seek state certification as a means of demonstrating the
quality of their programs and facilitating entry of their graduates
into Texas public colleges and universities. In an unpublished 1983
decision, the U.S. District Court for the Eastern District of Texas
decided that an eighteen-year-old graduate of an unaccredited private school was denied no constitutional right when she was refused
admission to Stephen F. Austin University (*Prater v. Stephen F. Austin University*). The student alleged a denial of religious freedom,
but the court found that attending nonaccredited schools was not
central to her religion and that the university had a strong reason to
make accreditation an admissions requirement.

Private schools are not exempt from basic health and safety
laws passed by local, state, and federal governments. While some in
the private sector may argue that these laws interfere with institutional autonomy, courts generally uphold them as appropriate governmental efforts to protect all persons regardless of religious belief.
Occasionally, the laws are welcomed. Thus, few object to a provision of the Texas Education Code first enacted in 1971 making dem-
onstrations and disruptive activities on the property of public or private schools criminal offenses (TEC §37.123).

The federal government has passed several civil rights laws that
regulate both private and public schools. Some of these laws have
exemptions for religiously affiliated private schools and some do

not. In an important 1976 case, *Runyon v. McCrary*, the U.S. Supreme Court ruled that under 42 U.S.C. §1981 a private school cannot discriminate in admissions on racial grounds. This decision had great significance for the so-called freedom schools, or "white academies," established during the desegregation of public schools in the South. As noted in Chapter 1, §1981 applies to discrimination occurring after a contract has been signed. Thus, a minority child subject to discrimination after being admitted to a private school would have a cause of action.

The *Runyon* case did not involve sectarian private schools that refuse to admit black or other minority children for religious reasons. That issue arose in a 1983 Supreme Court ruling, *Bob Jones University v. United States*, involving the Internal Revenue Service's curtailing tax-exempt status to discriminatory schools. In an eight-to-one decision, the Court upheld the IRS. Writing for the majority, Chief Justice Warren Burger rejected the contention that racial discrimination could be justified by religious doctrine, a view espoused by Bob Jones University and Goldsboro Christian Schools, another institution involved in the suit. "The government has a fundamental, overriding interest in eradicating racial discrimination in education. . . . [T]hat governmental interest substantially outweighs whatever burden denial of tax benefits places on petitioners' exercise of their religious beliefs" (p. 2035).

SUMMARY

In this chapter we have reviewed the somewhat stormy relationship between education and religion, a relationship which is still evolving. Both the Texas and U.S. constitutions make it very clear that public schools are to be neutral regarding religion. Thus, the U.S. Supreme Court has mandated that school-sponsored prayer, even at graduation ceremonies, violates the wall of separation between church and state. At the same time, both constitutions provide strong support for individual freedom of religious belief and exercise. Recent developments such as the federal Equal Access Act extend protection to students who want to engage in religious activities on campus, and Congressional enactment of the Religious Freedom Restoration Act in 1993 gives added support to those who want greater accommodation of their religious beliefs in public schools. The inherent tensions between avoiding endorsement of religion and accommodating religious activity make decision making particularly difficult for educators, policymakers, and judges alike. If there is any consistent line of reasoning running through the case law, it is that public schools must avoid either advancing or inhibiting religion. Teachers and administrators are best advised to fall back on this commonsense rationale when confronted with a complaint, using the cases discussed above as guidelines.

EIGHT
Student Discipline

NO AREA of school law was more significantly impacted by Senate Bill 1 than student discipline. Concerned over increasing violence and disruption in our schools, the 1995 legislature took bold steps designed to restore the teacher's authority in the classroom and to guarantee a safe school environment for each child. In this chapter we will examine the changes wrought by Senate Bill 1 in the larger context of federal and constitutional requirements of student discipline.

GUIDELINES FOR RULE MAKING

We begin with some general principles concerning the formulation and enforcement of rules in general. Regardless of the theoretical approach a particular district or school professional takes toward student discipline, rules are a fundamental component. In many ways, the school and classroom are a microcosm of society. Just as rules are necessary for society to function, so too are rules important for an orderly educational environment. As will be noted in the next section, the presence of rules is a prerequisite to due process, since accused persons are entitled to notice of the charges against them.

Rules should meet two basic requirements. First, rules should be effective in behavior control. Students must understand them in order to behave in the desired manner. Second, rules must be legally valid. Generally, courts defer to educators on the interpretation and application of rules. In 1982 the U.S. Supreme Court in *Board of Education of Rogers, Arkansas v. McCluskey* dealt with a case in which a local school board had expelled a student for drinking. The school rule in question prohibited drug use, and did not speak of alcohol. Nevertheless, the Supreme Court ruled for the school district. In a brief unsigned opinion, the Court noted that alcohol can be classified as a drug and concluded that "the District Court and the Court of Appeals plainly erred in replacing the Board's construction of [the rule] with their own notions under the facts of the case." The message was clear—local school boards can interpret their own rules and courts must defer to those interpretations, within reason.

Still, the school bears the burden of proving the legal validity of school rules when they touch on constitutionally or statutorily protected behavior. This point will be developed in more detail below. With these considerations in mind, the following guidelines are offered as a means of helping school administrators and teachers improve the rules they construct to maintain order in the school and classroom.

Rules Must Have a Rational Purpose

People are more inclined to follow rules if they can see that the rules are rationally related to providing a safe and orderly environment. In deciding which rules should be retained or developed in the context of student discipline, ask whether the rule in question is really necessary to prevent disruption and to safeguard the rights of others. Most discipline experts agree that the fewer the rules, the better the understanding of what behavior is appropriate and what is not.

The Meaning of Rules Must Be Clear

Rules that are so vague as to be meaningless are self-defeating. The U.S. Court of Appeals for the Seventh Circuit observed in an often-cited case that a school rule must not be so vague as to penalize activities that are free from any taint of impropriety (*Soglin v. Kauffman*, 1969). A clearly stated rule that describes the conduct to be avoided meets the threshold requirement of effective discipline by setting forth a standard of reference. Examples of vague rules abound: "Students exhibiting poor citizenship will be disciplined"; "Hazing in all forms is prohibited"; "Students are to conduct themselves at all times in a manner consistent with any public building." These rules are not likely to be very effective in behavior control, because they provide no standard of reference. What one person considers poor citizenship may be good citizenship to another. Hazing to one might be just a harmless prank to another. Behavior appropriate for a public building obviously depends upon the type of public building. What is tolerated at a municipal auditorium during a rock group performance is quite different from the behavior one would expect at a public hospital.

Other rules are defined in terms unfamiliar to students. This is most apparent when school districts reproduce sections from a criminal statute in their student handbooks. Criminal laws are often written in "legalese" and are very complex. Adults—even legal experts—have a hard time understanding them. Other times, the rules will include phrases or words beyond the comprehension of most students. For example, consider this rule from the student handbook of a rural North Texas school district: "Students are to observe good etiquette in the lunchroom at all times." Some of us would have a hard time defining "etiquette." Like a Supreme Court justice some years ago wrestling with the definition of "hard-core pornography," we might not be able to define it but know it when we see it. Unfortunately, such a definition is not conducive to promoting a good rule system.

How can we improve the clarity of rules? One way is to keep rules short, yet comprehensive, by including several diverse examples to illustrate meaning. Thus, the rule against hazing can be improved by giving examples of what is considered hazing and what is not. The rule promoting good etiquette in the lunchroom could also be improved by indicating that proper conduct does not include such behavior as . . . and then listing three or four specific examples of inappropriate lunchroom behavior. We would probably be better off dropping the term *etiquette* altogether and finding another term. Citing examples will clarify the meaning of broad rules without sacrificing brevity.

A second suggestion is to transpose the wording of complex terminology into terms understandable to students. A criminal statute can be easily simplified without losing its thrust. A reference could then be given to the statute, or the statute itself could be included in an appendix to the student handbook. A third suggestion is to have students help in rewording or constructing rules. What is meaningful to administrators and teachers may not be to students.

Equally self-defeating are rules that are never effectively brought to the students' attention. If students do not know what the rules are, they cannot comply. State discipline laws have helped in this regard by requiring that each student is to receive a copy of the student code of conduct upon publication. Changes during the year should be published and distributed to the students in a timely manner. It is wise to update and distribute the student code of conduct to each student and parent annually, and to new students and their parents at the time of enrollment.

Effective classroom management requires that teachers make a practice of periodically referring to rules. This is particularly important for younger students who cannot look them up for themselves. Many elementary school teachers construct a poster of four or five key rules and place it in a conspicuous place. The rules are carefully explained at the start of each school term and periodically thereafter, as for example when a rash of misbehavior breaks out.

Rules That Relate to Protected Behavior Must Be Carefully Developed

Rules that pertain to constitutionally or statutorily protected behavior, particularly free speech and press, must be drawn with special care so as not to "chill" the exercise of these rights. The development of a prior restraint system for reviewing student and teacher publications has already been discussed in Chapter 6. Legal validity comes into play most often with these rules. Legal validity relates primarily to issues of vagueness and overbreadth. Vagueness means that the rule is so ambiguously worded as to provide no guide to acceptable and unacceptable conduct. A rule against "misconduct" suffers from vagueness. Overbreadth means that the rule sweeps too broadly and penalizes protected behavior. A rule prohibiting "talking in the library" is overbroad, for, if taken literally, it prohibits all oral communication.

A good example of a rule whose legal validity is questionable is one stating that students will be disciplined for "upbraiding, insulting, or abusing any teacher on school property or at a school function." At first glance, such a rule seems perfectly reasonable and appropriate. Many schools include a variation of it in their student codes of conduct. The problem is that it touches communication, a constitutional right. Two courts in 1985, the Washington State Supreme Court (*State v. Reyes*) and the Court of Appeals of Kentucky (*Commonwealth v. Ashcraft*), struck down statutes to this effect as being both vague and overbroad, and thus in violation of freedom of expression. If the terms *upbraiding, insulting,* and *abusing* had been defined and/or illustrations provided, the rules may have survived constitutional attack. In Texas, the U.S. Court of Appeals for the Fifth Circuit ruled in 1972 that when the constitutionality of a school rule is questioned "it is settled law that the burden of justifying the regulation falls upon the school board" (*Shanley v. Northeast I.S.D.*, 1972, p. 969). It is wise, therefore, to be particularly sensitive to the wording of rules that relate to constitutional and statutory rights, such as expression, association, assembly, search and seizure, and privacy.

Rules That Apply Off Campus Must Be
Carefully Worded and Applied

Schools, of course, retain the same authority over students at school-sponsored activities occurring off campus as they have when students are on campus. But, frequently, the question arises as to whether student behavior occurring off campus at a non-school-sponsored activity is beyond the reach of the school. Senate Bill 1 expands school authority over off-campus conduct significantly. Students must be removed to an AEP (alternative education program) if they engage in conduct punishable as a felony off campus. This is discussed in more detail below.

But what about nonfelonious behavior? Can students be disciplined in any way for what they do away from school? While there is a tendency in this direction, it is not absolute. The U.S. Court of Appeals for the Fifth Circuit wrestled with this issue in the *Shanley* case. There, school officials had sought to punish students for circulating a newspaper of their own creation off campus before and after school. As described in Chapter 6, the court struck down the school rule as unconstitutionally vague and overbroad because it was too generally worded and failed to follow the requirements necessary for a legal prior-review system. Though the students argued that school officials should *never* be able to punish students for what they do off campus, the court refused to endorse this proposition. However, the opinion makes it clear that school officials must have a convincing reason for punishing students for what they do on their own time.

Examples of school rules likely to meet this criterion include those pertaining to athletic training, to behavior at spectator activities at another school, and to behavior at the bus stop. In most instances, school officials would be able to justify punishing students for misbehavior occurring in these situations because the relationship between the legitimate interests of the school and student misbehavior appears clear. However, when the relationship is not clear, the school would be acting outside its sphere of authority. The law uses the term *ultra vires* to apply to such situations, and an *ultra vires* action is null and void. This doesn't mean that students can't be held accountable for off-campus behavior, for, as the court noted in *Shanley*, students are also subject to the laws of the state and community.

What is important about rules pertaining to the behavior of students on their own time is that there must be a clear relationship between the off-campus conduct and the legitimate interests of the school, and the rules must be worded to apply to off-campus behavior. If students are not notified that their off-campus behavior may subject them to school discipline procedures, any action taken by the school may be overturned if challenged.

Rules Must Be Consistently Enforced

Unless rules are enforced, they lose their influence as behavior guides. Speed limits are a good example. Regardless of the reasons for lack of consistent enforcement, the fact that one is infrequently penalized for driving over most speed limits results in almost everyone's ignoring the law.

A good example of selective enforcement in the school setting is a 1979 State Board of Education ruling (*Green v. Troy I.S.D.*). (The State Board of Education no longer has jurisdiction over student discipline cases.) The case involved a student who was suspended from school for violating the dress code provision on hair length. He argued that he should not have been suspended, because other students who had hair just as long but kept it tucked behind their ears while in school were not suspended. Green preferred to wear his hair over his ears. The state board agreed with the student that the inconsistent enforcement denied him equal protection of the laws and was arbitrary and capricious.

Rules Must Be Fairly Enforced

Starting with the development and the promulgation of rules, school administrators and teachers should endeavor to see that all actions aimed at student behavior control are fair. A prerequisite, of course, is that classroom rules must be consistent with school policy and with state and federal law. Insofar as classroom management is concerned, state and federal laws leave a good deal of discretion to educators. But at the same time, courts reserve the right to intervene if fair play is not evident.

It thus makes good educational sense to bend over backward to guarantee fair play. Zechariah Chafee, a Harvard law professor, noted many years ago: "It is easy to understand how educational authorities believe that they will secure efficiency and desired standards through the possession of absolute powers. However, an institution which professes to prepare youth for life in a democracy might easily give them an example of fair play when it is conducting its own affairs" ("The Internal Affairs of Associations Not for

Profit," *Harvard Law Review* 43 [1930]: 1027). Professor Chafee's observation would seem to apply as much to our day as to his.

Fairness is not to be confused with permissiveness. A Texas federal court judge once told an audience of school attorneys and superintendents that even seemingly frivolous matters should be treated seriously in the interest of fairness. But once it is clear that the right student is being punished for the right reason and there are no mitigating circumstances, appropriate sanctions should be levied. Indeed, to ignore misbehavior is an evasion of professional responsibility and contributes to the collapse of effective classroom and school management.

DUE PROCESS GENERALLY

Due process is one of the most overworked and inaccurately used expressions in schools today. The expression comes from the Fifth and Fourteenth amendments to the U.S. Constitution, both of which require that the state provide "due process" to an individual prior to taking from that person "life, liberty, or property." There are three key concepts necessary to an understanding of the due process clauses in our Constitution.

First, there must be some action of the state. Generally speaking, actions by private entities do not implicate the due process clause. Thus, a teacher in a private school who is fired without notice or an opportunity for a hearing may rightly complain of a breach of contract, or that the school has violated its own policies. But the teacher has no due process case under the Constitution for the simple reason that the private school is not restrained by the Constitution. The same holds true for the private school student who is expelled without notice or a hearing.

Second, the state must have deprived the individual of "life, liberty, or property." We are not aware of any school in Texas that purports to take away anyone's life (the incremental loss of life on a daily basis suffered by teachers and administrators happens too slowly to count—the due process clause is concerned with more dramatic losses of life). So the educator or student who sues over a violation of due process must assert a "property interest" or a "liberty interest."

Third, the nature of the process due depends on the severity of the deprivation. Due process is a flexible term that fits a wide variety of situations. When the government withholds a certain amount from a paycheck for income tax purposes the state has taken action and brought about a deprivation of property. Therefore, some process is due. When the state charges a person with the crime of murder and seeks a life imprisonment or death penalty, the state is also taking action and bringing about a deprivation of life, liberty, and property. Some process is due. Both situations require due process. But since the second case involves a much greater deprivation than the first, the amount of process due is much greater in the second situation than the first.

To summarize, an analysis of a due process claim hinges on the answer to three questions: (1) Did the state take action? (2) Did the state deprive the individual of life, liberty, or property? and (3) Did the state provide the process that is due for such a deprivation?

The meaning of due process of law came early to Texas and other states within the jurisdiction of the U.S. Court of Appeals for the Fifth Circuit. In *Dixon v. Alabama State Board of Education,* a 1961 Fifth Circuit ruling, the court held that students at a public college are entitled to fair notice of the rules they were charged with breaking and a fair hearing before they could be expelled. The court then set forth what it considered to be the components of fair notice and a fair hearing. The notice should contain a statement of the specific charges and the grounds that, if proven, would justify expulsion. The court then pointed out that "the nature of the hearing should vary depending upon the circumstances of the particular case" (p. 158). Insofar as the circumstances of *Dixon* are concerned, the students first should be given the names of the witnesses against them and a report on the facts to which each witness testifies. Second, the students should be given an opportunity to present to the board of trustees or administrative officials of the college their own defense against the charges, including the right to call witnesses on their behalf. Finally, the students should be apprised of the results and findings of the hearing in a report open to their inspection.

The *Dixon* case involved expulsion from a public college. A 1975 U.S. Supreme Court ruling extended the *Dixon* principle to short-term suspensions from a public school (*Goss v. Lopez*). In *Goss,* the U.S. Supreme Court held that "the total exclusion from the educational process for more than a trivial period . . . is a serious event in the life of the suspended child." The Court continued, "Neither the property interest in educational benefits temporarily denied nor the liberty interest in reputation, which is also implicated, is so insubstantial that suspensions may constitutionally be imposed by any procedure the school chooses, no matter how arbitrary" (*Goss v. Lopez*, 1975). In other words, a deprivation of educational services must involve due process. In *Goss*, the Court concluded that, because the state provides compulsory schooling, even a short-term suspension deprives the student of a property right and, thus, requires due process. In cases of suspensions of ten days or less, the Court ruled that due process requires school officials to give the student informal notice of the misbehavior and an opportunity to offer an explanation. Such an informal give-and-take is also necessary lest school officials erroneously suspend the wrong student and thereby deprive that student of a protected liberty interest in his or her reputation.

The procedure outlined by the Court requires that "the student be given oral or written notice of the charges against him and, if he denies them, an explanation of the evidence the authorities have and an opportunity to present his side of the story" (p. 581). The interchange can take place minutes after the misconduct has occurred; there need be no time delay. Such a procedure prior to a short-term suspension will, the Court noted, provide a "meaningful hedge against erroneous action. At least the disciplinarian will be alerted to the existence of disputes about facts and arguments about cause and effect. He may then determine himself to summon the accuser, permit cross-examination, and allow the student to present his own witnesses. In more difficult cases, he may permit counsel. In any event, his discretion will be more informed and we think the risk of error substantially reduced" (pp. 583–584).

The greater the loss suffered by the student, the more sympathetic courts are likely to be to claims of lack of due process. Three cases involving grade disputes clearly illustrate this. In *Obersteller v. Flour Bluff I.S.D.*, a high school student claimed a denial of due process when he was "arbitrarily" assigned a grade of 70 in athletics for a six-week grading period. The court noted that the student still received a final grade of "A" and thus his injury, if any, was too trivial to invoke the due process clause of the Fourteenth Amendment.

The same result occurred in *Raymon v. Alvord I.S.D.* when the student complained of a lowering of her algebra grade by three points for the six-weeks grading period. The Fifth Circuit did not look at the six-weeks grade, but rather the overall effect of this three-point penalty. And the court appeared to be a bit put out:

> Ms. Raymon's claim that the insignificant decrease in her overall grade point average, from 95.478 to 95.413, constituted a deprivation of a

vested property or liberty interest without due process is patently insubstantial.

Thus the court dismissed the case.

In *New Braunfels I.S.D. v. Armke*, students suffered a more serious academic penalty. School policy called for a grade reduction of three points per day for each day of suspension. When the students were suspended for three days, their six-weeks grades were automatically lowered by nine points. Though the penalty was more severe, the result in this case was the same as the two cited above. The court determined that this did not deprive the students of property or liberty, and thus did not violate constitutional guarantees.

Having reviewed the philosophy of rule making as well as the basics of federal law, let's move to the specifics that apply between the Red River and the Rio Grande.

SENATE BILL 1 AND STUDENT DISCIPLINE: AN OVERVIEW

Most of the key players in the overhaul of the Texas Education Code, from Governor Bush on down, spoke of their strong desire to return to the notion of local control. Decisions should be made in local communities, not Austin. Texas is too diverse to have a one-size-fits-all approach to problems. Let the local people decide.

In many respects, that theme carried the day. In some significant ways, Senate Bill 1 does return control to the locals. But when the legislature got to Chapter 37, Safe Schools, the "local control" concept flew out the window. Senate Bill 1 gives state law more control over student discipline than ever before. Local discretion in student disciplinary matters is at a low ebb. The word "may" appears rarely in Chapter 37. "Shall" and "must," however, are frequent entries.

A second theme evident in Chapter 37 is the clear desire of the legislature to keep students in school if at all possible. Despite cries for "zero tolerance," the legislature has not made it easier for schools to expel students. On the contrary, Senate Bill 1 removed from the list of "expellable offenses" many of the reasons students were expelled in the past. In particular, minor assaults along with minor drug and alcohol offenses no longer constitute expellable conduct. Instead, students who commit these offenses will be placed in alternative education programs. Expulsion is reserved for only the most serious offenses.

A third theme, though not specifically articulated in the law, is the notion of "good kids" versus "bad kids." The legislature has placed great emphasis on "AEPs"—alternative education programs. Schools are required to establish at least one AEP, and are required to place students there in case of certain misconduct. Students assigned to the AEP must be separated from the other students. The notion seems to be that if we can keep the "bad kids" away from the "good kids" schools will be safer and better.

The fourth theme to emerge from Senate Bill 1 is the interplay between schools and the juvenile justice system. Never before has there been such mandated coordination of schools with law enforcement.

Finally, a much-ballyhooed provision in Senate Bill 1 is designed to empower teachers to teach, by giving them greater control over the classroom. The bill strengthens the hand of the teacher who wants to remove an unruly student from the classroom.

Now let's take a look at the current state of the law, post–Senate Bill 1.

Initial Intervention Strategies

State law does not address those strategies to be used for routine student discipline. This is a matter largely left to the local school district, its administrators, and its teachers. Research has shown that the most frequently used strategies include verbal reprimand, detention, and revocation of privileges. There are a host of others, including corporal punishment, work assignments, parent conferences, and counseling. The range of alternatives is limited only by the imagination and creativity of the disciplinarian.

Traditionally, teachers and administrators have exercised authority over students on the basis of the common law doctrine of *in loco parentis*, "in place of a parent." According to the theory, as long as educators use the same kind of authority a parent would be likely to use, they enjoy legal protection. However, the notion of *in loco parentis* has had to give way in the face of legal decisions recognizing student rights, such as expression and assembly within the public school. Due process requirements have also undercut it. However, *in loco parentis* remains a viable concept for routine classroom discipline. This is particularly true where the younger child is concerned.

While no hearing is legally required when using routine disciplinary techniques, it seems wise to inform the student of the infraction and give the student a chance to explain. Doing so will help build respect for the school teacher or official and for the discipline system. It will have the added benefit of helping safeguard the educator from a damage suit under state law when corporal punishment is involved.

Corporal Punishment

Due process is not required as a matter of constitutional law when students are paddled. The U.S. Supreme Court ruled in 1977 in *Ingraham v. Wright* that no Fourteenth Amendment procedural due process need be provided prior to the imposition of corporal punishment, because students are not removed from school (no property right is thus infringed) and because state law affords sufficient remedy through civil damage suits and criminal penalties for abuses (these state provisions are considered a form of due process satisfying whatever liberty right might be involved). The high court also ruled that corporal punishment used on school children does not constitute cruel and unusual punishment under the Eighth Amendment of the Constitution.

The position of most federal courts on corporal punishment challenges is well illustrated by a 1984 Fifth Circuit ruling involving a sixteen-year-old high school student who was given three "licks" for using abusive language to a school bus driver. The student was given a choice of corporal punishment or suspension; she chose the former. This decision was in contradiction of a parental request that the student not be spanked. The court rejected the challenge. "Every tort committed by a state official is not a violation of constitutional rights. Every deviation from a state agency regulation does not constitute a denial of due process. The Fourteenth Amendment did not make every trespass by a state government a deprivation of federal constitutional rights. Invocation of [42 U.S.C.] §1983 and the Fourteenth Amendment to obtain redress for three strokes of a paddle administered with the consent of the person paddled denigrates the fundamental values they embody. We, therefore, affirm the district court judgment dismissing the suit" (*Woodard v. Los Fresnos I.S.D.*, p. 1244).

Even when corporal punishment has been arguably excessive federal courts have stuck to their guns on this issue. In a case in which two kindergartners caught "snickering" were given swats with a wooden paddle by both the teacher and the principal, the Fifth Circuit found no constitutional violation of either due process or equal protection. The paddling left bruises on the two young girls, but the court concluded that if there was a violation of law, it was a matter for the state, and not a federal constitutional matter. The court reiterated its reasoning from the *Woodard* case and stated, "if the spankings . . . were unreasonable, the plaintiffs would be entitled to relief under Texas common law" (*Cunningham v. Beavers*, 1988).

The Fifth Circuit followed up on its *Cunningham v. Beavers* decision by issuing a similar decision involving the paddling of a sixth-grade special education student by the school's principal. The parents of the emotionally disturbed student had authorized the administering of three paddle swats to their child. But they filed a federal lawsuit against the school district and various school officials, contending that the paddling amounted to a severe beating, resulting in six months' psychiatric hospitalization at a cost of $90,000, thus denying their child substantive due process. They also contacted the sheriff's department, and although photographs were taken of the welts and scrapes on the child's body, no criminal action was instituted. The school contended the injuries were self-inflicted when the student resisted the punishment.

The appeals court affirmed the trial court's rejection of all federal claims. The availability of state civil and criminal remedies negated any claim of denial of substantive due process under federal law. The court also observed that the parents had given their consent, although parental consent is not necessary under constitutional law prior to imposition of corporal punishment. Nor did the teacher who observed the spanking have a duty under state law to intervene to stop it. The appeals court noted that the parents could pursue their excessive force lawsuit against the principal in state court and could also argue their negligence theory against the teacher in that forum (*Fee v. Herndon*, 1990).

Given the *Cunningham* and *Fee* decisions, it seems abundantly clear that public school children have no recourse in federal court under the due process clause of the Fourteenth Amendment for allegations of abuse of corporal punishment. The fact that prisoners do have such recourse is attributable to the different federal claims they can assert, e.g., cruel and unusual punishment under the Eighth Amendment, and to the fact that they are incarcerated and thus not free to escape the abusive conduct.

State law in Texas does not address corporal punishment. Though many states have abolished the practice, the Texas Legislature has not had the votes to do so. Consequently, corporal punishment remains a matter of local control, governed by policy adopted by the school board in each district.

To lessen the chances of damage suits in state or federal courts, most schools specify that corporal punishment can be used only under certain circumstances and in accord with certain procedures. The school administrator or teacher who administers corporal punishment should be careful. Though the practice is legal, it is highly controversial and subject to challenge. Moreover, the paddler is subject to criminal liability if the paddling was "excessive," or if the person was not authorized by school policy to administer corporal punishment. Civil liability can also be imposed for excessive or negligent administration of corporal punishment. Many school administrators have made the personal decision not to use corporal punishment. The cost of being the district's "designated hitter" often exceeds the benefit. See the extensive discussion of this subject in Chapter 10.

Suspension from Extracurricular Activities

What must a district do if a student is to be excluded from one such activity rather than suspended or expelled from the entire educational process? Early cases indicated that at least some sort of minimal due process was required. In *Ector County I.S.D. v. Hopkins*, a Texas court of appeals ruled that a student was entitled to notice and a hearing before permanent expulsion from the National Honor Society and the Permian Pepettes. A federal court reached a similar conclusion regarding an expulsion from the National Honor Society in *Warren v. National Association of Secondary School Principals*.

However, later decisions have drawn a sharper distinction between the student's right to attend school for academic purposes and the student's right to participate in extracurricular activities. Pursuant to *Goss*, we know that a student has a property and liberty interest, protected by the Fourteenth Amendment, in attending school. But courts, and the Fifth Circuit in particular, have specifically and repeatedly held that no such protection attaches to extracurricular activities (*Hardy v. University Interscholastic League*; *Walsh v. Louisiana High School Athletic Association*). Thus it appears that students can be removed from extracurricular activities without any formal due process measures.

This may be the law, but school administrators are well aware of the fact that removal of Muffy from the cheerleading squad, or Biff from the basketball team, can lead to a terrific fight in a school district. Consequently, most school administrators wisely provide minimal "due process" prior to removing a student from such programs. By minimal due process we mean (1) notice to the student of what the rules are and (2) an opportunity for the student to give his or her side of the story before being removed from the activity.

The authority of the school over extracurricular activities does have its limits. While the school does not have to offer any extracurricular activities, if it chooses to do so it cannot exclude students in a manner that discriminates against a class of students. For example, in the case of *Bell v. Lone Oak I.S.D.*, a court struck down a school district regulation which would have prohibited any married student from participating in extracurricular activities.

Student involvement with extracurricular activity is further affected by the student's status in school. Under Senate Bill 1, students who must be removed to an AEP must also be removed from participation in or attendance at extracurricular activities. This is discussed in more detail below.

Emergency Actions

School officials encounter emergencies almost daily. Texas law recognizes that there are occasions when a student must be removed from the school due to an emergency. Such action is authorized by Senate Bill 1. Section 37.019 authorizes the principal or designee to order the immediate, emergency expulsion of a student if the principal or designee "reasonably believes that action is necessary to protect persons or property from imminent harm." The student is to be given oral notice of the action, with more formal procedures to take place within a reasonable time thereafter.

Emergency removal to an AEP is also available, whenever the principal or designee "reasonably believes the student's behavior is so unruly, disruptive, or abusive that it seriously interferes with a teacher's ability to communicate effectively with the students in a class, with the ability of the student's classmates to learn, or with the operation of the school or a school-sponsored activity." Again, oral notice is all that is required, with appropriate procedures to follow.

Neither emergency placement nor emergency expulsion under §37.019 has a definite time limit. It appears to be a matter of local discretion, but school administrators should keep in mind that these actions are clearly designed to be used only when necessary due to an emergency, and should be limited to as short a time as is reasonable.

In most instances emergency action should not be viewed as an action to be taken in isolation. In most cases, the conduct of the student that caused an emergency AEP placement or expulsion will also provide a basis for further action of a disciplinary nature. For example, the student who brings a gun to school may be "emergency expelled" as a first step in dealing with the problem. But the second step would be a recommendation for a traditional expulsion, to be preceded with appropriate due process.

Student Code of Conduct

Senate Bill 1 requires each district to adopt a student code of conduct which will specify standards for student conduct, and outline the types of behavior which might get a student in trouble at school. The code of conduct is to be developed with the advice of the district-level committee, and jointly, as appropriate, with the juvenile board of each county in which the district is located.

The code of conduct is a familiar concept in school law. It is a basic rule of due process that students can only be punished for misconduct after they are advised that such conduct is prohibited. Most schools discharge this responsibility by distributing a "student handbook" containing all the rules and regulations of the school, including those pertaining to discipline. Most schools require parents and students to sign a receipt indicating that they have received and read the book.

Senate Bill 1, though, for the first time requires the district-level committee and the juvenile board of each county to be involved in the process. The involvement of the juvenile board makes sense, in light of the fact that the code of conduct is to "outline the responsibilities of each juvenile board concerning the establishment and operation of a juvenile justice alternative education program [JJAEP] under Section 37.011." The juvenile board is a statutorily created body for each county, usually consisting of judges of district and/or county courts in the county.

A code of conduct meeting all the requirements of Senate Bill 1 is not required until September 1, 1996. Thus school districts have the 1995–1996 school year to develop the code and work with the juvenile board toward the possible creation of a JJAEP. In an effort to make sure that parents are advised of misconduct, the law now requires reports from teachers. Any teacher who knows that a student has violated the student code of conduct must file with the principal, or other appropriate administrator, a written report, not to exceed one page, documenting the violation. The principal is then required to send a copy of this report to the parents within twenty-four hours of receipt from the teacher.

Teacher Initiated Removal

Senate Bill 1 provides three different types of teacher initiated removal. There is teacher removal for assistance; discretionary teacher removal; and mandatory teacher removal. We will examine each in turn.

Teacher removal for assistance is nothing more than a statutory assurance that teachers can do what they have always done—send kids to the principal's office. Section 37.002 authorizes the teacher to do this "to maintain effective discipline in the classroom." What happens next is up to the principal, who is to "respond by employing appropriate discipline management techniques consistent with the student code of conduct adopted under Section 37.001."

Discretionary teacher removal is authorized for a student:

(1) who has been documented by the teacher to repeatedly interfere with the teacher's ability to communicate effectively with the students in the class or with the ability of the student's classmates to learn; or
(2) whose behavior the teacher determines is so unruly, disruptive, or abusive that it seriously interferes with the teacher's ability to communicate effectively with the students in the class or with the ability of the student's classmates to learn. (TEC §37.002(b))

When the classroom teacher exercises this authority, the principal is required to conduct a hearing within three class days. The hearing should include the parent, the student, and the teacher, but the hearing is to go forward whether all parties are present or not, provided that "valid attempts" have been made to require the attendance of all parties. After conducting this hearing, the principal can order the student placed in another appropriate classroom, an in-school suspension program, or an AEP for a period of time consistent with the code of conduct. However, the principal cannot place the student back into the classroom of the teacher who initiated the removal without that teacher's consent. It is this last provision that is new. Pre–Senate Bill 1 law allowed teachers to remove unruly students from the classroom and demand a hearing by the principal. The new wrinkle in Senate Bill 1 is the power of the teacher to refuse to take the student back. Such a power could be abused if there were no limitation on it. Just think of the power of a teacher who knows that next year he is getting out of the profession and going to law school. Such a teacher, armed with a "who gives a flip" attitude along with the power of S.B. 1, could empty out of his classroom all but the most compliant and pleasant children.

To guard against such abuses, the legislature has created PRCs—Placement Review Committees. The primary function of the PRC will be to decide what to do when the principal orders the student back to the classroom of a teacher who refuses to take the student back. The PRC can override the teacher if the PRC decides that placement of the student in that classroom "is the best or only alternative available" (TEC §37.002(c)). PRCs will be composed of three persons. Two PRC members must be teachers, selected to the PRC by the campus faculty. The third member will be a member of the campus professional staff appointed by the principal.

The third type of teacher initiated removal, mandatory removal, arises only when the student commits an offense in the classroom which requires removal to an AEP or expulsion. In that event, the teacher must order the student's removal from class and the principal must assign the student to an AEP or seek expulsion. These procedures are described in more detail below.

Teachers will find that their ability to document student behavior and misbehavior in the classroom will be of tremendous significance. The statutory provisions authorizing teachers to remove a student from class will be effectively used only if the teacher is diligent in documenting in-class efforts to bring the student's behavior under control. Teachers must have a set of rules for the class as a whole. The rules should be clearly displayed, reviewed with the students in detail, and consistently enforced. In addition to the general rules, teachers are likely to have to deal with one or more individualized behavior plans. Children with a special education IEP may have an individualized BMP (Behavior Management Plan) that the classroom teacher will be responsible for.

Suspension

Senate Bill 1 contains just one short provision dealing with suspension. It states that a student may be suspended from school if the student engages in conduct for which the student may be placed in an alternative education program. Thus any time a student could be removed to AEP, the student can be suspended.

Besides the statutory reasons, a school can generate its own reasons for AEP removal, and thus, suspension. Section 37.001 of the Code states that the student code of conduct is to "specify conditions that authorize or require a principal or other appropriate administrator to transfer a student to an AEP." Since the conditions that require AEP placement are already spelled out in state law, it would appear that the local authorities can add additional offenses which would *authorize* AEP removal, and thus, suspension. Indeed, §37.001 goes on to say that the code of conduct is to specify conditions under which a student may be suspended.

Suspension is designed as a short-term disciplinary action. Prior to Senate Bill 1, Texas law limited suspensions to six days per semester, cumulatively. Thus, if a student were to be suspended for three days in September and another three days in October, the school could not suspend that student again for the remainder of that semester.

Under Senate Bill 1, suspension is limited to three days per offense. However, the limitation of cumulative suspensions has been removed. Thus, if a student commits ten separate offenses which call for suspension, the student could be suspended as many as thirty days. While there is no limit on accumulated days of suspension for most students, there are limitations regarding students with disabilities, discussed in more detail in Chapter 3.

Although the statute does not address the issue of due process, the Fourteenth Amendment requires that the student be afforded an informal hearing prior to suspension since the student is being deprived, albeit for a short time, of the property right in a public education. As the U.S. Supreme Court put it, "At the very minimum . . . students facing suspension and the consequent interference with a protected property interest must be given *some* kind of notice and afforded *some* kind of hearing" (*Goss v. Lopez*, 1975).

The *Goss* case requires nothing more than what the typical principal would do anyway. Students are entitled to be advised of what they are accused of; to be given an opportunity to tell their side of the story; and if they deny the charge, to be advised of the basis for it. This conference can be held immediately, can be done orally, does not require parental participation or lawyer representation. It has been described by some as nothing beyond a "thank you for sharing" conference. (This because the principal will usually respond to the student's excuses with "Thank you for sharing. Your suspension begins now.")

Under a 1984 ruling by the U.S. Court of Appeals for the Fifth Circuit, a student who is suspended over an examination period and receives zeroes on those days is not entitled to anything more than the *Goss* informal due process procedures (*Keough v. Tate County Board of Education*). The Fifth Circuit observed that "*Goss* makes no distinctions between [short-term] suspensions that occur during examination periods and those that do not, and it seems to us, for obvious reasons. In any school year, a number of examinations may take place at various times throughout a given semester which are crucial to a student's performance for the semester" (p. 1080). The court concluded that the informal conversation with the principal was all Chuck Keough was entitled to prior to his short-term suspension. The court hedged a bit, however, noting that the district later allowed Keough to take his tests and, as a result, no harm took place.

Under prior law, if a student was suspended, the absence had to be considered excused if the student satisfactorily completed the assignments for the period of suspension within a reasonable time. Senate Bill 1 has removed this provision. It will now be up to local districts to decide how and when to give credit to students who have been suspended.

For provisions dealing with suspensions of students with disabilities, see Chapter 3.

Removal to an AEP

It is clear from Senate Bill 1 that the legislature has high hopes for AEPs. AEPs are not new in Texas law, but this is the first time that state law has *required* that students be assigned to an AEP for certain offenses.

At School. Section 37.006 lists the offenses for which a student must be assigned to an AEP. They include assaults, terroristic threats, drug offenses, alcohol offenses, inhalant offenses, public lewdness, and indecent exposure. If the student engages in conduct containing the elements of any of these offenses at school, or at a school-related function, the student must be removed to an AEP.

Some of these offenses would have caused a student to be expelled under previous law. For example, most schools would have expelled a student who committed an assault at school or who possessed an illegal drug at school. Under Senate Bill 1, such conduct is not expellable. More serious assaultive or drug offenses are expellable, as described below.

Off-Campus Conduct. In addition to these on-campus offenses, Senate Bill 1 lists two off-campus offenses for which a student must be removed to AEP. First, "if the student engages in conduct punishable as a felony," the student must be removed to AEP. This provision is sure to lead to widely varying interpretations and applications. Some will challenge this as an unconstitutional extension of school district authority. Others will argue over what it takes to prove that a student has engaged in such conduct. Still others will debate the application of this provision to children under the age of ten—is it even possible for them to engage in conduct punishable as a felony?

None of these questions has clear answers at present. Schools will have to navigate these fog-enshrouded shoals with caution. What appears to be the legislative intent, however, is to remove from the main campus those students who have engaged in behavior off campus that indicates they are dangerous or disruptive.

The second type of off-campus conduct that requires AEP removal is engaging in conduct that contains the elements of the offense of retaliation against any school employee, under Penal Code §36.06. That provision of the Code defines retaliation as any unlawful conduct directed against a public servant or official in retaliation for the public servant or official's performance of official duties. In other words, the student who vandalizes or assaults a teacher off campus in retaliation for the teacher's performance of job duties must be removed to an AEP.

School districts can send students to AEPs for reasons other than those listed in state law, provided that the code of conduct advises the students that removal might occur. Most schools inform students that they can be sent to an AEP for any serious or persistent misconduct.

State law does not tell us how long an AEP placement is to last. This appears to be a matter of local discretion. A student can even be kept in an AEP beyond the end of the school year provided that the school determines that the student's presence on campus will be dangerous, or that the student has engaged in serious or persistent misbehavior. Also, the school is required to conduct a review of the student's status every 120 calendar days.

As one observer has pointed out, however, this is really no limitation at all. Consider the case of Jennifer, who was caught smoking in the bathroom her first week of high school. Most codes of conduct will describe smoking as "serious misconduct." Senate Bill 1 tells us that the student can be assigned to AEP beyond the end of the school year if the board or board's designee determines that the student has engaged in serious misconduct. While we do not recommend it, it appears the "zero tolerance" school could slap Jennifer into AEP for four years, with appropriate 120-day reviews.

Procedure. What type of hearing will a student receive prior to placement in AEP? State law leaves this largely to local discretion. We know from §37.009 that if a removal is initiated by the classroom teacher, then the principal must conduct the initial hearing. The law seems to contemplate an informal process involving the principal, teacher, parent, and student.

If the student is to be assigned to an AEP beyond the end of the next grading period, the school is required to give the parents notice and an opportunity to participate in a proceeding before the board or designee. But again the law is silent as to the formality of the proceeding.

It appears that the legislature desires disputes over AEP placement to end within the school district. Whatever decision is made about AEP placement by the board or designee is "final and may not be appealed." This means that the Texas Education Agency will not hear such an appeal. It does not necessarily prevent a parent or student from filing suit alleging that the AEP placement was discriminatory or unconstitutional.

Life in an AEP. AEPs are required to offer the core curriculum— English language arts, math, science, and history. In addition, an AEP is to focus on self-discipline. An AEP must offer counseling, and it must be supervised. Schools can put students into unsupervised settings only when the students are suspended or expelled.

Although an AEP is required to focus on core curriculum subjects, the law requires schools to meet the educational and behavioral needs of students in their AEPs. In light of this provision, school districts would be wise to make every effort to ensure that students are able to keep up with all courses while attending AEP, to the extent that this is possible.

In order to maintain safety, the AEP students must be separated from other students. Schools can operate an AEP on campus or off campus, but must ensure separation of AEP students from the others. Schools can cooperate to set up an AEP, and many small schools will certainly do so.

AEPs that are set up off campus—that is, physically removed from all district campuses—are exempt from most of the requirements of the Texas Education Code, including those pertaining to length of the school day and certification of teachers. Thus an off-campus arrangement is likely to offer the school district greater flexibility.

The prudent school administrator will put a good deal of thought into the setup of an AEP. The AEP should be capable of dealing with any student assigned to it, including special education students. Thus the school will have to think carefully about staffing, equipment, services, and location. The legislature wants to be sure that AEPs are not treated like stepchildren; thus the law mandates that school districts must allocate the same amount of money to an AEP that the school would have allocated for that student if he or she were assigned to the regular school program (TEC §37.008(g)).

Finally, students who are assigned to AEP as a result of commission of one of those offenses which require AEP removal must also be suspended from extracurricular activities. The students can neither participate in nor attend extracurricular events. Students who are assigned to an AEP as a result of violation of school rules which authorize but do not require AEP placement *may* be suspended from extracurricular activities.

Expulsion

Expulsion is the harshest penalty the school can impose, and thus is reserved for only the most serious offenses. This is particularly true after Senate Bill 1. Most expulsions prior to Senate Bill 1 resulted from assaults, or minor drug or alcohol offenses. No more. Such offenses now can lead to AEP removal, but not expulsion. Let's take a look at what the legislature believes to be serious enough to warrant expulsion from school.

Grounds. Section 37.007 spells out several types of conduct which *require* expulsion from school. They are:

1. Possession of weapons—firearms, illegal knives, clubs, or any other prohibited weapons.
2. Assaultive offenses—aggravated assault, sexual assault, or aggravated sexual assault.
3. Arson.
4. Murder, capital murder, criminal attempt to commit murder or capital murder.
5. Indecency with a child.
6. Aggravated kidnapping.
7. Drug or alcohol offenses if punishable as a felony.
8. Retaliatory commission of an expellable offense against a school employee.

The first seven of these reasons for expulsion must occur on school property or at a school-related function. Retaliation against a school employee, however, is expellable no matter where it took place.

Please note that the local district has no discretion as to these offenses. However, there are two additional expellable offenses where the district does have discretion:

1. Serious or persistent misconduct after being placed in an AEP; and
2. Criminal mischief (vandalism) if punishable as a felony.

Before moving on, we must point out that this is the first time the word "murder" has appeared in the Texas Education Code. We've come a long way.

Procedures. The procedures that must accompany expulsion are far more extensive than those involved in suspension or removal to an alternative education program. Since the student's "property right" to a public education is being taken, the Fourteenth Amendment requires that the student be afforded an appropriate level of due process. In the *Goss* case, the Court emphasized the informality of what was being required—"less than a fair-minded school principal would impose upon himself in order to avoid unfair suspensions" (p. 583). But the Court stated that, in unusual situations and for suspensions over ten days in length, more formal procedural due process would be necessary, as in the *Dixon* decision. Unfortunately, the Court did not give any examples.

The Education Code does not tell us how much process is due prior to an expulsion. Instead, it merely invokes federal constitutional standards. Section 37.009 provides, "Before a student may be expelled under Section 37.007, the board or the board's designee must provide the student a hearing at which the student is afforded appropriate due process as required by the federal constitution and which the student's parent or guardian is invited, in writing, to attend." State law imposes only two other requirements. First, the student must be represented at an expulsion hearing by some adult who can give guidance to the student. This individual would normally be the parent or guardian, but can be someone else, as long as it is not a school district employee. Second, if an expulsion is ordered by the board's designee, then it is appealable to the board, and then to the district court of the county in which the school's administrative office is located.

State law specifies that the appeal of a student expulsion is to be heard by the district court by "trial de novo," meaning, essentially, a new trial. However, the expression is misleading. Two courts have now held that the proper standard to be applied is "substantial evidence de novo review" rather than "pure trial de novo" *(Sanchez v. Huntsville I.S.D.* and *United I.S.D. v. Gonzalez).* The difference in the two standards is much more than semantic. In a "pure trial de novo" case the school district would bear the burden of proving its expulsion case all over again. In a "substantial evidence de novo review," the court is limited to a review of the record created in the proceedings before the school board. Moreover, the court presumes the findings of the school board are legal and valid, and puts the burden on the student to prove that those findings are not supported by substantial evidence. In simple terms, it is much easier for the school district to satisfy the "substantial evidence" test than to start from scratch and prove its case to the satisfaction of a district judge.

State board rules in the past have set forth with specificity the nature of the hearing, which must include the following: prior notice of the charges and the proposed sanctions so as to afford a reasonable opportunity for preparation, right to a full and fair hearing before the board or its designee, right to an adult representative or legal counsel, opportunity to testify and to present evidence and witnesses in his or her defense, and opportunity to examine the evidence presented by the school administration and to question the administration's witnesses (19 TAC §133.27(b)).

It is apparent from case law, however, that the right to "question administrators and witnesses" has some limitations. The question often arises, for example, as to the right of an accused student to confront his accusers when some of the accusers are other students. If a student is charged with selling drugs on campus and the only eyewitness is another student, does the school have to produce the witness to testify at the expulsion hearing? What if the witness has legitimate fears of retaliation? Courts have consistently held that the procedures for an expulsion hearing are not as strict as those in a criminal trial. School districts can rely on student or staff witnesses, and even read their written witness statements at an expulsion hearing, without a right to cross-examine by the accused student. Courts have decided that such prerecorded statements— considered "hearsay" and generally inadmissible in court—are admissible in student discipline matters.

In a 1988 case, a student was expelled for over two months for allegedly selling marijuana. At no time was the student allowed to learn the identity of the two accusing students or to cross-examine them. His attorney was not allowed to cross-examine the principal or the superintendent. Addressing the claim of failure of due process, the court stated:

> In this turbulent, sometimes violent, school atmosphere, it is critically important that we protect the anonymity of students who "blow the whistle." . . . Without the cloak of anonymity, students who witness criminal activity on school property will be much less likely to notify school authorities, and those who do will be faced with ostracism at best and perhaps physical reprisals. (*Newsome v. Batavia Local School District*, Sixth Circuit, 1988)

In another case, a student was expelled for striking a coach, and the coach did not testify at the student's hearing, but rather submitted a written account of the incident. A Texas federal court ruled that the failure of the coach to testify at the hearing did not amount to a violation of due process. The minimum due process requirements for a long-term expulsion consist of (1) oral and written notice of the charges against the student, (2) an explanation of the evidence, and (3) an opportunity for the student to present his side of the story. The opportunity to cross-examine is not required in this situation. The court held that the burden of cross-examination in a school discipline hearing outweighed any benefit the student might derive from that process in this case (*Johnson v. Humble I.S.D.*, 1992).

Courts have advanced many reasons for denying the right to cross-examine, including (1) the fact that the administrators who investigate the offenses are qualified to determine the truthfulness of student accusers, (2) that, if forced to testify, many students would fail to come forward, and (3) reasons associated with administrative convenience. This question seems relatively settled, with a consistent line of cases dating to the 1970s (for example, *Tasby v. Estes*, 1981; *Boykins v. Fairfield Board of Education*, 1974).

Due process concerns diminish, but do not disappear, when dealing with the student who has admitted guilt. The Fifth Circuit addressed this issue in a case involving a student who admitted possession of marijuana. He contested only the procedures used by the school district during the portion of his hearing where his punishment was determined. He argued that it was unfair for the district to consider evidence of prior misconduct in determining his punishment and that he should have been allowed to confront and cross-examine the three students who reported that he had sold drugs on campus during the preceding three months. The Fifth Circuit disagreed, noting that, once guilt is admitted, there need be only a rational relationship between the punishment and the offense. "We decline to escalate the formality of the suspension process even further by requiring school administrators to provide a fact hearing as to the accuracy of each bit of evidence considered in determining the appropriate length of punishment, a requirement that is not imposed even in criminal cases." The court noted that the statements from the three students were sufficiently detailed to allow the boy to confront the evidence (*Brewer v. Austin I.S.D.*, 1985).

Because of the constitutional dimensions of due process, it would appear that the best policy to follow when students are caught in the act of breaking a school rule and admit guilt is to give them notice of the rule violation and an opportunity in the presence of their parents or a representative to confirm their admission of guilt in writing and to waive formal due process rights. It is essential that coercion, direct or indirect, be absent. Coercion would both invalidate the admission of guilt and create evidence of bias on the part of the school officials. When bias is shown to exist, the constitutionality of the hearing process will be in question.

Are grade school children entitled to the same due process rights as older students? The answer appears to be yes. Writing in a 1975 case, Supreme Court Justice Harry A. Blackmun pointed out that "constitutional rights do not mature and come into being magically only when one attains the state-defined age of majority. Minors, as well as adults, are protected by the Constitution and possess Constitutional rights" (*Planned Parenthood v. Danforth*, 1976, p. 74). In *Sullivan v. Houston I.S.D.* (1969) the Federal District Court for the Southern District of Texas noted that, when younger students are involved, parents should be included in due process procedures. When students are too young to exercise the rights themselves, their parents will exercise them on their behalf.

Interaction with the Juvenile Justice System

Senate Bill 1 contemplates a high degree of coordination between the public schools and the juvenile justice system, beginning with the adoption of a code of conduct. The code of conduct to be developed by each school district must be adopted "jointly, as appropriate" with the juvenile board of each county in which the district is located (TEC §37.001). Thereafter, joint meetings of the school board and the juvenile board, or their designees, are to be held at the call of the school board president (TEC §37.013).

Communication between schools and law enforcement is required in Chapter 37. School districts are required to notify the juvenile board of students who commit an offense which requires placement in AEP or expulsion. A copy of the school's order of removal or expulsion must be sent to the authorized officer of the juvenile court (TEC §37.010). Furthermore, the principal of any school—public or private—is required to notify law enforcement officials if the principal has reasonable grounds to believe that a student has engaged in certain types of illegal behavior at school or at a school-related function. The violations required to be reported include drug and weapons offenses.

Texas law also requires local law enforcement officials to give oral notice to the school superintendent within twenty-four hours after students are arrested or taken into custody in connection with certain offenses. These include terroristic threats, drug offenses, and weapons offenses. The superintendent is then required to promptly notify "all instructional and support personnel who have regular contact with the student." Within seven days after the oral notice, law enforcement personnel are required to give written notice to the superintendent.

A Juvenile Justice AEP (JJAEP) is required in any county with a population in excess of 125,000. Smaller counties may develop a JJAEP, but are not required to do so. JJAEPs will serve students who have been expelled and found to have engaged in delinquent conduct. Other students may be admitted to the JJAEP depending on the agreement between the juvenile board and the school district. The JJAEP program will be a full-fledged educational program, operating seven hours per day, 180 days per year, and focusing on the core curriculum along with self-discipline.

A final provision in Chapter 37 that will be of interest to school administrators limits the power of a court to order an expelled student back on campus. Here is the typical scenario as it has played out in the past: the student commits an expellable offense and is expelled. The student is also charged with criminal misconduct, is found guilty, and placed on probation. As a condition of probation, the student is ordered right back to the campus from which he was expelled. Senate Bill 1 prohibits a judge from placing an expelled student back in any school program, including a school-operated AEP, unless the juvenile board and the school board have entered into a memorandum of understanding concerning the juvenile probation department's role in supervising and providing other support services for students in AEPs (TEC §37.010(c)).

SUMMARY: GUIDELINES FOR EFFECTIVE STUDENT DISCIPLINE

Student discipline has changed considerably in Texas with the passage of the Education Reform Act of 1984 and Senate Bill 1 in 1995. In this chapter we have reviewed the key provisions of Texas laws relating to discipline, as well as the important decisions of state and federal courts that help to shape the contours of due process required for student discipline decision making.

While there is no one perfect solution to the problem of student discipline, both teachers and administrators can improve their chances of making effective discipline decisions by adhering to the following five guidelines:

1. Have good rules and enforce them consistently.
2. Make careful investigations when infractions occur.
3. Assume that your decision will be challenged and prepare accordingly.
4. Remember to document infractions as soon as possible after they occur. A memorandum to the file is well worth the effort later on.
5. Follow school policies and procedures carefully, especially with respect to due process provisions.

NINE

Privacy Issues: Community, Educators, Students

THE MOST OFTEN quoted definition of the "right to privacy" is simply "the right to be left alone." Except for searches and seizures by government officials, which is the subject of the Fourth Amendment to the U.S. Constitution, the law of privacy is of recent origin. What complicates this area of the law is that, at the same time the right of privacy has developed as a legal concept, the countervailing "right of the public to know" has appeared. In Texas, the public's "right to know" is reflected in the Texas Open Meetings and Public Information acts.

Our purpose in this chapter is to provide an overview of privacy rights and the public's right to know in the context of education. We begin with a discussion of the legal framework of the law of privacy and then look at the Texas Open Meetings and Public Information acts, educator privacy rights, and student privacy issues. Included in the latter is a discussion of student search and seizure and personal grooming.

THE LEGAL FRAMEWORK

The U.S. Constitution

The most specific reference to privacy in the U.S. Constitution is found in the Fourth Amendment, which states that "the right of the people to be secure in their persons, houses, papers, and effects, against unreasonable searches and seizures, shall not be violated, and no warrants shall issue but upon probable cause, supported by oath or affirmation, and particularly describing the place to be searched, and the persons or things to be seized." The U.S. Supreme Court has ruled that public school students are entitled to the protections of the Fourth Amendment, which is now applicable to state governments and their political subdivisions through the Fourteenth Amendment. But, at the same time, the Court has also recognized that school officials must have sufficient discretion to maintain order. Thus, as we will see, the standards for a lawful search are less stringent than would be the case if the police were to conduct the search.

Federal courts have also found a right of family and personal privacy inherent in the word *liberty* of the Fourteenth Amendment due process clause ("nor shall any State deprive any person of life, liberty, or property, without due process of law"). In the 1920s, the U.S. Supreme Court construed the word *liberty* to include the right of parents to control the upbringing of their children (*Meyer v. Nebraska*, 1923; *Pierce v. Society of Sisters*, 1925). In 1971, the Court ruled that people have a liberty right from unwarranted government stigmatization of their reputation (*Wisconsin v. Constantineau*). In 1965, the Court ruled that a state law prohibiting the use of contraceptive devices by married couples violates the zone of personal privacy (*Griswold v. Connecticut*). Later, in a very controversial decision, the Court extended the right to include a woman's choice to have an abortion (*Roe v. Wade*, 1973). The right of privacy in the context of the public school is dependent to some extent on the reasoning expressed in these rulings.

Federal Statutes

The federal privacy law affecting education is the 1974 Family Educational Rights and Privacy Act (FERPA), also known as the Buckley Amendment. Unlike the Fourth and Fourteenth amendments, FERPA applies to any educational institution receiving federal funds. Public, as well as some private, schools and colleges are subject to its provisions. The FERPA regulates student record-keeping activities by giving parents and students access to student records, the right to challenge material contained therein, and the right to restrict publication of personally identifiable information. Its provisions are discussed in detail in the section on student rights of privacy later in this chapter.

Shortly after it was enacted, FERPA was amended to provide parents and guardians with the right to inspect material used in connection with any federally sponsored research or experimental program designed to improve teaching in the nation's schools. Known as the Hatch Amendment after its sponsor, Senator Orrin Hatch of Utah, a second section was added in 1978 prohibiting use of psychiatric or psychological examinations that involve students' privacy in connection with this research. A flurry of controversy greeted U.S. Education Department regulations promulgated in 1984 to implement the Hatch Amendment. The regulations listed some thirty-four off-limit classroom topics and activities, including alcohol and drugs, instruction in nuclear war or weaponry, evolution, human sexuality, and student diaries or journals. Conservative groups began a letter-writing campaign to enforce the law, threatening that if such topics and activities were not avoided federal funds could be terminated. The letter-writing campaign misrepresented the statute by implying that it applies to classroom teaching in general. Such is not the case. Application of the Hatch Amendment is limited to experimental teaching programs sponsored by federal funds. Senator Hatch took to the Senate floor early in 1985 to emphasize this fact and to assert that federal involvement in local curriculum decision making would be "anathema to both parents and educators."

In 1994 the Hatch Amendment was modified by Goals 2000: Educate America Act. The Goals 2000 provision requires schools to make available to parents for inspection instructional material that will be used in connection with any survey, analysis, or evaluation as part of any applicable program. "Applicable program" means a program for which the U.S. Secretary of Education has administrative responsibility. Schools also must obtain prior written parental approval before requiring students to respond to surveys that request information about political affiliations, potentially embarrassing mental and psychological problems, illegal or demeaning behavior, sexual behavior and attitudes, critical appraisal of family members, legally recognized privileged relationships, or income. Proposed regulations developed by the U.S. Department of Education in 1995 to implement the Goals 2000 provision appeared to limit its application to federally funded surveys.

State Law

The law of torts (civil wrongs committed by one person against another) has had the most to do with privacy. The so-called common law of torts, meaning generally accepted case law as it has developed in Texas and elsewhere, has included the familiar tort of defamation. Defamation through libel or slander traditionally involves the knowing communication of false information to a third party such as to cause the person defamed significant loss, e.g., being fired from a job or suffering a divorce. Other torts related to privacy include trespass and false arrest. A person who can prove in court that he or she has suffered loss because of these torts may recover monetary damages, though as noted in the next chapter, the immunity provisions in Texas law afford some protection to school districts and school professional personnel.

Aside from these traditional torts, state constitutions, statutes, and case law generally were silent on a personal right of privacy until well into the twentieth century. Industrialization and urban growth produced an array of privacy threats, ranging from unwarranted noise to newspaper gossip stories and, now, computerized data banks.

By 1960 enough state statutory and case law had developed for commentators to identify the chief components of the evolving state law against personal privacy invasion to include:

1. Intrusion upon a person's seclusion or solitude or into the person's private affairs.
2. Public disclosure of embarrassing private facts about a person.
3. Publicity that places a person in a false light in the public eye.
4. Appropriation of a person's name or likeness for personal advantage.

Texas courts have recognized these four personal privacy torts but have restricted damage awards to situations where the person bringing suit (the plaintiff) can show:

1. That publicity was given to matters concerning his or her private life.
2. That the publication would be highly offensive to a person of ordinary sensibilities.
3. That the matter publicized was not of legitimate public concern.

By "publicized," the Texas Supreme Court has indicated that "the matter must be communicated to the public at large, such that the matter becomes one of public knowledge" (*Industrial Foundation of the South v. Texas Industrial Accident Board*, 1976, pp. 683–684). Invasion of personal privacy overlaps somewhat with the traditional tort of defamation and tends to increase the situations in which suits can be brought. Personal privacy torts surface most often in the context of employee references, a topic to be discussed later in the chapter.

TEXAS SUNSHINE LEGISLATION

The Texas Open Meetings Act (TOMA) and the Texas Public Information Act (TPIA) seem to be in a state of tension with evolving privacy law because they are designed to further public access to government business. Both are reviewed in detail here.

Texas Open Meetings Act

Chapter 551 of the Texas Government Code requires that meetings of governmental bodies, such as the school board, be open to the public. Section 551.002 of the act states: "Every regular, special, or called meeting of a governmental body shall be open to the public, except as provided by this chapter."

A Texas court of appeals in 1985 construed the law to apply under certain circumstances to meetings involving both staff members and school board members (*Hitt v. Mabry*). In 1989, the Texas Attorney General advised that the law applies to a committee composed of one or more members of the board of trustees of a school district that meets to discuss public business or policy (*Att'y. Gen. Op. JM-1072*). However, the law does not apply to meetings composed only of staff members. Thus, in 1985 the attorney general issued an advisory opinion that "governmental body" does not include subordinate committees composed only of employees (*Att'y. Gen. Op. JM-340*). Nor is a grievance committee subject to the terms of the TOMA, since it is without powers accorded to a governmental body (*City of Austin v. Evans*, 1990).

The law is explicit in spelling out the notice requirements regarding open meetings. One important requirement is that written notice of the date, place, and subject of each meeting must be posted on a bulletin board convenient to the public in the central administration building at least seventy-two hours before the meeting. Action taken at a meeting on any item not appearing on the posted agenda may be voided.

The TOMA does, however, allow emergency meetings to be held, if two hours' public notice is given stating the nature of the emergency. Emergencies are by statute limited to imminent threats to public health and safety or reasonably unforeseeable situations requiring immediate action.

The law also allows additional items to be placed on the agenda of a nonemergency meeting after the seventy-two-hour posting requirement if an emergency or urgent public necessity warrants it. Again, the reason for the additions must be given. With respect to the seventy-two-hour posting requirement, strict compliance is required (*Smith County v. Thornton*, 1985).

Public meetings are those at which public business or public policy is discussed or at which formal action is taken. Closed sessions are permitted in the following situations (quoting from the law):

Section 551.071: CONSULTATION WITH ATTORNEY; CLOSED MEETINGS. A governmental body may not conduct a private consultation with its attorney except:
  (1) when the governmental body seeks the advice of its attorney about:
     (A) pending or contemplated litigation; or
     (B) a settlement or offer; or
  (2) on a matter in which the duty of the attorney to the governmental body under the Texas Disciplinary Rules of Professional Conduct of the State Bar of Texas clearly conflicts with this chapter.

Section 551.072: DELIBERATION REGARDING REAL PROPERTY; CLOSED MEETING. A governmental body may conduct a closed meeting to deliberate the purchase, exchange, lease, or value of real property if deliberation in an open meeting would have a detrimental effect on the position of the governmental body in negotiations with a third person.

Section 551.073. DELIBERATION REGARDING PROSPECTIVE GIFT; CLOSED MEETING. A governmental body may conduct a closed meeting to deliberate a negotiated contract for a prospective gift or donation to the state or governmental body if deliberation in an open meeting would have a detrimental effect on the position of the governmental body in negotiations with a third person.

Section 551.074. PERSONNEL MATTERS; CLOSED MEETING. (a) This chapter does not require a governmental body to conduct an open meeting:
  (1) to deliberate the appointment, employment, evaluation, reassignment, duties, discipline, or dismissal of a public officer or employee; or
  (2) to hear a complaint or charge against an officer or employee.
(b) Subsection (a) does not apply if the officer or employee who is the subject of the deliberation or hearing requests a public hearing.

Section 551.076. DELIBERATION REGARDING SECURITY DEVICES; CLOSED MEETING. This chapter does not require a governmental body to conduct an open meeting to deliberate the deployment, or specific occasions for implementation, of security personnel or devices.

Section 551.082. SCHOOL CHILDREN; SCHOOL DISTRICT EMPLOYEES; DISCIPLINARY MATTER OR COMPLAINT. (a) This chapter does not require a school board to conduct an open meeting to deliberate in a case:

(1) involving discipline of a public school child; or

(2) in which a complaint or charge is brought against an employee of the school district by another employee and the complaint or charge directly results in a need for a hearing.

(b) Subsection (a) does not apply if an open hearing is requested in writing by a parent or guardian of the child or by the employee against whom the complaint or charge is brought.

Section 551.083. CERTAIN SCHOOL BOARDS; CLOSED MEETING REGARDING CONSULTATION WITH REPRESENTATIVE OF EMPLOYEE GROUP. This chapter does not require a school board operating under a consultation agreement authorized by Section 13.901, Education Code [this section was not carried over by Senate Bill 1 to the revised Code in 1995; §11.251(g) of the current Code allows districts to consult with teacher groups and others outside of the district-level committee process], to conduct an open meeting to deliberate the standards, guidelines, terms, or condition the board will follow, or instruct its representatives to follow, in a consultation with a representative of an employee group.

Note that students and teachers are accorded the right under the TOMA to have board meetings involving their disciplinary and personnel status, respectively, open if they so desire.

After the start of a public meeting, the law requires the presiding officer to announce the intention to hold a closed session and identify the reason from the above list before doing so. Failure to do so will render actions taken at the meeting voidable (*Rickaway v. Elkhart I.S.D.*, 1995). The posted agenda need not state that a particular subject will be discussed in closed session (*Att'y. Gen. Op. LO-90-27*, 1990). However, the notice requirements regarding specificity (to be discussed below) are the same for an open or closed meeting. No formal, final action may be taken at a closed session. Matters may be discussed during this time, but formal action must take place in open sessions. A Texas court of appeals has ruled that the law allows tape recording of public sessions but not at closed sessions against the objection of those present (*Zamora v. Edgewood I.S.D.*).

Governmental bodies must keep a tape recording or minutes of open meetings and make them available to the general public. Furthermore, video recording of public meetings is allowed under the act. For meetings closed to the public, the keeping of a certified agenda or tape recording is mandated. The certified agenda or tape recording is not available to the general public but is to be kept for a period of at least two years for possible use in legal proceedings involving challenges to closed meetings.

Section 551.075 allows a quorum of a governmental body to confer with its employees, provided no discussion of business or policy takes place among members of the governmental body. The attorney general has concluded that these "briefing sessions," in which board members receive information from and ask questions of staff but do not engage in discussions among themselves, are not subject to the terms of the TOMA (*Att'y. Gen. Op. JM-1058*, 1989). In effect, conversation at these meetings "can go north and south, but not east or west."

A Texas court of appeals likewise has ruled that meetings closed to the public where third parties provide information to a governmental body are not subject to the act provided that the governmental body does not engage in verbal exchange with the third party or engage in verbal exchange among its own members on any issue (*Dallas Morning News v. Board of Trustees of Dallas I.S.D.*, 1993). The case involved a closed meeting between DISD board members and TEA officials who gave an exit accreditation report. The court overruled an attorney general opinion to the contrary (*Att'y. Gen. Op. DM-191*, 1992).

The character of the business that can be conducted in private session was clarified somewhat in a 1984 ruling by the Texas Court of Appeals–Texarkana. In *Board of Trustees of Austin I.S.D. v. Cox Enterprises*, the appeals court began by stating that, while board members can express opinions on issues and announce how they intend to vote in closed session, the actual vote or decision must be made in public session. The court observed that "to allow public officials to make their actual decisions in private sessions and then merely report their decision or present a formal, unanimous front to the public in an open meeting would thwart much of [the purpose of the law]" (p. 89). Thus, the Austin I.S.D. board violated the law by conducting a straw vote for selection of a chairman in closed session and then voting unanimously in open session for the candidate with the most straw votes. The school board also violated the law by selecting in closed session a consultant and a search committee composed of nonboard members to screen candidates for the superintendency. The court noted that even a discussion of their selection in a closed meeting was prohibited, since consultants are not school employees under §551.074 above. However, the board did not violate the law by deciding in executive session to make public the names and qualifications of candidates for the superintendent's position, by deciding to offer some surplus property for sale, or in discussing the possibility of employing a particular candidate as superintendent where no vote was taken.

The above points were affirmed when the ruling was appealed to the Texas Supreme Court in 1986. However, the Texas Supreme Court disagreed with the appeals court that posting notices of meetings with business items indicated in general terms, such as *personnel, litigation,* and *real estate,* did not violate the provision regarding posting of agendas. Whether the meeting is open or closed, advance notice adequately must describe the subject matter to be considered. "Our prior judgments should have served as notice to all public bodies that the Open Meetings Act requires a full disclosure of the subject matter of the meetings." A Texas appellate court expanded on this point in a 1990 decision involving the selection of a principal. Given the special interest of the public in the principalship, posted agendas must specify this position rather than include it within a general "employment of personnel" category. Failure to do so will void the board's selection in a contested case. The court noted that "as expected public interest in a particular subject increases, notice must become more specific" (*Point Isabel I.S.D. v. Hinojosa*).

On the other hand, the TOMA does not create a right for employees to have specific notice of discussion or action pertaining to their own employment. A case in point involved a band instructor in Bridgeport I.S.D. who alleged that board failure to specify in the notice that his particular contract would be discussed in closed session denied him an opportunity to request an open hearing. The Texas Court of Appeals–Austin was not persuaded, noting that the purpose of the act is to alert the public to the workings of government, not to provide due process protections to individual employees. The teacher had not demonstrated a special public interest that would require the board to list his specific position as the topic of discussion (*Stockdale v. Meno*, 1993).

A good way to follow the general thrust of the TOMA regarding agenda items is to apply the "Joe Citizen" test: Will the average citizen who does not follow school matters as a rule understand the significance of an item on the posted agenda? If not, specificity is lacking. Thus, a grievance filed by a teacher should include the name of the grieving party and may also contain the subject matter of the grievance (*Att'y. Gen. Op. JM-1112*, 1989).

In the *Cox Enterprises* case, the Texas Supreme Court also found that the convening of closed sessions without a quorum physically present violates the law. "The public is entitled to know which members are present for the closed session and whether there is a quorum." However, in 1995 a federal district court ruled that nothing precludes board members from discussing matters at a pre-board meeting conference when a quorum is not present and when there is no evidence of an intent to circumvent the requirements of the law. The act applies only to meetings at which a quorum is present. The case involved a closed meeting of less than a quorum of Houston I.S.D. school board members. At the meeting, one of the members was asked to consider being appointed to the position of general superintendent. Some time later at an open meeting with all board members present, the member was selected. The court noted that the act allows board members to meet in closed meetings to discuss personnel, and the expression of interest in the board member and the terms of his employment contract were personnel issues (*Hispanic Education Committee v. Houston I.S.D.*). The Fifth Circuit affirmed the lower court decision without opinion.

Section 551.125 of the TOMA was amended in 1995 to allow governmental bodies to hold meetings by telephone conference call, provided that an emergency or public necessity exists and the convening of a quorum at one location would be difficult or impossible. Such meetings are subject to the TOMA notice requirements. The notice must specify as the location of the meeting the place where meetings of the governmental body are usually held. At this location, each portion of the conference call that is required to be open to the public must be audible and tape recorded. Two-way communication must be provided during the full course of the meeting, and the identity of the speakers must be clearly stated prior to their speaking. In an earlier decision, the attorney general advised that the TOMA does not permit attendance via live video transmission. Rather, the TOMA requires that members must be physically present at the meeting location designated in the notice, unless the act provides a specific exception otherwise (*Att'y. Gen. Op. DM-207*). Nor can school board members vote by proxy at a school board meeting, whether or not a quorum of board members is present (*Att'y. Gen. Op. LO-94-028*, 1994).

The Texas Supreme Court has ruled that, once a quorum is in place, there can be no informal discussion outside of a meeting when a majority of a public decision-making body is considering a pending issue. "There is either formal consideration of the matter in compliance with the Open Meetings Act or an illegal meeting" (*Acker v. Texas Water Commission*). The case involved two members of the three-member Texas Water Commission who were overheard in the restroom conversing about an impending application of a water treatment plant. However, the attorney general has concluded that nothing precludes members of a governmental body or other persons in attendance at a closed session from making public statements about the subject matter of the session (*Att'y. Gen. Op. JM-1071*, 1989).

A board's action in violation of the TOMA is voidable, but a violation of one item does not affect the validity of other actions taken during the meeting. Only courts can declare governmental actions void. Persons that substantially prevail in a lawsuit under TOMA are entitled to recover court costs and legal fees. Releasing a certified agenda or tape recording of a closed meeting may result in money damages as well (Government Code §551.146). There are also criminal penalties for violating the act. Holding an illegally closed meeting, for example, constitutes a misdemeanor punishable by a fine of not less than $100 nor more than $500 or imprisonment in the county jail for not less than one month nor more than six months, or both. Knowingly conspiring to deliberate in numbers less than a quorum for the purpose of secret deliberations is subject to the same penalty (Government Code §§551.143–144).

Texas Public Information Act

Formerly known as the Texas Open Records Act, the Texas Public Information Act (TPIA) is a companion to the complex open meetings measure. Its provisions are found in Chapter 552 of the Texas Government Code. The TPIA rests on the proposition that "government is the servant of the people" and thus "each person is at all times entitled, unless otherwise expressly provided by law, to full and complete information regarding the affairs of government and the official acts of public officials and employees." The declaration of policy in §552.001 goes on to note that "the people, in delegating authority, do not give their public servants the right to decide what is good for the people to know and what is not good for them to know. The people insist on remaining informed so that they may retain control over the instruments they have created."

The TPIA's declaration of purpose ends by noting that the "provisions of this Act shall be liberally construed" in favor of granting people access to government information. Included in the definition of "governmental body" are boards of trustees of school districts. "Public information" is broadly defined to include media on which public information is recorded such as paper, film, magnetic tape, and even silk and linen. Thus a book, paper, letter, document, photograph, map, drawing, and videotape fall within the ambit of the TPIA.

The law specifically excludes information deemed confidential by constitutional, statutory, or judicial decision. Thus, information that is protected from disclosure by the federal Family Educational Rights and Privacy Act cannot be released, nor can information that would violate someone's personal right of privacy as recognized by Texas law. Section 552.102(a) specifically exempts "information in a personnel file, the disclosure of which would constitute a clearly unwarranted invasion of personal privacy." At the same time, this provision grants public employees, including teachers or their designated representatives, access to their own personnel files.

Among the other types of information that are exempted from disclosure are information related to litigation; information that if released would give advantage to competitors or bidders; interagency or intra-agency memoranda or letters that would not be available by law to a party other than one in litigation with the agency; the performance evaluation of a teacher or administrator; and the home addresses, telephone numbers, Social Security numbers, and information about family members of current or former employees. However, the latter may opt to make this information available. Also exempted from disclosure are transcripts from institutions of higher education maintained in the personnel files of professional public school employees. The TPIA does allow disclosure, from the information contained in these transcripts, of the degree obtained, the name of the institution attended, and the curriculum studied. Test items developed by educational institutions funded in whole or part by the state need not be disclosed, nor do library records identifying those who have checked out books or obtained other services, with limited exceptions. In 1995 the legislature exempted the name of an applicant for a superintendent's position, though the board must provide notice of the names of finalists at least twenty-one days before the date of the meeting when the selection will be made.

A public body may recover the actual cost of reproducing requests exceeding fifty pages and may set established time limits for examining the requested material. However, the attorney general has concluded that TPIA only limits the time period during which public records may be physically inspected; it does not authorize governmental bodies to deny requests for copies of public records (*Att'y. Gen. Op. ORD-512*, 1988).

The law also exempts from disclosure student records at institutions "funded wholly, or in part, by state revenue." This provision

in effect extends the protections of the federal Family Educational
Rights and Privacy Act, which applies to educational institutions
receiving federal funding, to schools which are only state funded.
Another section of the TPIA, §552.022, lists information that *is* to
be released upon request to the public. Some of the items relevant
to education include (by subsection number):

(2) the name, sex, ethnicity, salary, title, and dates of employment of each employee and officer of a governmental body;

(3) information in an account, voucher, or contract relating to
the receipt or expenditure of public or other funds by a governmental body, if the information is not otherwise made
confidential by law;

(4) the name of each official and the final record of voting on all
proceedings in a governmental body;

(13) a policy statement or interpretation which has been adopted
or issued by an agency;

(14) administrative staff manuals and instructions to staff that affect a member of the public;

(15) information that is in a bill for attorneys' fees and that is not
privileged under the attorney-client privilege or confidential
under other law.

The act establishes the chief administrative officer or designee
of each governmental unit as the officer for public information and,
among other requirements, states that the only inquiry to be made
of persons requesting information is that they produce proper identification. If a large amount of information is requested, the officer
for public information is allowed to discuss with the requester how
the request might be narrowed. No inquiry is to be made about the
purpose for which the information will be used.

Extensive requirements as to the care and disposition of public
records are delineated in the Local Government Records Act (Sub-
title C, Title 6, of the Local Government Code). The act defines a
local government record as any document, paper, letter, book, map,
photograph, sound or video recording, microfilm, magnetic tape,
electronic medium, or other information recording medium, regardless of physical form or character and regardless of whether public
access to it is open or restricted under the laws of the state, created
or received by a local government or its officers or employees. The
law details when records can be destroyed and who is authorized to
destroy them.

Quite naturally, uncertainty arises from time to time as to
whether a specific item falls in the exempted from disclosure cate-

gory. The law provides that requests for clarification are to be made to the attorney general, who will issue an advisory opinion. Needless to say, there have been hundreds of such requests. Some of the attorney general responses, usually in the form of an Open Records Decision (ORD), directly related to education are the following:

1. A student cannot be denied access to, or the right to make copies of, his or her records, including a transcript, because of failure to pay fees (ORD-152, 1977; ORD-431, 1985).
2. Student-initiated, subjective, handwritten comments evaluating a named professor are not required to be revealed. (The attorney general's office has issued a number of opinions that subjective evaluations of identifiable personnel are not required to be made public. See, for example, item 8 below.) However, statistical compilations of anonymous student evaluations of teachers can be made public (ORD-224, 1979; JM-36, 1983).
3. Prospective employees who are not hired do not have access to their files (ORD-326, 1982).
4. Employees have the right of access to memoranda to the file made by their superiors if the latter have been directed to make such notes for use in the evaluation process. This decision has significant implications for administrators and others involved in evaluation and documentation activities (ORD-327, 1982).
5. Letters sent to a school board complaining about a teacher are to be made available to the teacher, provided the names of the students and parents are deleted (ORD-332, 1982).
6. Employee names and documents relating to an employee's resignation, as well as the names of all employees taking sick leave and the dates they took it, must be made available (ORD-336, 1982).
7. A school board member has an absolute right to access to school information in his or her official capacity as a board member (Att'y. Gen. Op. JM-119, 1984).
8. Section 552.111 exempts from disclosure "inter-agency or intra-agency memorandums or letters which would not be available by law to a party other than one in litigation with the agency." Prior to 1992, this provision was interpreted broadly. For example, the report of a review committee established to conduct an investigation of the activities of a high school principal was considered intra-agency memoranda and exempted from disclosure. The testimony of witnesses also

was exempted from disclosure, as were the documents they presented. The attorney general opined that when factual information is so intertwined with advice, opinion, and recommendation, none of the information had to be disclosed (*ORD-470*, 1987). Similarly, while objective observations of facts and events as contained in an appraiser's notes must be released upon request, subjective commentary—advice, opinion, and recommendations—were exempt from disclosure under §552.111 (*ORD-450*, 1986). (Note that the evaluation of a teacher or administrator is now listed as confidential in the TPIA. This means that while the employee has access to the evaluation, the general public does not.) In 1990 the attorney general advised that ratings sheets evaluating candidates for administrative positions on a series of characteristics are exempted from disclosure under §552.111. Earlier opinions that required disclosure if the identity of the evaluators could not be ascertained were overruled (*ORD-538*, 1990).

In recent years, the inter- and intra-agency memorandum exception has been the source of litigation that has yet to clarify its meaning. In 1992, the Texas Court of Appeals–Austin ruled that all documents pertaining to the employment application of an unsuccessful applicant for a position as a Texas Ranger had to be disclosed after the attorney general had stipulated at trial that this kind of information is routinely available in litigation (*Texas Department of Public Safety v. Gilbreath*). The practical effect of the ruling was to narrow the inter- or intra-agency exception to material directly related to agency policy making. In subsequent decisions, the attorney general has followed the thrust of the *Gilbreath* decision with respect to releasing information under the inter- and intra-agency memorandum exception. Thus, a parent is entitled to see most of the internal administrative notes and memoranda pertaining to the conduct record of his child (*ORD-615*, 1993). In 1996 the Texas Court of Appeals, Houston, ruled that a parent has access to internal school documents relating to a bad conduct grade given to the parent's daughter (*Lett v. Klein I.S.D.*).

9. The minutes of meetings attended by administrators, teachers, and employee representatives—such as a consultation or campus-based committee—are subject to disclosure. The attorney general considers that, while the meetings may be closed to the public because they do not involve board members, the minutes and recordings of such meetings must be disclosed if the committee has the authority to take final ac-

tion on the matter and the minutes reflect its having done so. If the minutes reflect only deliberation and no final action, they need not be disclosed. If the committee serves only in an advisory capacity to the governmental agency (school board) and the minutes constitute "advice, opinion, or recommendation," they need not be disclosed under §552.111 (ORD-491, 1988).

10. Except for those assigned to law enforcement officers, the general rule is that cellular car telephone numbers have to be released if the telephones are paid for by public funds, just as they would be for telephones in the school. (ORD-506, 1988).

11. The records of deceased students are not exempt from public disclosure and must be provided to the requester (ORD-524, 1989).

12. The public has no right under the act to use the school's computer to inspect records (in this case, American Express Company receipts) as an alternative to receiving a computer printout (ORD-571, 1990).

13. Unless exempted by statute from disclosure (for example, candidates for college presidencies and the superintendency), names of applicants for employment must be disclosed (ORD-585, 1991).

14. When information is requested, a copy of the actual document must be released with any confidential information excised. The document may not be retyped with asterisks to indicate the excised material unless the person making the request consents (ORD-606, 1992).

15. Since law enforcement records created and maintained by campus police are not educational records, they are not subject to the Family Educational Rights and Privacy Act and are subject to disclosure (ORD-612, 1992).

16. An applicant's personal financial history is exempt from disclosure; notes taken during an oral employment interview are not confidential (ORD-626, 1994).

17. Records and documents resulting from the investigation of sexual harassment allegations against a principal must be released with deletion of identities of victims and witnesses but including references to the principal's name because of the public's interest in sexual harassment in the workplace (OR-95-348, 1995).

Note that the legislature significantly increased access of parents to information about their children by enacting TEC §§26.001–

26.012 in 1995. See Chapter 2 for a detailed discussion of these provisions. See also the discussion of the federal Family Educational
Rights and Privacy Act later in this chapter for more information
about parental access to information in student records.

EDUCATOR PRIVACY RIGHTS

As we have seen, considerable information about public employees
and their work is readily available to the public under the Texas
Public Information Act. The zone of employee privacy is largely determined by traditional forms of tort law, such as libel and slander.
In Texas, state courts have recognized the tort of personal privacy
invasion. A teacher in the Houston I.S.D. tried unsuccessfully to assert this right in connection with the videotaping of her classroom
performance. The state appeals court observed that "Appellant has
not cited any authority, and we have found none, relating to her
claim of 'involuntary videotaping' of her performance as a teacher"
(p. 111). The court went on to note that teaching in a public classroom does not fall within the zone of protected privacy, since public
school teaching is by its nature open to public view (*Roberts v.
Houston I.S.D.*, 1990).

Life-Style Issues

Life-style behaviors related to marriage and procreation, which have
long been recognized as Fourteenth Amendment liberty rights, are
usually accorded at least some constitutional protection. Thus, the
U.S. Court of Appeals for the Fifth Circuit in 1981 ruled that teachers have the right to breast-feed a baby on school grounds, though
school officials can determine where it can take place (*Dike v.
School Board of Orange County*). In 1995 the Texas Legislature
added a section to the Health and Safety Code declaring that "a
mother is entitled to breast-feed her baby in any location in which
the mother is authorized to be" (§165.022).

Insofar as unwed mothers are concerned, the Fifth Circuit ruled
in 1975 that a blanket rule against their employment in a public
school district violates their Fourteenth Amendment due process
and equal protection rights (*Andrews v. Drew Municipal Separate
School District*). The Fifth Circuit specifically stated that it was not
deciding the case on the basis of privacy rights. The case involved
two teacher aides who were not rehired, because they were mothers
of illegitimate children. The court found the rule created an "irre-
buttable presumption" that all unwed mothers are immoral and im-

proper role models. The court noted the availability of "alternative means through which to remove or suspend teachers engaging in immoral conduct; means that guarantee the teacher a public hearing on the merits and right of appeal" (pp. 615–616). In a related decision in 1982, the Fifth Circuit ruled that a teacher's out-of-wedlock pregnancy is constitutionally protected (*Avery v. Homewood City Board of Education*). Since the school board had no other reason to justify her dismissal, the court ordered the lower court decision vacated. Both decisions serve to tighten up the definition of "immorality."

Is living with a friend of the opposite sex a constitutionally protected privacy right? Two federal district court decisions provide some guidance to judicial thinking in this area, though neither applies to Texas. The first, *Sullivan v. Meade City I.S.D.* (1975), involved an unmarried teacher who was living with her boyfriend in a mobile home furnished by the school only one-eighth of a mile from the school. The smallness of the community, together with the facts that the living arrangement was well known in and out of school and that 140 persons had signed a petition protesting the teacher's conduct, convinced both school officials and the court that the teacher's effectiveness in the classroom had been undermined. The court in the second case, *Thompson v. Southwest School District* (1980), distinguished *Sullivan*, observing that the community there was small and that the teacher refused to get married before she was dismissed. By contrast, the teacher in *Thompson* got married on the eve of her suspension. The court, however, did not decide the case on the basis of the teacher's alleged constitutional right of privacy but rather on the absence of evidence produced by the school board that her teaching effectiveness was undermined.

In the *Thompson* case, the court was faced with a state law allowing a school board to dismiss a teacher for "immoral conduct." Texas school districts often list immoral conduct as a reason for contract nonrenewal or termination. The Missouri teacher argued that the state law was unconstitutionally vague, an argument the court explored in some depth. The judge concluded that, standing alone, the phrase "immoral conduct" could well be unconstitutionally vague but found that, when read in conjunction with other provisions, immoral conduct relates to conduct that would render the teacher unfit to perform her duties. So interpreted, the law was valid.

In 1980 a federal district court in Texas had no trouble concluding that adultery is not entitled to constitutional protection. In *Johnson v. San Jacinto Junior College*, the court concluded from its review of the case law that "at this stage in the development of the right of privacy, the protection of actual sexual intimacy appears to be confined to those persons in the marital relationship" (p. 575). The case involved the demotion of the college registrar to a teaching position for engaging in an extramarital affair. The court found that, while procedural violations involved in the demotion entitled the plaintiff to damages, he was not entitled to reinstatement as registrar.

The judicial response to moral turpitude as grounds for terminating an educator is well illustrated by a 1980 ruling of the Texas Court of Appeals in Austin. In *Board of Regents v. Martine*, a college professor was dismissed from his tenured position on the basis of a board policy against "moral turpitude." The court affirmed the district court order reinstating the faculty member, observing that "an agency is not empowered to dismiss an employee whose personal or private conduct incurred the agency's displeasure" (p. 642). The behavior must be related to the job. "In the teaching profession, the inquiry becomes one of whether the teacher's private conduct bears a direct relationship to his ability to teach. In different terms, what is the likelihood that the employee's conduct may have adversely affected students or fellow teachers." Under this analysis, the board was acting illegally in dismissing him for "moral turpitude."

As noted in Chapter 4, teachers are considered role models for their students, and life-style behavior on or off campus that endangers students or undermines teaching effectiveness can serve as good cause for termination. Clearly, sexual behavior with students falls into this category. A few examples from recent commissioner decisions will prove the point. A continuing contract teacher's writing a student notes, going over to her house when her parents are not home, and kissing her on the lips constitute good cause for termination on grounds of immorality (*Rabe v. Lewisville I.S.D.*, 1994). Even if the student consents to the relationship, grounds for termination may be established. As the commissioner noted in a 1989 decision, "Even if the student were an adult, the fact that a student was a *student* is the controlling point. It is this status and this relationship that constitute immoral conduct" (*Molina v. Pasadena I.S.D.*).

Like sexual relations outside marriage, sexual orientation enjoys no constitutional protection. However, case law suggests that unless that orientation negatively impacts students or the employee's ability to perform the job, no adverse action should be taken. For example, the California Supreme Court in 1977 ruled that an isolated incident of solicitation in a public restroom did not impair the teacher's ability to teach, because the conduct was not known to students (*Board of Education v. Jack M.*). A ruling of the U.S. Court of Appeals for the Tenth Circuit is also instructive. The court upheld an Oklahoma statute declaring public homosexual conduct to be grounds for dismissal of a teacher but disallowed application of the provision to advocacy, encouragement, or promotion of public or private homosexual conduct as overly broad and a violation of free speech and association (*National Gay Task Force v. Board of Education, City of Oklahoma City*, 1985). The decision was later affirmed by an equally divided Supreme Court.

Insofar as personal grooming is concerned, while the U.S. Court of Appeals for the Fifth Circuit has ruled that a teacher in a public high school (and presumably in the lower grades as well) has a constitutional liberty right in choosing how to wear his or her hair, "the right may be regulated so long as the deprivation is not arbitrary." Thus, a teacher hairstyle regulation is a reasonable means of furthering the school's interest in "teaching hygiene, instilling discipline, asserting authority, and compelling uniformity." The court noted that the same rationale applies to other employees who come into contact with students, such as bus drivers (*Domico v. Rapides Parish School Board*, 1982).

The law is different for the public community and four-year college. In *Hander v. San Jacinto Junior College*, the Fifth Circuit concluded that a faculty member has a constitutional right to wear a beard and that a community college regulation to the contrary is unjustified. Instrumental in the decision is the Fifth Circuit's 1972 ruling that community college students have the right to wear long hair (*Lansdale v. Tyler Junior College*). As the court noted, if students have such a right, surely their teachers do, too.

Finally, with regard to employee privacy rights, §81.102(a) of the Texas Health and Safety Code spells out the conditions and requirements for testing persons with AIDS and related disorders. Employers can test employees only when there is a bona fide occupational qualification justifying the testing. The statute sets forth the conditions for confidentiality of test results.

Personnel Records and Employee References

The law of defamation and privacy invasion is most likely to surface in the education setting in the context of revealing the content of personnel records. The problem for educational officials is that other laws—most notably federal antibias legislation and the state's

Public Information Act—often mandate disclosure. Thus, educators are sometimes caught between a "rock and a hard place," where reconciliation is not easily accomplished.

As noted earlier, defamation can be either oral (slander) or in writing (libel). For defamation to be actionable, several conditions must be met, the most important of which are: (1) the words must meet the definition of defamation, (2) the words must be communicated to a third person, (3) the words must be false, (4) the communication of the words must have resulted in injury to the person. These conditions suggest some defenses to claims of defamation. For example, if there has been no communication to a third party, there is no viable claim of defamation. Truth is always a defense to a claim of defamation. Mere statements of opinion also are protected as free speech.

In addition, two Texas statutes convey a qualified privilege to employers with respect to employee decision making. Article 5206 of the Texas Civil Statutes states that "Any written statement of cause of discharge, if true, when made by such agent, company, or corporation, shall never be used as the cause of an action for libel, either civil or criminal, against the agent, company, or corporation furnishing same." And TEC §22.051(a) shields school professional employees from liability from damage suits in most situations. Section 101.051 of the Civil Practices and Remedies Code does the same for school districts. These laws will be discussed in some detail in the next chapter. The qualified immunity granted professional employees by §22.051 requires that the person sued be acting in the scope of his or her public employment. Statutory protection would not otherwise be available. For example, a school official who releases information about an employee that constitutes a "clearly unwarranted invasion of personal privacy" under the Texas Public Information Act would have difficulty claiming immunity under TEC §22.051.

The U.S. Court of Appeals for the Fifth Circuit cited the qualified privilege provided by TEC §22.051 (then codified as TEC §21.912(b)) in ruling in 1992 that administrators in the Houston I.S.D. were immune from liability for circulating a memorandum within the district relating to the alleged deficiencies of a substitute teacher (*Jones v. Houston I.S.D.*). A Texas appeals court ruled similarly in a 1991 decision, noting that "a letter of reference written by a professional supervisor of a public school merely expressing his professional *opinion* on an employee's work performance under his supervision is an act within the scope of the employee's duties with the school district and is, consequently, not subject to a libel action by virtue of section 21.912(b) unless such statements are false statement of *fact* or are libelous *per se"* (*Hammond v. Katy I.S.D.*, p. 180).

Probably the best protection against defamation lawsuits in the context of employee references is to secure the employee's permission to release information. An employee who authorizes release of employment information by the former employer limits his or her ability later to prevail in a defamation action. In the *Jones* case above, the substitute teacher had signed a release form and thus was precluded from seeking damages for libel when the memorandum was sent to a prospective employer. In the absence of release forms, many personnel administrators provide only factual information to prospective employers, e.g., the dates of employment and salary. (For a detailed discussion of release forms in Texas, see *Smith v. Holley*, a 1992 decision of the Texas Court of Appeals–San Antonio. A sample release form is provided in F. R. Kemerer and J. A. Crain's *The Documentation Handbook*, Second Edition, available from the *Texas School Administrators' Legal Digest*.)

Telephone conversations can present special concerns for administrators. A case in point is *Sitzler v. Babers*, a 1992 decision of the Texas Commissioner of Education. In that case, the teacher filed several grievances in the district prior to resigning. After her resignation, Glenda Sitzler had difficulty securing employment. She contacted her sister, the branch manager of an employment agency. The sister contacted the principal by telephone for a reference check and learned that the principal could not give a positive reference, in part because of Sitzler's tendency to file grievances. The teacher's cousin, an advocate for the U.S. Small Business Administration, also obtained the same information. The commissioner revoked the principal's certificate for penalizing the teacher for exercising her right to file grievances (see Chapter 5).

As noted in the employment chapter, public school employees have the right to clear their names if their reputations are stigmatized in the context of being nonrenewed (*Dennis v. S & S Consolidated Rural High School District*, U.S. Court of Appeals for the Fifth Circuit, 1978). However, the stigmatizing has to occur in the context of a loss or a denial of a state-conferred status (here, employment). The U.S. Supreme Court has ruled that stigmatizing by public officials unaccompanied by any loss of status does not trigger a Fourteenth Amendment liberty right violation (*Paul v. Davis*, 1976). Serious stigmatizing, however, might constitute an invasion of personal privacy under state law.

Occasionally, school officials themselves are targets of consid-

erable criticism. To what extent can they seek redress by filing defamation suits? Because the law affords great leeway to critics of public officials, school authorities will generally be unsuccessful unless
they can establish "actual malice"—that is, that the statements
were made with knowledge that they were false or with reckless
disregard of their truth or falsity. Thus, an irate Texas football coach
was unsuccessful in suing the town newspaper for libel over criticism it printed about his performance (*Johnson v. Southwestern
Newspapers Corp.*, 1993).

STUDENT PRIVACY RIGHTS

Issues involving parent and student privacy rights involve both
statutory and judicial law, and can be separated into several
categories.

Student Records

Enacted in 1974, the Family Educational Rights and Privacy Act
(FERPA) applies to most educational institutions in the country and
gives parents practically unlimited rights of access to personally
identifiable information contained in their child's education records. Also known as the Buckley Amendment, FERPA restricts the
release of this information to third parties without permission of
parents or eligible students. Since the Texas Public Information Act
incorporates FERPA's provisions, TPIA must be read in harmony
with the federal statute. The penalty for illegal disclosure is withholding of federal funds from the school district. In addition, parents and eligible students may seek money damages under a federal
statute discussed in the next chapter, 42 U.S.C. §1983.

The FERPA provisions require annual notice to parents of their
rights under the statute. Further, such notice "shall effectively notify parents of students who have a primary or home language other
than English." The basic provisions of this law are these:[1]

1. Parents exercise the rights conveyed by the law until the student is attending college or is eighteen years of age. Rights under FERPA then transfer to the student. Even then, however,

---

[1] For a detailed discussion, see Chris Elizalde, "Legal Issues Involved in Releasing Student Records," in *The Texas School Administrators' Legal Digest* 11, no. 6
(June 1995).

the parents retain a right of access to the student's records if
the student is a dependent for federal income tax purposes. A
"parent" includes a natural parent, guardian, or any person acting as a parent in the absence of a parent or guardian. A parent
has access to student records even if the parent does not have
custody of the child, unless there is a court order to the contrary. See the discussion of child custody issues in the next
section.

2. The term "education records" is defined much more broadly
than just the information in the student's cumulative folder.
Included within the definition are "records, files, documents,
and other materials that contain information directly related to
the student" maintained by the school or its personnel. For example, a parent would be entitled to see the evaluation forms
for the parent's child following cheerleader tryouts. The parent
would also be entitled to see the videotape made of her performance, provided the videotape does not include personally
identifiable information about other students. In addition, new
state law provisions resulting from the passage of Senate Bill 1
give parents access to such information as student attendance
records, test scores, counseling records, reports about behavior-
ial patterns, and teaching materials (TEC §§26.004, 26.006).
Only a few items are excluded under FERPA's education records definition. Included among them are records made by district personnel kept in the sole possession of the person and not
revealed to anyone else other than a temporary substitute for
the maker of the record, e.g., a substitute teacher.

3. Parents have a right in most instances to inspect student records and a right to consent to disclosure of personally identifiable information to third persons. They have a right to challenge the accuracy or content of the records and to request that
an amendment be added if the records are not accurate or are
misleading. Parents also have a right to know what kinds of so-
called directory information (names, phone numbers, addresses, height, weight, athletic team rosters, and the like) the
school assembles and to request that it not be released with respect to their children. After informing parents of their rights
to withhold directory information, a school district thereafter
must provide third parties with the requested information
(Att'y. Gen. Ops. ORD-242, ORD-244, 1980). Thus, if a community group wants a roster of all students in the school, the
school must release the information, excluding only the names

of students whose parents requested this information not be disclosed.

4. School employees are among the relatively few persons allowed access to student records by the law without written consent of the parent or eligible student. The district, however, must include in its policies the criteria for determining who has a "legitimate educational interest" in looking at a student's record. Access is also provided to school officials in a district to which the student has transferred, providing the sending district has notified the parent and student that it provides such information. Schools may make limited disclosure to state and local law enforcement personnel to whom criminal activities must be reported under TEC §37.015. Limited disclosure also may be made to organizations conducting certain evaluative studies, and officials of the Department of Human Services investigating allegations of child abuse or neglect.

5. Records must be kept of every person who requests or obtains access to a particular student's record, except for the student's parents and school district officials. No record need be kept of requests accompanied by prior written parental consent and requests for directory information only.

When a parent requests a record about the parent's child and information about other children is also contained in the record, personally identifiable information about the other students must be deleted. While parents and eligible students can waive their FERPA rights, as in the case of confidential recommendations for college or employment, the waiver must be a knowing one. That is, the waiver must be completely voluntary and must be made with full knowledge of what is being waived.

In situations where it is not clear whether requested information should be released to parents or third parties under provisions of FERPA and the Texas Public Information Act, it is best to request an open records decision from the Texas Attorney General. For example, recently the Burnet school district was not sure whether it should release the ridership lists for school bus routes to a parent who asked for the information. The district requested an attorney general opinion to clarify the law. The attorney general concluded that the ridership lists contained personally identifiable information about individual students and could not be released. However, the bus driver's name and bus number did have to be released (*Att'y. Gen. Op. OR-94-138*, 1994).

Child Custody Issues

When a divorce case is concluded, the divorce decree will usually name one parent to be the managing conservator (the one with custody) and one parent to be the possessory conservator (the parent with visitation rights) or name both parents as joint managing conservators. Section 153.012 of the Family Code allows the court to order the custodian of records to delete all references to the place of residence of either party appointed as a conservator before releasing the records to another party appointed as conservator.

Occasionally, school personnel are faced with a request from a divorced parent for a special arrangement involving the child—for example, visitation on the campus. It is preferable in these situations to have on file a copy of the divorce settlement and to ask the parent with custody to add a note for the child's file showing that parent's consent to deviate from the court order.

It should be noted that §42.003 of the Texas Family Code makes one who assists a person to take or retain possession of a child or to conceal the whereabouts of a child in violation of a court order liable for damages. This provision of the Family Code protects all persons who have either custody or visitation rights under a court order. Thus, it is especially important for school officials to have all relevant court orders on file for review when disputes about release of the child arise.

Student Search and Seizure

For the first time, the U.S. Supreme Court ruled in 1985 that the Fourth and Fourteenth amendments, protecting persons from unreasonable searches and seizures, apply to public school students. The Court in *New Jersey v. T.L.O.* rejected arguments that school officials have the same authority to search that parents do (the *in loco parentis* theory).

However, given the school's need to preserve order, the full protections of the Constitution do not apply. Thus, the Court specifically held that neither a warrant nor probable cause is required. To search a student, a school official must (1) establish reasonable cause that the student is violating or has violated a student rule or a law, and (2) make sure that the search that is conducted is reasonable in scope in light of the age and sex of the student and the nature of the offense.

Using these standards, the Court upheld the pocketbook searches of T.L.O., who was reported to the principal to be smoking in the restroom in violation of school rules. When she denied it, the principal searched her purse and found both cigarettes and a package of rolling papers (the first search). The presence of the rolling papers justified searching further (the second search). The principal found marijuana and a list of names suggesting drug dealing. The student was then turned over to the police and subsequently adjudged a juvenile delinquent. Both searches were justified because there was reasonable cause to conduct them and because they were not excessively intrusive.

Reasonable cause to believe is a lesser standard than the probable cause standard for the issuing of warrants as stated in the Fourth Amendment, but more than a hunch that wrongdoing might be involved. Searching a truant student who is seen hanging around the school bleachers where illicit activity occasionally takes place or searching a student who tries to hide a bulging calculator behind his back falls into the "hunch" category (*Matter of Pima County Juvenile Action*, 1987, and *In re William G.*, 1985). Generally, as in the *New Jersey v. T.L.O.* decision, "reasonable cause" means that there exists some articulable grounds to conduct the search. Further elucidation of the standard was provided by the Texas Court of Appeals–Eastland in 1988 and by the Texas Court of Appeals–Houston in 1989.

The 1988 case involved the conviction of a seventeen-year-old high school student for possession of two ounces of marijuana. The student, Sean Irby, argued that there was no reasonable cause to conduct the search. A teacher had overheard a conversation among students that a certain student had marijuana with him at school. The teacher told the assistant principal, who confronted the student. The student, an unidentified informant, admitted that he did have marijuana and handed it over to the assistant principal. The student indicated that he had obtained it from Irby. The assistant principal confronted Irby, who agreed to a search. Marijuana was found concealed in the lining of his coat. Reviewing the words of the majority in the *T.L.O.* decision carefully, the appeals court concluded that the search was "justified at its inception" because the teacher had informed the principal of the conversation regarding the student informant and because the student informant then identified Irby as the person who provided him with the drug (*Irby v. State*).

The 1989 case involved the refusal of a student to stop in the hall when asked by the assistant principal to produce a hall pass. The school official, Bart Busker, had disciplined the student several times in the past. Busker testified that when he continued to inquire about the pass, the student, Bryan Coffman, jumped back and clutched his book bag and became "excited and aggressive." The student then said he had been in the parking lot. Busker knew the parking lot had been the scene of recent thefts. When Busker asked Coffman to open the book bag, Coffman tried to push past him to get away. Busker threatened to contact the police if Coffman did not comply. The student then agreed to open the bag, but not in the hall. On the way to the principal's office, the student tried to grab the bag. Busker held onto both the bag and Coffman's arm. Once in the office, Busker discovered a .22-caliber pistol in the bag and contacted police. He did not search further. Coffman was indicted and convicted for the felony offense of carrying a weapon on school premises. The appeals court affirmed the trial court's judgment that reasonable cause was present to conduct the search because the student's behavior was erratic and suspicious, the student admitted being in an area where recent thefts had occurred, and the student had exhibited aggressive behavior in trying to retain control of the book bag (*Coffman v. State*).

What happens when a student refuses to comply with a request to empty his pockets or turn over her purse? In the absence of an emergency situation, rather than force a search, the best strategy is probably to call the parents or, where weapons or drugs are suspected, the police. If the parent, when called, also refuses to consent to the search, the matter can then be turned over to the police.

The excessively intrusive component of the *T.L.O.* guidelines was addressed in a 1992 decision by the Texas Court of Criminal Appeals. High school student José Coronado told the school secretary that he was leaving campus to attend his grandfather's funeral. The assistant principal, Kim Benning, then saw Coronado at a pay phone outside the building. The assistant principal was suspicious, since several days earlier he had confronted Coronado regarding a tip that the student was selling drugs on campus. The student had denied it. Benning asked Coronado to accompany him to the office. He learned from the boy's relatives that the grandfather had not died. Car keys were found when Benning "patted down" Coronado, though the student said he did not drive. Then the assistant principal had the student remove his socks and shoes and pull down his pants. Nothing was found. Following a fruitless locker search, the assistant principal, deputy sheriff, and campus security guard accompanied Coronado to the parking lot. Benning testified that he demanded Coronado open the car. The student did so, and drugs and drug paraphernalia were found in the trunk. The student was arrested. He sought to suppress use of the evidence against him in a criminal prosecution for possession of cocaine.

The Court of Criminal Appeals concluded that there was reasonable cause for the assistant principal to suspect Coronado of attempting to skip school and for initially patting him down for safety reasons. Indeed, the assistant principal had testified at trial that he was trying to determine if Coronado was truant. However, the subsequent search of the student's clothing, person, locker, and car were excessively intrusive. These searches were not related to suspicion about skipping school. Further, nothing surfaced in the searches justifying expansion of the search to the car. The high court distinguished both the *Irby* and *Coffman* cases. "[W]e find no connection whatsoever between Benning's original stop of [Coronado] to determine whether [Coronado] was skipping school, and the unproductive, progressively intrusive searches culminating in the search of appellant's vehicle" (p. 641). The evidence found in the car search could not be used in the subsequent trial against the student (*Coronado v. State*).

The *T.L.O.* case is also important for what it does *not* say about searches of lockers and desks, use of sniffer dogs, general luggage and metal detector searches, searches where the police are involved, and strip searches. The Court refused to take up these matters. Thus, we must look to lower court rulings and legal commentary.

Searches of lockers and desks are considered permissible upon reasonable cause to believe that they contain illegal items or for periodic inspection purposes—for example, a search for overdue library books or spoiled food at the end of a semester. Since lockers and desks are jointly held property, schools may limit student expectation of privacy. *Caution*: Board policy may restrict locker searches to times when individualized suspicion is present. If so, then general searching is impermissible. If board policy does permit general searches, students should be notified through the student code of conduct that lockers and desks are jointly held property and that the school reserves the right to conduct searches. Students should be put on notice that any illicit items "in plain view" will be confiscated and may subject the student to disciplinary measures. Commentators in this area of the law advise school personnel against conducting general "fishing expeditions," which are not conducted for health or safety reasons. General searches have always been frowned upon. Indeed, the Fourth Amendment was added to the Bill of Rights to prevent government officials from carrying out blanket searches as the British had done during colonial times.

Sniffer dogs can be used to conduct general searches of lockers and automobiles on school property if the dogs are reliable. The U.S. Court of Appeals for the Fifth Circuit has ruled that the use of sniffer dogs in this context is not a "search." At the same time, the dogs must be sufficiently reliable to indicate reasonable suspicion that contraband is present at the time the sniff occurs (*Horton v. Goose Creek I.S.D.*, 1982). In the *Horton* decision, the Fifth Circuit observed in a footnote that it was not ruling on whether sniffer dogs might be used to conduct a general search of students at a distance. The use of sniffer dogs in this fashion could be analogized to the use of metal detectors in airports and electronic scanners in libraries. In neither case is the person being touched. Whether sniffer dogs could be used in the same way has yet to be determined, as is the relevance of this observation to the use of metal detectors and magnetometers in school.

Under the *Horton* ruling, individualized suspicion is required in conducting pocket and purse searches of students. While the Supreme Court in the *T.L.O.* decision did not rule on the general student search, it did note in a footnote that "exceptions to the requirement of individualized suspicion are generally appropriate only where the privacy interests implicated by a search are minimal" and where other safeguards are available to assure that the individual's reasonable expectation of privacy is not subject to the discretion of school officials. We next examine the developing law in other jurisdictions regarding luggage and metal detector searches, since the law in Texas is silent on these searches.

In the past, courts have been reluctant to support suspicionless general searches of student luggage prior to school-sponsored field trips. For example, the Washington State Supreme Court ruled in 1985 that such searches violate student privacy rights, pointing out that there are less intrusive means of assuring that contraband is not present, e.g., requiring parents to examine and vouch for their own children's luggage (*Kuehn v. Renton School District No. 403*). However, a trend in the opposite direction may be occurring. For example, in 1993, a New Jersey appellate court upheld a school policy allowing school officials to search carry-on luggage to discover alcohol, drugs, or weapons (*Desilets v. Clearview Regional Board of Education*). The court noted that between 1978 and 1991, such searches had turned up contraband in six instances. Further, parents signed a permission form, which contained a statement that hand luggage would be searched. The New Jersey court took its cue from a footnote in the *T.L.O.* decision indicating that individualized suspicion is not the *sine qua non* of all student searches. The court likened the luggage search to airport searches, sobriety checkpoints, and border crossings.

Some Texas school districts now use hand-held metal detectors or magnetometers through which all students pass as they enter school to screen for weapons. Like luggage searches, there is no Texas law on the practice. In fact, at this writing, only one court in the country has considered the legality of metal detector/magnetometer searches. In *People v. Dukes* (1992), a New York City criminal court upheld a carefully developed metal detector search policy. The policy had been implemented in light of a serious and growing weapons problem in New York City schools. The policy informs students that metal detector searches of their persons and their bookbags and parcels might occur periodically. Signs are posted outside the building on the day of the search. The searches are conducted by police officers using hand-held metal detectors that never touch the student's person. If the device activates, the officer reminds the student to remove metal objects from the student's pockets or parcels. If activated again, the officer then leads the student to a private area for a pat-down. If an object is detected, the student is given a chance to remove it before the officer does so. In upholding the practice, the judge likened the search to the use of magnetometer searches in airports and courts, which have been routinely upheld, and noted even greater governmental justification for such searches in the school setting.

Given the sparsity of law on the subject of both luggage and metal detector searches, Texas school districts should be particularly cautious in employing them in situations where student safety issues are not paramount. Their legality will depend upon the factual justification for their use and the extent to which search procedures minimize intrusion on student personal privacy.

Where evidence found in a search is to be turned over to the police, it seems preferable to have either probable cause for the search or a warrant, if there is time to secure one. Better yet, the police should conduct the search themselves. This is because courts are troubled when police benefit from evidence secured in a search that they themselves could not have conducted without adhering to more stringent standards. While the Supreme Court in *T.L.O.* specifically declined to comment on this issue, the Fifth Circuit in *Horton* observed in a footnote that when the police are involved the standards for a student search may well be higher. Unfortunately, the court did not specify what they are. Police involvement came to the aid of school officials in the *Irby* case discussed earlier. The court rejected Irby's contention that the chain of custody on the contraband had not been established. The assistant principal had not put his initials on the bag containing the marijuana and conceded that the exhibits at trial might not be the same as found in Irby's jacket. However, he handed the items over to an Abilene police officer, who testified that he had placed them in the evidence vault and had retrieved them for the trial. The appeals court concluded that "the evidence is sufficient to support the trial court's finding that the State proved the chain of custody and that the marijuana produced at the trial was the same as the contraband taken from appellant's jacket."

Turning the matter over to police has another advantage: it limits the liability of the school district and school officials. A case in point is *Jennings v. Joshua I.S.D.*, a decision of the Fifth Circuit in 1989. In *Jennings*, sniffer dogs alerted school officials to the presence of substances in a car in the school parking lot during a general sweep. The student's father had directed his daughter not to permit a search. When he was contacted, the father also refused to consent, whereupon the school officials turned the matter over to the police. A search warrant was obtained, but nothing illegal surfaced when the car was searched. The father later filed a civil rights lawsuit against the school district, school officials, the dog handling company, the police officer, and the city. The Fifth Circuit upheld dismissal of the lawsuit against the school district and school officials. Because the matter had been turned over to the police when the father refused to unlock the car, school officials "cannot be liable for any constitutional violation that followed." The appeals court also upheld dismissal of the lawsuit against the dog handlers and upheld a jury verdict in favor of the policeman.

The most intrusive search, of course, is the strip search. When punitive damages have been assessed against school officials in connection with student searches, it has usually been in the context of the strip search. For example, in *M.M. v. Anker*, a 1979 decision of the U.S. Court of Appeals for the Second Circuit, the appeals court upheld a lower court award of $7,500 damages to a fifteen-year-old student who was subjected to a strip search in a New York City public school. The dean of women thought there was drug paraphernalia among the girl's pocketbook belongings. She ordered the search after some of the items fell off the desk onto the floor and the girl stooped to pick them up. The dean claimed she suspected the girl had hidden a marijuana pipe among her clothing in the process of retrieving the contents. The trial court had awarded damages on the basis of the student's "angrily helpless humiliation."

In a decision remanding a strip search case back to the trial court for a calculation of damages, the U.S. Court of Appeals for the

Seventh Circuit observed that "it does not require a constitutional scholar to conclude that a nude search of a thirteen-year-old child is an invasion of constitutional rights of some magnitude. More than that, it is a violation of any known principle of human decency" (*Doe v. Renfrow*, 1980, pp. 92–93).

More recently, several courts have permitted nude searches. In *Williams by Williams v. Ellington*, the U.S. Court of Appeals for the Sixth Circuit upheld a strip search of a sixteen-year-old Kentucky female high school student after the student had surrendered a vial containing "rush," a volatile substance that can be purchased over the counter. Similarly, the Seventh Circuit upheld a nude search of a sixteen-year-old special education student who was observed by several teachers with a suspicious bulge in his crotch. Earlier reports had tied the student to drug-related activity. At one point, he had bragged about "crotching" drugs during a raid on his mother's house. The student was taken to the boys' locker room, where a teacher and the dean, both males, asked him to change from street clothes into his gym uniform. The officials visually inspected his naked body and physically inspected his clothes. No contraband was found. While observing that the trauma of a search increases with the age of the student, the appeals court also noted that older students have increased capacity to conceal contraband in their private areas. Given the justification for the search and the careful manner in which it was conducted, the court ruled in favor of the school (*Cornfield by Lewis v. Consolidated High School District No. 230*, 1993). In the absence of similar case rulings in Texas, most commentators advise leaving strip searches to parents or to the police.

In June 1995 the U.S. Supreme Court revisited the student search and seizure area, this time in the context of drug testing. By a six-to-three margin the Court upheld a school district drug-testing policy for students participating in interscholastic sports (*Vernonia School District v. Acton*). In the face of a serious drug problem among student athletes, the district implemented the testing program in 1989. Only those students involved in interscholastic sports are tested and then only after a consent form has been signed. Those taking medication provide a copy of the prescription or a doctor's authorization. The Court assumed that students could convey this information in a sealed envelope that is forwarded to the testing agency. Testing is done at the beginning of the season and then randomly on a weekly basis thereafter. Adult monitors of the same sex accompany students to the locker room. Male students produce a sample at a urinal with their backs to the monitor; female students produce a sample in an enclosed stall. The samples are checked for temperature and tampering, then turned over to the testing agency. Testing results are made available only to selected school personnel and are 99.94 percent accurate.

Penalties are limited. If the first test is positive, a second test is administered. If the second test is also positive, the student is given a choice of participating in a six-week assistance program that includes weekly urinalysis or being dropped from athletics for the remainder of the current season and the next athletic season. Second and third offenses result in longer suspension from athletics. Testing results are not used for internal school disciplinary measures and are not turned over to the police.

With these features, the Vernonia drug-testing policy passed constitutional muster as a reasonable search under the Fourth Amendment, even though it lacks individualized suspicion. The Court based its ruling on three factors. First, students have a diminished right of privacy in public schools, particularly in the context of athletics. "School sports are not for the bashful," wrote Justice Scalia. Scalia pointed out that students who volunteer for athletics willingly subject themselves to a greater amount of regulation than other students. Second, the Court noted that the Vernonia drug-testing procedures adequately protect student privacy. And third, the Court noted the strong interest of the school district in deterring drug use among athletes. The Court decided only the constitutionality of the Vernonia policy and cautioned against assuming that suspicionless drug testing in other contexts would pass constitutional muster.

So far, we have been considering the "search" component of the Fourth Amendment's prohibition on unreasonable search and seizure. The "seizure" component is rarely litigated in the schooling context. However, one recent decision is worthy of note. In *Hassan v. Lubbock I.S.D.*, the Fifth Circuit was confronted with an odd case in which school officials conducting a field trip through a juvenile detention center placed one of their misbehaving sixth graders in a holding room for the duration of the trip. Other than a toilet and bed, the room was bare. The metal door had a glass viewing panel. Ameen Hassan's parents filed suit against the district, alleging in part that the placement violated their son's right to be free from unreasonable seizures under the Fourth Amendment. The Fifth Circuit was not persuaded, concluding that the seizure of the student by confining him to the room was a reasonable disciplinary measure that did not endanger his welfare. The sixth grader was continuously monitored during his incarceration and was released as soon as the other students completed their visit. Further, his confinement protected him from possible harm by dangerous juveniles in the center. The seizure thus met the reasonable cause/reasonable scope requirements of the *T.L.O.* decision.

Student Personal Privacy

We have already looked at student personal privacy in the context of strip searches. Another area concerns tests and testing insofar as the questions intrude on a student's personal and family life. In addition to the provisions of the Family Educational Rights and Privacy Act previously discussed, the 1973 ruling of a federal district court in Pennsylvania has gained wide acceptance and has been cited in support of a zone of personal privacy by the Texas Supreme Court (*Merriken v. Cressman*). *Merriken* involved the administering of a testing program to identify potential drug abusers among eighth graders in Norristown, Pennsylvania. The test, called the Critical Period of Intervention (CPI), purported to identify, through questionnaire responses, behavioral patterns similar to those in users of marijuana, LSD, barbiturates, or amphetamines. Students were asked questions about their backgrounds and family life and were also asked to identify others in the class who got into fights or quarrels, made unusual or inappropriate remarks, or had to be coaxed or forced to work with other students. Once identified, potential student drug abusers were to be assigned to peer groups for behavioral modification or were to be referred to outside specialists.

The court agreed with plaintiffs that the test was an unconstitutional invasion of family privacy and of the juvenile's right to privacy. The court noted, "There is probably no more private a relationship, excepting marriage, which the Constitution safeguards than that between parent and child. This court can look upon any invasion of that relationship as a direct violation of one's Constitutional right to privacy" (p. 918). What particularly troubled the court was that the parents were not given complete information about the test, that those who refused to participate were likely to be scapegoated, and that confidentiality could not be assured. "When a program talks about labeling someone as a particular type and such a label could remain with him for the remainder of his life, the margin of error must be almost nil."

Note that the court in *Merriken* above refers to marriage as a constitutionally protected right. The recognition by the U.S. Supreme Court that marriage falls within the ambit of the Fourteenth Amendment liberty provision is one of the main reasons schools can no longer discriminate against married students (*Skinner v. Oklahoma*, 1942; *Loving v. Virginia*, 1967). The prohibition extends to extracurricular activities. As a Texas court of appeals noted in a 1974 decision, it "seems illogical to say that a school district can make a rule punishing a student for entering into a status authorized and sanctioned by the laws of the state" (*Bell v. Lone Oak I.S.D.*). In addition to constitutional provisions, Title IX of the Education Amendments of 1972 restricts discrimination based on gender, as do provisions of state law (see especially §106.001, Title 5 of the Texas Civil Practices and Remedies Code).

The U.S. Supreme Court has struck down state attempts to prohibit the sale of contraceptives to minors, holding that the decision to beget a child is a liberty right protected by the Fourteenth Amendment (*Carey v. Population Services International*, 1977). In 1983 the Court unanimously struck down a federal law making it a crime to send unsolicited advertisements for contraceptives through the mail (*Bolger v. Youngs Drug Products Co.*). The Justice Department defended the law as a means to help parents shield their children from birth control information. But writing for himself and four others, Justice Marshall noted "a pressing need for information about contraception" for adolescent children, given the high rate of unwanted pregnancies. He based his ruling on the First Amendment, holding that the law unconstitutionally restricts free speech. "The level of discourse reaching a mailbox simply cannot be limited to that which would be suitable for a sandbox," he wrote.

It is apparent from these rulings that students have considerable freedom in sexual practices and may not be disciplined by the school for life-style behavior unless school officials can show material disruption of the educational environment or substantial interference with the rights of others. School officials sometimes seek to isolate unwed mothers from other students, viewing the unwed status as indicative of lack of moral character and potentially harmful to other students. Such isolation is inherently discriminatory because it singles out females for punishment. Both federal and state law prohibit discrimination based on sex unless the school can show a compelling reason. Thus, if a physician advises that participation in extracurricular activities by a pregnant student would endanger the health of the student and/or the fetus, the school would be justified in restricting her participation. Whenever school officials contemplate such discriminatory action, they should be prepared to defend that action against a possible legal challenge.

Hair Length and Grooming

Some students in the early 1970s tried to convince the U.S. Court of Appeals for the Fifth Circuit that personal grooming is a Fourteenth Amendment liberty right, like privacy. The Fifth Circuit rejected the claim, upholding the right of public elementary and secondary schools to have dress codes (*Karr v. Schmidt*, 1972). Interestingly, in another 1972 case, the Fifth Circuit ruled that students at public community colleges do have a liberty right to personal grooming (*Lansdale v. Tyler Junior College*). This led one wag to remark that, "apparently, high school students in the southern United States are handed a new constitutional right along with their diploma at commencement."

State law also does not support a right to personal grooming preferences in Texas public schools. While there was some inconsistency on this point in the past, the Texas Supreme Court clarified the matter in 1995 by following the Fifth Circuit's precedent in the *Karr* case. In a decision ironically styled *Barber v. Colorado I.S.D.*, the Texas high court ruled that the Equal Rights Amendment in the Texas Constitution, Article I, §3a, does not restrict school districts from having grooming codes that discriminate on the basis of gender—in this case, a rule restricting boys from having long hair or wearing earrings. The court was not persuaded that the law should apply differently to a public school student who has reached the age of majority. Disclaiming any interest to "micro-manage" Texas high schools, the court noted that "It is a matter of common sense that the state judiciary is less competent to deal with students' hair length than a parent, school board, administrator, principal, or teacher." Despite a plea for an exacting scrutiny under the Texas Equal Rights Amendment of the school's purposes in discriminating on the basis of gender, the two dissenters could not prevent a trip to the barber for Barber.

While dress codes are thus legally permissible, school officials must be careful not to intrude upon the right of symbolic expression upheld by the U.S. Supreme Court in *Tinker v. Des Moines School District* (see Chapter 6). In that case, the Court ruled that students had a constitutional right to wear armbands to school to protest the Vietnam War so long as they did not create material disruption or substantially interfere with the rights of others. Later, the high court ruled that student speech which is indecent, lewd, or profane is not entitled to any constitutional protection (*Bethel School District No. 403 v. Fraser*). Thus, while a student who wears a sweatshirt emblazoned with a profane slogan could be appropriately disciplined, a student who wears a T-shirt with the words "you can force me to attend school, but you can't force me to learn" is engaging in protected speech. Unless the sweatshirt proves disruptive or interferes with the rights of others, school officials may not be able to restrict it.

Gang attire presents special problems for some school districts. An initial question is whether the attire is a form of expression. If not, then provisions of the dress code apply. If it is, the school district still has the right under the *Tinker* ruling to restrict the attire if there is a reasonable basis to forecast disruption or interference with the rights of others. See Chapter 6 for an extended discussion. Religious expression may also be implicated in some personal grooming issues. As noted in Chapter 7, a federal district court in Texas upheld the right of Native Americans to wear long hair in violation of the school's personal grooming code (*Alabama and Coushatta Tribes of Texas v. Big Sandy I.S.D.*). Tracking the case law, the U.S. Department of Education issued guidelines in 1995 regarding permissible and impermissible accommodation of religion on campus, including student wearing of religious attire. The relevant guideline provides that "Students may display religious messages on items of clothing to the same extent that they are permitted to display other comparable messages." Further, if wearing particular attire, such as yarmulkes and head scarves, during the school day is part of students' religious practice, then under the Religious Freedom Restoration Act (RFRA) schools generally may not prohibit their doing so. RFRA is discussed in Chapter 7.

Students have been unsuccessful in claiming that sex-based grooming requirements are a form of illegal sex discrimination under either the Fourteenth Amendment or Title IX. While at one time schools receiving federal funds were not allowed to have different grooming codes for males and females under Title IX regulations, the regulations have been revoked and the Office of Civil Rights no longer pursues dress code complaints.

SUMMARY

While the right of privacy has evolved slowly, so, too, has the public's right to know what its government is doing. In Texas, the Open Meetings and Public Information acts shine a light not only on the activities of school boards but also on operations internal to the school and classroom. There is a very real tension between personal privacy and the public's need to know, one which suggests that caution, legal advice, and common sense are the best guides when privacy-related issues surface.

The Fourth Amendment to the U.S. Constitution has provided some degree of protection for students in the context of searches and seizures, and courts have found a personal right to privacy for both students and teachers in the word *liberty* of the Fourteenth Amendment. However, the protection is limited, especially for employees. Courts have also recognized the responsibility of school officials to maintain an orderly educational environment and have not been sympathetic to student claims of invasion of personal privacy in the context of interscholastic sports drug testing and regulation of personal grooming.

TEN
Legal Liability

MOST EDUCATORS do not realize that the law is different in Texas from what it is in other states with respect to personal injury and property damage lawsuits. Complicating the matter is the rapid development of damage suit liability in federal courts for certain types of actions. The purpose of this chapter is to sort out the confusion.

IDENTIFYING AREAS OF LEGAL LIABILITY

Basically, legal liability can be separated into two distinct categories. The first, criminal law, involves crimes against the state. Penalties for the convicted range from fines to lengthy imprisonment or death (in some states), depending upon the severity of the crime. School professionals are infrequently involved in criminal actions. Most of the cases in this area involve abuse of office as, for example, misappropriation of public funds.

The second category of legal liability relates to the civil law and includes everything that is not classified as criminal. Most civil cases involve a lawsuit brought by one person against another and usually involve monetary damages. We have already looked briefly at contract violations related to employment. The focus of our concern in this chapter is the law of torts, that is, civil wrongs against another that cause the injured party to go to court seeking compensation from the wrongdoer for damages. There are many kinds of torts, among them defamation, negligence, assault, and invasion of privacy. Negligence, which involves the failure to use reasonable care to avoid causing harm to someone, is the most common in the educational setting. All of these we can classify as state torts. Federal torts involve the infringement of a person's recognized constitutional or federal statutory rights. Each will be discussed in turn.

STATE TORTS

School District Immunity

The Texas Tort Claims Act represents a waiver of the general immunity from liability enjoyed by the state and its political subdivisions. The Act permits injured parties to recover damages from governmental entities caused by the negligent acts of employees arising from the operation of motor vehicles or from some condition of public property—for example, an unsafe stairwell. School districts and community colleges, however, were specifically excluded from the Act except with respect to the operation of motor vehicles. Hence, unless motor vehicles are involved, a school district is shielded by Texas law from tort liability. A 1978 Texas Supreme Court case makes this clear. In *Barr v. Bernhard*, a student was severely injured when a calf he was tending in conjunction with a voc-ag course bumped a pole supporting the roof of a barn, causing the roof to collapse upon him. The barn was part of a seventy-three-acre facility maintained by the Kerrville I.S.D. The parents of Mark Bernhard sued the school district for negligence, claiming the barn was in disrepair and improperly supervised. The Texas Supreme Court dismissed this part of his suit, stating that "the law is well settled in this state that an independent school district is an agency of the state and, while exercising governmental functions, is not answerable for its negligence in a suit sounding in tort" (p. 846). The court relied on the section of the Tort Claims Act which exempts school districts from liability except as to motor vehicles. That section can now be found at §101.051 of the Civil Practices and Remedies Code.

Note that the court referred to the school district "exercising governmental functions." Tort cases involving governmental entities have long turned on the distinction between the entity's "governmental functions" as opposed to its "proprietary functions." The general rule was that the entity was liable for negligence in carrying out proprietary functions, but immune from liability when performing governmental functions. Fortunately for the taxpayers of Texas, our courts have consistently ruled that virtually everything a school does is classified as a governmental function. For example, a Texas court of appeals decided in 1979 that interscholastic football is a governmental function, rather than a proprietary function, and thus denied money damages to an athlete who was seriously injured (*Garza v. Edinburg C.I.S.D.*).

Similarly, the Texas Court of Appeals–El Paso held in 1981 that furnishing swings for the use of school children on the playground is a governmental function and dismissed a damage suit against the district over injuries suffered by a child while using the swings. The court observed that the school exemption under the Texas Tort Claims Act is a rational and reasonable means of assuring that the quality and availability of public education are not impaired through the diversion of funds to cover private claims (*Duson v. Midland County I.S.D.*).

In 1987, the Texas Supreme Court had another occasion to consider the extent of school district liability under the Tort Claims Act. Celeste Adeline Hopkins, a student in the Spring I.S.D., allegedly was left unsupervised and sustained head injuries after being pushed into a stack of chairs in a room at the school. At the end of the day, the child rode on the school bus to the day-care center, and during the ride she suffered severe convulsions. In the subsequent lawsuit, the mother argued that the school district could not claim the defense of governmental immunity, because the child's injuries were aggravated when she had seizures on the bus and the district personnel failed to provide adequate medical care. Thus, the mother argued that the injuries arose from the "use or operation of a motor vehicle."

The Texas Supreme Court rejected the argument. The Court observed that previous cases had denied liability for injuries that occur on a bus unless they are also caused by the negligent use or operation of the bus. The court concluded, "Applying the common and ordinary meaning of the words 'operation' or 'use,' Celeste Adeline's injury could not have arisen from the use of a motor vehicle as contemplated by the statute" (*Hopkins v. Spring I.S.D.*).

Almost a decade passed between *Barr v. Bernhard* and *Hopkins v. Spring*. During that time, Texas courts indeed had numerous occasions to adjudicate disputes involving governmental immunity of school districts and the motor vehicle exception in the Tort Claims Act. In 1987 we learned that the motor vehicle causing the damage must be operated by a school employee. In *Heyer v. North East I.S.D.*, the court considered the case of a student who was "power braking" his car, a practice involving simultaneously applying the brakes and stepping on the accelerator, in the school parking lot. The car careened out of control and struck another student, who was seriously injured. The court held that, since the vehicle involved was not owned or operated by any agent of the school district, the injury did not arise from the operation or use of a motor vehicle contemplated by the Tort Claims Act exception and the school district was not liable.

As noted in the *Hopkins* case, even when a school bus is involved, the school district may be immune from liability. In 1981, a court of appeals considered the extent of school district liability for the death of one student and the injury to his brother resulting from a knife fight aboard a school bus. Was the school district liable for damages in this instance because the fight occurred aboard a motorized vehicle and the bus driver was allegedly negligent in supervision? The court concluded that the school district was immune. The injuries occurred *on* the school bus, but they were not *caused by the negligent use or operation* of the school bus (*Garza v. McAllen I.S.D.*, Texas Court of Appeals–Beaumont).

Much the same rationale applied in the Texas Supreme Court case of *LeLeax v. Hamshire-Fannett I.S.D.* The student in that case jumped up into the rear door frame of the bus and hit her head, causing injury. Her suit against the school district failed, largely because the bus was parked and the motor was turned off when the student injured herself. Indeed, the injury did appear to be more self-inflicted than the result of the negligent use or operation of a motor vehicle.

In another interesting twist, a suit was filed over a bus driver's decision to make a stop at a location which was not designated for bus stops. Two girls disembarked from the bus to get into a car with a friend. Subsequently there was a tragic car accident, killing one of the girls and seriously injuring the other. But again the Texas Tort Claims Act intervened to protect the district. The court concluded that the decision to let the girls off at a nondesignated stop raised issues as to the negligent supervision of the students. However, Texas school districts are not liable for negligent supervision. They are liable for injuries arising from the negligent use or operation of a motor vehicle. None was proved in the case of *Goston v. Hutchison* (1993).

This does not mean that liability concerns vanish the moment the student steps off the bus. For example, negligence by the bus driver may have been involved in the case of *Hitchcock v. Garvin and Plano I.S.D.* (1987). There, the injury occurred when a Plano I.S.D. student got off a school bus, attempted to cross the street, and was struck by a car. Rather than alleging "negligent supervision," the Hitchcocks alleged that the bus driver failed to activate the flashers on the bus to indicate that the bus was slowing and that this negligence caused the injury. The court held that the failure to activate flashers or warning signals of a school bus when children are exiting constitutes an act of omission arising from the operation or use of a motor vehicle within the meaning of the Tort Claims Act exception. Accordingly, the Hitchcocks had stated a cause of action and were entitled to a trial on the merits of their claim that the bus driver's conduct was negligent and had caused the injury to the child.

Even when a school district is liable, there are limitations on the extent of that liability. In 1983 the Texas Supreme Court recognized the liability of districts in conjunction with the operation of a school bus in *Madisonville I.S.D. v. Kyle* but reversed the lower court with respect to the extent of liability. The high court pointed out that, under the Tort Claims Act, school district liability is limited to $100,000 per person and $300,000 per occurrence for losses arising from bodily injury. Property damage losses are limited to a maximum of $100,000. The case involved the death of a child who had disembarked from a school bus and was struck by a car when crossing the street. The court limited district liability to $100,000.

As another protection of the public trough, the courts have ruled that school bus drivers are not to be held to the same high standard of care that applies to commercial bus or taxi drivers. The case of *Estate of Lindburg v. Mount Pleasant I.S.D.* concerned the standard of care to which school bus drivers are to be held. The case involved a child who was struck and killed by a pickup truck after getting off a school bus. The Texarkana appeals court held that the bus driver should have been held to a high degree of care, defined as "that degree of care which would have been used by a very cautious, competent, and prudent person under the same or similar circumstances." This is the standard of care required of common carriers who transport goods or people from place to place for hire.

On appeal, the Texas Supreme Court reversed the appeals court and held that a Texas school bus driver is held to the standard of ordinary care, defined as "that degree of care which would be used by a person of ordinary prudence under the same or similar circumstances." Thus, the standard of care required of a bus driver is that required of the general public and not that of drivers for common carriers (*Estate of Lindburg v. Mount Pleasant I.S.D.*).

The same rationale applies when a school contracts with a private company to transport students. In *Durham Transportation Inc. v. Valero*, the school district contracted with Durham to provide bus service. Again, the issue of "standard of care" arose, and again the court ruled that the lower, ordinary negligence standard should apply. The court distinguished Durham's services from those of a commercial carrier based on the fact that the commercial carrier makes its services available to the public at large. Here, Durham transported only school children pursuant to a contract with the school district.

Sometimes what looks like a motor vehicle is not. In 1989, the San Antonio court of appeals issued a significant decision in the case of *Naranjo v. Southwest I.S.D.* The school district was not liable for injuries suffered by a student who was repairing an immobilized car in an auto mechanics class. For liability to attach for the negligent operation or use of a motor vehicle, the vehicle must be used for transporting persons: "[A] teaching tool or teaching equipment, as was this immobilized Ford, is not such a 'motor vehicle' . . ." Other decisions have excluded from the definition a motorized forklift and a boat that has a motor.

Suppose a school employee is furnished an automobile by the school district and is then negligent in operating the automobile on the way home from work. Can the employer be liable? In a case involving the City of Houston, the answer was no when the city established that the employee was not acting within the scope of his duties of employment. The employee had been furnished the car on a twenty-four-hour basis, since he was "on call" during that time period. The employee could not use the car for personal business. "In this case, the evidence was presented that the employee had completed his task for his employer at the time of the accident, was on his way home from work and was not engaged in serving his [employer] when the accident occurred" (*Garcia v. City of Houston,* 1990).

Governmental immunity is a controversial subject. Various states have abolished it entirely. In Texas the courts have taken the view that any change in the current status of governmental immunity should come through the legislative process. Indeed, this happened when the legislature passed the Tort Claims Act. Although governmental immunity has its critics, thus far the legislature has not seen fit to impose further burdens of liability upon public schools. In effect, Texas law places the risk in question upon the individual families rather than the school district. One way school districts help families to meet this burden is by providing inexpensive insurance, which the families may purchase to protect against the costs of injuries at school. The commissioner of education ruled in a 1980 case that school districts cannot force students to purchase accident insurance, since the Education Code authorizes only a voluntary student health and accident plan (*Bertics v. Premont I.S.D.;* see TEC §11.158(a)(7)). TEC §33.085 authorizes school districts to purchase insurance for their athletes if they desire to do so. Prior to Senate Bill 1, these insurance policies could only be funded out of gate receipts. Senate Bill 1 changed that by asserting that "The cost of the insurance is a legitimate part of the total cost of the athletic program of the district."

Qualified Immunity for Public School Professional Employees

Since school districts are shielded from liability in Texas, injured parties are apt to sue school professionals. What protection do school administrators and teachers have? Let us return to *Barr v. Bernhard*, for there school officials were also sued. Attorneys for Bernhard claimed that school employees were negligent in maintaining the ag barn and in supervising its use. No school professional had been present when the structure collapsed. Once again, the suit was unsuccessful because of a provision of the Texas Education Code that provides professional school employees with what is called "qualified immunity" from tort liability. The specific provision, now found at TEC §22.051, provides in part that a professional employee of a school district is not "personally liable for any act that is incident to or within the scope of the duties of the employee's position of employment and that involves the exercise of judgment or discretion on the part of the employee." The majority on the court observed that this statute (then codified at TEC §21.912(b)) goes on to list excessive use of force in student discipline and negligence resulting in injury to a student as exceptions, but the majority tied the negligence clause in with student discipline. Thus, the Texas Supreme Court determined that the only exception to immunity for professional employees under the statute relates to the use of excessive force in disciplining students or being negligent in disciplining students so as to cause an injury. Since Mark Bernhard was not being disciplined when the injury occurred, school employees were not liable. The dissenters disagreed, reading the negligence clause as referring to any negligent action resulting in student injury, not just negligence in disciplining students. This ruling demonstrates the importance of courts in interpreting the actual meaning of statutes.

Thus, unlike the situation in many states where school employees are legally liable when students are injured at school, school professionals in Texas are shielded by law from such liability. Those who have damage claims against school districts and school professionals have little recourse but to shoulder the costs themselves.

Note, however, that only "professional employees" are covered by TEC §22.051. The statute has an expansive definition of the term. It includes superintendents, principals, teachers, supervisors, social workers, counselors, nurses, teacher's aides, student teachers, DPS-certified bus drivers, and anyone else whose employment requires certification and an exercise of discretion.

The immunity protection afforded school employees in Texas does not cover everyone. Keep in mind that some school employees remain potentially liable for student injuries. Cafeteria and maintenance workers, for example, are not "professional employees" and thus enjoy no special protection. However, many school districts now have broad insurance policies protecting all paid employees.

Yet another provision in the Code protects volunteers. Section 22.053 provides that "direct service volunteers" in the district enjoy the same immunity from civil liability that professional employees have under TEC §22.051. A volunteer is defined as "a person providing services for or on behalf of a school district on the premises of the district or at a school-sponsored or school-related activity on or off school property, who does not receive compensation in excess of reimbursement for expenses." Volunteers can be liable for intentional misconduct or gross negligence.

Furthermore, those who do enjoy the protection of the statute must remember that the immunity, though broad, is not absolute. To be protected, professional employees must be acting in the scope of their duties, must be exercising judgment or discretion, and must not be using excessive force in disciplining students or have been negligent in disciplining students sufficiently to cause bodily injury. Statutory immunity is weakest when force is used in student discipline, a topic explored in detail below.

The final limitation of the qualified immunity defense under state law is that it does not apply to the operation, use, or maintenance of motor vehicles. Faced with the same potential liability as a private operator, school employees involved in the transportation of students should make sure they have adequate insurance protection through a personal and/or school policy. So suppose a school bus driver is negligent while operating the bus. Can the school and the driver both be held liable? Yes—but due to yet another peculiarity of the Tort Claims Act, the chances of recovery against both parties are somewhat diminished. In *Thomas v. Oldham* and *Gibson v. Spinks* the Texas Supreme Court considered the portion of the Act that reads:

> A judgment in an action or a settlement of a claim under this chapter bars any action involving the same subject matter by the claimant

against the employee of the governmental unit whose act or omission gave rise to the claim. (Civil Practices and Remedies Code §101.106)

Injured parties in the two cases had been awarded judgments against both a city and an individual employed by the city. Both cases involved automobile accidents. The Supreme Court held that the statute quoted above precluded such a result. A judgment against the city bars any claim against the employee. Thus the Supreme Court reversed the decision by releasing the individual employees from liability. In other words, if you settle up with the government, or win a case against the government, you cannot later sue the employee individually. The savvy plaintiff will sue one or the other, or sue the employee first, and then the government.

Even when an employee is held liable in a court of law for damages, state law imposes limits on the amount of damages. Section 108.002 of the Civil Practice and Remedies Code limits the damages that can be assessed against a governmental employee to $100,000, so long as the employee was acting within the scope of employment and is covered by insurance or an indemnity arrangement. This provision appears to be designed to guarantee that governmental employees will be covered by insurance up to $100,000 so that injured parties will have a "deep pocket" from which to recover.

The notion of qualified immunity for school professionals is well established in Texas law. Courts have had numerous opportunities since *Barr v. Bernhard* to reconsider the matter, but have continued to uphold the doctrine. For example, in *Hopkins v. Spring I.S.D.*, discussed above in connection with district immunity, the Texas Supreme Court also took another look at qualified individual immunity under the Education Code. The plaintiff asked the court to overrule *Barr v. Bernhard* and hold that school district personnel can be held liable for their negligent acts that result in serious bodily injury to students. A majority of the court declined to do so, stating that any waiver of governmental immunity is a matter to be addressed by the legislature. Three justices dissented, arguing that *Barr v. Bernhard* should be overruled and that professional school employees should be held liable for their negligence.

A review of the case law shows that Texas state courts generally interpret the qualified immunity statute liberally in favor of protecting school professionals, who must oversee the activities of numerous students on a daily basis. For example, in *Schumate v. Thompson*, a 1979 court of appeals case, the court dismissed a suit for personal injuries against a teacher over a playground incident.

The teacher, an employee of Cypress Fairbanks School District, instructed her aide, a mentally handicapped person, to take the class outside to play. The aide directed a student to high jump a stick held by herself and a classmate. The injury occurred when the student fell. A similar decision was reached in a 1980 court of appeals case, *Wagner v. Alvarado I.S.D. Wagner* involved a damage suit against the school district and several of its employees over injuries sustained when a student fell while carrying a jar full of acid from one physics lab to another. The physics teacher was one of the employees sued. The court upheld dismissal of the suit against both the school and the professional employees, citing the immunity of each under Texas law.

In *Stout v. Grand Prairie I.S.D.*, the injured student attacked the constitutionality of the qualified immunity statute. The student alleged that such a statute deprived injured parties of any recourse, while providing no public benefit whatsoever. The statute, it was argued, benefited teachers only, but not the general public. The court rejected that argument, noting that "if competent people are discouraged from entering the teaching profession because of potential tort liability, the public education system will be adversely affected." Thus the statute served a public purpose and was constitutional.

The most recent illustration of the qualified immunity doctrine arose from a tragic set of facts. A student in the Cypress Fairbanks School District was suspected of selling drugs on campus. School administrators investigated the matter, sent the student home with her parents, and gave notice of proposed expulsion. When her parents left her alone at home, the girl committed suicide. The parents subsequently sued two assistant principals and the principal, alleging that their improper handling of the matter caused the distraught young girl to kill herself. The Court of Appeals granted summary judgment for the school administrators, citing the qualified immunity statute once again (*Fowler v. Szostek*).

While most of the reported cases deal with physical injuries of some sort, the professional employee's qualified immunity applies to suits alleging slander as well. When a newspaper reported that one high school baseball coach had accused a rival coach of violating UIL rules, the accused coach sued, alleging slander, defamation, and intentional infliction of emotional distress. The federal court dismissed all these claims, citing the qualified immunity statute (*Anderson v. Blankenship*). Similar decisions are discussed in Chapter 9.

School employees are not always acting "within the scope of

employment." When they step outside that protective bubble, they stand to lose their qualified immunity. There are at least two good illustrations of this, the first being the 1981 Texas court of appeals case of *O'Haver v. Blair*. The case involved a teacher at Madison High School in San Antonio who struck a student in the course of trying to halt use of the school's football field on a Sunday afternoon in October. The teacher, Tommy Blair, was attending a coaches' meeting at the high school. When the coaches learned that a group of people were using the football field, they attempted to get them to leave. Coach Blair pushed Shaun O'Haver, whereupon O'Haver started pushing back. The two began to struggle, and Coach Blair struck O'Haver in the mouth, knocking out two of his teeth and loosening several others. The trial court refused to hear the case, agreeing with Coach Blair that he was protected from civil liability under the qualified immunity statute. But the appeals court disagreed and remanded the case back to the lower court. The appeals court held that it was not clear that Coach Blair had fulfilled all the elements necessary to claim immunity under the statute. Specifically, the court questioned whether Coach Blair was acting in the scope of his duties when the incident occurred, whether he was employing judgment or discretion, and whether he was not in fact disciplining the student. Noting the rulings in *Barr v. Bernhard, Schumate v. Thompson*, and *Wagner v. Alvarado I.S.D.*, the court pointed out that "the distinctions between these cases and the present case are obvious. In the case at bar there is no dispute that a teacher struck a student with his fist with enough force to knock out teeth" (p. 469).

It should be clear from *O'Haver v. Blair* that the immunity conferred upon Texas public school professional employees by the qualified immunity statute is not automatic. Furthermore, protection from civil liability is weakest when hands-on discipline is involved.

The second illustration of the "scope of employment" provision is *Stimpson v. Plano I.S.D.* In that case the plaintiff elementary school principal alleged that the superintendent and teacher had intentionally interfered with her teaching contract by wrongfully conspiring to force her out of the school system. The individual defendants asserted as a defense the immunity provided by the statute. The appeals court held that the plaintiff had pled sufficient facts to be entitled to a trial on the question of whether the superintendent and principal were acting within the scope of their duties in their actions regarding the plaintiff. Any action taken outside the scope of duties would not be shielded by the statute.

Besides §22.051, there are other statutes designed to provide a measure of immunity to public school employees in various situations. TEC §22.052 provides civil immunity from damages or injuries resulting from the administering of medication to students if the school district has adopted a policy on the administering of medication to students, the school has received a written request from the parent or guardian, and the medication appears to be in the original container and to be properly labeled. However, the statute does not provide immunity "from civil liability for injuries resulting from gross negligence."

The 1989 legislature passed a bill providing that a school employee is not liable in civil damages for reporting to a school administrator or governmental authority, in the exercise of professional judgment within the scope of duties, a student whom the person suspects of using, passing, or selling on school property marijuana, a dangerous drug, an abusable glue or aerosol paint, a chemical inhalant, or an alcoholic beverage. Again, the critical point is that the report must be made within the scope of duties (TEC §37.016).

Those who contemplate suits versus schools or school employees must also take into account two statutes designed to protect the public from defending frivolous suits. Section 11.161 of the Education Code authorizes a court to require the payment of court costs and attorneys' fees by a person who files a frivolous suit against a school district or school officer. A similar provision applies to suits versus school employees (TEC §22.055).

Even with all that protection, suits will be filed and legal costs will be incurred. Consequently, state law authorizes school districts to purchase insurance policies protecting the district and its employees against legal claims (Tex. Civ. Prac. & Rem. Code §101.027). Also, in 1985 the legislature authorized school districts to pay actual damages awarded against employees if the damages result from an act or omission of the employee in the course and scope of employment and arise from a cause of action for negligence. The statute further authorizes a district to pay the court costs and attorneys' fees awarded against such an employee. Also, the district may provide legal counsel to represent the employee. Payments are limited to $100,000 per person or $300,000 per occurrence in the case of personal injury or death or $10,000 per occurrence of property damage.

There are some exceptions to the grant of authority. A district may not pay damages awarded against an employee that arise from official misconduct, willful or wrongful act or omission, or gross negligence (Tex. Civ. Prac. & Rem. Code §§102.001–102.004). Since we can anticipate that lawsuits will continue to be brought against school districts and school professionals, and since we cannot be sure that Texas professional employees will always be so well protected in the future, the best advice is to observe school policies and rules carefully and to be sure to act within the ethical standards of one's profession in carrying out assigned duties. When all else fails, good common sense usually offers excellent protection.

The Special Case of Corporal Punishment

As noted in the chapter on student discipline, the U.S. Supreme Court has ruled that no due process is necessary prior to the imposition of corporal punishment (*Ingraham v. Wright*, 1977). Since that ruling, the courts have been reluctant to become involved in corporal punishment cases on constitutional grounds, as illustrated by the decisions discussed in Chapter 8.

Despite these rulings, it makes good sense to comply with minimal due process procedures, given the limited protection from damage suits that public school professionals enjoy under Texas law where student discipline is involved. Recall that the relevant provision in the Texas Education Code states that professional employees are not personally liable for their acts as employees "except in circumstances in which a professional employee uses excessive force in the discipline of students or negligence resulting in bodily injury to students." The best way to avoid falling into the "excessive force" or "negligence" categories of TEC §22.051 is to follow school policy scrupulously. Most schools now require that corporal punishment be administered only by certain persons and only under certain circumstances. The most frequently mentioned procedural steps prior to its administration are these:

1. The rules state what offenses may result in corporal punishment.
2. Corporal punishment is used only as a last resort.
3. Punishment is to be administered in front of a witness and away from other students. Both the student and the witness are to be informed of the reason for the paddling.
4. Parents are to be notified as soon as possible of the punishment and the reasons for it and are to be given the name of the witness. Some schools allow parents who are opposed to corporal punishment to choose alternative means of discipline. Under an earlier federal district court ruling, which the U.S. Supreme Court subsequently affirmed, it is not legally required that this be done (*Baker v. Owen*, 1975). The court ruled that the inter-

est of the school in maintaining an orderly environment outweighs the liberty rights of parents to control their children's
upbringing. Of course, granting parents this option does serve
to siphon off the kind of resentment that brews lawsuits.

It is particularly important for teachers and administrators to
follow school policy explicitly with respect to administering corporal punishment, for failure to do so could well constitute "negligence" within the meaning of §22.051 if injury resulted. Those professional educators who serve as the campus "designated hitter"
should be aware that a flagrant abuse of the educators' right to use
hands-on discipline may constitute a criminal offense as an assault
as well as a civil wrong (tort). Thus, not only might professional employees find themselves involved in a civil suit for money damages
in such a situation, but they might also be subject to criminal prosecution. Texas Penal Code §22.04 states in part that

(a) A person commits an offense if he intentionally, knowingly, recklessly, or with criminal negligence by act or intentionally, knowingly, or
recklessly by omission causes to a child, elderly individual, or disabled
individual:
   (1) serious bodily injury;
   (2) serious mental deficiency impairment, or injury; or
   (3) bodily injury.

Another section of the Penal Code, §9.62, does recognize that
educators may use force, "but not deadly force," with regard to students under their charge "when and to the degree the actor reasonably believes the force is necessary to further the special purpose or
to maintain discipline in a group." However, the Court of Appeals
for Texarkana has ruled that the use of force "must be that which
the teacher *reasonably* believes necessary (1) to enforce compliance
with a *proper* command issued for the purpose of controlling, training, or educating the child, or (2) to punish the child for prohibited
conduct; and in either case, the force or physical contact must be
reasonable and not disproportionate to the activity or the offense"
(*Hogenson v. Williams*, 1976, p. 460). The court specifically stated
that "we do not accept the proposition that a teacher may use physical violence against a child merely because the child is unable or
fails to perform, either academically or athletically, at a desired
level of ability, even though the teacher considers such violence to
be 'instruction and encouragement.' " The case involved a football
coach at Terrell Middle School in Denison, Texas, who used physi-

cal force on a student during a practice session of the seventh-grade football team, causing injury. The coach claimed that he was trying to "fire up" the student and instill spirit in him. Based on the broadened definition of assault given by the court of appeals, the case was sent back to the trial court for a new trial. The coach had been exonerated on the basis of §9.62 at the first trial. It should be emphasized that the qualified immunity conveyed by TEC §22.051 from damage suits would not immunize an employee in the event of a challenge under criminal law.

Whether the strong endorsement given the qualified immunity from tort suit by the more recently decided *Barr v. Bernhard* and *Hopkins v. Spring I.S.D.* cases would protect a professional employee today who uses force to "fire up" students on the athletic field is open to speculation, particularly because such use of force may be construed as "excessive force in the discipline of students" under TEC §22.051 and thus be unprotected.

Two 1995 decisions indicate that courts will continue to protect school employees who use some degree of physical force in handling students. In *Doria v. Stulting* the student alleged he was physically injured by his teacher when the teacher physically escorted the student out of the classroom. The departure from the classroom was occasioned by student misbehavior, and the teacher was taking the student to the vice-principal's office for the imposition of disciplinary consequences. Thus it would appear to be a use of force in the context of discipline. Nevertheless, the court ruled that the teacher was entitled to immunity under the qualified immunity statute. The court observed that the term "discipline" normally refers to punishment. The court reasoned that the teacher was not disciplining the student—the teacher was acting "to protect the school learning process from disruption by a wrongdoer by physically removing the wrongdoer to the public official designated by rule, regulation, or law to impose the necessary and proper 'discipline-punishment'—the vice principal." Since the teacher was not disciplining the student, the teacher could not be held liable even if the student was injured in the process.

The second case involved a student-to-student injury. When a student assaulted another student during class and broke the jaw of the second student, the second student sued the teacher and principal. The allegation was that these professional employees knew or should have known that the assaulting student was a delinquent with a propensity for violence. The school employees were charged with negligent failure to discipline the student who committed the assault. Once again, the courts protected the school employees from liability. The court ruled that the qualified immunity statute applied in this context (*Pulido v. Dennis*).

So it is reasonably clear that personal liability for student injuries under state law can be applied to the professional school employee only for the excessive or negligent use of discipline as punishment. However, this is not limited to paddling. Such is the lesson of *Diggs v. Bales*, a case in which the court offered some important commentary about the liability of professional employees for injuries resulting from student discipline. Both trial and appeals courts decided in favor of the Plano school district and its employee in a suit involving a student who was struck in the eye by an object allegedly shot at him by another student. The appeals court observed that liability of professional employees is restricted to situations involving student discipline, and here discipline was not an issue. However, the court also observed that *direct* use of force need not be necessary for an actionable case to arise. As an example, the court noted that, if a teacher's assignment for students to run laps around an athletic field is the proximate cause of a student injury, the teacher may be liable despite the qualified immunity statute.

Finally, in a related matter, the Texas Commissioner of Education has revoked the certificate of a teacher who injured a child by striking the student with a wooden paddle. The teacher was indicted and later pled guilty to a reduced charge of assault. The commissioner observed that while the teacher's action might have constituted corporal punishment and been excused under Penal Code §9.62, "the fact that respondent was indicted and pled guilty to assault leads this decision maker to conclude that the actions were not legally excusable." The incident underscores the need to be especially careful when using corporal punishment, given the legal consequences under state law (*Texas Education Agency v. Darthard*, 1991).

Law and the School Counselor

School counselors often ask if they have special protection under state or federal law from legal liability. Specifically, they are concerned about the degree of confidentiality they and their student clients are entitled to. Do they have to reveal the substance of confidential conversations to parents upon request? If they fail to do so, are they likely to be sued? Do counselors have to testify about a confidential conversation in court?

Regarding disclosures to parents, Senate Bill 1 contains strong language which appears to require disclosure of materials upon request. Section 26.004 tells us that a parent is entitled to access to "all written records of a school district concerning the parent's child," including counseling records and psychological records. Section 26.001 describes parents as "partners with educators, administrators, and school district boards of trustees in their children's education." With that in mind, it would seem that a counselor would have to disclose any notes or other records which have been made in connection with counseling sessions with the student.

This is somewhat ironic, since state law does not require counselors to have parental consent to meet with children in certain situations. Section 35.03(g) of the Texas Family Code permits a minor to meet with a counselor without parental consent if the counseling concerns "sexual abuse, physical abuse, suicide prevention, or chemical addiction, dependency or abuse." In effect, this means that a student can meet with a counselor at school to discuss physical or sexual abuse going on in the family. Parental consent would not be required by state law. But if the parent later asks for copies of the counselor's notes pertaining to the counseling sessions, the counselor would have to provide access to those notes.

While state law does not require parental consent for counseling regarding certain sensitive issues, a local school district may. Section 33.003 of the Education Code requires each board of trustees to adopt guidelines to ensure that written consent is obtained "for the student to participate in those activities for which the district requires parental consent." This is a curious provision, in that it does not require parental consent for counseling, but merely requires that the district obtain consent when the district requires consent. Apparently, local school board policy will have to deal with the issue of consent.

Regarding disclosure of confidential information to people other than the student's parents, the relevant law is the Family Educational Rights and Privacy Act (FERPA), which is discussed in detail in Chapter 9. The issue that arises most often with counselors concerns the disclosure of information to other school personnel. Can the counselor share information about a student with other members of the staff?

Under FERPA, such disclosures are permitted. FERPA requires parental consent for the disclosure of confidential information, subject to several exceptions. One of those exceptions permits school officials to release confidential information to other school officials who have "a legitimate educational interest" in the student and in the information. This provision is designed to facilitate the sharing of relevant information by school officials. This provision applies to the records of a counselor just as it does to the records of a teacher. If there is a legitimate educational reason why information pertaining to a particular student, or records concerning that student, should be shared with other school officials, the counselor can do so.

Counselors are often concerned about the scope of other laws that appear to require a higher degree of confidentiality. However, those laws defer to FERPA. For example, the Texas Health and Safety Code requires that counseling records be kept confidential, but allows an exception if the disclosure is "to a governmental agency if the disclosure is required or authorized by law" (Health and Safety Code §611.004(a)). Since FERPA authorizes the disclosure of information to other school officials with a legitimate educational interest, then such a disclosure is permissible under the Health and Safety Code as well.

Likewise the statutes pertaining to the Licensed Professional Counselor (LPC) do not appear to restrict intraschool disclosures. The regulations governing LPCs permit disclosure of records if such disclosure is permitted by the Health and Safety Code or any other state or federal statute or rules.

This is not to suggest that counselors should be careless or thoughtless about the disclosure of information. The point is that the school counselor does stand in a different position than the counselor's private counterpart, at least insofar as intraschool disclosures are concerned. Furthermore, the school counselor, like any counselor, can be sued for *not* disclosing information in certain situations. The case of *Tarasoff v. Regents of the University of California* best illustrates the point. In that case a distraught student met with a counselor employed by the university. The student told the counselor of his desire to kill his ex-girlfriend. Two months later, he did just that. The girl's parents sued the psychologist and the university for the failure to warn of this threat. The Supreme Court of California held that the special nature of the relationship between a psychologist and a patient created a legal duty to use reasonable care to protect third parties from serious bodily injury or death.

Texas law appears to acknowledge such a duty as well. The Texas mental health law referred to above provides that confidentiality does not extend to disclosure of information "to medical or law enforcement personnel if the professional determines that there is a probability of imminent physical injury by the patient to the patient or others or there is a probability of immediate mental or emotional injury to the patient" (Health and Safety Code §611.004(b)).

Faced with a *Tarasoff*-type situation, we do not know if the

Texas Supreme Court would reach the same result as the California court did. Nor do we know if the court would apply this standard to a counselor, as opposed to a licensed psychologist. Nevertheless, the California case, along with other out-of-Texas cases, has put counselors and psychologists on notice of a potential liability. Personal liability would appear a fairly remote possibility, however, for the Texas school counselor, given the protections of §22.051 of the Education Code.

State law will not, however, protect the school employee who wrongfully discloses confidential student information. In fact, recent case law has indicated the seriousness of this business of confidentiality. There is no "private right of action" under FERPA. That is, an individual cannot sue in court for damages or injunctive relief because the school district has violated FERPA. The only remedy available to the aggrieved under that statute is to have the federal funds of the institution withheld.

However, the aggrieved can slide around this apparent limitation by framing the suit as a §1983 suit alleging a violation of FERPA under color of law. Such allegations appear to open the courthouse door, though prevailing in that arena remains difficult. For example, one case involved a college student's suit over his physics grade. The court held that FERPA was intended to allow parents and adult students to challenge school records which are inaccurate, misleading, or invade privacy. However, FERPA does not permit a student to challenge a teacher's method of grading (*Tarka v. Cunningham*, 1990).

Indeed, much of the foregoing discussion of qualified immunity under state law should be tempered by the fact of potential liability under federal law. Lawyers are a creative and persistent lot. When state law avenues are closed, a good lawyer will explore the possibility of framing the suit to fit federal law. So let us now turn to an examination of liability under federal law under Section 1983.

FEDERAL CIVIL RIGHTS LIABILITY

School administrators are aware that many of the federal lawsuits filed against school districts and their employees are referred to as "§1983" suits. While other federal statutes protect more specific rights, the federal statute codified as §1983 of volume 42 of the United States Code (hence, 42 U.S.C. §1983) provides a broad basis for litigation in federal court. Section 1983 was enacted in 1871 shortly after the Civil War and was designed to protect the civil rights of citizens. It reads as follows: "Every person who, under color of any statute, ordinance, regulation, custom, or usage, of any State or Territory, subjects, or causes to be subjected, any citizen of the United States or other person within the jurisdiction thereof to the deprivation of any rights, privileges, or immunities secured by the Constitution and laws, shall be liable to the party injured in an action at law, suit in equity, or other proper proceeding for redress."

In essence, §1983 grants the litigant the right to hold liable every person who has deprived the litigant of rights protected by the U.S. Constitution or by federal law, when that person has done so acting under color of state law. Section 1983 does not reach purely private conduct, because such conduct is not taken "under color of state law" as is required. Liability attaches under §1983 only to a person who carries a "badge of authority" of a state or local government.

A §1983 suit thus basically involves a charge of an abuse of governmental authority that deprives someone (e.g., a student, a teacher) of federally protected rights. The rights at stake can range from a student's Fourth Amendment right to be free from an unreasonable search to an employee's First Amendment right to speak out as a citizen on matters of public concern. While §1983 speaks of holding "every person" liable, the scope of liability under the statute is not unlimited. The federal courts apply different tests to determine the liability of the government, itself, as opposed to the personal liability of officers and employees of the government. That difference is the subject of this section.

Governmental Liability

The landscape of federal civil rights liability changed dramatically in 1978, when the U.S. Supreme Court handed down its decision in *Monell v. New York City Department of Social Services*. At issue in *Monell* was whether §1983's language that "every person" could be held liable included governmental entities, such as municipalities and school districts. Reversing its own prior decisions, the Supreme Court in *Monell* held that governments are indeed "persons" and subject to liability for damages under §1983. With that single decision, the Court ushered in a new era of spirited federal civil rights litigation.

There is, however, one critical limitation upon governmental liability. As the Court explained in *Monell* and often thereafter, government is not liable merely because a governmental employee commits a wrong that deprives someone of his or her federal rights. That sort of liability is referred to in the law as *respondeat superior*, a Latin term meaning, roughly, "hang the boss." It is *respondeat superior* that allows the injured party to sue the deep-pocket brewery when a shallow-pocket driver runs over the plaintiff with the beer delivery truck. Such is not the case with civil rights liability.

Under *Monell* and its ample progeny, the governmental entity can be held liable *only* if the wrong is committed pursuant to either an official policy of the government or a "custom," even though the custom has not received formal approval through the governmental body's official decision-making channels. Thus, the entity may be held liable only when the injury is inflicted by a government's "lawmakers or by those whose edicts or acts may fairly be said to represent official policy."

The theory behind the *Monell* case is that the taxpayers should not be held liable merely because they have employed a wrongdoer. They should be held liable only if the wrong is attributable to the policy or custom of the governmental entity itself. The theory is reasonable and even admirable. In practice, however, whether a particular wrong involves a policy or custom has proven to be an inquiry of much complexity. A few cases will illustrate.

Generally speaking, it is difficult for an injured party to pin liability on the government arising from a single incident of unconstitutional conduct of an employee. Such was the case of *Oklahoma City v. Tuttle*. The case involved an Oklahoma City policeman who used excessive force in dealing with a drunk, the force in question being shooting and killing the man. The bereaved widow sued the policeman, but also attempted to impose liability on the city.

The Supreme Court in *Tuttle* concluded that proof of a single incident of unconstitutional activity is not sufficient to hold the government liable under *Monell*, unless it also includes proof that the incident was caused by an existing, unconstitutional governmental policy that can be attributed to a governmental policymaker.

While it is difficult to hold the city liable for a single action of a police officer, there are times when a single incident can lead to liability. If the person who took that single action can be characterized as a "policymaker" for the governmental entity, then that person's actions are attributable to the governmental entity.

So who is a policymaker? Let us begin to attempt to answer that question by looking at the 1986 Supreme Court case of *Pembaur v. City of Cincinnati*. In this case, a county prosecutor ordered the police to "go in and get" two witnesses who were believed to be in a doctor's clinic. Since Dr. Pembaur had refused the police entry, the police grabbed an ax and broke down the door. Pembaur alleged that the warrantless search of his clinic violated the Fourth Amendment to the U.S. Constitution, and he sought to impose liability upon the city and the county for the actions of the police officers and deputies.

In light of *Monell*, the issue before the Supreme Court in *Pembaur* was whether the search of the doctor's clinic had been pursuant to official policy. While this case was like *Tuttle* in that it involved a single incident, it was unlike *Tuttle* in that that single incident was ordered by a high-ranking county official, the county attorney. The Court in *Pembaur* determined that governmental liability may be imposed for a single unconstitutional decision by a policymaker under appropriate circumstances, as for example a single decision by the governmental body itself. In the absence of formal action by the governmental body, however, liability may still attach where a governmental official has been granted or delegated final authority to establish policy with respect to the particular action at issue. That governmental officials have discretion in how they exercise their functions, does not make their decisions those of a policymaker for which the government is responsible. Rather, governmental liability under §1983 attaches where the official or officials responsible for establishing final governmental policy for a particular activity make a deliberate choice from among various alternatives and order or authorize an unconstitutional act.

In the particular facts of *Pembaur*, the Court held that the county prosecutor made a considered decision based on his understanding of the law and commanded the officers forcibly to enter Pembaur's clinic. That decision directly caused the violation of Pembaur's Fourth Amendment rights. Finally, the Court held that, in ordering the police officers and deputy sheriffs to go in and get the supposed witnesses, the county prosecutor "was acting as the final decision maker for the county, and the county may therefore be held liable under §1983." In other words, the county prosecutor was a person "whose edicts or acts may fairly be said to represent official policy."

Both *Tuttle* and *Pembaur* involved a single, wrongful act. In *Tuttle* the wrongful act was committed by a nonpolicymaker under circumstances offering no proof that he was acting pursuant to a policy or custom of the city. In *Pembaur* the wrongful act was committed by a policymaker, the county prosecutor, and because he was a policymaker the county could be held liable.

In the school context, a leading case is the 1987 Fifth Circuit decision of *Lopez v. Houston I.S.D.* In this case a student alleged that he was beaten unconscious on a school bus while the bus driver did nothing to intervene or stop the beating. The student sued the Houston school district. Before the case went to trial the school district moved for summary judgment, arguing that even if the student's allegations turned out to be true, the district would not be liable. The federal district court granted the school district's motion, dismissing the case against the school. The Fifth Circuit upheld that decision, noting that (1) the school district could not be held liable merely because it hired someone who used poor judgment; (2) there was no indication in the record that the district's training program for bus drivers was so inadequate that it could be the cause of this incident; and (3) clearly a substitute bus driver is not a "policymaker."

In sorting out this complex area of the law, no case is more helpful to school districts than the Supreme Court's 1988 decision *Saint Louis v. Praprotnik.* Having noted the *Monell* precedent and the different holdings of *Tuttle* and *Pembaur,* the Supreme Court in *Praprotnik* took another stab at the question of who qualifies as a policymaker. The situation in *Praprotnik* involved a personnel dispute, a more familiar and mundane set of facts than those in *Tuttle* and *Pembaur.* The question turned on who had the authority to establish "final" policy for the transfer and layoff of city employees.

The Court began by noting that the identification of a policymaker is a question of state and local law. Official policy can only be adopted by those legally charged with doing so. The Court observed that, when a governmental employee's discretionary decisions are constrained by policies not of that employee's making, those policies, rather than the employee's conduct in departing from them, are the act of the government. Similarly, when a subordinate's decision is subject to review by the government's authorized policymakers, they have retained the authority to measure the official's conduct for conformance with the authorized policymaker's policies. Further, the mere failure of policymakers to investigate the basis of a subordinate's discretionary decisions does not amount to a delegation of policy-making authority, especially where the wrongfulness of the subordinate's decision arises from a retaliatory motive or other unstated rationale. In none of these instances is the subordinate employee's conduct that of a policymaker for which the government is liable. However, if the authorized policymakers approve a subordinate's decision and the basis for it, their ratification would be chargeable to the government because their decision is final.

Relating this language to the typical school district situation, then, it would appear to be very difficult to make the school district liable for the acts of principals, central office personnel, or even the superintendent. All of those officials make decisions which are constrained by policies not of their making; their decisions are subject to review by the school board; the school board has retained the authority to measure the official's conduct for conformance with board policy. The mere fact that the school board fails to investigate the basis for a principal's or superintendent's decision does not create liability for the district. Only when the board hears the matter and approves of the handling of it does the school district expose itself to potential liability.

The preceding discussion of governmental liability began with *Monell*'s holding that government could be held liable in §1983 actions, but only if the wrong was done pursuant to a policy or custom of the entity, and ended with *Prapotnik*'s refinements. Taken together, these cases impose a heavy burden upon a plaintiff who seeks to hold a Texas school district liable for an alleged wrong done by one of its employees. On the one hand, a school superintendent's "edicts and acts may fairly be said to represent official policy" in some circumstances. On the other hand, how can the superintendent be a policymaker in most situations in view of *Praprotnik*'s teaching that (1) the authority to make governmental policy is necessarily the authority to make *final* policy; (2) when an official's discretionary decisions are constrained by policies not of the official's making, those policies, rather than the subordinate's departures from them, are the act of the government; and (3) when a subordinate's decision is subject to *review* by the government's authorized policymakers, they have retained the authority to measure the official's conduct for conformance with *their* policies? In Texas, by both state law and local policy and custom, the trustees have the "exclusive power and duty to govern and oversee the management of the public schools of the district" (TEC §11.151(b)). So who, other than the trustees themselves, in official session, can be a policymaker in Texas? Whatever arguments may be made in the case of a superintendent who serves as the chief executive officer of the district, it is virtually certain that no other employee comes even close to being a policymaker. For example, in a recent case a parent sued the school district, alleging that the principal wrongfully had her arrested and prosecuted. The Fifth Circuit granted a summary judgment in favor of the school district, noting that under Texas law, the final policymaking authority rests with the school board. Though the principal may have decision-making authority, that does not mean that the principal has policy-making authority. Rather, the principal must make decisions in conformity with the policies adopted by the school board (*Eugene v. Alief I.S.D.*).

Having exhausted the subject of governmental liability, and perhaps the reader as well, let us turn to the more personally critical issue of individual liability. Under what circumstances can personal liability be imposed upon an individual trustee or employee of a school district?

Individual Liability

Individuals who operate under a "badge of authority" may be held personally liable for violating constitutional rights under Section 1983. The "badge of authority" should not be confused with a police badge. Public school teachers and administrators perform their duties "under color of law," and thus have the badge of authority that could trigger §1983 liability.

However, individuals have one defense available to them that is not available to the governmental entity itself: qualified good faith immunity.

Governmental entities cannot avoid liability by claiming that they were acting in good faith (*Owen v. City of Independence,* 1980). If it is determined that a person's rights were violated pursuant to a policy or custom of the entity, including the acts of those identified by the court as being final governmental policymakers, the entity itself is liable. The "But we meant well" defense does not work.

The law is different, however, for individuals who are sued in their individual capacities. Individual employees can escape personal liability by asserting and proving the defense of qualified good faith immunity. The leading case on this subject is the Supreme Court's decision of *Harlow v. Fitzgerald,* decided in 1982. The Harlow in the case is Bryce N. Harlow, one of the senior officials in the Nixon administration.

The Court noted that qualified or good faith immunity is an affirmative defense that must be pleaded by a governmental official or employee. The heart of the defense is this: " . . . government officials performing discretionary functions generally are shielded from liability for civil damages insofar as their conduct does not violate clearly established statutory or constitutional rights of which a reasonable person would have known." The Court declared that the judge may determine whether the law in question was clearly established at the time the employee acted. If the law at that time was not clearly established, an official cannot reasonably be expected to anticipate subsequent legal developments and cannot fairly be said to "know" that the law forbade conduct not previously identified as unlawful. If the law was clearly established, the immunity defense should fail, since a reasonably competent public official should know the law governing his or her conduct.

Again, the theory behind this is great. In effect, this is a "knew or should have known" standard. For example, the right of students to refuse to salute the American flag has been "clearly established" since the 1943 Supreme Court case of *West Virginia State Board of Education v. Barnette*. Every school administrator should be aware of this. Suppose, then, that Patty Principal, acting in complete good faith as well as total ignorance of the *Barnette* case, were to suspend a student for refusing to salute the flag. The "qualified good faith immunity" defense would not rescue Patty from personal liability. If it did, we would be rewarding ignorance among our educational leaders. Thus, school teachers and administrators are expected to have a basic understanding of what the law requires.

In practice, however, the matter gets a lot murkier. Most cases are not as neat and clean as the hypothetical in the paragraph above. No doubt the most celebrated case in Texas concerning the qualified good faith immunity defense was *Doe v. Taylor I.S.D.* In that case, the student alleged that the principal and superintendent acted with deliberate indifference toward her right to be free from invasions of bodily integrity. To put the matter more plainly, Jane Doe had a sexual affair with a teacher/coach. She alleged that both the principal and superintendent knew of the affair and did nothing about it. Both administrators denied any wrongdoing, but also asserted their qualified good faith immunity.

Here, the arguments got pretty technical. While all parties conceded that teacher-student sex was wrong, and should be prevented, the superintendent and principal argued that as of the time of the affair and their alleged nonaction, it was not at all clear that a student had a constitutionally protected right to be free from sexual abuse at school. This argument is not as bizarre as it may sound at first. The administrators were not arguing that such relationships were permissible. They merely asserted that before they should be held personally liable, the student should have to prove that her right to be free of such mistreatment at school was protected by the Constitution. Section 1983 imposes liability only for constitutional wrongs, not simple acts of negligence. Thus the question was presented: does a student have a right to be free from sexual abuse at school? If so, is this a right protected by the U.S. Constitution? If so, was this right clearly established so as to make all school employees accountable for its protection?

In *Doe v. Taylor I.S.D.* the Fifth Circuit answered all three questions with a "yes." A student has a right to be free from invasions of bodily integrity—specifically, physical sexual abuse. This right is protected by the U.S. Constitution's guarantee of due process of law. The student's rights were clearly established, and thus both the principal and superintendent were potentially liable. A further discussion of this case follows in the next section.

Before we leave the matter of qualified good faith immunity, however, we should point out that teachers also are held to a standard of knowledge of certain constitutional principles. Teachers are generally not as knowledgeable of school law as are administrators, but the courts expect classroom teachers to have a basic understanding of key concepts. Thus the defense of qualified good faith immunity failed in the case of *Jefferson v. Ysleta I.S.D.* The facts alleged are unfortunate to say the least. Allegedly, a teacher tied a second-grader named Jardine to a chair, using a jump rope and securing her by the waist and legs. During the first day Jardine was tied to the chair for the entire school day, except for the lunch hour. On the second day she was tied to the chair for protracted periods. While tied, Jardine was denied access to the bathroom. This treatment allegedly was not intended as punishment but, rather, as "an instructional technique." Jardine claimed damages, including humiliation, mental anguish, and an impaired ability to study productively.

The teacher raised the defense of qualified good faith immunity, a defense that was rejected by the trial judge. The Fifth Circuit Court of Appeals began its analysis by citing the precedent of *Harlow v. Fitzgerald*. The court noted that the teacher would be immune from personal liability for Jardine's damages unless her alleged conduct, tying Jardine to a chair for nearly two days, violated one or more of Jardine's constitutional or statutory rights of which the teacher reasonably should have been aware. The court stated that, in determining what a reasonable teacher should know, it is not necessary to point to a court case that is factually identical with the case in question. It suffices that a reasonable teacher be aware of general, well-developed principles. The court declared itself persuaded that at the time of the incident a competent teacher should have known that to tie a second-grade student to a chair for an entire school day and for a substantial portion of a second day, as an educational exercise with no suggested justification, was constitutionally impermissible. The court concluded that a young student has a constitutional right not to be lashed to a chair through the school day and denied, among other things, the basic liberty of access to the bathroom when needed. The court found Jardine's constitutional right in the Fifth and Fourteenth Amendment rights to substantive due process, specifically her right to be free from bodily restraint.

The *Ysleta* case, along with the *Doe v. Taylor I.S.D.* case, is significant for several reasons. First, these cases illustrate the scope of knowledge required of school employees. While reasonable employees no doubt would have known that the conduct they were alleged to have engaged in was wrongful, it probably came as a surprise to the school employees to learn that they were charged with violating well-established substantive due process rights of the students under the Fourteenth Amendment to the U.S. Constitution. A second significant aspect of the *Ysleta* case is the fact that the person charged with knowledge of constitutional law is a teacher rather than an administrator. While administrators routinely are hailed into court over constitutional allegations, the *Ysleta* case illustrates that classroom teachers also are charged with knowledge of and adherence to federal constitutional principles.

Qualified good faith immunity is certainly no guarantee against individual liability. It is significant that under *Harlow* the issue is not what the particular defendant knew about the law but, rather, whether there has been a violation of a well-settled right of which a *reasonable* person would have known. Public school employees frequently are exhorted to keep abreast of the law. That is good advice.

The defense, however, is of value to individuals who are sued. It is often said that the individual is not required to predict the future course of the law, and that is true. The individual school employee or trustee is entitled to escape any personal liability for damages if at the time of the action there was no well-settled principle of law to the contrary of which a reasonable person would have known.

Personal Injuries and the Constitution

A person who sues the local school district or school official over a personal injury faces yet another problem that a typical plaintiff who falls down in a grocery store does not encounter. The person who sues under §1983 must establish that he or she has suffered an injury of a constitutional nature. A short explanation is in order.

State law is, by tradition and long-standing practice, the protector of broken arms and dented fenders. Until recently, suits involving §1983 concerned injured rights rather than injured bodies.

Section 1983 suits generally involved deprivation of due process, freedom of speech, equal protection, or the right of privacy. Of late, however, attorneys have attempted to convert garden-variety personal injury suits into matters of constitutional law. And there has been some success. However, such suits must establish (1) that a constitutional right is involved; and (2) that the actions of school officials exceeded mere negligence.

Frequently the constitutional right cited is the right to work or attend school in a safe environment. But in a 1992 case the Supreme Court seemed to cool on the idea of city liability for injured workers, particularly in those cases where state law provides a remedy. In *Collins v. City of Harker Heights* the Court was faced with a case in which a widow alleged that her husband's death while working for the city was evidence of the city's violation of his right "to be free from unreasonable risks of harm." The widow alleged that the city showed deliberate indifference toward its employees in failing to train them for certain dangerous work assignments.

The Court rejected the notion that the Constitution imposes on local governments any affirmative duty to provide a safe and secure working environment. The Court indicated that the government takes on such a duty only when it has taken steps to deprive an individual of normal personal liberties. So the government does have a duty to protect the safety of prisoners and involuntarily committed mental patients. But city workers—and school employees—are there by choice, and cannot use the Constitution to hold the government responsible for failing to provide a safe working environment.

While employees have little chance of holding the school district liable under §1983 for work-related injuries, students may have more success. There have been numerous cases over the past five years in which students have sued teachers, administrators, and school districts over sexual misconduct in the schools. Let us now turn to a review of some of those cases.

The cases can be divided into (1) those that arise out of sexual misconduct by a teacher or other employee, and (2) those that arise out of sexual misconduct by other students. The leading precedent regarding teacher-student sexual misconduct is *Doe v. Taylor I.S.D.*, which was discussed above in connection with qualified good faith immunity. In the *Taylor I.S.D.* case the Fifth Circuit ruled, for the first time, that students do have a constitutional right to be free from physical sexual abuse in the public schools. School administrators who supervise the wrongdoer can be personally liable if (1) they knew of the sexual misconduct, or of a pattern of inappropriate behavior pointing plainly toward that conclusion; (2) they were deliberately indifferent about it; and (3) their actions and/or inactions were the cause of injury to the student. How does this play out in the real world? If a teacher has a sexual relationship with the student, the teacher can be held liable under §1983 because the teacher is acting under color of state law in causing injury to the student. In addition, the principal can be liable if the student can show the three elements outlined above.

In *Doe v. Taylor I.S.D.* the Fifth Circuit exonerated the superintendent of any possible liability. The court ruled that there was no way that a reasonable jury could conclude that the superintendent was deliberately indifferent. The superintendent did not know for certain that a sexual relationship existed. Every time some piece of information aroused his suspicions, the superintendent took some action. The court noted that the superintendent may not have been as persistent or thorough as one would hope, but he always did something. He was not "deliberately indifferent."

The court ruled that the principal, however, may have been deliberately indifferent. There were times, according to the student, that the principal became aware of certain facts and simply did not respond. The court did not rule that the principal was deliberately indifferent, it simply said that a reasonable jury could conclude that he was. Therefore, the case would not be dismissed as to the principal.

Doe v. Taylor I.S.D. sent a clear message to school administrators. The message was to make more of an effort to protect students from the sexual misconduct of school employees. Supervisors became more vigilant in their oversight and their documentation.

But what about teachers who know of the sexual misconduct? Can they be held liable under federal law even though they are not in a supervisory capacity? According to *Doe v. Rains I.S.D.* the answer is no. In this case, a student confided in a teacher that she was having an affair with a coach at the school. The teacher tried to persuade the young girl to end the affair and report the misconduct. However, for five months, the teacher did not report the matter to child abuse authorities. The federal district court swept aside the teacher's arguments for immunity. The court ruled that a reasonable jury could conclude that this five-month delay amounted to deliberate indifference, thus making the teacher liable for the misconduct of her fellow teacher. The court noted that state law requires school teachers to report suspected child abuse within forty-eight hours. However, the Fifth Circuit reversed that decision, noting that the teacher had no supervisory responsibility for the actions of the coach and thus was not acting under color of state law when she failed to report the matter.

Liability of school employees for student-to-student sexual misconduct is another matter, however. Why should the law be different? What difference does it make who inflicted the injury, isn't the school expected to protect students from harm while attending school? The reason for the distinction is the language of Section 1983. Recall that it provides legal recourse for parties injured by persons "acting under color of law." The state, or its political subdivision, must be the wrongdoer. When a student assaults, rapes, or murders another student, the injury is just as damaging, but the crucial element of "state action" is missing. Thus the courts have consistently held that schools are generally not liable for student-inflicted injuries.

In light of that, plaintiffs have argued that the school has a constitutional duty affirmatively to protect students from harm inflicted from any wrongdoer—those who are on the payroll as well as those who are not. Thus, the argument goes, when the state fails to protect those for whom it is responsible, there is "state action" sufficient to justify §1983 liability. This argument has not had much success in the public school context. The Supreme Court has ruled that the state takes on the duty to protect an individual whenever the state takes affirmative acts to restrain that person's freedom to act on his or her own behalf, through "incarceration, institutionalization, or other similar restraint of personal liberty" (*DeShaney v. Winnebago County Department of Social Services*, 1989). Thus the state clearly owes some duty of protection to prisoners and involuntarily committed mental patients.

What about school children? State law requires students to attend school. Does this amount to a deprivation of normal personal liberties serious enough to warrant a constitutional right to a safe school environment? The law on that score is evolving, but to date, every circuit court that has addressed the issue has ruled that compulsory attendance laws are not a sufficient deprivation of personal liberty to impose additional liabilities on a school district. The most recent pronouncement of the Fifth Circuit came in the case of *Walton v. Alexander.*

First, a little background. As early as 1982 the Fifth Circuit referred to the duty of school officials "to protect [school children] from dangers posed by anti-social activities—their own and those of other students—and to provide them with an environment in which education is possible" (*Horton v. Goose Creek I.S.D.*). Later, in the *Lopez* case discussed above, the Fifth Circuit held that the substitute bus driver could be held liable for Lopez's injuries because the driver was "entrusted with the care of students attending school under Texas' compulsory education statute."

In 1995, however, the Fifth Circuit reversed course, overruled its holding in the *Lopez* case, and settled this issue by ruling in the case of *Walton v. Alexander*. The case involved a sexual assault of a student at the Mississippi School for the Deaf by another student. The injured student alleged that the school had a duty to protect him from injuries inflicted by other students. Therefore, the argument went, the school and the superintendent were liable under Section 1983. The Fifth Circuit, sitting *en banc*, meaning that all fifteen circuit judges participated, rejected that argument. The court concluded that compulsory attendence laws do not create a duty to protect one student from another. The key discussion was contained in a footnote:

> Prior to *DeShaney*, in *Lopez v. Houston Indep. Sch. Dist.*, [cite omitted], we found that a school bus driver was entrusted with the care of students attending school under the state's compulsory education statute. . . . Clearly, this is not the type of restraint on personal liberty nor the type of affirmative act by the state intended by *DeShaney*. To the extent the holding in *Lopez* is directly contrary to our holding today, as well as the holding in *DeShaney*, we overrule it.

Bear in mind that Walton was a student at a residential school, the School for the Deaf. If the state has no legal duty to protect a child in that setting, it surely has no duty to protect a child in a regular public school, when the child goes home to her parents every night.

Indeed, the dissenting opinion in the *Walton* case drew a stark picture:

> Following this decision, parents should be aware when the school bus doors close that if their child is sexually or physically assaulted, the driver of the bus has no constitutional duty to intervene, stop the assault, summon assistance, or attend to any injuries that may have been sustained. Under the majority's reasoning, he may with full knowledge of the assault be totally indifferent to it.

The *Walton* case is a good illustration of a situation where moral duties and legal duties do not coincide. The indifferent bus driver described by the dissent violates his moral duty, but not his legal duty. His actions lead to moral consequences, not legal judgments.

In cases involving sexual misconduct, that is, actual physical sexual abuse, students are able to establish that a constitutional right is involved. Since the *Doe v. Taylor I.S.D.* case that has been clearly established.

But the next question arises: what standard of conduct applies to the school and its officials? Will the student be successful if the evidence shows that the school and its officials were negligent? Or does the student have to prove something more intentional?

The Supreme Court resolved that issue in two 1986 cases, *Daniels v. Williams* and *Davidson v. Cannon*. In *Daniels*, the plaintiff sued a deputy sheriff, alleging that, while an inmate, the plaintiff had slipped on a pillow negligently left on a stairway by the deputy. Plaintiff claimed that the alleged negligence deprived him of a liberty interest without due process in violation of the Fourteenth Amendment. The Supreme Court concluded, "To hold that injury caused by such conduct is a deprivation within the meaning of the Fourteenth Amendment would trivialize the centuries old principle of due process law." Thus garden variety negligence claims are not sufficient to impose §1983 liability. Instead, the injured party must establish "deliberate indifference" on the part of the defendant. This is difficult to prove.

A case in point is a 1993 Fifth Circuit decision involving an Ysleta I.S.D. teacher who was accused of sexually molesting a first grader. School officials had conducted a cursory investigation after two previous reports of the teacher's improper contact with students, such as letting them sit on his lap and putting his arm around their waists. Following the investigation, the school board decided to transfer the teacher to a different school rather than terminate the teacher's contract, as was customary in the district when instances of child abuse arose. The molestation occurred after the transfer. The parents of the student sued the school district in federal court, alleging that by not terminating the teacher, the district was deliberately indifferent to the student's welfare. The Fifth Circuit ruled that the district's transfer action constituted official policy under 42 U.S.C. §1983. The appeals court viewed the transfer decision to be "not only negligent but also inconsistent with the district's handling of other cases of suspected sexual abuse." However, because the board had not ignored the previous allegations but had ordered an investigation, the board was not deliberately indifferent to the welfare of the students when it made the transfer decision. The lesson seems to be that doing the wrong thing is preferable to doing nothing. You may be accused of negligence, but that alone will not impose liability. Doing nothing could lead to an accusation of deliberate indifference, which could lead to liability (*Gonzalez v. Ysleta I.S.D.*).

Cases involving student injuries, of course, do not always revolve around sexual misconduct. In *Leffall v. Dallas I.S.D.* a student was shot and killed by random gunfire at a school-sponsored dance. The Fifth Circuit absolved the Dallas I.S.D. of any potential liability due to two critical factors. First, the death was not caused by a school official, but rather by the wrongful act of a third party who was not acting "under a badge of authority." In so holding, the court rejected the theory that the school district had a legal duty to protect students from other students, thus anticipating the later *en banc* decision of the Fifth Circuit in the *Walton* case. Second, the most that could be said of school officials in this case is that they were negligent, and that simply is not sufficient to impose liability under §1983.

A more mundane example of this arose in *Myers v. Troup I.S.D.*, in which a football player was allegedly injured due to the negligence of school officials. The student asserted that school officials sent him back into the game five minutes after he was knocked unconscious, and that the school was negligent in doing so, particularly since the school had no medical personnel on the sidelines. The federal district court, citing its desire not to trivialize the Fourteenth Amendment, said: "Plaintiff's claims are grounded in negligence; they do not raise a constitutional question." Thus the case was dismissed from federal court.

SUMMARY

Texas public school educators have no immunity from violations of criminal law. However, insofar as civil damage suits are concerned, educators are shielded by state law from tort suits as long as they are acting in the scope of their duties and are exercising discretion. Only in disciplinary matters or in the operation, use, or maintenance of a motor vehicle are school professionals vulnerable to damage suits. All school officials should have a basic understanding of the notion of confidentiality of student records, but this is perhaps most important for the school counselor. School districts, under Texas law, are immune from tort suits except in matters involving motor vehicles.

Of growing concern to school professionals and school districts is increasing liability for federal constitutional and statutory rights violations. It is important for everyone in a position of professional responsibility to avoid actions that might trigger them.

How to Find and Read
a Court Case

MOST LIBRARIES have at least one of the three sets of volumes (called "reporters") containing the decisions of the U.S. Supreme Court. The official set, *United States Reports*, is printed by the U.S. Government Printing Office. The two commercial sets, *Supreme Court Reporter* and *Lawyers' Edition*, augment their coverage of Supreme Court decisions by adding headnotes, digests, and other material of importance to practicing attorneys and legal researchers. Both the official set and the *Supreme Court Reporter* are cited interchangeably for U.S. Supreme Court cases in the Index of Cases of this book.

The published decisions of the lower federal courts are usually available at larger libraries, including those at public and private universities and, of course, at law schools. The decisions of the federal courts of appeals can be found in the *Federal Reporter* (2d series). Federal district court decisions are printed in the *Federal Supplement*.

The appellate decisions of Texas courts, along with the courts of several other states, can be found in the *Southwestern Reporter* (2d series), a set of volumes that is generally available in larger libraries. There are also regional reporters for the court decisions of other states.

Specific cases can be easily located once one knows how the citation system operates. Both federal and state cases are cited the same way. The citing pattern consists of the name of the case, the volume number, the name of the volume, page, and date—in that order. Thus, the U.S. Supreme Court decision *Tinker v. Des Moines School District*, the so-called black armband case, is cited 393 U.S. 503 (1969). This means that in volume 393 of the *United States Reports* the reader will find the case beginning on page 503. The two commercial reporters containing the decisions of the U.S. Supreme Court are abbreviated "S.Ct." for *Supreme Court Reporter* and "L.Ed." for *Lawyers' Edition*. The *Tinker* case citations to these volumes are 89 S.Ct. 733 and 21 L.Ed.2d 731, respectively.

The federal courts of appeals decisions are cited as "F.2d," meaning they are printed in volumes of the *Federal Reporter* (2d series), while the decisions of the federal district courts are cited as "F.Supp." for *Federal Supplement*. Texas appellate court decisions to be found in the *Southwestern Reporter* (2d series) are abbreviated "S.W.2d" in citations. Thus, the important Texas Supreme Court decision regarding tort liability of school districts and professional employees, *Barr v. Bernhard*, 562 S.W.2d 844, can be found in volume 562 of the *Southwestern Reporter* (2d series) beginning on page 844.

In a case citation, the name appearing on the left is that of the initiator of the suit, or plaintiff, and the name on the right is that of the defendant. The adversary character of our legal system is clearly evidenced by the "v." or "vs." appearing between the names, abbreviations for *versus*. Frequently, the order of the names will reverse on appeal, since, if the plaintiff wins in the trial court, the defendant (or now appellant) is the initiator of the appellate review action in this situation. In this event, the plaintiff becomes the appellee.

Once a case is located in a reporter, the reader will first be confronted with a brief syllabus of the opinion and a series of short headnotes. The latter are for the benefit of the legal researcher, as they call attention to important points of law reflected in the decision. Following the headnotes is the actual opinion of the court. And following the majority opinion may be one or more concurring or dissenting opinions. The concurring and dissenting opinions have no value aside from setting forth the views of a particular judge or a group of judges. It is often said, however, that today's dissent may become tomorrow's majority opinion, so these should not be completely ignored.

Opinions are sometimes very readable and sometimes not. Much depends on the importance of the case, its complexity, and the judge's writing style. The lay reader will quickly see how influential precedent is in judicial decision making, for judges repeatedly cite other cases, statutes, and secondary sources, such as law review articles and legal encyclopedias, to back up their points. The law is anchored by precedent; this keeps it from "lurching after the day's passing fancy," as one federal judge put it. Consistency and stability over time are the hallmarks of a sound legal system. Generally, lower court decisions tend to be shorter than those of higher courts—some recent opinions of the U.S. Supreme Court run over a hundred pages. The lay reader quickly develops the knack of skimming over the opinion first to see how it is laid out. Often, only a few pages or paragraphs will reflect the essence of the case—what the decision is and why the court decides it this way.

Readers should be aware that the law is never static. It is constantly growing and changing. Thus, the opinion one reads today may eventually be overturned on appeal to a higher court. Those skilled in legal research are well aware of the transitory nature of case law and will utilize techniques of legal research to track a case through the judiciary to determine its continuing validity and its influence on other courts.

One final word of advice. Do not be afraid to ask the librarian for help. Your time is too valuable to be spent wandering around a legal reference section or attempting to master the intricacies of a computerized legal retrieval system. If you are particularly shy or inclined toward doing it yourself, one handy paperback worth purchasing is Morris L. Cohen's and Kent Olson's *Legal Research in a Nutshell*. For using a computerized legal retrieval system, Penny Hazelton's short monograph *Computer Assisted Legal Research: The Basics* presents a fine introduction. Both are among the sources listed in Appendix C.

Glossary of Legal Terminology

THE WORDS and definitions below are intended to help the lay reader better understand this guide, case reports, and other materials on school law. Only a few of the many terms related to law are included; for a more extensive list, consult Daniel Oran's *Law Dictionary for Non-Lawyers* (see Appendix C).

Amicus curiae: "Friend of the court"; a person or organization allowed to appear in a lawsuit, usually to file arguments in the form of a brief supporting one side or the other, even though not a party to the dispute.

Appellant: See *plaintiff*.

Appellee: See *defendant*.

Attorneys' fees: Refers to the practice of according the winning party's costs to the losing party in a civil case. The 1976 Civil Rights Attorneys' Fees Awards Act gives courts this power in civil rights suits.

Back pay: Lost wages that must be paid to employees who have been illegally discharged or laid off.

Cause of action: Facts sufficient to support a valid lawsuit.

Certiorari: A writ issued by a court asking the lower court to submit the record in a case, thus indicating the willingness of the higher court to entertain the appeal; "cert." for short.

Civil case: Every lawsuit other than a criminal proceeding. Most civil cases involve a lawsuit brought by one person against another and usually concern money damages.

Civil liberties: Fundamental individual freedoms that are constitutionally protected. Provisions listed in the Bill of Rights to the U.S. Constitution, such as freedom of speech and religious exercise, are considered civil liberties.

Civil rights: Rights that provide access to the legal system and equitable treatment before the law. Civil rights can be provided by a constitution or action of a legislative body. Thus, one is entitled to freedom from discrimination based on race, color, religion, sex, or national origin in public and private employment by provisions of Title VII of the 1964 Civil Rights Act.

Class action: A lawsuit brought by one person on behalf of himself or herself and all other persons in the same situation.

Code: A collection of laws. The Texas Education Code is a grouping of state statutes affecting education.

Common law: Law that develops by custom and is given expression through court rulings. Many student and teacher rights have developed this way, as has the tort of personal privacy invasion. Many common law principles have been incorporated into legislative enactments (statutes).

Compensatory damages: Damages that relate to the actual loss suffered by a plaintiff, as opposed to punitive damages (q.v.).

Complaint: The first main paper filed in a civil lawsuit in federal court. It includes, among other things, a statement of the wrong or harm supposedly done to the plaintiff by the defendant and a request for specific help from the court. The defendant responds to the complaint by filing an "answer." The equivalent term in state court is "original petition."

Contract: An agreement that affects the legal relationship between two or more persons. To be a contract, an agreement must involve persons legally capable of making binding agreements, at least one promise, consideration (i.e., something of value promised or given), and a reasonable amount of agreement between the persons as to what the contract means.

Criminal case: Cases involving crimes against the laws of the state; unlike in civil cases, the state is the prosecuting party.

De facto: "In fact, actual"; a situation that exists in fact, whether or not it is lawful. De facto segregation is that which exists regardless of the law or the actions of civil authorities (see *de jure*).

Defamation: Injuring a person's character or reputation by false or malicious statements. This includes both libel and slander (see these terms).

Defendant (appellee): The person against whom a legal action is brought. This legal action may be civil or criminal. At the appeal stage, the party against whom an appeal is taken is known as the appellee. Usually, the appellee is the winner in the lower court.

De jure: "Of right"; legitimate; lawful, whether or not in actual fact. De jure segregation is that which is sanctioned by law (see *de facto*).

De minimis: "Trivial, small, unimportant."

Dictum: See *obiter dictum*.

Disclaimer: The refusal to accept certain types of responsibility. For example, a college catalog may disclaim any responsibility for guaranteeing that the courses contained therein will actually be offered since courses, programs, and instructors are likely to change without notice.

En banc: The hearing of a case by a Circuit Court's full membership rather than by a small panel.

Expunge: Blot out. For example, a court order requesting that a student's record be expunged of any references to disciplinary action during such and such a time period means that the references are to be "wiped off the books."

Fiduciary: A relationship between persons in which one person acts for another in a position of trust. Some courts hold private schools to a fiduciary relationship with students and may intervene if the school has not acted fairly, as for example, in expelling a student.

Forum: A place for communication. In the context of the First Amendment to the U.S. Constitution, a *public forum* means a place where First Amendment rights are almost unlimited in their scope, a *limited public forum* allows government some restriction over speakers and content of expression, and a *closed forum* refers to government property traditionally not open to public communication.

Grievance: An employee complaint concerning wages, hours, or conditions of work, i.e., literally anything connected with employment. A grievance system consists of steps by which an individual employee or a group of employees seeks a solution to a complaint. First, the grievance is brought to the attention of the employee's immediate superior. If no satisfactory adjustment is made, the employee may continue to appeal to higher levels. While virtually all collective bargaining contracts contain a grievance system, they are also increasingly part of organizational life whether or not a union is present, since they afford the means to channel and resolve disputes.

Hearing: An oral proceeding before a court or quasi-judicial tribunal.

Holding: The rule of law set forth in a case to answer the issues presented to the court.

Informed consent: A person's agreement to allow something to happen (such as surgery) that is based on a full disclosure of facts needed to make the decision intelligently. Certain types of student searches are best carried out with informed consent of the student being searched or the parents.

Infra: Later in the article or book. For example, *infra*, p. 235, means to turn to that page, which is further on. Opposite of *supra*.

Injunction: A court order requiring someone to do something or to refrain from taking some action.

In loco parentis: "In place of a parent"; acting as a parent with respect to the care, supervision, and discipline of a child. The development of student rights law has curtailed the common law *in loco parentis* powers of public school officials.

Ipso facto: "By the fact itself"; by the mere fact that.

Jurisdiction: Right of a court to hear a case; also the geographic area within which a court has the right and power to operate. Original jurisdiction means that the court will be the first to hear the case; appellate jurisdiction means that the court reviews cases on appeal from lower court rulings.

Jurisprudence: Philosophy of the law; the rationale for one's legal position.

Justiciable: Proper for a court to decide. For example, a justiciable controversy is a real dispute that a court may handle.

Law: Basic rules of order. Constitutional law reflects the basic principles by which government operates. Statute law consists of laws passed by legislatures and recorded in public documents. Administrative laws are the decisions of administrative agencies, for example, a State Board of Education ruling. Case law consists of the pronouncement of courts.

Libel: Written defamation; published false and malicious written statements that injure a person's reputation.

Litigation: A lawsuit or series of lawsuits.

Mandamus: A court order commanding some official duty to be performed.

Mediation: The involvement of a neutral third party to facilitate agreement.

Moot: Abstract; for the sake of argument; not a real case involving a real dispute.

Negligence: A tort or civil wrong that involves failure to exercise reasonable care when one has a duty to do so and as a result someone or something is harmed. Different degrees of negligence trigger different legal penalties.

Obiter dictum: A digression from the central focus of a discussion to consider unrelated points; often shortened to *dictum*.

Parens patriae: The historical right of all governments to take care of persons under their jurisdiction, particularly minors and incapacitated persons. Thus, states have acted *parens patriae* in establishing public schooling systems for the benefit of all people within their borders.

Per curiam: An unsigned decision and opinion of a court, as distinguished from one signed by a judge.

Petitioner: The one bringing an action; similar to *plaintiff*. Opposite of *respondent*.

Plaintiff: The person who brings a lawsuit against another person. At the appeal stage, the person bringing the appeal is called the "appellant" and is usually the one losing in the lower court action.

Plenary: Complete or full in all respects.

Police power: The traditional power of governments to establish criminal laws and to enforce them.

Precedent: A court decision on a question of law that gives authority or direction on how to decide a similar question of law in a later case with similar facts. Ruling by precedent is usually conveyed through the term *stare decisis*.

Prima facie: Clear on the face of it; presumably, a fact that will be considered to be true unless disproved by contrary evidence. For example, a prima facie case is one that will win unless the other side comes forward with evidence to dispute it.

Punitive damages: Money awarded to a person by a court that is over and above the damages actually sustained. Punitive damages are designed to serve as a deterrent to similar acts in the future.

Quasi-judicial: The case-deciding function of an administrative agency. Thus, a school board is a quasi-judicial body when it holds a formal hearing on a teacher dismissal case.

Remand: To send back; for example, a higher court may send a case back to the lower court, asking that certain action be taken.

Res judicata: "A thing decided." Thus, if a court decides the case, the matter is settled and no new lawsuit can be brought on the same subject by the same parties.

Respondent: The party responding to an action; similar to defendant. The opposite of *petitioner*.

Right to work: The term used to apply to laws that ban union-security agreements, such as the union shop, by rendering it illegal to make employment conditional on membership or nonmembership in a labor organization. Unions are particularly opposed to these state laws because they allow "free riders"—those who share in the collective benefit but pay nothing for it.

Sectarian: Of or relating to religion or a religious sect.

Secular: Of or relating to worldly concerns; opposite of *sectarian*.

Slander: Oral defamation; the speaking of false and malicious words that injure another person's reputation, business, or property rights.

Sovereign immunity: The government's freedom from being sued for money damages without its consent. At present, Texas school districts enjoy a kind of sovereign immunity from most damage suits involving torts under state laws, for example, negligence.

Standing: A person's right to bring a lawsuit because he or she is directly affected by the issues raised.

Stare decisis: "Let the decision stand"; a legal rule that, when a court has decided a case by applying a legal principle to a set of facts, the court should stick by that principle and apply it to all later cases with clearly similar facts unless there is a good, strong reason not to. This rule helps promote fairness and reliability in judicial decision making and is inherent in the American legal system (see *precedent*).

State action concept: For the Fourteenth Amendment of the U.S. Constitution to apply to a given situation, there must be some involvement by a state or one of its political subdivisions. A public school falls into the latter category. Wholly private action is not covered by the Fourteenth Amendment. Thus, private schools and colleges, like corporate organizations and private clubs, are not subject to its strictures.

Statute: A law enacted by a legislative body.

Summary judgment: A decision for one side in a lawsuit rendered on the pleadings and before the trial begins.

Supra: Earlier in an article or book. For example, *supra*, p. 11, means to turn to that page, which appeared earlier. Opposite of *infra*.

Tort: A civil wrong done by one person to another. For an act to be a tort, there must be a legal duty owed by one person to another, a breach of that duty, and harm done as a direct result of the action. Examples of torts are negligence, battery, and libel. Texas school districts are immune under state law from most nonconstitutional tort damage suits but not from constitutional tort claims, for example, damage claims resulting from deprivation of a constitutional or federal statutory right. Texas public school professional employees also enjoy substantial immunity from nonconstitutional tort damage suits.

Trial: A process occurring in a court whereby opposing parties present evidence, subject to cross-examination and rebuttal, pertaining to the matter in dispute.

Trial de novo: A completely new trial ordered by a judge or appeals
court.

Ultra vires: Going beyond the specifically delegated authority to
act; for example, a school board that is by law restricted from
punishing students for behavior occurring wholly off campus
acts *ultra vires* in punishing a student for behavior observed at
a private weekend party.

Waiver: The means by which a person voluntarily gives up a right or
benefit. To be valid, waivers have to be worded very carefully.
Thus, in a case where a parent is asked to sign a waiver absolv-
ing the school or teacher from liability in the event of an accident to his or her child on a field trip, waivers must make it
clear what the parent is giving up, for example, the right to sue
even if the school or teacher is negligent. Some courts have
ruled that, even if parents sign such a knowing waiver, the
child may recover damages in his or her own right. The services
of an attorney are best secured in drawing up waivers.

Reference Sources

THE FOLLOWING materials will provide more information about topics discussed in this volume. Some are designed for the lay reader, while others require a trip to the library and the assistance of a librarian.

Cohen, Morris L., and Kent Olson. *Legal Research in a Nutshell,* Fifth Edition. St. Paul: West Publishing Company, 1993. Excellent paperback for the lay person who wishes to learn how to use a law library. For a less comprehensive research source, see Lowe and Watters below. Order from West Publishing Company, 50 W. Kellogg Blvd., P.O. Box 64526, St. Paul, MN 55164-0526.

Guide to American Law. St. Paul: West Publishing Company, 1985. This twelve-volume encyclopedia of American law with annual supplements is geared to the layperson. It is an excellent, easy-to-use reference source for a variety of legal topics. Handsomely illustrated; written by experts in the field. Recommended as a starting place for research on a legal topic.

Hazelton, Penny A. *Computer-Assisted Legal Research: The Basics.* St. Paul: West Publishing Company, 1993. This seventy-three-page monograph provides a nontechnical introduction to the Lexis-Nexis and Westlaw computerized legal retrieval systems.

The Individuals with Disabilities Education Law Report (IDELR). Horsham, PA: LRP Publications. This is a comprehensive loose-leaf service, updated twenty-four times annually. It provides copies of all relevant laws, court cases, interpretations of law by the Office of Special Education Programs, Office of Civil Rights, and some state hearing officer decisions. This set is comprehensive, but expensive to maintain. Order from LRP Publications, P.O. Box 980, Horsham, PA 19044-0980.

Kemerer, Frank R., and John A. Crain. *The Documentation Handbook,* Second Edition, 1995. Available from the *Texas School Administrators' Legal Digest* (see this reference below). The handbook provides a detailed discussion of the mechanics of effective documentation for employee appraisal, nonrenewal, and termination. Included are sample forms, including a series of focused observation instruments for targeted classroom data-gathering.

Lowe, David, and Annette Jones Watters. *Legal Research for Educators.* Bloomington, IN: Phi Delta Kappa, 1984. This thirty-nine-page paperback will help the uninitiated unlock the mysteries of a legal collection but does not provide the detailed discussion evident in the Cohen volume. Order from PDK at Eighth and Union, P.O. Box 789, Bloomington, IN 47402.

Oran, Daniel. *Law Dictionary for Non-Lawyers*, Third Edition. St. Paul: West Publishing Company, 1991. Excellent dictionary for the person unversed in legal terminology.

Students with Disabilities and Special Education, Twelfth Edition. Rosemont, MN: Data Research Inc., 1995. This is a handy, paperback desk reference which includes summaries of major court cases covering the entire spectrum of special education law. It also includes copies of the statutes and regulations. Order from Data Research, P.O. Box 490, Rosemont, MN 55068.

Texas Digest. St. Paul: West Publishing Company. A multivolume reference source to Texas federal and state case law. Look up "Schools and School Districts" in the appropriate volume; consult pocket parts at the rear of the volume for recent cases; available at larger libraries.

Texas Register. Published twice a week, the *Register* is a state publication containing various facets of state government, including announcements of administrative rules, attorney general opinions, executive orders of the governor, bills introduced into the legislature, and other information of value to the public. Available at larger libraries.

Texas School Administrators' Legal Digest. This monthly legal periodical features articles written by leading Texas attorneys and commentators, as well as digests of court rulings, commission decisions, and attorney general opinions affecting Texas education. Published by Frank Kemerer, Jim Walsh, and Eric Schulze. Available by writing the *Legal Digest* at UNT Box 13855, Denton, TX 76203-3855. The *Legal Digest* also offers a series of law charts and videotapes that describe legal requirements in complex areas.

Texas School Law Bulletin. St. Paul: West Publishing Company, latest edition. This large paperback is a Texas Education Agency–sponsored collection of Texas statutes directly affecting education. Published biennially. About one-half of the book is devoted to the Texas Education Code. It is the single best source for statutory information short of visiting a law library. Many schools make the *Bulletin* routinely available to principals; it is also a standard feature of most school law courses taught in the state. Its chief limitation is that it does not contain administrative rules, decisions by administrative agencies, or court rulings. One should be cautious about relying on the wording of statutes alone, since they are subject to interpretation by administrative agencies and courts.

Vernon's Texas Codes Annotated — Education. St. Paul: West Publishing Company. This multivolume source contains the provisions of the Texas Education Code and supplements them with interpretive case law, attorney general opinions, and legal commentary. Be sure to consult the pocket parts for recent developments; available at larger libraries.

Index of Cases

Note: For the benefit of the lay reader, citations are given only to the court actually referenced in the text, along with the pages where the reference appears. Virtually all citations included here represent the final judicial word on the case at the time of this book's publication. Readers should be aware, however, that some of the recent lower court rulings are likely to have been appealed to higher courts.

Index of Topics